Labor and Monopoly Capital
25th Anniversary Edition

Labor and Monopoly Capital

The Degradation of Work in the Twentieth Century

Harry Braverman

25th Anniversary Edition

Foreword by Paul M. Sweezy

New Introduction by John Bellamy Foster

Monthly Review Press

New York

Library of Congress Cataloging-in-Publication Data
Braverman, Harry.
    Labor and monopoly capital : the degradation of work in the
twentieth century / by Harry Braverman ; foreword by Paul M. Sweezy
: new introduction by John Bellamy Foster. — 25th anniversary ed.
        p.   cm.
    Includes bibliographical references and index.
    ISBN 0-85345-940-1 (pbk.)
    1. Labor—History—20 century. 2. Capitalism—History—20th
century.   6. Working class—History—20th century.
I. Title.
HD4851.B66
331'.09'04—dc21   98-46497
                                                                              CIP

Monthly Review Press
146 West 29th Street Room 6W
New York NY 10001

Manufactured in Canada
10 9 8

Acknowledgments

To the following, for permission to reproduce short passages from the works named: Oxford University Press, from *White Collar* by C. Wright Mills, copyright © 1951 by Oxford University Press; Division of Research of Harvard Business School, from *Automation and Management* by James Bright, copyright © 1958 by the President and Fellows of Harvard College; University of Minnesota Press, from *The Sociology of Work* by Theodore Caplow, copyright © 1954 by the University of Minnesota; Harvard Business Review, from "Does Automation Raise Skill Requirements?" by James Bright, July-August 1958, copyright © 1958 by the President and Fellows of Harvard College; Columbia University Press, from *Women and Work in America* by Robert W. Smuts, copyright © 1959 by Columbia University Press; Public Affairs Press, from *Automation in the Office* by Ida R. Hoos.

Contents

Part IV: The Growing Working-Class Occupations

Introduction to the New Edition

John Bellamy Foster

Work, in today's society, is a mystery. No other realm of social existence is so obscured in mist, so zealously concealed from view ("no admittance except on business") by the prevailing ideology. Within so-called popular culture—the world of TV and films, commodities and advertising—consumption occupies center stage, while the more fundamental reality of work recedes into the background, seldom depicted in any detail, and then usually in romanticized forms. The harsh experiences of those forced to earn their living by endless conformity to boring machine-regulated routines, divorced from their own creative potential—all in the name of efficiency and profits—seem always just beyond the eye of the camera, forever out of sight.

In social science, the situation is hardly better. The dismal performance of legions of orthodox economists and sociologists in the area of work is testimony to the dominance of ideological imperatives within mainstream social science, despite its scientific pretensions. There is no other realm requiring as much concealment to permit the continued dominance of capitalist relations of production. What must remain impenetrable is not so much the stultifying character of modern working life: that is hard to deny in a time when the neologism "McJob" has entered the language to describe a form of employment experienced by millions. The secret is the prevailing social order's *systematic tendency* to create unsatisfying work.

Orthodox economists have consistently steered clear of issues of production and the organization of work, viewing these from the distant standpoint of the exigencies of the market (the buying and selling of "factors of production"). They almost never engage directly with the realm of production itself, in which capital and labor struggle over the control of working time and the appropriation of surplus product—issues discretely left to those concerned with the everyday practical realities of business and management. As the heterodox economist Robert Heilbroner has written, "The actual social process of production—the flesh and blood act of work, the relationships of sub- and superordination by which work is organized and controlled—are almost strangers to the conventional economist."[1]

Sociologists, it is true, have analyzed occupational reality, looking for signs of alienation. But sociology, like economics, has usually been divorced from any real understanding of the way in which working life is objectively organized around the division of labor and profitability. All too often academic investigators have assumed that the essence of working life is to be discovered simply in the subjective responses of "scientifically selected samples" of workers to carefully constructed questionnaires. Even radical theorists, familiar with the results of such economic and sociological research but lacking direct experience of their own with the capitalist labor process, have frequently fallen prey to illusions generated in this way, as Paul Sweezy eloquently explains in his foreword to the present volume.

When it was published in 1974, Harry Braverman's *Labor and Monopoly Capital: The Degradation of Work in the Twentieth Century* immediately stood out among twentieth-century studies in the degree to which it penetrated the hidden abode of the workplace, providing the first clear, critical understanding in more than a century of the labor process as a whole within capitalist society. It thus opened the way to the flood of radical investigations of the labor process that followed. Braverman's success, where so many others had failed, was not simply fortuitous. Much of the basis for his achievement is to be found in his personal background.

Braverman was born on December 9, 1920, in New York City, the son of Morris Braverman, a shoeworker, and Sarah Wolf Braverman. Caught up in the fervent radical intellectual spirit of the Depression years, he aspired to a college education and enrolled at Brooklyn College, only to be forced to terminate his schooling within a year due to the hard economic times. Beginning in 1937, Braverman apprenticed at the Brooklyn Naval Shipyard, where he began as a coppersmith, branched out into pipefitting, and eventually supervised a team of eighteen to twenty workers at refitting pipes of docked ships. Drafted near the end of the war in 1945, he was sent by the Army to Cheyenne, Wyoming, where as a sergeant he taught and supervised locomotive pipefitting. In 1947, he and his wife Miriam settled in Youngstown, Ohio, where he worked in steel layout and fitting at Republic Steel (where he was quickly fired at the instigation of the FBI), William B. Pollock Co., and Owen Structural Steel.[2]

From his teenage years in Brooklyn on, Braverman had identified with socialism, participating first in the Young People's Socialist League and later in the Socialist Workers Party (SWP), as part of a small but vibrant Trotskyist movement. During the 1940s and early 1950s, he wrote frequently for various SWP publications under a party name, Harry Frankel. But in 1953, Braverman broke with the SWP and left his job in the steel industry to establish, along with Bert Cochran, a new independent periodical, *The American Socialist*, which lasted until 1960. Braverman's editorial experience on *The American Socialist* opened the way to a new career from 1960 to 1967 as editor and later vice president and general manager at Grove Press, where he was credited with publishing *The Autobiography of Malcolm X*. During his Grove years, he picked up a B.A. at the New School for Social Research. In 1967, he became director of Monthly Review Press, a position he held until his death on August 2, 1976.

This unique background as a socialist intellectual who had been a worker and an activist within the productive core of world industry, one who rose by dint of his political struggles and intellectual brilliance to executive positions within two important presses, gave Braverman unique qualifications to take on the difficult task of stripping the veil away from the capitalist labor process. Braverman's Marxist training gave him the intellectual and political compass for his perceptive analysis of the entire history of managerial literature, culminating in an investigation of work under monopoly capital—the economic and social regime dominated by the giant corporation.[3] He wrote with a sophisticated understanding of Marx's dialectical method and with a clarity rarely equaled in modern social science, and he dealt with a fundamental realm of everyday existence—the very foundation of wealth and power in modern society, long lost behind a veil of obscurity. *Labor and Monopoly Capital* immediately inspired tens of thousands of readers, liberating them from enslavement to the conventional wisdom. Based on this single treatise, Braverman is now renowned worldwide as one of the great social scientists of the twentieth century: a legendary figure who arose from the depths of production to combat "the great god Capital," armed only with what he had learned while working with his own two hands and through his struggles as an organic intellectual, a human embodiment of the unification of theory and practice.

It is a measure of the tremendous influence exerted by Harry Braverman and successive radical labor process analysts that only a quarter-century after the publication of *Labor and Monopoly Capital* it is difficult to recall the absolute confidence with which the orthodox view of work relations was espoused in the early post-Second World War years.[4] At that time the preeminent interpretation of work in modern society was the one presented by Clark Kerr, John Dunlop, and others in a book entitled *Industrialism and Industrial Man* (1960). These authors provided a description of industrial society that can be summarized as follows:

(1) Industrialization has displaced capitalism.

(2) New technology requires rising levels of skill and responsibility.

(3) A growing proportion of technological and managerial personnel is transforming class relations.

(4) New wealth and leisure mean increased well-being rather than increased misery.

(5) There is a decline of overt protest.

(6) A larger role is assumed by enterprise managers and humanistic professionals, who constitute the "vanguard" of the future.

(7) The state is omnipresent and modern industry demands bureaucratization.

(8) Classes are eternal.

(9) There are many roads to industrialism.

(10) Industrialism is pluralistic, and power is diffuse.

"One of the central traits" of industrial society, declared Kerr and his co-authors, "is the inevitable and *eternal* separation of industrial men into managers and the managed" (emphasis added).[5]

In this orthodox view, technological changes in the organization of production are socially neutral. As sociologist Robert Blauner argued in his influential study *Alienation and Freedom* (1964), technological change is shaped by three factors: the state of scientific and mechanical processes, the nature of the product, and the engineering and economic resources specific to particular firms. Class and other forms of social conflict were either overlooked or excluded as factors by Blauner, like most conventional analysts of work.

Job dissatisfaction was not entirely ignored in the orthodox view of work relations, but it was seen as diminishing and in no way contradicting the reality of increasing skill levels, more humanistic management, and the diffusion of power and responsibility. "Alienation," Blauner wrote, "has traveled a course that could be charted on a graph by means of an inverted U-curve." It reached its height, he suggested, with the assembly-line industries of the early twentieth century. But as more and more industries have become automated, alienation has diminished—"thus the inverted U." Moreover, "the average worker," his readers were told, "is able to make an adjustment to a job which, from the standpoint of an intellectual, appears to be the epitome of tedium." Because of this, "empirical studies show that the majority of industrial workers are satisfied with their work and with their jobs." (The "empirical studies" consisted of numerous questionnaires collected for various industries by sociologists and business organizations concerned with the issue of overt job dissatisfaction.)[6]

Those who claimed that alienation was fading as a social problem, however, found this position difficult to maintain consistently. Blauner wrote, somewhat tortuously, that, "The typical worker in modern industrial society is probably satisfied *and* self-estranged."[7] Indeed, it is here that the orthodox academic approach ran into trouble as alienation became a hot issue in the 1960s and 1970s. A special task force selected by the secretary of health, education, and welfare declared in its 1973 report, *Work in America,* that "Significant numbers of American workers are dissatisfied by the quality of their working lives. As a result, the productivity of the worker is low—as measured by absenteeism, turnover rates, wildcat strikes, sabotage, poor-quality products, and a reluctance by workers to commit themselves to their work tasks." One job design consultant quoted in the *New York Times* explained the increase in active job dissatisfaction this way: "We may have created too many dumb jobs for the number of dumb people to fill them."[8]

For Braverman, all of this was simply illustrative of the contradiction at the heart of the orthodox approach to work and occupations. As he explained in the opening pages of *Labor and Monopoly Capital:*

> The more I read in the formal and informal literature of occupations, the more I became aware of a contradiction that marks much of the current writing in this area. On the one hand, it is emphasized that modern work, as a result of the scientific-technical revolution and "automation," requires ever higher levels of education, training, the greater exercise of intelligence and mental effort in general. At the same time, a mounting dissatisfaction with the conditions of industrial and office labor appears to contradict this view. For it is also said—sometimes by the same people who at other times support the first view—that work has become increasingly subdivided into petty operations that fail to sustain the interest or engage the capacities of humans with current levels of education; that these petty operations demand ever less skill and training; and that the modern trend of work by its "mindlessness" and "bureaucratization" is "alienating" ever larger sections of the working population.[9]

In the process of investigating this contradiction, Braverman turned the prevailing assumptions concerning the work process upside down, putting the orthodox position on the defensive within the social sciences and humanities. For the last quarter-century, the terms of the debate have been defined not by the orthodox conception of work, but by Braverman's critique. A generation of historians stimulated by E. P. Thompson's *The Making of the English Working Class* (1964) to explore labor history from radically new perspectives drew heavily upon Braverman in the 1970s. In sociology, an entire body of literature inspired by Braverman arose, now known familiarly as "the labor process debate." In Britain, social scientists spoke of "Bravermania." One measure of Braverman's lasting influence is that for the period 1976-1980 the *Social Science Citations Index* lists around 500 citations to *Labor and Monopoly Capital*, and for 1992-1996 the level was practically identical.[10]

In more recent, more conservative times, of course, the orthodox view of work has begun to reassert itself, but not with the same confidence with which it was espoused before Braverman. Instead the form that much of this takes is a steady attempt to chip away at Braverman—insisting that he emphasized "deskilling" unduly and neglected "reskilling," asserting that he did not pay attention to the subjective side of work and workers' struggles, stressing the growth of humanistic management techniques that supposedly qualify Braverman's conclusions, and arguing that Taylorism (which Braverman analyzed so devastatingly) was merely one stage, now bypassed, in worker-management relations.[11]

In order to evaluate these criticisms, it is necessary first to take a close look at the development of Braverman's argument, which arose out of the earlier critique of the capitalist division of labor by Marx. Kerr, Dunlop, and their collaborators in *Industrialism and Industrial Man* had introduced their own conception of work in industrial society as a refutation of "the Marxist interpretation" of capitalist development which pointed to the "degradation of the industrial worker." "An interpretation of the industrialization process developed during the early stages of the first instance of industrialization," they wrote, "is not likely to be appropriate or applicable after a century of experience." From their point of view, standard for the establishment, Marx was simply wrong in envisaging "greater intensity of work, the destruction of hierarchy of specialized workmen in pre-industrial society and the leveling of skill, a minor number of skilled labor, engineers, and managers, and the use of women and children for a growing number of unskilled tending and feeding jobs."[12]

Labor and Monopoly Capital, however, refuted this by means of an updated analysis corroborating Marx's conclusion that the reduction of the vast quantity of workers to a homogeneous grouping of "interchangeable parts," mere appendages to machines requiring little on-the-job training, was one of the fundamental tendencies of capitalist development. Like Marx, Braverman began with the distinction between labor and labor power. When hired for a particular job, the worker sells "not an agreed amount of labor, but the power to labor over an agreed period of time" for a wage. Humans bring to work the "infinitely malleable character of human labor." But once workers driven by necessity have "been forced to sell their labor power to another," Braverman observed, "the workers also surrender their interest in the labor process, which has now been 'alienated.' *The labor process has become the responsibility of the capitalist. . . .* It thus becomes essential for the capitalist that control over the labor process pass from the hands of the worker into his own. This transition presents itself in history as the *progressive alienation of the process of production* from the worker; to the capitalist, it presents itself as the problem of *management.* " Hence, under capitalism management is war by other means, sharing "from the first the characterization which Clausewitz assigned to war; it is *movement in a resistant medium* because it involves the control of refractory masses."[13]

The advantages arising from the division of labor have traditionally been conceived in the terms introduced by Adam Smith in the opening pages of *The Wealth of Nations* (1776), according to which savings in labor are obtained through the maximization of learning acquired by doing.[14] Each individual worker theoretically becomes more adept at a given task when the work is subdivided, with each worker responsible for a single operation. In Smith's famous example of pin manufacture, "one man draws out the wire, another straights it, a third cuts it, a fourth points it, . . . and the important business of making a pin is, in this manner, divided into about eighteen distinct operations, which, in some manufactories, are all performed by distinct hands." Increased dexterity on the part of the individual worker, the saving in labor time through the elimination of the time previously spent going from task to task, and the ease with which this division of labor facilitated the introduction of machinery: all were considered by Smith to be advantages obtained by the master manufacturer through the division of labor. For Smith, this kind of detailed division of labor was a mere matter of technical efficiency; the promotion of job-specific work skills led in each and every case to "a proportionate increase of the productive powers of labour."[15]

Yet there was considerable ambiguity in Smith's description. The extreme form of the division of labor he depicted could more readily be seen as embodying the reduction of skill—in any meaningful sense, beyond mere dexterity—rather than its enhancement. Thus, further along in *The Wealth of Nations,* Smith painted an entirely different picture of the effects of the division of labor in capitalist society:

> In the progress of the division of labour, the employment of the far greater part of those who live by labour, that is, of the great body of the people, comes to be confined to a few very simple operations, frequently to one or two. But the understandings of the greater part of men are necessarily formed by their ordinary employments. The man whose whole life is spent performing a few simple operations, of which the effects too are, perhaps, always the same, or very nearly the same, has no occasion to exert his understanding, or to exercise his invention in finding out expedients for removing difficulties which never occur. He naturally loses, therefore, the habit of such exertion, and generally becomes as stupid and ignorant as it is possible for a human creature to become.[16]

Indeed, the Industrial Revolution that arose in the late eighteenth century at around the time Smith completed *The Wealth of Nations* resulted in the degradation, not enhancement, of human labor. The classical liberal theorists of management, Charles Babbage and Andrew Ure, writing a half-century after Smith, understood the division of labor in a way that sharply contradicted Smith's earlier assumption of skill enhancement through job specialization.[17] It was obvious to Babbage and Ure that the detailed division of labor within the factory meant for the vast majority of workers not so much the creation of job-specific work skills as the breaking down of previous skills—a process that could only be justified by the greater profits it brought to employers.

Deliberately choosing the very same example of pin-making as Smith, Babbage argued in *On the Economy of Machinery and Manufactures* (1832) that the "the most important and influential cause" of the division of labor under capitalism was to be found in the *minimization* of job-specific knowledge on the part of the worker. "By dividing the work to be performed into different processes each requiring different degrees of skill or of force," Babbage wrote, the owner "can purchase exactly that precise quantity of both which is necessary for each process; whereas, if the whole work were executed by one workman, that person must possess sufficient skill to perform the most difficult, and sufficient strength to execute the most laborious, of the operations into which the art is divided."[18] Given that the higher the worker's skill level, the higher the wages that had to be paid, this process of systematic deskilling by breaking down work tasks into simpler components had the effect, Babbage argued, of cheapening labor.

Ure identified the same overall tendency toward diminishing skill requirements for the great bulk of workers in his *Philosophy of Manufactures* (1835). Ure explained that "the division, or rather adaptation of labour to the different talents of men, is little thought of in factory employment": with the introduction of machinery, processes formerly conducted by "the cunning workman, who is prone to irregularities of many kinds" are placed under the "charge of a peculiar mechanism, so self-regulating, that a child may superintend it." The whole tendency of manufacturing industry, according to Ure, was, if not "to supersede human labour altogether," at least "to diminish its cost, by substituting the industry of women and children for that of men; or that of ordinary labourers, for trained artisans."[19]

These criticisms of the Smithian theory of the division of labor by the early proponents of capitalist management were subsequently incorporated by Marx into his critique of capitalist political economy, in which he argued that the key to understanding the development of the detailed division of labor under capitalism was to be found not in Smith's learning by doing, demanding ever greater technical specialization as a means of enhancing the skill levels of workers, but in the opposite principle enunciated by Babbage and Ure in the early nineteenth century: reducing labor costs through the systematic degradation of human labor.[20] "Babbage's principle," Braverman wrote, "eventually becomes the underlying force governing all forms of work in capitalist society, no matter in what setting or at what hierarchical level."[21]

While these tendencies of the capitalist division of labor were already evident in the nineteenth century, it was not until the maturation of monopoly capitalism in the twentieth century that they came to be applied systematically. The development of the division of labor, as Adam Smith observed, was dependent on the extent of the market and the scale of production. Its full development was therefore impracticable for the small family firm that still predominated in the nineteenth century. With the rise of the giant corporation in the late nineteenth century, however, all of this changed. It is in this context that one has to understand the rise to prominence of Frederick Winslow Taylor and scientific management, or Taylorism, in the early twentieth century.

Taylorism was summarized by Braverman in the form of three distinct principles: "dissociation of the labor process from the skills of the workers," "separation of conception from execution," and "use of this monopoly over knowledge to control each step of the labor process and its mode of execution." Although Taylor claimed wage increases were integral to his system, so too were reduced employers' labor costs, to be accomplished by eliminating jobs and saving labor time. "Taylor," Braverman wrote, "understood the Babbage principle better than anyone of his time, and it was always uppermost in his calculations. . . . In his early book, *Shop Management,* he said frankly that the 'full possibilities' of his system 'will not have been realized until almost all of the machines in the shop are run by men who are of smaller calibre and attainments, and who are therefore cheaper than those required under the old system.' "[22] In the end, thus, the Babbage principle and Taylor's scientific management led to the same result. Taylor's distinctive contribution was to articulate a full-scale managerial imperative for increased job control, to be implemented primarily through deskilling. Hence, within Taylorism, Braverman maintained, "lies a theory which is nothing less than the explicit verbalization of the capitalist mode of production."[23]

The essential elements of the capitalist division of labor, Marx and Braverman each insisted, could be analyzed prior to the consideration of machinery. Taylor likewise abstracted from machinery in his analysis of scientific management. Once labor has been simplified, the substitution of machines for labor becomes increasingly possible. Moreover, in carrying out such substitutions, management is at least as interested in the capacity of certain types of machinery to centralize their control over the labor process as it is in the productivity of labor. The particular production technology introduced into the work process under capitalism is therefore designed to maximize managerial control. Capitalism is characterized by "the incessant drive to enlarge and perfect machinery on the one hand, and to diminish the worker on the other."[24]

There was, however, nothing inevitable about such a process, according to Braverman. The development of modern technology itself often reunified processes that had previously been divided by the division of labor, completely undermining Adam Smith's original justification for the detailed division of labor, and generating the possibility of creating a more rewarding work environment for socialized labor. Ironically, the best illustration of this was to be found in the further evolution of the very pin manufacturing process that Smith had originally discussed. Pins, as Braverman pointed out, were no longer produced by workers divided into discrete tasks. Rather,

> The entire process is re-unified in a single machine which transforms great coils of wire into millions of pins each day already papered and ready for sale. Now go back and read Adam Smith's arguments for the division of labor,

arguments having to do with the dexterity gained in the constant application to one operation of a hand process over and over again and so on. You will notice that this modern technology has made a complete hash of these arguments. Not one remains with any force today. The re-unified process in which the execution of all the steps is built into the working mechanism of a single machine would seem now to render it suitable for a collective of associated producers, none of whom need spend all of their lives at any single function and all of whom can participate in the engineering, design, improvement, repair and operation of these ever more productive machines. Such a system would entail no loss of production, and it would represent the re-unification of the craft in a body of workers far superior to the old craftsworkers.[25]

If such radical possibilities were not realized, it was due not to the technical requirements of modern machine production and engineering but rather to the economic mandates of the capitalist system. For Braverman, the essence of the development of labor under capitalism lay in the fact that "a structure is given to all labor processes that at its extremes polarizes those whose time is infinitely valuable and those whose time is worth almost nothing. This might even be called the general law of the capitalist division of labor."[26]

Since some subsequent commentators have reduced Braverman's contribution to a fairly simplistic conception of generalized deskilling, it is vital to recognize that Braverman did not argue that the average level of skill in society would decline as a result of the further development of the division of labor under capitalism. Instead, he insisted,

Since, with the development of technology and the application to it of the fundamental sciences, the labor processes of society have come to embody a greater amount of scientific knowledge, clearly the "average" scientific, technical, and in that sense "skill" content of these labor processes is much greater now than in the past. But this is nothing but a tautology. The question is precisely whether the scientific and "educated" content of labor tends toward *averaging,* or, on the contrary, toward polarization. . . . The mass of the workers gain nothing from the fact that the decline in their command over the labor process is more than compensated for by the increasing command on the part of managers and engineers. On the contrary, not only does their skill fall in an absolute sense (in that they lose craft and traditional abilities without gaining new abilities adequate to compensate the loss), but it falls even more in a *relative* sense. The more science is incorporated into the labor process, the less the worker understands of the process; the more sophisticated an intellectual product the machine becomes, the less control and comprehension of the machine the worker has.[27]

Braverman's analysis, then, is not simply about "deskilling" in some generalized, abstract sense, divorced from capitalist exploitation and accumulation.

It is worth noting that Braverman himself did not employ that term, writing instead of "the destruction of craftsmanship" and maintaining that "the capitalist mode of production systematically destroys all-round skills where they exist."[28] Although "deskilling" may be a useful shorthand designation for this theory, the term has often been invoked mistakenly, as an all-encompassing notion obviating any need for a reconstruction of the whole of Braverman's argument. Braverman was primarily concerned with the degradation of work as it affected the *working class*, not the entire society. His real subject, as he emphasized on the opening page of his book, was "the structure of the working class, and the manner in which it had changed." He was concerned with uncovering the primary relationships of workers to the means of production under monopoly capitalism. Much of his analysis was therefore directed at the changing occupational characteristics of the working class, including the rise of service work (made possible by the development of "the universal market"), the transformation of clerical work, and so forth. Indeed, *Labor and Monopoly Capital* was greeted on its appearance as making "a major contribution, perhaps unbeknownst to its author, to feminist analysis" as a result of its portrait of the shift in clerical work from a predominantly male to a predominantly female occupation.[29]

Labor and Monopoly Capital has inspired an enormous and continuing body of research on the labor process in capitalist society. Much of this research, usually taking the form of specific case studies, has verified Braverman's conclusions. Not only has it been shown that struggles over job control are the central feature of work under capitalism, but also that to a considerable extent the labor of most workers has been degraded. A statistical assessment first published in *The American Journal of Sociology*, for example, showed that "there was a systematic tendency for those positions with relatively little control over their labor processes to expand during the 1960s and for those positions with high levels of autonomy to decline." The advent of "lean production" on an increasingly global scale in the 1980s and 1990s has further accelerated this tendency towards the degradation of work for most workers.[30]

Needless to say, proponents of the orthodox view of work still dispute these conclusions. Braverman is often criticized for oversimplifying the direction of change and for ignoring the "reskilling" that accompanies deskilling. Such arguments, however, miss the point. The main question is whether there is a general tendency toward the deskilling of most workers. Has there been a polarization of working conditions, with the greatest number of workers occupying positions that are less and less skilled? As a general tendency, resulting from the managerial imperatives of capitalism, this may be modified by other tendencies and forces. But as a general trend it nonetheless exists; and as the central imperative of management, it is always present. It derives its force not from any mere technical imperative but from the unending quest for profitability, which requires as its basis a continual reduction in unit wage costs, the relative cheapening of labor.[31]

Braverman is also criticized for paying too little attention to the subjective side of work and workers' own struggles. As a former working-class activist, Braverman obviously did not undervalue the issue of workers' consciousness. On the contrary, he believed that "the value of any analysis of the composition and social trends within the working population can only lie in precisely how well it helps us to answer questions about class consciousness." Marxism, he held, is after all "a theory of revolution and thus a tool of combat."[32] In *Labor and Monopoly Capital* itself, however, he imposed, as any careful author will do, certain limitations on his own research. Workers' political sensibilities, trade union organization, working-class parties, socialist strategy, and comparable issues lay beyond the designated scope of *Labor and Monopoly Capital*.

Nonetheless, *Labor and Monopoly Capital*, far from avoiding the question of class struggle, actually deepens our appreciation of the struggle between classes. Like Marx, Braverman considered class related above all to the process of exploitation, to the way in which the surplus product is extracted from the direct producer. Class struggle does not simply occur within the wider public sphere in which classes become self-conscious and operate as political actors, but also in daily life, within the labor process itself, where control over production, as measured in units of time as small as ten-thousandths of a second (or even smaller), is bitterly contested. Case study after case study has shown that Braverman's analysis illuminates the class struggle at a deeper, more intensive level—a level seldom comprehended by intellectuals but well known to workers.

Others claim, in opposition to Braverman, that Taylorism was a passing managerial strategy, later replaced by Fordism, bureaucratic control, "humanistic" control, or what have you. No doubt there have been important modifications in managerial practice since the time of Taylor.[33] Management is quite willing to use more elaborate work rules, credentialism, and so on, to further divide the workers and centralize control. And "worker participation" schemes will be used up to a point if they do not contradict the real centralization of authority within management or the final object of lowering labor costs. But a good case can nonetheless be made that Taylor's principles of scientific management remain "the explicit verbalization of the capitalist mode of production." All these other strategies are therefore mere modifications of the tendency toward the polarization of working conditions under monopoly capitalism—that is, the degradation of work for the vast majority and the upgrading of work for a relative few. Braverman, indeed, anticipated the farce of "Quality Work Circles" when he wrote, referring to comparable reforms, "They represent a style of management rather than a genuine change in the position of the worker. They are characterized by a studied pretense of worker 'participation,' a gracious liberality in allowing the worker to adjust a machine, replace a light bulb, move from one fractional job to another, and to have the illusion of making decisions by choosing among fixed and limited alternatives designed by a management which deliberately leaves insignificant matters open to choice."[34]

There is enormous pressure to conform to the orthodox view of work, which, though rendered hollow by Braverman's analysis, still remains dominant since it suits the needs of the dominant interests in society. The same John Dunlop who co-authored *Industrialism and Industrial Man* with Clark Kerr and others went on to become U.S. Secretary of Labor (1975-1976) and, more recently, chair of the Commission on the Future of Worker-Management Relations of the U.S. Department of Labor and the Department of Commerce. In its May 1994 report, the Dunlop Commission concluded, "Some technological changes require more skilled workers. Others downgrade existing skills. The current consensus is that the former predominates, so that technology has raised the demand for skills, responsibility, and knowledge."[35] In the face of this kind of ongoing official obfuscation, Braverman's *Labor and Monopoly Capital* remains a truly revolutionary work—as revolutionary today as it was when it was first published a quarter-century ago.

Notes

1. Robert Heilbroner, "Men at Work," review of *Labor and Monopoly Capital* by Harry Braverman, *The New York Review of Books*, 23 January 1975: 6.
2. These biographical notes owe much to Bryan D. Palmer, "Before Braverman: Harry Frankel and the American Workers' Movement" (paper presented to the conference on "Work, Difference, and Social Change," State University of New York at Binghamton, May 1998); and Miriam Braverman, telephone conversation with author, 5 August 1998.
3. Braverman saw his book as a contribution to the general theory of monopoly capital (capitalism in the age of the giant firm), elements of which had been previously explored in Paul Baran and Paul Sweezy, *Monopoly Capital* (New York: Monthly Review Press, 1966) and Harry Magdoff, *The Age of Imperialism* (New York: Monthly Review Press, 1969).
4. Part of what follows is adapted from my article "*Labor and Monopoly Capital* Twenty Years After: An Introduction," *Monthly Review* 46 (November 1994): 1-13.
5. Clark Kerr, John T. Dunlop, Frederick Harbison, and Charles A. Myers, *Industrialism and Industrial Man* (Cambridge: Harvard University Press, 1969), 28-32; see also Paul Thompson, *The Nature of Work* (London: Macmillan, 1983), 11-13.
6. Robert Blauner, *Alienation and Freedom* (Chicago: University of Chicago Press, 1964), 6, 117, 182-83. Blauner intended his study as a refutation of the Marxist theory of work and alienation. Later in the 1960s, Blauner began to

contribute to the analysis of race in the United States. Many radical students studied under him, and his work took a more progressive form through his advocacy of the "internal colonialism" thesis. See, for example, Robert Blauner, *Racial Oppression in America* (New York: Harper and Row, 1972).

7. Blauner, *Alienation and Freedom,* 29.

8. Harry Braverman, *Labor and Monopoly Capital*, 21-25. (All page references to *Labor and Monopoly Capital* are to the present edition.)

9. Ibid., 3.

10. Histories that creatively amplified Braverman's findings include David Montgomery, *Workers' Control in America: Studies in the History of Work, Technology, and Labor Struggles* (Cambridge: Cambridge University Press, 1979) and David F. Noble, *Forces of Production* (New York: Alfred A. Knopf, 1984). On "Bravermania," see Graeme Salaman, *Working* (New York: Tavistock, 1986), 17.

11. These specific criticisms of Braverman's analysis are advanced in the articles on "Labor Process" and "Proletarianization" in each of the following dictionaries of sociology: Nicholas Abercrombie, Stephen Hill, and Bryan S. Turner, *The Penguin Dictionary of Sociology* (Harmondsworth: Penguin, 1988); Gordon Marshall, ed., *The Oxford Dictionary of Sociology* (New York: Oxford University Press, 1994); and David Jara and Julia Jara, eds., *The Harper-Collins Dictionary of Sociology* (New York: Harper-Collins, 1991). For a critique of such interpretations, see Peter Meiksins, "*Labor and Monopoly Capital* for the 1990s: A Review and Critique of the Labor Process Debate," *Monthly Review* 46 (November 1994): 45-59.

12. Kerr and others, *Industrialism and Industrial Man*, 24-25, 32.

13. Braverman, *Labor and Monopoly Capital*, 37-39, 46.

14. This interpretation of Smith is partly inspired by Ugo Pagano, "Harry Braverman (1920-1976)," in *A Biographical Dictionary of Dissenting Economists*, ed. Philip Arestis and Malcolm Sawyer (Brookfield, VT: Edward Elgar, 1992), 60-61.

15. Adam Smith, *The Wealth of Nations* (New York: Modern Library, 1937), 4-5.

16. Ibid., 734.

17. This interpretation draws upon Ugo Pagano, *Work and Welfare in Economic Theory* (New York: Basil Blackwell, 1985), 12-18.

18. Charles Babbage, *The Economy of Machinery and Manufactures,* vol. 8 of *Works* (New York: New York University Press, 1989), 124-25.

19. Andrew Ure, *The Philosophy of Manufactures* (New York: Augustus M. Kelley, 1967), 19-23.

20. See Karl Marx, *Capital,* vol. 1 (New York: Vintage, 1976), 470.

21. Braverman, *Labor and Monopoly Capital*, 57. The term "Babbage principle" was employed by the great British economist Alfred Marshall at the time of the First World War. Marshall saw scientific management as prefigured by the Babbage principle, which had only needed the proper economic scale to be

fully applied (and which Marshall believed that the war was providing, at long last). See Alfred Marshall, *Industry and Trade* (London: Macmillan, 1920), 224-25, 376-78.

22. Braverman, *Labor and Monopoly Capital*, 77-82. Despite Taylor's frequent call for "high wages," scientific management in actuality culminated usually in wage reductions once the system was wholly instituted in any given sector. Taylor himself made it clear that wage incentives were to be only marginally higher, and that wages should be carefully calibrated according to grades of work. "For their own good," Taylor wrote, "it is as important that workmen should not be very much overpaid, as it is that they should not be underpaid." Frederick Winslow Taylor, *Shop Management* (New York: Harper and Brothers, 1912), 27-29.

23. Braverman, *Labor and Monopoly Capital*, 59-60. Some have mistakenly concluded that Taylorism was itself a form of radicalism, but, as Robert Kanigel has written, "Taylor fancied himself a radical; he was not. Management scholar Harlow Person saw . . . 'evidence that Taylor was not thinking of management for a new social order. . . . He was concerned only with better management under the present system.' " Robert Kanigel, *The One Best Way: Frederick Winslow Taylor and the Enigma of Efficiency* (New York: Viking, 1997), 549.

24. Braverman, *Labor and Monopoly Capital*, 134, 157.

25. Braverman, "The Degradation of Work," appendix 2 to this edition, 320.

26. Braverman, *Labor and Monopoly Capital*, 57-58.

27. Ibid., 294-95.

28. Ibid., 94, 57.

29. Rosalyn Baxandall, Elizabeth Ewen, and Linda Gordon, "The Other Side of the Paycheck," in *Technology, the Labor Process, and the Working Class*, by Baxandall and others (New York: Monthly Review Press, 1976), 8.

30. Eric Olin Wright and Joachim Singleman, "Proletarianization in the Changing American Class Structure," in *Marxist Inquiries: Studies of Labor, Class and States*, ed. Michael Burawoy and Theda Skocpol (Chicago: University of Chicago Press, 1982), S198. For further studies confirming Braverman's findings, see Andrew Zimbalist, ed., *Case Studies on the Labor Process* (New York: Monthly Review Press, 1979); Craig Heron and Robert Storey, eds., *On the Job* (Montreal: McGill-Queens University Press, 1986); and Joan Greenbaum, *Windows on the Workplace: Computers, Jobs, and the Organization of Office Work in the Late Twentieth Century* (New York: Monthly Review Press, 1995). On the effects of "lean production," see Kim Moody, *Workers in a Lean World* (New York: Verso, 1997), 87-90.

31. Malcolm Sawyer, *The Challenge of Radical Political Economy* (Brighton: Harvester Wheatsheaf, 1989); Pagano, "Harry Braverman," 63-64; Sheila Cohen, "A Labour Process to Nowhere?," *New Left Review*, no. 165 (September-October 1987), 34-50.

32. Harry Braverman, "Two Comments," appendix 1 to this edition, 313.
33. See John Bellamy Foster, "The Fetish of Fordism," *Monthly Review* 39 (March 1988): 14-33.
34. Braverman, *Labor and Monopoly Capital*, 26-27.
35. U.S. Department of Labor and U.S. Department of Commerce, Commission on the Future of Worker-Management Relations, *Fact Finding Report* (Washington, D.C.: GPO, May 1994), 6.

Foreword to the Original Edition

by Paul M. Sweezy

In the Introduction to our book *Monopoly Capital*, published in 1966, Paul Baran and I wrote that the approach we had adopted was not calculated to give a complete picture of the form of society under study. We continued:

> And we are particularly conscious of the fact that this approach, as we have used it, has resulted in almost total neglect of a subject which occupies a central place in Marx's study of capitalism: the labor process. We stress the crucial role of technological change in the development of monopoly capitalism but make no attempt to inquire systematically into the consequences which the particular kinds of technological change characteristic of the monopoly capitalist period have had for the nature of work, the composition (and differentiation) of the working class, the psychology of workers, the forms of working-class organization and struggle, and so on. These are all obviously important subjects which would have to be dealt with in any comprehensive study of monopoly capitalism.

Now at last, in Harry Braverman's work published nearly a decade later, we have a serious, and in my judgment solidly successful, effort to fill a large part of this gap. It would be hard to describe this effort more accurately or concisely than as "an attempt to inquire systematically into the consequences which the particular kinds of technological change characteristic of the monopoly capitalist period have had for the nature of work [and] the composition (and differentiation) of the working class." Harry Braverman, however, does not attempt to pursue the inquiry into what may be called the subjective aspects of the development of the working class under monopoly capitalism. That task remains to be tackled. Whoever undertakes it will find in the present work a firm and indispensable foundation on which to build.

I want to make quite clear that the reason Baran and I did not ourselves attempt in any way to fill this gap was not only the approach we adopted. A more fundamental reason was that we lacked the necessary qualifications. A genius like Marx could analyze the labor process under capitalism without ever having been immediately involved in it, and do so with unmatched brilliance and insight. For lesser mortals, direct experience is a *sine qua non*, as the dismal record of various academic "experts" and "authorities" in this area so eloquently testifies. Baran and I lacked this crucially important direct experience, and if we had ventured into the subject we would in all probability have been taken in by many of the myths and fallacies so energetically promoted by capitalism's ideologists. There is, after all, no subject on which it is so important (for capitalism) that the truth should be hidden. As evidence of this gullibility I will cite only one instance—our swallowing whole the myth of a tremendous decline during the last half century of the percentage of the labor force which is unskilled (see *Monopoly Capital*, p. 267). Harry Braverman has had a wealth of direct experience—he summarizes it briefly in his Introduction—and is therefore admirably equipped to combat and expose the distortions and lies of capitalism's apologists. Nowhere is this done more crushingly than in the eloquent final chapter where the myth of the increasingly skilled labor force is destroyed once and for all.

But it is not only direct experience that is needed for the scientific study of the labor process under monopoly capitalism. Equally important is a thorough mastery of Marx's pioneering work in this field and of his dialectical method. Harry Braverman has this too, and it is the combination of practical experience and theoretical acumen—a combination excluded almost by definition from our academic social sciences—which has enabled him to produce a contribution of surpassing importance to the understanding of the society we live in.

Everyone who reads this book will benefit from it. But those who will benefit particularly are the ones who read it along with Volume I of *Capital*, and especially Part IV ("The Production of Relative Surplus Value"), for it is here that the analysis of the labor process under capitalism was first put on a genuinely scientific foundation. All the essential concepts and tools were provided by Marx, and indeed he used them to such good effect that for a long time his followers took it for granted that nothing new needed to be added in this field of investigation. As far as theory is concerned, they were right. But of course the outward manifestations of capitalism, though not its inner nature, have undergone tremendous changes in the last century. Capital accumulation has assumed new organizational forms; it has invaded old branches of the economy and flowed into many new ones. What needed to be done was to apply Marx's theory to the new methods and occupations invented or created by capital in its restless expansion. This is the task Harry Braverman has set himself. In terms of theory, as he would be the first to say, there is very little that is new in this book. In terms of knowledge gained from the creative application of theory there is an enormous amount that is new, and much of it in direct contradiction to what capitalist ideology has succeeded in establishing as the society's conventional wisdom.

I hasten to add, and here again I am sure Harry Braverman would be the first to agree, that in important respects the function of this work is to pose rather than answer questions, to open (or re-open) lines of inquiry which have been neglected and which cry out for research and elaboration. There is hardly an occupation or other aspect of the labor process which would not repay a great deal more detailed historical and analytical investigation than are accorded to it in this broad survey. In this sense, Harry Braverman's book is to be considered an invitation and a challenge to a younger generation of Marxist economists and sociologists to get on with the urgent task of destroying bourgeois ideology and putting in its place an honest picture of the social reality within which we are forced to live.*

I must conclude these remarks with a confession: for me reading this book has been an emotional experience, somewhat similar, I suppose, to that which millions of readers of Volume I of *Capital* have been through. The sad, horrible, heart-breaking way the vast majority of my fellow countrymen and women, as well as their counterparts in most of the rest of the world, are obliged to spend their working lives is seared into my consciousness in an excruciating and unforgettable way. And when I think of all the talent and energy which daily go into devising ways and means of making their torment worse, all in the name of efficiency and productivity but really for the greater glory of the great god Capital, my wonder at humanity's ability to create such a monstrous system is surpassed only by amazement at its willingness to tolerate the continuance of an arrangement so obviously destructive of the well-being and happiness of human beings. If the same effort, or only half of it, were devoted to making work the joyous and creative activity it can be, what a wonderful world this could be.

But first of all must come widespread popular understanding of what capitalism really is, and why its seeming necessity and inevitability are in reality only ideological fig leaves to hide the naked self-interest of a tiny minority. This book, I am convinced, can make a vital contribution to that much-needed enlightenment.

---

* In this connection let me call attention to Chapter 17 ("The Structure of the Working Class and Its Reserve Armies"), where the thesis is put forward that Marx's "General Law of Capitalist Accumulation," according to which the advance of capitalism is characterized by the amassing of wealth at one pole and of deprivation and misery at the other, far from being the egregious fallacy which bourgeois social science has long held it to be, has in fact turned out to be one of the best founded of all Marx's insights into the capitalist system. How much more coherent and useful the voluminous literature of recent years on poverty and related questions would be if it had started from this solid foundation!

Labor and Monopoly Capital

Denn die einen sind im Dunkeln
Und die andern sind im Licht
Und man siehet die im Lichte
Die im Dunkeln sieht man nicht. *

—Bertolt Brecht

(To the tune of *Mack the Knife)*

* Some there are who live in darkness / While the others live in light / We see those who live in daylight / Those in darkness, out of sight.

Introduction

This book first took shape in my mind as little more than a study of occupational shifts in the United States. I was interested in the structure of the working class, and the manner in which it had changed. That portion of the population employed in manufacturing and associated industries—the so-called industrial working class—had apparently been shrinking for some time, if not in absolute numbers at any rate in relative terms. Since the details of this process, especially its historical turning points and the shape of the new employment that was taking the place of the old, were not clear to me, I undertook to find out more about them. And since, as I soon discovered, these things had not yet been clarified in any comprehensive fashion, I decided that there was a need for a more substantial historical description and analysis of the process of occupational change than had yet been presented in print.

The more I read in the formal and informal literature of occupations, the more I became aware of a contradiction that marks much of the current writing in this area. On the one hand, it is emphasized that modern work, as a result of the scientific-technical revolution and "automation," requires ever higher levels of education, training, the greater exercise of intelligence and mental effort in general. At the same time, a mounting dissatisfaction with the conditions of industrial and office labor appears to contradict this view. For it is also said—sometimes even by the same people who at other times support the first view—that work has become increasingly subdivided into petty operations that fail to sustain the interest or engage the capacities of humans with current levels of education; that these petty operations demand ever less skill and training; and that the modern trend of work by its "mindlessness" and "bureaucratization" is "alienating" ever larger sections of the working population. As generalizations, these two views cannot easily be harmonized. On the other hand, I was not able to find in the vast literature any attempt to reconcile them by careful specification of the manner in which various occupations have evolved, perhaps in contrast to one another.

Thus my interests began to broaden to include the evolution of labor processes *within* occupations as well as the shifts of labor *among* occupations. And as both these varieties of change became gradually clearer in my mind, I was led into the search for the causes, the dynamic underlying the incessant transformation of work in the modern era. In particular, this led me to include in my investigation the evolution of management as well as of technology, of the modern corporation as well as of changes in social life. Before long I found myself attempting a study of the development of the capitalist mode of production during the past hundred years.

The literature which presents and interprets technical and management trends for the general reader exists primarily in two forms: journalism and social science. In the course of a fairly extensive reading of this literature, I was particularly struck by the vagueness, generality of wording, and on occasion egregious errors of description of the concrete matters under discussion. It seemed to me that many widely accepted conclusions were based on little genuine information, and represented either simplifications or outright misreadings of a complex reality. Since much of what appears here will challenge this conventional picture of work and the working population, I feel that I owe the reader an account of my own background insofar as it plays a role in this book. For although I spent on this study the largest part of my spare time during more than four years, my interest in many of the subjects discussed in it dates from many years earlier.

I began my working life by serving a four-year apprenticeship in the coppersmith's trade, and worked at this trade for a total of seven years. These seven years were spent in a naval shipyard, a type of industrial enterprise which, at that time, was probably the most complete product of two centuries of industrial revolution. Almost all the mechanic crafts which had arisen in the course of these centuries (some of which, like my own, were rooted in the handicrafts of classical antiquity and earlier) were practiced in such a shipyard in close association with each other. Because of this propinquity and the interlocking processes practiced by the crafts, and also because of the gathering together of apprentices of all crafts in a trade school for semi-weekly sessions, I learned not only my own trade but gained a concrete understanding of most of the others.

The extremely limited nature of employment in my trade, and its rapid decline with the substitution of new processes and materials for the traditional modes of copper working, made it difficult for me to continue to work as a coppersmith when I moved to other parts of the country or from job to job. But because the trade of working copper provided a foundation in the elements of a number of other crafts, I was always able to find employment in other trades, such as pipefitting, sheetmetal work, and layout, and I did work of these sorts for another seven years: in a railroad repair shop, in sheetmetal shops, and especially in two plants which fabricated heavy steel plate and structural steel into equipment for the basic steel industry, including blast furnaces.

This background of craftsmanship may lead some readers to conclude, after they have read this book, that I have been influenced by a sentimental attachment to the outworn conditions of now archaic modes of labor. I have been conscious of this possibility, but I have tried not to let any of my conclusions flow from such a romanticism, and on the whole I do not believe that this criticism would be warranted. It is true that I enjoyed, and still enjoy, working as a craftsman, but since I grew up during the years of rapid change in the mechanic crafts, I was always conscious of the inexorable march of science-based technological change; moreover, in my reflections upon this subject and in the many discussions among craftsmen debating the "old" and the "new" in which I took part, I was always a modernizer. I believed then, and still believe now, that the transformation of labor processes from their basis in tradition to their basis in science is not only inevitable but necessary for the progress of the human race and for its emancipation from hunger and other forms of need. More important, throughout those years I was an activist in the socialist movement, and I had assimilated the Marxist view which is hostile not to science and technology as such, but only to the manner in which these are used as weapons of domination in the creation, perpetuation, and deepening of a gulf between classes in society.

I had the opportunity of seeing at first hand, during those years, not only the transformation of industrial processes but the manner in which these processes are reorganized; how the worker, systematically robbed of a craft heritage, is given little or nothing to take its place. Like all craftsmen, even the most inarticulate, I always resented this, and as I reread these pages, I find in them a sense not only of social outrage, which was intended, but also perhaps of personal affront. If this is so, it is, as I say, unintended, but I do not think it does any harm. However, I repeat that I hope no one draws from this the conclusion that my views are shaped by nostalgia for an age that cannot be recaptured. Rather, my views about work are governed by nostalgia for an age that has not yet come into being, in which, for the worker, the craft satisfaction that arises from conscious and purposeful mastery of the labor process will be combined with the marvels of science and the ingenuity of engineering, an age in which everyone will be able to benefit, in some degree, from this combination.

In later years, I was able to gain first-hand experience of some of the most typical office processes of our times, again at the moment when they were beginning to undergo rapid changes. Some years of experience in socialist journalism led eventually to my employment in book publishing as an editor, and this in turn led to more than a dozen years as an operating executive in two publishing houses. Here I was able to see, and in fact design, some of the administrative processes involved in modern marketing, distributing, account-ing, and book production routines; and this experience twice included the transition from conventional to computerized office systems. I would not pretend that this background is as extensive as that of many others who have worked for longer periods of time in larger organizations, but at least it does enable me to understand, in some detail and concreteness, the principles by which labor processes are organized in modern offices.

As the reader will see in the appropriate chapters, I have tried to put this experience to some use in this book. I have also had the benefit of many conversations—with friends, acquaintances, strangers met at social gatherings or while traveling—about their work (and it may be that some of them, if they chance to read this, will now understand why I was curious to the point of rudeness). But while this occupational and conversational background has been useful, I must emphasize that nothing in this book relies upon personal experience or reminiscences, and that I have in the formal sense included almost no factual materials for which I could not give a reference which can be checked independently by the reader, as is proper in any scientific work.

Throughout the period of study and composition, I discussed the ideas that were taking shape in my mind with a number of friends, and I want to thank them here for their interest and patience. The manuscript was also read in draft by friends, associates, and otherwise interested persons, and I must thank them all for valuable suggestions which improved the clarity of presentation of a sometimes complex subject matter, and saved me from some blunders of conception and expression. In particular, I must acknowledge my debt to Paul Sweezy and Harry Magdoff, who were especially helpful in starting me on a number of tracks which I might otherwise have neglected, and in suggesting readings which I might otherwise have missed; but I would like also to add that my chief debt to them, and one which I feel most keenly, is the force of their example as Marxists attempting a grasp of modern social reality. My acknowledgments to writers whose work had a special value will be found in the text, footnotes, and reference notes. The intellectual influence under which this work was composed is that of Marx and, as the reader will see, little that has been written by any Marxists since Marx plays a direct role in those portions of this book concerned with the labor process, for reasons which I must now try to explain.

The central place in the first volume of Marx's *Capital* is occupied by the labor process as it takes place under the control of capital, and the subtitle describes it accurately as a "critical analysis of capitalist production." In this volume, the only part of his projected study of capitalism that he was able to realize fully, Marx shows how the processes of production are, in capitalist society, incessantly transformed under the impetus of the principal driving force of that society, the accumulation of capital. For the working population, this transformation manifests itself, first, as a continuous change in the labor processes of each branch of industry, and second, as a redistribution of labor among occupations and industries.

Marx completed this work in the mid-1860s. During the past century this very same dynamic has been far more powerful than the manifestations of it which Marx witnessed in his own lifetime and upon which he based his critical analysis of capitalist production. Yet the extraordinary fact is that Marxists have added little to his body of work in this respect. Neither the changes in productive processes throughout this century of capitalism and monopoly capitalism, nor the changes in the occupational and industrial structure of the working population have been subjected to any comprehensive Marxist analysis since Marx's death. It is for this reason that I cannot, as I have already said, attribute to any Marxists other than Marx himself a strong intellectual influence upon this study: there simply is no continuing body of work in the Marxist tradition dealing with the capitalist mode of production in the manner in which Marx treated it in the first volume of *Capital*. Since the reasons for this are bound to be of interest, we must ask why this is so.

The answer probably begins with the extraordinary thoroughness and prescience with which Marx performed his task. He subjected labor processes, and their development in the factory system, to the most knowledgeable and systematic study they have ever received. So well did he understand the tendencies of the capitalist mode of production, and so accurately did he generalize from the as yet meager instances of his own time, that in the decades immediately after he completed his work Marx's analysis seemed adequate to each special problem of the labor process, and remarkably faithful to the overall movement of production. It may thus have been, in the beginning, the very prophetic strength of Marx's analysis that contributed to the dormancy of this subject among Marxists. The development of the factory system seemed to bear out Marx in every particular, and to render superfluous any attempt to repeat what he had already accomplished. It is true that by the early part of the twentieth century the increase in commercial, administrative, and technical labor seemed to cut across Marx's bipolar class structure and introduce a complicating element, and this occasioned a discussion in the Second International and especially in its German section. But the discussion was abortive, in part because the tendencies had not yet ripened sufficiently, and it faded away without conclusive results even while the substance of the problem increased in scope.

Meanwhile, the cataclysmic events of this century—two world wars, fascism, the successive disintegrations and restabilizations of capitalist economies in the aftermaths of wars and in the Great Depression, and revolutions both proletarian and nationalist—dominated the analytical work of Marxism. The front of this violent stage was taken and held by monopoly, militarism, imperialism, nationalism, the "crisis" or "breakdown" tendencies of the capitalist system, revolutionary strategy, and the problems of the transition from capitalism to socialism.

The extraordinary development of scientific technology, of the productivity of labor, and to some extent of the customary levels of working-class consumption during this century have had, as has often been noted, a profound effect upon the labor movement as a whole. The unionized working class, intimidated by the scale and complexity of capitalist production, and weakened in its original revolutionary impetus by the gains afforded by the rapid increase of productivity, increasingly lost the will and ambition to wrest control of production from capitalist hands and turned ever more to bargaining over labor's share in the product. This labor movement formed the immediate environment of Marxism; and Marxists were, in varying degrees, compelled to adapt themselves to it.

The adaptation took various forms, many of which can now be seen as ideologically destructive. The working philosophy of Marxism, as distinguished from its holiday pronouncements, focused increasingly not upon the profound inner nature of capitalism and the worker's position within it, but upon its various conjunctural effects and crises. In particular, the critique of the mode of production gave way to the critique of capitalism as a mode of distribution. Impressed, perhaps even overawed, by the immense productivity of the labor process, baffled by its increasing scientific intricacy, participating in the struggles of workers for improvements in wages, hours, and conditions, Marxists adapted to the view of the modern factory as an inevitable if perfectible form of the organization of the labor process. In the Social Democracy, the pre-World-War-I socialist movement, the evolution of unions and Marxist parties went hand in hand, as part of the close association between the two and their joint drift toward a thoroughly nonrevolutionary outlook.

The revival of revolutionary Marxism in the Communist movement after the Russian Revolution arrested the drift toward reformism in many other fields but seems only to have exacerbated it in this respect. The Soviet Communists had taken power, in a turn of history unexpected by classical Marxism, in a barely capitalist country where, except in a few industrial centers, technology, production, and even mere organized and disciplined labor processes were weak. The Soviet Union faced catastrophe unless it could develop production and replace the ingrained traditions of the Russian peasantry with systematic habits of social labor. In this situation, the respect and even admiration of Marxists for the scientific technology, the production system, and the organized and regularized labor processes of developed capitalism was if anything heightened. If the old Social Democracy tended to view the capitalist mode of production as an immensely powerful and successful enterprise with which it was necessary to compromise, the Communists tended to view it with equal awe as a source from which it was necessary to learn and borrow, and which would have to be imitated if the Soviet Union were to catch up with capitalism and lay the foundations for socialism.

We need only recall that Lenin himself repeatedly urged the study of Frederick W. Taylor's "scientific management," with an eye toward utilizing it in Soviet industry. The Taylor system, he said, "like all capitalist progress, is a combination of the refined brutality of bourgeois exploitation and a number of the greatest scientific achievements in the field of analyzing mechanical motions during work, the elimination of superfluous and awkward motions, the elaboration of correct methods of work, the introduction of the best system of accounting and control, etc. The Soviet Republic must at all costs adopt all that is valuable in the achievements of science and technology in this field. The possibility of building socialism depends exactly upon our success in combining the Soviet power and the Soviet Organization of administration with the up-to-date achievements of capitalism. We must organize in Russia the study and teaching of the Taylor system and systematically try it out and adapt it to our ends."[1] In practice, Soviet industrialization imitated the capitalist model; and as industrialization advanced the structure lost its provisional character and the Soviet Union settled down to an organization of labor differing only in details from that of the capitalist countries, so that the Soviet working population bears all the stigmata of the Western working classes. In the process, the ideological effect was felt throughout world Marxism: the technology of capitalism, which Marx had treated with cautious reserve, and the organization and administration of labor, which he had treated with passionate hostility, became relatively acceptable. Now the revolution against capitalism was increasingly conceived as a matter of stripping from the highly productive capitalist mechanism certain "excrescences," improving the conditions of work, adding to the factory organization a formal structure of "workers' control," and replacing the capitalist mechanisms of accumulation and distribution with socialist planning.

At any rate and whatever the precise factors at work, the critique of the capitalist mode of production, originally the most trenchant weapon of Marxism, gradually lost its cutting edge as the Marxist analysis of the class structure of society failed to keep pace with the rapid process of change. It has now become a commonplace to assert that Marxism was adequate only for the definition of the "industrial proletariat," and that with the relative shrinkage of that proletariat in size and social weight, Marxism, at least in this respect, has become "outmoded." As a result of this uncorrected obsolescence, Marxism became weakest at the very point where it had originally been strongest.

During the past decade there has been a renewal of interest on the Left in work processes and the ways in which they are organized. This may be attributed to a number of causes. The headlong rush of capital accumulation which has proceeded relatively without check since World War II in Western Europe, the United States, and Japan has removed from the center of radical attention those notions of the imminent "breakdown" and "collapse" of the capitalist system which dominated radical thought during the decades following World War I. The bankruptcy of Soviet Communist ideology has opened the way for a neo-Marxism which has attempted fresh approaches to the problems of capitalism and socialism. In particular, the discussions of the organization of labor in Cuba in the mid-sixties, and the Cultural Revolution in China shortly thereafter, went beyond the preoccupation with the equalitarian distribution of the products of social labor and brought to the fore the idea of a revolution in the organization of social production. And finally, the new wave of radicalism of the 1960s was animated by its own peculiar and in some ways unprecedented concerns. Since the discontents of youth, intellectuals, feminists, ghetto populations, etc., were produced not by the "breakdown" of capitalism but by capitalism functioning at the top of its form, so to speak, working at its most rapid and energetic pace, the focus of rebellion was now somewhat different from that of the past. At least in part, dissatisfaction centered not so much on capitalism's inability to provide work as on the work it provides, not on the collapse of its productive processes but on the appalling effects of these processes at their most "successful." It is not that the pressures of poverty, unemployment, and want have been eliminated—far from it—but rather that these have been supplemented by a discontent which cannot be touched by providing more prosperity and jobs because these are the very things that produced this discontent in the first place.

Technology and Society

In this book, we will be concerned entirely with the development of the processes of production, and of labor processes in general, in *capitalist* society. The question at once arises as to the place of the countries of the Soviet bloc in relation to this analysis. I have already briefly indicated my view that the organization of labor in the Soviet Union (to which I refer for convenience in the singular although its characteristics are to be found in all the countries of the Soviet bloc and, in some degree, in all countries where capitalist property relations have been overthrown) differs little from the organization of labor in capitalist countries. Commenting on this aspect of Soviet life, Georges Friedmann, the French sociologist and long-time student of the anatomy of work, wrote:

> . . . it appears that planned economies of the Soviet type, including those of the peoples' democracies of Eastern Europe, and more and more of communist China,* contain large sectors in which technical progress has multiplied the number of simplified jobs . . . and has thus started, and is developing, that separation between planning and execution which seems to be in our day a common denominator linking all industrial societies together, however different their populations and structures.[2]

An American sociologist reports that "Soviet economists and social scientists I met in Moscow . . . insisted that job satisfaction studies are irrelevant

---

* This was written during the 1950s, before China's break with the Soviet Union and before the Cultural Revolution.

in a society in which the workers own the means of production."[3] At the same time, a growing body of Westernized sociological and management literature in the Soviet Union seeks to make explicit the debt of Soviet society to capitalist industrial practice.* This debt need hardly be demonstrated, since the descriptive and apologetic literature of Soviet society, while it presents claims of superiority to capitalist practice in terms of worker "ownership" of the means of production, health and safety practices, rational planning, and the like, does not claim substantial differences in terms of the organization and division of labor.

The similarity of Soviet and traditional capitalist practice strongly encourages the conclusion that there is no other way in which modern industry can be organized. And this conclusion had already been sufficiently encouraged by the tendency of modern social science to accept all that is *real* as *necessary*, all that exists as inevitable, and thus the present mode of production as eternal. In its most complete form, this view appears as a veritable technological determinism: the attributes of modern society are seen as issuing directly from smokestacks, machine tools, and computers. We are, as a result, presented with the theory of a *societas ex machina*, not only a "determinism" but a *despotism* of the machine. In a book by four social scientists (among them Clark Kerr), we read: "Industrialization in any country displays many of the same features. Industrializing countries are more nearly like each other, however varied they may be, than they are like commercial or agricultural or hunting and fishing economies. . . . One of the central traits is the inevitable and eternal separation of industrial men into managers and the managed."[5] This leaves nothing to the imagination. The antagonistic relations of production are not only inevitable, but, we are told in almost religious language, *eternal*.**

The problem which this presents is obviously an important one for a work such as this, but it is doubtful that it can be illuminated or solved by vaulting

---

* See, for example, a recent influential volume called *Organization and Management: A Sociological Analysis of Western Theories*. The author adopts as his formal framework Lenin's attitude toward Taylorism (which condemned its use in "bourgeois exploitation" but urged that it be studied and everything of value adopted). Bearing this convenient warrant, he makes the expected condemnations in a perfunctory way, but the total spirit of the book is one of absorption in Western management theory and fascination with its administrative and manipulative aspects. Thus he adopts not just the spirit but the language, and Marx's investigation of capitalist society becomes for the enthusiastic author "a splendid example of a systems analysis," while Marx himself, "in creating dialectical materialism also laid the foundations of systems analysis."[4]

** In a polemic against anarchism called "On Authority," Frederick Engels wrote in 1873: "If man, by dint of his knowledge and inventive genius, has subdued the forces of nature, the latter avenge themselves upon him by subjecting him, in so far as he employs them, to a veritable despotism independent of all social organization. Wanting to abolish authority in large-scale industry is tantamount to wanting to abolish industry

conclusions which achieve their plausibility only by worship of the existing fact. The problem can be fruitfully attacked, it seems to me, only by way of concrete and historically specific analysis of technology and machinery on the one side and social relations on the other, and of the manner in which these two come together in existing societies. Such an analysis could well start with the possibility that the present mode of the organization and control of labor arose in capitalist society for reasons specific to *that* society, and was transferred to Soviet society and imitated by it for reasons that have to do with the specific nature of that society. Recognizing that there are very few "eternal" or "inevitable" features of human social organization in an abstract sense, such an analysis would proceed by way of an understanding of the *historical evolution* which produced modern social forms. And most important, such an analysis must not simply accept what the designers, owners, and managers of the machines tell us about them, but it must form its own independent evaluation of machinery and modern industry, in the factory and in the office; otherwise it will create not a social science but merely a branch of management science.

I must at this point devote a few pages to some discussion of Marx's view of the relation between technology and society before saying something more about the Soviet Union. A clarification of Marx's views on this relationship is necessary because orthodox social science, although it is, as we have just seen, itself prone to the most vulgar and superficial technological determinism, often misunderstands Marx in exactly this respect, and accuses him of this very sin.

In the first published essay in which his approach to history and society was outlined, the reply to Proudhon written in 1846-1847 and called *The Poverty of Philosophy*, Marx at one point says:

> M. Proudhon the economist understands very well that men make cloth, linen or silk materials in definite relations of production. But what he has not understood is that these definite social relations are just as much produced by men as linen, flax, etc. Social relations are closely bound up with productive forces. In acquiring new productive forces men change their mode of production; and in changing their mode of production, in changing the way of earning

---

itself, to destroy the power loom in order to return to the spinning wheel."[6] One may agree wholeheartedly with Engels that in mastering natural forces and using them in social production, humanity has altered the terms of its social life and introduced organizational limits to the free and individual activity of the isolated producer. But in postulating "a veritable despotism," and in making this "independent of all social organization," Engels was so carried away by his polemic that he used terminological generalities uncharacteristic of the body of his, and especially Marx's, writings. In particular, the use of the term "authority" as a supra-historical concept, independent of the various forms which it may assume—individual or collective, antagonistic or harmonious, alienated or retained in the hands of the direct producers—can only be a source of confusion.

their living, they change all their social relations. The hand-mill gives you society
with the feudal lord; the steam-mill, society with the industrial capitalist.[7]

The final sentence has the striking quality and broad historical fidelity
characteristic of Marx's best aphorisms. But unfortunately it is its other quality,
that of appearing to be a ready-made formula, that has attracted the attention
of many and caused them to try to use it as a substitute for the immense
historical and analytical labors Marx performed on this theme. "Science,"
Marx says of Proudhon only a few pages later, "for him reduces itself to the
slender proportions of a scientific formula; he is the man in search of formulas."[8]
In spite of such warnings, there are those who have tried to understand Marx
as a provider of formulas, and in that way labeled him a "technological
determinist."

Marx did, of course, give a position of primacy to the "means of production" in social evolution. But this was never conceived as a simple and
unilateral determinism which "causes" a specific mode of production to issue
automatically from a specific technology. Such a determinism is false to history
in general, and particularly useless in confronting revolutionary and transitional epochs, with which Marx was especially concerned. In such epochs,
clearly, societies exhibiting a variety of forms of social relations coexist on the
basis of substantially the same technology. Marx's solution to the problem of
transition turns upon his conception of the development of the productive
forces *within* a system of social relations, until they outgrow it, come into
conflict with it, and burst its bounds. This has two important implications
which clash with the interpretation of Marx as a "technological determinist"
wielding a simple formula. On the one hand, it means that the same productive
forces that are characteristic of the *close of one epoch* of social relations are
also characteristic of the *opening of the succeeding epoch*; indeed, how could
it be otherwise, since social and political revolutions, although they may come
about in the last analysis because of the gradual evolution of the productive
forces, do not on their morrow provide society with a brand-new technology.
And on the other hand, it provides for the growth and evolution of the forces
of production within the bounds of a single social system, a feature of all social
systems but especially significant for capitalism. Thus if steam power "gives
us" the industrial capitalist, industrial capitalism "gives us," in turn, electric
power, the power of the internal combustion engine, and atomic power.

On the basis of this sketch, we would expect the technology and organization of production of early capitalism to be much closer to those of the late
feudal epoch, and those of late capitalism much closer to those of early
socialism, than they are to each other. This is of course true, and serves as an
elementary demonstration of the fact that the relations between technology and
society are beyond the reach of any simpleminded "determinism." The treatment of the interplay between the forces and relations of production occupied

Marx in almost all his historical writing, and while there is no question that he gave primacy to the forces of production in the long sweep of history, the idea that this primacy could be used in a formulistic way in the analysis of history on a day-to-day basis would never have entered his mind.*

Those who know Marx's historical method only from a few scattered aphorisms would do well to study *Capital* in order to see how the relationship between capital as a social form and the capitalist mode of production as a technical organization is treated. Within the historical and analytical limits of capitalism, according to Marx's analysis, technology, instead of simply *producing* social relations, *is produced by* the social relation represented by capital. The capitalist mode of production is traced by Marx from its beginnings, when it "is hardly to be distinguished, in its earliest stages, from the handicraft trades of the guilds, otherwise than by the greater number of workmen simultaneously employed by one and the same individual capital,"[10] through domestic industry, the manufacturing division of labor, machinery and modern industry, and the factory system, in which the capitalist mode of production is at last fully created and the inherent social form of labor under capitalism "for the first time acquires technical and palpable reality."[11] From this point of view, the first volume of *Capital* may be considered a massive essay on how the commodity form, in an adequate social and technological setting, matures into the form of capital, and how the social form of capital, driven to incessant accumulation as the condition for its own existence, *completely transforms technology.***

In this analysis the conditions of the oft-quoted aphorism are reversed. If Marx was not in the least embarrassed by this interchange of roles between social forms on the one side and material production processes on the other, but on the contrary moved comfortably among them, it was because—apart from his genius at dialectic—he never took a formulistic view of history, never

---

* In his "Introduction to the Critique of Political Economy," uncompleted and never published by Marx and described by Kautsky as "a fragmentary sketch of a treatise that was to have served as an introduction to his main work," Marx set down for himself eight paragraphs as "notes on the points to be mentioned here and not to be omitted." The fifth reads: "The dialectics of the conceptions productive force (means of production) and relation of production, dialectics whose limits are to be determined and which does not do away with the concrete difference."[9] His elaboration of this theme would have been of considerable interest in this connection.

** The rediscovery of Marx by bourgeois social science in recent years has brought Marx friends who are almost as little help as his enemies. Thus William L. Zwerman, in a recent book on technology and "organization theory," summarizes the Marxian view as follows: "Marxians presuppose the primacy of industrial technology, treating social relationships (in the first instance the individual organization itself) as secondary, i.e., superstructures."[12] This he then attempts to apply to the *capitalist firm*, precisely the arena in which it has little relevance and in fact where the terms of this relationship

played with bare and hapless correlatives, "one-to-one relationships," and other foolish attempts to master history by means of violent simplifications. Social determinacy does not have the fixity of a chemical reaction, but is a *historic process*. The concrete and determinate forms of society are indeed "determined" rather than accidental, but this is the determinacy of the thread-by-thread weaving of the fabric of history, not the imposition of external formulas.

The relevance of these observations for the subject matter of this book is simply this: As the reader will have already understood, it will be argued here that the "mode of production" we see around us, the manner in which labor processes are organized and carried out, is the "product" of the social relations we know as capitalist. But the shape of our society, the shape of any given society, is not an instantaneous creation of "laws" which generate that society on the spot and before our eyes. Every society is a moment in the historical process, and can be grasped only as part of that process. Capitalism, a social form, when it exists in time, space, population, and history, weaves a web of myriad threads; the conditions of its existence form a complex network each of which presupposes many others. It is because of this solid and tangible existence, this concrete form produced by history, no part of which may be changed by artificial suppositions without doing violence to its true mode of existence—it is precisely because of this that it appears to us as "natural," "inevitable," and "eternal." And it is only in this sense, as a fabric woven over centuries, that we may say that capitalism "produced" the present capitalist mode of production. This is a far cry from a ready-made formula which enables us to "deduce" from a given state of technology a given mode of social organization.

What is said of capitalism may also be said of "socialism," which does not yet exist anywhere in the classic Marxist sense. The Soviet Union had a revolution, but a revolution under specific social conditions, and almost all of its subsequent history combines progress in technology and production with a retreat from its original revolutionary objectives. This special combination requires its own very specific analysis. In Soviet society, we have the first phenomenal form of an epoch of transition which may well last for centuries and will undoubtedly exhibit many contradictory, complex, and transitional forms. Whatever view one takes of Soviet industrialization, one cannot conscientiously interpret its history, even in its earliest and most revolutionary period, as an attempt to organize labor processes in a way fundamentally different from those of capitalism—and thus as an attempt that came to grief

---

are reversed. In this effort, he resembles a neo-Darwinian attempting to apply to a given *social* evolution those *biological* terms which in that context no longer apply. Within the capitalist firm it is the social forms that dominate technology, rather than the other way around.

on the rocks of Clark Kerr's eternal verities. One would be hard put to demonstrate that any of the successive Soviet leaderships *has ever claimed that such an attempt should be made at this stage of Soviet history.* * (Here there is an enormous distinction between Soviet and recent Chinese programmatic literature; Khrushchev ridiculed the Chinese plan of incorporating the building of communism into the very process of industrialization as trying to "eat soup with an awl." His wit was engaging within the limits of an orthodox Communist conception that dates back, in some respects, to Lenin and before, but his remark is not half so funny now that the Chinese have made their remarkable conception clearer.)

If there is no automatic and immediate transformation of the mode of production as a result of a change in social forms, then such hybrid formations as we see in the Soviet Union should not come as a surprise. It took capitalism centuries to develop its own mode of production, which, as we shall see later in these pages, is still being worked out and developed. Socialism, as a mode of production, does not grow "automatically" in the way that capitalism grew in response to blind and organic market forces; it must be brought into being, on the basis of an adequate technology, by the conscious and purposive activity of collective humanity. And this activity must overcome not just the customary conditions of the previous mode of production, but those of the many millennia during which class societies of all sorts have existed, since with the decline of capitalism we come to the end not merely of a single form of society but of the "last antagonistic form of the social process of production," in Marx's words, the "closing chapter of the prehistoric stage of human society."[14] Considered from this point of view, the notion that the labor processes to be discussed in this book can be divested of their capitalist character by the simple expedient of citing the Soviet Union seems to me the worst sort of slot-machine science.

In any event, the purpose of this book is the study of the labor processes of capitalist society, and the specific manner in which these are formed by capitalist property relations. I cannot offer here any parallel study of the specific manner in which this structure has been imitated by the hybrid societies of the Soviet bloc. The latter study forms its own and considerably different subject matter, and has enormous interest in its own right. But since this mode of production was *created* by capitalism and not by Sovietism, where it is only a reflexive, imitative, and one hopes transitional form, it is with capitalism that the study of the labor process must begin.

---

* In an essay on the origins and functions of hierarchy in capitalist production, Stephen A. Marglin says: "In according first priority to the accumulation of capital, the Soviet Union repeated the history of capitalism, at least as regards the relationship of men and women to their work. . . . The Soviets consciously and deliberately embraced the capitalist mode of production. . . . Now, alas, the Soviets have the 'catch-up-with-and-surpass the-U.S.A.' tiger by the tail, for it would probably take as much of a revolution to transform work organization in that society as in ours."[13]

The "New Working Class"

The term "working class," properly understood, never precisely delineated a specified body of people, but was rather an expression for an ongoing social process. Nevertheless, to most people's minds it represented for a long time a fairly well-defined part of the population of capitalist countries. But with the coming of broad occupational shifts (which will be described in later chapters), and a growing consciousness of these shifts in recent decades, the term has lost much of its descriptive capacity. I can therefore sympathize with those readers who would want me to begin with a concise and up-to-date definition of the term "working class." Such a definition, if it could easily be managed, would be helpful to the writer as well as the reader, but I cannot help feeling that an attempt to provide it at the outset would result in more confusion than clarification. We are dealing not with the static terms of an algebraic equation, which requires only that quantities be filled in, but with a dynamic process the mark of which is the *transformation* of sectors of the population. The place of many of these sectors in class definition is rather more complex than otherwise, and cannot be attempted until much has been described and the standards of analysis clarified.

To make this a little more concrete: I have no quarrel with the definition of the working class, on the basis of its "relationship to the means of production," as that class which does not own or otherwise have proprietary access to the means of labor, and must sell its labor power to those who do. But in the present situation, when almost all of the population has been placed in this situation so that the definition encompasses occupational strata of the most diverse kinds, it is not the bare definition that is important but its application. I can only say at this point that I hope a reasonable and useful picture of the structure of the working class emerges from this study. If readers will indulge me this far, I think they may see the necessity for this course later in the exposition, as I came to see it in the course of the investigation.*

For purposes of clarity, however, I should note at the start that although I will be describing the immense changes in the shape of the working class during the past century, I cannot accept the arbitrary conception of a "new working class" that has been developed by some writers during the past decade. According to this conception, the "new working class" embraces

---

* "Though extremely precise, [Marx] was not much inclined to define his concepts in set terms. For instance, the present treatise on capitalist production does not contain a formal definition of 'capital'. . . . The fact is that the whole book is his definition."[15] This comment by the translators of the Everyman edition of *Capital* is important, especially as a hint to the beginner in the study of Marxism. It holds true, with all proportions guarded, in the present case as well, if we are to arrive at a "definition" of the working class that will go beyond the elements that most students of this subject already know well.

those occupations which serve as the repositories for specialized knowledge in production and administration: engineers, technicians, scientists, lower managerial and administrative aides and experts, teachers, etc. Rather than examine the entire working population and learn how it has been altered, which portions have grown and which have declined or stagnated, these analysts have selected one portion of employment as the sole focus of their analysis. What saves this procedure from being completely arbitrary in the eyes of its practitioners is that they use the word *new* in a double sense: it refers to occupations that are new in the sense of having been recently created or enlarged, and also in the sense of their gloss, presumed advancement, and "superiority" to the old.

The results of an investigation based upon such a postulate are contained in advance in the chosen definition. The "new working class" is thus "educated labor," better paid, somewhat privileged, etc. Manual labor, according to this definition, is "old working class," regardless of the actual movement of occupations and the increase of various categories of labor of this sort. So far have these writers been governed by their definition that it has escaped their notice, for example, that the occupations of engineer on the one side and janitor-porter on the other have followed similar growth curves since the start of the century, each beginning at a level between 50,000 and 100,000 (in the United States in 1900), and expanding to about 1.25 million by 1970. Both now rank among the largest occupations in the United States, and both have developed in response to the forces of industrial and commercial growth and urbanization. Why is one to be considered "new working class" and the other not? That this single example is not at all fortuitous will be clear to anyone who makes a study of the long-term occupational trends in the capitalist countries. These trends— from their beginnings, which, if one must choose a starting point for something that is more realistically a continuous process, date back to the last decades of the nineteenth century—indicate that it is the *class as a whole* that must be studied, rather than an arbitrarily chosen part of it.

Having so broadened the scope of the investigation, let me hasten to limit it sharply in another way. No attempt will be made to deal with the modern working class on the level of its consciousness, organization, or activities. This is a book about the working class as a class *in itself*, not as a class *for itself*. I realize that to many readers it will appear that I have omitted the most urgent part of the subject matter. There are those who hope to discover, in some quick and simple manner, a replacement for the "blue-collar workers" as an "agency for social change," to use the popular phrases. It is my feeling, to put it bluntly, that this constitutes an attempt to derive the "science before the science," and I have tried to dismiss such preoccupations from my mind on the theory that what is needed first of all is a picture of the working class as it exists, as the shape given to the working population by the capital accumulation process.*

This self-imposed limitation to the "objective" content of class and the omission of the "subjective" will, I fear, hopelessly compromise this study in the eyes of some of those who float in the conventional stream of social science. For them, by long habit and insistent theory, class does not really exist outside its subjective manifestations. Class, "status," "stratification," and even that favorite hobby horse of recent years which has been taken from Marx without the least understanding of its significance, "alienation"**—all of these are for bourgeois social science artifacts of consciousness and can be studied only as they manifest themselves in the minds of the subject population. At least two generations of academic sociology have so elevated this approach into a dogma that only rarely is the need felt to substantiate it. This dogma calls for the delineation of various layers of stratification by means of questionnaires which enable the respondents to choose their own class, thereby relieving sociologists of the obligation. The results have been extraordinarily variable. For example, in the many polls conducted according to the conceptions of W. Lloyd Warner—by Gallup, by *Fortune* in 1940, etc.—in which the population is classified into "upper," "middle," and "lower" classes, and into subgroups of these, vast majorities of up to 90 percent predictably volunteered themselves as the "middle class." But when Richard Centers varied the questionnaire only to the extent of including the choice "working class," this suddenly became the majority category by choice of the respondents.[17] Here we see sociologists measuring not popular consciousness but their own. Yet the superiority of the questionnaire as the means for measuring social phenomena remains an article of faith. Michel Crozier, the French sociologist, says in criticism of C. Wright Mills' *White Collar*:

---

* These criticisms of both "new working class" theory and of the search for an "agency of social change" are not intended to disparage the useful materials that have been assembled by some of those, Europeans and Americans, who have worked along these lines, and whose work has been helpful to me in the present study. In particular, these writers have drawn attention to the importance of, and to the discontent among, various "professional" strata, and to the special features of ghetto populations, young workers, and women. While my own approach does not proceed by way of such sectoral considerations, the manner in which they fit into the analysis as a whole will, I think, be apparent.

** Alfred Schmidt notes that "Marx gave up using such terms as 'estrangement,' 'alienation,' 'return of man to himself,' as soon as he noticed that they had turned into ideological prattle in the mouths of petty-bourgeois authors, instead of a lever for the empirical study of the world and its transformation." He adds to this the observation that "Marx's general abandonment of such terms does not mean that he did not continue to follow theoretically the material conditions designated by them."[16]

Unfortunately Mills's work . . . is not a true research study. In effect, it is not the feelings of alienation which may actually be suffered by the salesgirl or by the intellectual at an advertising agency that interest Mills, but rather objective alienation of these persons as it might be reconstructed by analyzing the forces which exert pressure on them. This attitude pretends to be more scientific than a poll of opinions, but it is so only in appearance.[18]

On the basis of Mills' approach, Crozier argues, "social life without alienation would in effect be impossible," because "the individual is always necessarily limited by his place in the social structure." This is the genteel form of an argument made more bluntly by Robert Blauner when he said: "The average worker is able to make an adjustment to a job which, from the standpoint of an intellectual appears to be the epitome of tedium."[19] In this line of reasoning we see the recognition on the part of sociology that modern labor processes are indeed degraded; the sociologist shares this foreknowledge with management, with whom he also shares the conviction that this organization of the labor process is "necessary" and "inevitable." This leaves to sociology the function, which it shares with personnel administration, of assaying not the nature of the work but the degree of adjustment of the worker. Clearly, for industrial sociology the problem does not appear with the degradation of work, but only with overt signs of dissatisfaction on the part of the worker. From this point of view, the only important matter, the only thing worth studying, is not work itself but the reaction of the worker to it, and in that respect sociology makes sense.

It is not my purpose in these comments to deprecate the importance of the study of the state of consciousness of the working class, since it is only through consciousness that a class becomes an actor on the historic stage. Nor do I believe that the feeble results achieved by questionnaire-sociology indicate that the mind of the working class is unknowable, but merely that this particular method of trying to know it is superficial, remote, and mechanistic. Class consciousness is that state of social cohesion reflected in the understanding and activities of a class or a portion of a class. Its *absolute expression* is a pervasive and durable attitude on the part of a class toward its position in society. Its *long-term relative expression* is found in the slowly changing traditions, experiences, education, and organization of the class. Its *short-term relative expression* is a dynamic complex of moods and sentiments affected by circumstances and changing with them, sometimes, in periods of stress and conflict, almost from day to day. These three expressions of class consciousness are related: changes of mood draw upon and give expression to the underlying reservoir of class attitudes which, while it may be deep below the surface, is never entirely exhausted.

Thus a class cannot exist in society without in some degree manifesting a consciousness of itself as a group with common problems, interests, and prospects—although this manifestation may for long periods be weak, confused, and subject to manipulation by other classes. The interpretation of the opinions, feelings, sentiments, and changing moods of the working class is best accomplished by experienced and well-attuned observers and participants, who know the history of a particular group, are acquainted with its circumstances, background, and relation to other parts of the working class, and form their assessments from intimate contact and detailed information. It is for this reason that the most astute interpreters of the moods of submerged and ordinarily voiceless populations have often been union organizers, agitators, experienced revolutionaries—and police spies. While these have always had among them a percentage of fools, illusionaries, and the otherwise error-prone, at their best such active and interested parties, whose interpretations are enriched by their efforts at practice, convey a solidity, a depth and subtlety of observation, an anticipation of changing moods, and an ability to disentangle the durable from the ephemeral that is entirely absent from the tabulations of sociology. It should be added, however, that where some sociologists have themselves gone to work in factories either as part of their professional training or out of necessity, or where as sometimes happens they have put aside their questionnaires and listened to workers with both ears, they have often established relationships of trust, learned to comprehend the milieu, and written creditable accounts.

Job Dissatisfaction in the 1970s

In the years that have passed since this study was begun, dissatisfaction with work has become what can only be called a "fashionable topic." Almost every major periodical in the United States has featured articles on the "blue-collar blues" or "white-collar woes." Books have been published, commissions set up, conferences organized, experiments conducted. Sociologists have caught the wind in their sails and, reinterpreting their questionnaire statistics, now view with alarm the very percentages of dissatisfied workers which yesterday they found comfortingly small. A Special Task Force selected by the Secretary of Health, Education, and Welfare has prepared a report under the title *Work in America* which found that "significant numbers of American workers are dissatisfied with the quality of their working lives":

> As a result, the productivity of the worker is low—as measured by absenteeism, turnover rates, wildcat strikes, sabotage, poor-quality products, and a reluctance by workers to commit themselves to their work tasks. Moreover, a growing body of research indicates that, as work problems increase, there may be a consequent decline in physical and mental health, family stability, community participation and cohesiveness, and "balanced" sociopolitical attitudes, while there is an increase in drug and alcohol addiction, aggression, and delinquency.

The report deals with what it calls "the effects of work problems on various segments of our society":

> Here we find the "blues" of blue-collar workers linked to their job dissatisfactions, as is the disgruntlement of white-collar workers and the growing discontent among managers. Many workers at all occupational levels feel locked-in, their mobility blocked, the opportunity to grow lacking in their jobs, challenge missing from their tasks. Young workers appear to be as committed to the institution of work as their elders have been, but many are rebelling against the anachronistic authoritarianism of the workplace. Minority workers similarly see authoritarian worksettings as evidence that society is falling short of its democratic ideals. Women, who are looking to work as an additional source of identity, are being frustrated by an opportunity structure that confines them to jobs damaging to their self-esteem. Older Americans suffer the ultimate in job dissatisfaction: they are denied meaningful jobs even when they have demonstrable skills and are physically capable of being productive.[20]

Absenteeism and the quit rate, cited as evidence of a "new worker attitude," tend to vary with the availability of jobs and may have partly reflected the decline in unemployment rates at the end of the 1960s. But in the atmosphere of discontent of that period these were interpreted, no doubt with some truth, as an indication of a new resistance to certain forms of work. The automobile plants, and especially their assembly lines, were cited as a prime example, as witness this 1970 report in *Fortune*:

> For management, the truly dismaying evidence about new worker attitudes is found in job performance. Absenteeism has risen sharply; in fact it has doubled over the past ten years at General Motors and at Ford, with the sharpest climb in the past year. It has reached the point where an average of 5 percent of G.M.'s hourly workers are missing from work without explanation every day. . . . On some days, notably Fridays and Mondays, the figure goes as high as 10 percent. Tardiness has increased, making it even more difficult to start up the production lines promptly when a shift begins—after the foreman has scrambled around to replace missing workers. Complaints about quality are up sharply. There are more arguments with foremen, more complaints about discipline and overtime, more grievances. There is more turnover. The quit rate at Ford last year was 25.2 percent. . . . Some assembly-line workers are so turned off, managers report with astonishment, that they just walk away in mid-shift and don't even come back to get their pay for the time they have worked."[21]

At the Chrysler Corporation's Jefferson Avenue plant in Detroit, a daily average absentee rate of 6 percent was reported in mid-1971, and an annual average turnover of almost 30 percent. In its 1970 negotiations with the union, Chrysler reported that during 1969 almost half its workers did not complete their first ninety days on the job. In that same year, the Ford assembly plant at

Wixom, on the outskirts of Detroit, with an 8 percent quit rate *each month*, had to hire 4,800 new workers in order to maintain a work force of 5,000. For the automobile industry as a whole, the absentee rate doubled in the second half of the 1960s, and turnover doubled as well.* Only with the increase in unemployment in 1971 and thereafter was the situation stabilized to some degree.[23]

A much-discussed strike in January 1972 at the Lordstown, Ohio, General Motors plant gave the world a glimpse of the conditions in this "most advanced" and "automated" plant in the industry, which General Motors regarded as a pilot plant for the future. At its designed speed, the assembly line at Lordstown turns out 100 Vegas an hour, giving each worker 36 seconds to complete work on each car and get ready for the next car. The immediate issue in the dispute was an increase in the pace of operations the previous October. "What the company is discovering is that workers not only want to go back to the pre-October pace, but many feel that the industry is going to have to do something to change the boring, repetitive nature of the assembly line work or it will continue to have unrest in the plant. An official familiar with the sessions said, 'What they're saying is you've got to do something. I don't know what it is but you've got to do something.' "[24]

Accounts of this kind are not confined to the assembly line, or even to the factory. The Special Task Force report attempts a summary of office trends in the following comments:

> The auto industry is the *locus classicus* of dissatisfying work; the assembly-line, its quintessential embodiment. But what is striking is the extent to which the dissatisfaction of the assembly-line and blue-collar worker is mirrored in white-collar and even managerial positions. The office today, where work is segmented and authoritarian, is often a factory. For a growing number of jobs, there is little to distinguish them but the color of the worker's collar: computer keypunch operations and typing pools share much in common with the automobile assembly line.
>
> Secretaries, clerks, and bureaucrats were once grateful for having been spared the dehumanization of the factory. White-collar jobs were rare; they had a higher status than blue-collar jobs. But today the clerk, and not the

---

* A number of European reports indicate that this situation was not limited to the United States. For example, a report from Rome said the Fiat Motor Company, Italy's largest private employer with more than 180,000 employees, 147,000 of whom are factory workers, had 21,000 employees missing on a Monday and a daily average absenteeism of 14,000. Throughout the Italian economy, an Italian management association reported, an average of at least 800,000 workers out of a total of nearly 20 million were absent daily. This was attributed to "the increasing disgust of younger people with assembly-line discipline and the recent influx of untrained southern Italians into northern factories." [22]

operative on the assembly-line, is the typical American worker, and such positions offer little in the way of prestige. . . .

Traditionally, lower-level white-collar jobs in both government and industry were held by high school graduates. Today, an increasing number of these jobs go to those who have attended college. But the demand for higher academic credentials has not increased the prestige, status, pay, or difficulty of the job. For example, the average weekly pay for clerical workers in 1969 was $105.00 per week, while blue-collar production workers were taking home an average of $130.00 per week. It is not surprising, then, that the Survey of Working Conditions found much of the greatest work dissatisfaction in the country among young, well-educated workers who were in low paying, dull, routine, and fractionated clerical positions. Other signs of discontent among this group include turnover rates as high as 30% annually and a 46% increase in white-collar union membership between 1958 and 1968. . . . These changing attitudes . . . may be affecting the productivity of these workers: a survey conducted by a group of management consultants of a cross section of office employees found that they were producing at only 55% of their potential. Among the reasons cited for this was boredom with repetitive jobs.[25]

The apparent increase in active dissatisfaction has been attributed to a number of causes, some having to do with the characteristics of the workers—younger, more years of schooling, "infected" by the new-generational restlessness—and others having to do with the changing nature of the work itself. One reporter cites the belief that "American industry in some instances may have pushed technology too far by taking the last few bits of skill out of jobs, and that a point of human resistance has been reached." He quotes a job design consultant at Case Western Reserve University, who said with disarming candor: "We may have created too many dumb jobs for the number of dumb people to fill them."[26]

Various remedies and reforms have been proposed, and some have been tested among small groups of workers by corporations with particularly pressing problems. Among these are job enlargement, enrichment, or rotation, work groups or teams, consultation or workers' "participation," group bonuses and profit-sharing, the abandonment of assembly line techniques, the removal of time clocks, and an "I Am" plan (short for "I Am Manager of My Job").

Behind the characteristic faddishness of these approaches it is possible to sense a deep concern, the reason for which is readily apparent. The ruling establishments of Western Europe and the United States, having just passed through a period when they were alarmed and even shaken by an incandescent revolt of student youth and third world nationalism within their own borders, were bound to ask themselves what would happen if to this were added a rebellion against the conditions of labor in the workplace. The fright occasioned by such a prospect gave rise to a discussion over the "quality of work," the purpose of which was in part to determine whether discontent among workers was at the usual level, endemic to life under capitalism, or whether it was rising threateningly; and in part to encourage reforms in the hope of forestalling such a rise in discontent. But as in almost all discussions of major issues of public policy, this one too has a certain air of hollow unreality, reflecting the gulf between the capitalist as statesman and the capitalist in command of corporate enterprise.

The problem as it presents itself to those managing industry, trade, and finance is very different from the problem as it appears in the academic or journalistic worlds. Management is habituated to carrying on labor processes in a setting of social antagonism and, in fact, has never known it to be otherwise. Corporate managers have neither the hope nor the expectation of altering this situation by a single stroke; rather, they are concerned to ameliorate it only when it interferes with the orderly functioning of their plants, offices, warehouses, and stores. For corporate management this is a problem in costs and controls, not in the "humanization of work." It compels their attention because it manifests itself in absentee, turnover, and productivity levels that do not conform to their calculations and expectations. The solutions they will accept are only those which provide improvements in their labor costs and in their competitive positions domestically and in the world market.

It is interesting to note that although the discussion of job enrichment, job enlargement, and the like began in connection with factory work, most actual applications have taken place in offices (three-quarters of them, according to an estimate by Roy H. Walters, a management consultant and pioneer of "job enrichment").[27] Industrial installations represent heavy investments in fixed equipment, and industrial processes as they now exist are the product of a long development aimed at reducing labor costs to their minimum. In office and service processes, by contrast, the recently swollen mass of employment has not as yet been subjected to the same extremes of rationalization and mechanization as in the factories, although this is under way. For these reasons, management decisions to reorganize work processes are made more readily and voluntarily in the office and are made in the factory only in situations that offer little choice. Corporate management is convinced that it is chiefly outside the factory that payrolls are "fat," productivity is low, and there is most need for reorganization.

Office rationalization has in part been taking place, in the most recent period, under the banner of job enlargement and the humanization of work. One need only look at reports such as one in the *Wall Street Journal* in the summer of 1972 to get the flavor of this duplicitous campaign: the article is headed "The Quality of Work," but consists almost entirely of a discussion of cost cutting, productivity drives, and staff reductions in banks, insurance companies, and brokerage houses.[28] In a typical case, a bank teller who is idle when the load at the counter is light will be pressed into service handling other routine duties, such as sorting returned checks. The First National Bank of Richmond, Indiana, put such a plan into operation under the guidance of a consulting firm called Science Management Associates, and its "first-year savings alone exceeded the fee by almost 40%." The bank's staff was reduced from 123 to 104, and a number of the remaining workers were cut back to part-time work. The "humanization" aspect was handled by quoting one worker as saying: "There's never a dull moment. It makes the job more interesting."[29]

A number of management consulting firms have taken this sort of "humanization" as their field and are pressing schemes upon managers. Whatever their phraseology, these consulting organizations have only one function: cutting costs, improving "efficiency," raising productivity. No other language is useful in conversation with management, unless it be with the public relations department.* These consultants possess, at the moment, a valuable stock in trade in the knowledge that the principle of the division of labor, as it has been applied in many large offices, banks, insurance companies, in retailing and in service industries, has been pursued with such fanaticism that various jobs have been broken into fragments of fragments and can be partially reassembled without injury to the present mode of organizing the work process and at a certain saving of labor costs. The hard-headed manner in which this is being done and the simpleminded manner in which these pathetic "enlargements" from one unvarying routine to two or three are being hailed make an interesting contrast.

Since it focuses attention upon this long-neglected aspect of capitalist society, the current discussion of work cannot help but be useful, no matter how meager its results. But like most such discussions in which a basic characteristic of our society is "discovered," accorded a superficial "analysis," given a facile "solution," and then once more forgotten, this one too has not begun to touch the roots of the matter. We are dealing with one of the fundamentals of capitalist society, and this means that even while slight ameliorations are accepted by corporations, *the structure and mode of functioning of capitalism reproduces the present processes of labor a thousandfold more rapidly, more massively, and more widely.*

The reforms that are being proposed today are by no means new ones, and have been popular with certain corporations (IBM, for instance) and certain management theorists for a generation. They represent a style of management rather than a genuine change in the position of the worker. They are characterized

---

* Academic sociologists dare not forget it either. The Special Task Force report introduces its chapter on the redesign of jobs by saying: "The burden of this chapter is to show that not only can work be redesigned to make it more satisfying but that significant increases in productivity can also be obtained."[30]

by a studied pretense of worker "participation," a gracious liberality in allowing the worker to adjust a machine, replace a light bulb, move from one fractional job to another, and to have the illusion of making decisions by choosing among fixed and limited alternatives designed by a management which deliberately leaves insignificant matters open to choice. One can best compare this style of management with the marketing strategy followed by those who, having discovered that housewives resent prepared baking mixes and feel guilty when using them, arrange for the removal of the powdered egg and restore to the consumer the thrill of breaking a fresh egg into the mix, thereby creating an "image" of skilled baking, wholesome products, etc. Peter F. Drucker, one of the early propagandists for job enlargement, wrote in a critique of scientific management in 1954: "It does not follow from the separation of planning and doing in the analysis of work that the planner and the doer should be two different people. It does not follow that the industrial world should be divided into two classes of people; a few who decide what is to be done, design the job, set the pace, rhythm and motions, and order others about; and the many who do what and as they are being told." These are bold words, especially from a management consultant; the proposal for changing the world, however, as it comes to us from Mr. Drucker, is somewhat less bold: ". . . even the lowliest human job should have some planning; only it should be simple planning and there should not be too much of it."[31] Just so did Adam Smith once recommend education for the people in order to prevent their complete deterioration under the division of labor, but, as Marx comments, "prudently, and in homeopathic doses."[32]

Notes

1. V. I. Lenin, "The Immediate Tasks of the Soviet Government" (1918), *Collected Works*, vol. 27 (Moscow, 1965), P. 259.
2. Georges Friedmann, *The Anatomy of Work* (London, 1961, and Glencoe, Ill., 1964), Foreword.
3. Harold L. Sheppard and Neal Q. Herrick, *Where Have All the Robots Gone? Worker Dissatisfaction in the '70s* (New York and London, 1972), p. 96.
4. D. Gvishiani, *Organization and Management: A Sociological Analysis of Western Theories* (Moscow, 1972), pp. 144-46.
5. Clark Kerr, John T. Dunlop, Fredrick Harbison, and Charles A. Myers, *Industrialism and Industrial Man* (Cambridge, Mass., 1960), P. 15.
6. Frederick Engels, "On Authority," in Karl Marx and Frederick Engels, *Selected Works*, vol. II (Moscow, 1969), p. 377.
7. Karl Marx, *The Poverty of Philosophy* (New York, n.d.), p. 92.
8. Ibid., p. 107.
9. Karl Marx, *A Contribution to the Critique of Political Economy* (Chicago, 1904), p. 309.
10. Karl Marx, *Capital*, vol. I (Moscow, n.d.), p. 305.

11. Ibid., P. 399.
12. William L. Zwerman, *New Perspectives on Organization Theory: An Empirical Reconsideration of the Marxian and Classical Analyses* (Westport, Conn., 1970), p. 1.
13. Stephen A. Marglin, "What Do Bosses Do? The Origins and Functions of Hierarchy in Capitalist Production," mimeographed (Cambridge, Mass., Harvard University Department of Economics).
14. Marx, *A Contribution to the Critique of Political Economy*, p. 13.
15. Eden and Cedar Paul, Translators' Preface to *Capital* (London and New York, 1930), P. xxxiv.
16. Alfred Schmidt, *The Concept of Nature in Marx* (London, 1971), pp. 129, 228.
17. See Joseph A. Kahl, *The American Class Structure* (New York, 1957), chapter VI.
18. Michel Crozier, *The World of the Office Worker* (Chicago and London, 1971), pp. 27-28.
19. Robert Blauner, *Alienation and Freedom: The Factory Worker and His Industry* (Chicago, 1964), p. 117.
20. Special Task Force to the Secretary of Health, Education, and Welfare, *Work in America* (Cambridge, Mass., 1973), pp. xvi-xvii.
21. Judson Gooding, "Blue-Collar Blues on the Assembly Line," *Fortune* (July 1970), p. 70.
22. *New York Times*, August 23, 1972.
23. *Wall Street Journal*, July 16, 1971; *New York Times*, April 2, 1972.
24. *New York Times*, February 3, 1972.
25. Special Task Force, *Work in America*, pp. 38-40.
26. *New York Times*, April 2, 1972.
27. *Wall Street Journal*, August 21, 1972.
28. Ibid.
29. Ibid., April 25, 1972.
30. Special Task Force, *Work in America*, p. 94.
31. Peter F. Drucker, *The Practice of Management* (New York, 1954), pp. 284, 296.
32. Marx, *Capital*, vol. I, p. 342.

Part I

Labor and Management

Chapter 1

Labor and Labor Power

All forms of life sustain themselves on their natural environment; thus all conduct activities for the purpose of appropriating natural products to their own use. Plants absorb moisture, minerals, and sunlight; animals feed on plant life or prey on other animals. But to seize upon the materials of nature ready made is not work; work is an activity that alters these materials from their natural state to improve their usefulness. The bird, the beaver, the spider, the bee, and the termite, in building nests, dams, webs, and hives, all may be said to work. Thus the human species shares with others the activity of acting upon nature in a manner which changes its forms to make them more suitable for its needs.

However, what is important about human work is not its similarities with that of other animals, but the crucial differences that mark it as the polar opposite. "We are not now dealing with those primitive instinctive forms of labour that remind us of the mere animal," wrote Marx in the first volume of *Capital*. "We pre-suppose labour in a form that stamps it as exclusively human. A spider conducts operations that resemble those of a weaver, and a bee puts to shame many an architect in the construction of her cells. But what distinguishes the worst architect from the best of bees is this, that the architect raises his structure in imagination before he erects it in reality. At the end of every labour-process, we get a result that already existed in the imagination of the labourer at its commencement. He not only effects a change of form in the material on which he works, but he also realises a purpose of his own that gives the law to his modus operandi, and to which he must subordinate his will."[1] *

---

* Thus labor in its human form was called by Aristotle *intelligent* action; Aristotle, despite his vain effort to find a single cause underlying all the products of nature, animals, and humans, gave the earliest form to this distinctive principle of human labor: "Art indeed consists in the conception of the result to be produced before its realization in the material."[2] In recent times, the artistic mind has often grasped this special feature of human activity better than the technical mind; for example, Paul Valéry: "Man acts; he exercises his powers on a material foreign to him; he separates his operations from their material infrastructure, and he has a clearly defined awareness of this; hence he can think out his operations and co-ordinate them

Human work is conscious and purposive, while the work of other animals is instinctual.* Instinctive activities are inborn rather than learned, and represent a relatively inflexible pattern for the release of energy upon the receipt of specific stimuli. It has been observed, for example, that a caterpillar which has completed half of its cocoon will continue to manufacture the second half without concern even if the first half is taken away. A more striking illustration of instinctual labor is seen in the following:

> The South African weaverbird builds a complicated nest of sticks, with a knotted strand of horsehair as foundation. A pair was isolated and bred for five generations under canaries, out of sight of their fellows and without their usual nest-building materials. In the sixth generation, still in captivity but with access to the right materials, they built a nest perfect even to the knot of horsehair.[5]

In human work, by contrast, the directing mechanism is the *power of conceptual thought,* originating in an altogether exceptional central nervous system. As anthropologists have pointed out, the physical structure of the anthropoid ape is not entirely unsuited to tool making and tool using. The ape's hand is an adequate, if relatively coarse, instrument, and because the lower limbs as well as the upper are fitted with opposable thumbs, it has been said that the ape has four hands. But it is not, first of all, in the hands or posture that the human advantage lies. Among the physical differences between humans and apes, it is the relative enlargement of nearly all parts of the brain, and especially the pronounced enlargement of the frontal and parietal parts of the cerebral hemispheres, which is most important in accounting for the human

---

with each other before performing them; he can assign to himself the most multifarious tasks and adapt to many different materials, and it is precisely this capacity of ordering his intentions or dividing his proposals into separate operations which he calls intelligence. He does not merge into the materials of his undertaking, but proceeds from this material to his mental picture, from his mind to his model, and at each moment exchanges *what he wants* against *what he can do,* and *what he can do* against *what he achieves.* "[3]

* Fourier thought he recognized in this the cause of "happiness" among animals and the "anguish of repugnant labor" among humans: "Labour, nevertheless, forms the delight of various creatures, such as beavers, bees, wasps, ants. . . . God has provided them with a social [he might have said biological] mechanism which attracts to industry, and causes happiness to be found in industry. Why should he not have accorded us the same favour as these animals? What a difference between their industrial condition and ours!"[4] But to see in the noninstinctual character of human labor the *direct* cause of the "anguish of repugnant labor," one must skip over all the intervening stages of social development which separate the early emergence of human labor out of pre-human forms, from labor in its modern form.

capacity for work well-conceptualized in advance and independent of the guidance of instinct.* "Men who made tools of standard type," as Oakley says, "must have formed in their minds images of the ends to which they laboured. Human culture . . . is the outcome of this capacity for conceptual thought."[7]

It is true, as experiments in animal behavior have shown, that animals are not entirely devoid of the power to learn, or to conceive rudimentary ideas, or to solve simple problems. Thus, a creature with as primitive a nervous system as the angleworm can learn to thread a maze; chimpanzees can be stimulated to "invent" and make tools, such as extensions of sticks, that enable them to reach food, or to stack boxes for the same purpose. As a result, some anthropologists and physiologists have concluded that the difference between the human and the nonhuman animal is not a difference in *kind* but in *degree*. But when a difference of degree is so enormous as the gap that exists between the learning and conceptual abilities of humans and even the most adaptable of other animals, it may properly be treated, for the purposes of our present discussion, as a difference in kind. And, we may add, whatever learning capacities may be stimulated in animals through ingenious forms of human tutelage, it has not proved possible to stimulate in them an ability to manage symbolic representation, especially in its highest form, articulate speech. Without symbols and speech, conceptual thought must remain rudimentary and, moreover, cannot be freely transmitted throughout the group or to succeeding generations:

> Culture without continuity of experience is, of course, impossible. But what sort of continuity of experience is prerequisite to culture? It is not the continuity which comes from the communication of experience by imitation, for we find this among apes. Clearly, it is continuity on the subjective side rather than on the objective, or overt, that is essential. As we have shown, it is the symbol, particularly in word form, which provides this element of continuity in the tool-experience of man. And, finally, it is this factor of continuity in man's tool-experience that has made accumulation and progress, in short, a material culture, possible.[8]

---

* The general increase in brain size is important, but "certain parts of the brain have increased in size much more than others. As functional maps of the cortex of the brain show, the human sensory-motor cortex is not just an enlargement of that of an ape. The areas for the hand, especially the thumb, in man are tremendously enlarged, and this is an integral part of the structural base that makes the skillful use of the hand possible. . . .

"The same is true for other cortical areas. Much of the cortex in a monkey is still engaged in the motor and sensory functions. In man it is the areas adjacent to the primary centers that are most expanded. These areas are concerned with skills, memory, foresight and language; that is, with the mental faculties that make human social life possible."[6]

Thus work as purposive action, guided by the intelligence, is the special product of humankind. But humankind is itself the special product of this form of labor. "By thus acting on the external world and changing it, he at the same time changes his own nature," wrote Marx.[9] Writing in 1876, Frederick Engels had worked out, in terms of the anthropological knowledge of his time, the theory that: "First labour, after it and then with it speech—these were the two most essential stimuli under the influence of which the brain of the ape gradually changed into that of man." "The hand," he maintained, "is not only the organ of labour, *it is also the product of labour."*[10] His essay, called "The Part Played by Labour in the Transition from Ape to Man," was limited by the state of scientific knowledge of his day, and some of its details may be faulty or wrong—as for example his implication that the "undeveloped larynx of the ape" is inadequate to produce speech sounds. But his fundamental idea has again found favor in the eyes of anthropologists, particularly in the light of recent discoveries of stone tools in association with "near-men" or "man-apes." In an article on tools and human evolution, Sherwood L. Washburn says:

> Prior to these findings the prevailing view held that man evolved nearly to his present structural state and then discovered tools and the new ways of life that they made possible. Now it appears that man-apes—creatures able to run but not yet walk on two legs, and with brains no larger than those of apes now living—had already learned to make and use tools. It follows that the structure of modern man must be the result of the change in the terms of natural selection that came with the tool-using way of life. . . . It was the success of the simplest tools that started the whole trend of human evolution and led to the civilizations of today."[11]

Labor that transcends mere instinctual activity is thus the force which created humankind and the force by which humankind created the world as we know it.

The possibility of all the various social forms which have arisen and which may yet arise depends in the last analysis upon this distinctive characteristic of human labor. Where the division of function within other animal species has been assigned by nature and stamped upon the genotype in the form of instinct, humanity is capable of an infinite variety of functions and division of function on the basis of family, group, and social assignment. In all other species, the directing force and the resulting activity, instinct and execution, are indivisible. The spider which weaves its web in accordance with a biological urge cannot depute this function to another spider; it carries on this activity because that is its nature. But for men and women, any instinctual patterns of work which they may have possessed at the dawn of their evolution have long since atrophied or been submerged by social forms.* Thus in humans, as distinguished from animals, the

---

* Veblen's "instinct of workmanship" can be understood only in a figurative sense, as a desire or proclivity to work well. A British "social psychologist" expresses himself somewhat agnostically on this matter: "Animals work too . . . and do so largely through

unity between the motive force of labor and the labor itself is not inviolable. *The unity of conception and execution may be dissolved.* The conception must still precede and govern execution, but the idea as conceived by *one* may be executed by *another*. The driving force of labor remains human consciousness, but the unity between the two may be broken in the individual and reasserted in the group, the workshop, the community, the society as a whole.

Finally, the human capacity to perform work, which Marx called "labor power," must not be confused with the power of any nonhuman agency, whether natural or man made. Human labor, whether directly exercised or stored in such products as tools, machinery, or domesticated animals, represents the sole resource of humanity in confronting nature. Thus for humans in society, labor power is a special category, separate and inexchangeable with any other, *simply because it is human.* Only one who is the *master of the labor of others* will confuse labor power with any other agency for performing a task, because to him, steam, horse, water, or human muscle which turns his mill are viewed as equivalents, as "factors of production." For *individuals who allocate their own labor* (or a community which does the same), the difference between using labor power as against any other power is a difference upon which the entire "economy" turns. And from the point of view of the species as a whole, this difference is also crucial, since every individual is the proprietor of a portion of the total labor power of the community, the society, and the species.

It is this consideration that forms the starting point for the labor theory of value, which bourgeois economists feel they may safely disregard because they are concerned not with social relations but with price relations, not with labor but with production, and not with the human point of view but with the bourgeois point of view.

Freed from the rigid paths dictated in animals by instinct, human labor becomes indeterminate, and its various determinate forms henceforth are the products not of biology but of the complex interaction between tools and social relations, technology and society. The subject of our discussion is not labor "in general," but labor in the forms it takes under capitalist relations of production.

Capitalist production requires exchange relations, commodities, and money, but its *differentia specifica* is the purchase and sale of labor power. For this purpose, three basic conditions become generalized throughout society. First, workers are separated from the means with which production is carried

---

instinctive patterns of behaviour, which are the product of evolutionary processes. It is not clear whether man has innate patterns of work behaviour or not." He adds: "It is possible that man's capacity for learnt, persistent, goal-directed behaviour in groups is such an innate pattern."[12] But the sum of the wisdom in this statement is that the human capacity to work *noninstinctually* may itself be called an instinct. This seems to be a useless and confusing attempt to force an assimilation of human and animal behavior.

on, and can gain access to them only by selling their labor power to others. Second, workers are freed of legal constraints, such as serfdom or slavery, that prevent them from disposing of their own labor power. Third, the purpose of the employment of the worker becomes the expansion of a unit of capital belonging to the employer, who is thus functioning as a capitalist. The labor process therefore begins with a contract or agreement governing the conditions of the sale of labor power by the worker and its purchase by the employer.

It is important to take note of the historical character of this phenomenon. While the purchase and sale of labor power has existed from antiquity,* a substantial class of wage-workers did not begin to form in Europe until the fourteenth century, and did not become numerically significant until the rise of industrial capitalism (that is, the *production* of commodities on a capitalist basis, as against mercantile capitalism, which merely *exchanged* the surplus products of prior forms of production) in the eighteenth century. It has been the numerically dominant form for little more than a century, and this in only a few countries. In the United States, perhaps four-fifths of the population was self-employed in the early part of the nineteenth century. By 1870 this had declined to about one-third and by 1940 to no more than one-fifth; by 1970 only about one-tenth of the population was self-employed. We are thus dealing with a social relation of extremely recent date. The rapidity with which it has won supremacy in a number of countries emphasizes the extraordinary power of the tendency of capitalist economies to convert all other forms of labor into hired labor.

The worker enters into the employment agreement because social conditions leave him or her no other way to gain a livelihood. The employer, on the other hand, is the possessor of a unit of capital which he is endeavoring to enlarge, and in order to do so he converts part of it into wages. Thus is set in motion the labor process, which, while it is in general a process for creating useful values, has now also become specifically a process for the expansion of capital, the creation of a profit.** From this point on, it becomes foolhardy to view the labor process purely from a technical standpoint, as a mere mode of labor. It has become in addition a process of accumulation of capital. And,

---

* Aristotle includes "service for hire—of this, one kind is employed in the mechanical arts, the other in unskilled and bodily labor" along with commerce and usury as the three divisions of exchange which form an unnatural mode of wealth-getting, the natural or "true and proper" modes being through livestock raising and husbandry. He seems, however, to have in mind the *sale of one's labor power* rather than the *purchase of that of others* as a means to wealth, an attitude the precise opposite of that which is characteristic in the capitalist era.[13]

** Thus Marx says of the process of production that "considered . . . as the unity of the labour-process and the process of producing surplus-value, it is the capitalist process of production, or capitalist production of commodities."[14]

moreover, it is the latter aspect which dominates in the mind and activities of the capitalist, into whose hands the control over the labor process has passed. In everything that follows, therefore, we shall be considering the manner in which the labor process is dominated and shaped by the accumulation of capital.*

Labor, like all life processes and bodily functions, is an inalienable property of the human individual. Muscle and brain cannot be separated from persons possessing them; one cannot endow another with one's own capacity for work, no matter at what price, any more than one can eat, sleep, or perform sex acts for another. Thus, in the exchange, the worker does not surrender to the capitalist his or her capacity for work. The worker retains it, and the capitalist can take advantage of the bargain only by setting the worker to work. It is of course understood that the useful effects or products of labor belong to the capitalist. But what the worker sells, and what the capitalist buys, is *not an agreed amount of labor, but the power to labor over an agreed period of time.* This inability to purchase labor, which is an inalienable bodily and mental function, and the necessity to purchase the power to perform it, is so fraught with consequences for the entire capitalist mode of production that it must be investigated more closely.

When a master employs the services of a beast of burden in his production process, he can do little more than direct into useful channels such natural abilities as strength and endurance. When he employs bees in the production of honey, silkworms in the making of silk, bacteria in the fermentation of wine, or sheep in the growing of wool, he can only turn to his own advantage the instinctual activities or biological functions of these forms of life. Babbage gave a fascinating example:

> A most extraordinary species of manufacture . . . has been contrived by an officer of engineers residing at Munich. It consists of lace, and veils, with open patterns in them, made entirely by caterpillars. The following is the mode of proceeding adopted:—He makes a paste of the leaves of the plant, which is the usual food of the species of caterpillar he employs, and spreads it thinly over a stone, or other flat substance. He then, with a camel-hair pencil dipped in olive oil, draws upon the coating of paste the pattern he wishes the insects to

---

* This is not the place for a general discussion of the capital-accumulation process, and the economic laws which enforce it on the capitalist regardless of his wishes. The best discussion remains that of Marx, and occupies much of the first volume of *Capital,* especially Part VII. A very clear and compressed exposition of the capitalist drive for accumulation, considered both as subjective desire and objective necessity, is to be found in Paul M. Sweezy, *The Theory of Capitalist Development* (New York, 1942), pp. 79-83 and 92-95. This should be supplemented with Paul M. Sweezy and Paul A. Baran, *Monopoly Capital,* which is devoted to the conditions of accumulation in the monopoly period of capitalism (New York, 1966; see especially pp. 42-44 and 67-71).

leave open. This stone is then placed in an inclined position, and a number of the caterpillars are placed at the bottom. A peculiar species is chosen, which spins a strong web; and the animals commencing at the bottom, eat and spin their way up to the top, carefully avoiding every part touched by the oil, but devouring all the rest of the paste. The extreme lightness of these veils, combined with some strength, is truly surprising."[15]

Notwithstanding the ingenuity displayed by this officer, it is evident that the entire process is circumscribed by the capacities and predisposition of the caterpillar; and so it is with every form of the use of nonhuman labor. It is implied in all such employments that the master must put up with the definite natural limitations of his servitors. Thus, in taking the *labor power* of animals, he at the same time takes their *labor,* because the two, while distinguishable in theory, are more or less identical in practice, and the most cunning contrivances can get from the labor power of the animal only minor variations of actual labor.

Human labor, on the other hand, because it is informed and directed by an understanding which has been socially and culturally developed, is capable of a vast range of productive activities. The active labor processes which reside in potential in the labor power of humans are so diverse as to type, manner of performance, etc., that for all practical purposes they may be said to be infinite, all the more so as new modes of labor can easily be invented more rapidly than they can be exploited. The capitalist finds in this infinitely malleable character of human labor the essential resource for the expansion of his capital.

It is known that human labor is able to produce more than it consumes, and this capacity for "surplus labor" is sometimes treated as a special and mystical endowment of humanity or of its labor. In reality it is nothing of the sort, but is merely a prolongation of working time beyond the point where labor has reproduced itself, or in other words brought into being its own means of subsistence or their equivalent. This time will vary with the intensity and productivity of labor, as well as with the changing requirements of "subsistence," but for any given state of these it is a definite duration. The "peculiar" capacity of labor power to produce for the capitalist after it has reproduced itself is therefore nothing but the extension of work time beyond the point where it could otherwise come to a halt. An ox too will have this capacity, and grind out more corn than it will eat if kept to the task by training and compulsion.

The distinctive capacity of human labor power is therefore not its ability to produce a surplus, but rather its intelligent and purposive character, which gives it infinite adaptability and which produces the social and cultural conditions for enlarging its own productivity, so that its surplus product may be continuously enlarged. From the point of view of the capitalist, this many-sided potentiality of humans in society is the basis upon which is built the enlargement of his capital. He therefore takes up every means of increasing the output of the labor power he has purchased when he sets it to work as labor. The means he employs may vary from the enforcement upon the worker of the longest possible working day in the early period of capitalism to the use of the most productive instruments of labor and the greatest intensity of labor, but they are always aimed at realizing from the potential inherent in labor power the greatest useful effect of labor, for it is this that will yield for him the greatest surplus and thus the greatest profit.

But if the capitalist builds upon this distinctive quality and potential of human labor power, it is also this quality, by its very indeterminacy, which places before him his greatest challenge and problem. The coin of labor has its obverse side: in purchasing labor power that can do much, he is at the same time purchasing an undefined quality and quantity. What he buys is infinite in *potential,* but in its *realization* it is limited by the subjective state of the workers, by their previous history, by the general social conditions under which they work as well as the particular conditions of the enterprise, and by the technical setting of their labor. The work actually performed will be affected by these and many other factors, including the organization of the process and the forms of supervision over it, if any.

This is all the more true since the technical features of the labor process are now dominated by the social features which the capitalist has introduced: that is to say, the new relations of production. Having been forced to sell their labor power to another, the workers also surrender their interest in the labor process, which has now been "alienated." *The labor process has become the responsibility of the capitalist.* In this setting of antagonistic relations of production, the problem of realizing the "full usefulness" of the labor power he has bought becomes exacerbated by the opposing interests of those for whose purposes the labor process is carried on, and those who, on the other side, carry it on.

Thus when the capitalist buys buildings, materials, tools, machinery, etc., he can evaluate with precision their place in the labor process. He knows that a certain portion of his outlay will be transferred to each unit of production, and his accounting practices allocate these in the form of costs or depreciation. But when he buys labor time, the outcome is far from being either so certain or so definite that it can be reckoned in this way, with precision and in advance. This is merely an expression of the fact that the portion of his capital expended on labor power is the "variable" portion, which undergoes an increase in the process of production; for him, the question is how great that increase will be.

It thus becomes essential for the capitalist that control over the labor process pass from the hands of the worker into his own. This transition presents itself in history as the *progressive alienation of the process of production* from the worker; to the capitalist, it presents itself as the problem of *management.*

Notes

1. Karl Marx, *Capital,* vol. I (Moscow, n.d.), p. 174.
2. Aristotle, *De Partibus Animalium,* i.1.64O^{a}32.
3. Paul Valéry, *Über Kunst* (Frankfurt, 1959), p. 69; quoted in Alfred Schmidt, *The Concept of Nature in Marx* (London, 1971), p. 101.
4. Charles Fourier, *Design for Utopia: Selected Writings* (New York, 1971), pp. 163-164.
5. Kenneth P. Oakley, "Skill as a Human Possession," in Charles Singer, E. J. Holmyard, and A. R. Hall, eds., *A History of Technology,* vol. I (New York and London, 1954), pp. 2-3.
6. Sherwood L. Washburn, "Tools and Human Evolution," *Scientific American* (September 1960), pp. 71-73.
7. Oakley, "Skill as a Human Possession," p. 27.
8. Leslie A. White, *The Science of Culture* (New York, 1949), p. 48.
9. Marx, *Capital,* vol. 1, p. 173.
10. See Karl Marx and Frederick Engels, *Selected Works,* vol. III (Moscow, 1970), pp. 66-77.
11. Washburn, "Tools and Human Evolution," p. 63.
12. Michael Argyle, *The Social Psychology of Work* (London, 1972), p. 1.
13. Aristotle, *Politics,* i.11.1258^{b}9-38.
14. Marx, *Capital,* vol. I, p. 191.
15. Charles Babbage, *On the Economy of Machinery and Manufactures* (London, 1832; reprint ed., New York, 1963), pp. 110-11.

Chapter 2

The Origins of Management

Industrial capitalism begins when a significant number of workers is employed by a single capitalist. At first, the capitalist utilizes labor as it comes to him from prior forms of production, carrying on labor processes as they had been carried on before. The workers are already trained in traditional arts of industry previously practiced in feudal and guild handicraft production. Spinners, weavers, glaziers, potters, blacksmiths, tinsmiths, locksmiths, joiners, millers, bakers, etc. continue to exercise in the employ of the capitalist the productive crafts they had carried on as guild journeymen and independent artisans. These early workshops were simply agglomerations of smaller units of production, reflecting little change in traditional methods, and the work thus remained under the immediate control of the producers in whom was embodied the traditional knowledge and skills of their crafts.

Nevertheless, as soon as the producers were gathered together, the problem of management arose in rudimentary form. In the first place, functions of management were brought into being by the very practice of cooperative labor. Even an assemblage of independently practicing artisans requires coordination, if one considers the need for the provision of a workplace and the ordering of processes within it, the centralization of the supply of materials, even the most elementary scheduling of priorities and assignments, and the maintenance of records of costs, payrolls, materials, finished products, sales, credit, and the calculation of profit and loss. Second, assembly trades like shipbuilding and coach making required the relatively sophisticated meshing of different kinds of labor, as did civil engineering works, etc. Again, it was not long before new industries arose which had little prior handicraft background, among them sugar refining, soap boiling, and distilling, while at the same time various primary processes like iron smelting, copper and brass working, and ordnance, paper and powder making, were completely transformed. All of these required conceptual and coordination functions which in capitalist industry took the form of management.

The capitalist assumed these functions as manager by virtue of his ownership of capital. Under capitalist exchange relations, the time of the workers he hired was as much his own as were the materials he supplied and the products that issued from the shop. That this was not understood from the beginning is attested by the fact that guild and apprenticeship rules and the legal restraints common to feudal and guild modes of production all persisted for a period, and had to be gradually stripped away as the capitalist consolidated his powers in society and demolished the juridical features of pre-capitalist social formations. It was partly for this reason that early manufacturing tended to gravitate to new towns which were free of guild and feudal regulations and traditions. In time, however, law and custom were reshaped to reflect the predominance of the "free" contract between buyer and seller under which the capitalist gained the virtually unrestricted power to determine the technical modes of labor.

The early phases of industrial capitalism were marked by a sustained effort on the part of the capitalist to disregard the difference between labor power and the labor that can be gotten out of it, and to buy labor in the same way he bought his raw materials: as a definite quantity of work, completed and embodied in the product. This attempt took the form of a great variety of subcontracting and "putting-out" systems.* In the form of domestic labor, it was to be found in textile, clothing, metal goods (nailing and cutlery), watch-making, hat, wood and leather industries, where the capitalist distributed materials on a piecework basis to workers for manufacture in their own homes, through the medium of subcontractors and commission agents. But even in industries where work could not be taken home, such as coal, tin, and copper mines, mine workers themselves, working at the face, took contracts singly or in gangs, either directly or through the mediation of the "butty" or subcontracting employer of mine labor. The system persisted even in the early factories. In cotton mills, skilled spinners were put in charge of machinery and engaged their own help, usually child assistants from among their families and acquaintances. Foremen sometimes added to their direct supervisory function the practice of taking a few machines on their own account and hiring labor to operate them. Pollard identifies practices of this sort not only in mines and textile mills, but also in carpet and lace mills, ironworks, potteries, building and civil engineering projects, transport, and quarrying.[2] In the United States, it has been pointed out, the contract system, in which puddlers and other skilled iron and steel craftsmen were paid by the ton on a sliding scale pegged to market prices, and hired their own help, was characteristic of this industry until almost the end of the nineteenth century.[3] The following description, by Maurice Dobb, of the prevalence of such systems well past the middle of the nineteenth century points to this important fact: that the specifically capitalist mode of management and thus of production did not become generalized until relatively recent times, that is, within the last hundred years:

---

* Sidney Pollard, to whose *The Genesis of Modern Management* I am indebted for materials used in this chapter, calls this effort "if not a method of management, at least a method of evading management."[1]

As late as 1870 the immediate employer of many workers was not the large capitalist but the intermediate sub-contractor who was both an employee and in turn a small employer of labour. In fact the skilled worker of the middle nineteenth century tended to be in some measure a sub-contractor, and in psychology and outlook bore the marks of this status.

It was not only in trades still at the stage of outwork and domestic production that this type of relationship prevailed, with their master gunmakers or nail-masters or saddlers' and coachbuilders' ironmongers, or factors and "foggers" with domestic workers under them. Even in factory trades the system of sub-contracting was common: a system with its opportunities for sordid tyranny and cheating through truck and debt and the payment of wages in public houses, against which early trade unionism fought a hard and prolonged battle. In blast-furnaces there were the bridge-stockers and the stock-takers, paid by the capitalist according to the tonnage output of the furnace and employing gangs of men, women, boys and horses to charge the furnace or control the casting. In coal-mines there were the butties who contracted with the management for the working of a stall, and employed their own assistants; some butties having as many as 150 men under them and requiring a special overseer called a "doggie" to superintend the work. In rolling mills there was the master-roller, in brass-foundries and chainfactories the overhand, who at times employed as many as twenty or thirty; even women workers in button factories employed girl assistants. When factories first came to the Birmingham small metal trades, "the idea that the employer should find, as a matter of course, the work places, plant and materials, and should exercise supervision over the details of the manufacturing processes, did not spring into existence."[4]

While all such systems involved the payment of wages by piece rates, or by subcontract rates, it must not be supposed that this in itself was their essential feature. Piece rates in various forms are common to the present day, and represent the conversion of time wages into a form which attempts, with very uneven success, to enlist the worker as a willing accomplice in his or her own exploitation. Today, however, piece rates are combined with the systematic and detailed control on the part of management over the processes of work, a control which is sometimes exercised more stringently than where time rates are employed. Rather, the early domestic and subcontracting systems represented a transitional form, a phase during which the capitalist had not yet assumed the essential function of management in industrial capitalism, control over the labor process; for this reason it was incompatible with the overall development of capitalist production, and survives only in specialized instances.

Such methods of dealing with labor bore the marks of the origins of industrial capitalism in mercantile capitalism, which understood the buying and selling of commodities but not their production, and sought to treat labor like all other commodities. It was bound to prove inadequate, and did so very rapidly, even though its survival was guaranteed for a time by the extreme unevenness of the development of technology, and by the need for technology to incessantly retrace its own steps and recapitulate, in newer industries, the stages of its historic development. The subcontracting and "putting out" systems were plagued by problems of irregularity of production, loss of materials in transit and through embezzlement, slowness of manufacture, lack of uniformity and uncertainty of the quality of the product. But most of all, they were limited by their inability to change the processes of production.* Based, as Pollard points out, upon a rudimentary division of labor, the domestic system prevented the further development of the division of labor. While the attempt to purchase finished labor, instead of assuming direct control over labor power, relieved the capitalist of the uncertainties of the latter system by fixing a definite unit cost, at the same time it placed beyond the reach of the capitalist much of the potential of human labor that may be made available by fixed hours, systematic control, and the reorganization of the labor process. This function, capitalist management soon seized upon with an avidity that was to make up for its earlier timidity.

The control of large bodies of workers long antedates the bourgeois epoch. The Pyramids, the Great Wall of China, extensive networks of roads, aqueducts, and irrigation canals, the large buildings, arenas, monuments, cathedrals, etc., dating from antiquity and medieval times all testify to this. We find an elementary division of labor in the workshops which produced weapons for the Roman armies, and the armies of pre-capitalist times exhibit primitive forms of later capitalist practices.** Roman workshops for metalwork, pottery, leather, glassblowing, brickmaking, and textiles, as well as large agricultural estates, brought together scores of workers under a single management.[7] These predecessors, however, were undertaken under conditions of slave or other unfree forms of labor, stagnant technology, and the absence of the driving capitalist need to expand each unit of capital employed, and so differed markedly from capitalist management. The Pyramids were built with the

---

* On this, David Landes writes: ". . . the manufacturer who wanted to increase output had to get more work out of the labour already engaged. Here, however, he again ran into the internal contradictions of the system. He had no way of compelling his workers to do a given number of hours of labour; the domestic weaver or craftsman was master of his time, starting and stopping when he desired. And while the employer could raise the piece rates with a view to encouraging diligence, he usually found that this actually reduced output." Landes also summarizes other "internal contradictions" of this mode of industrial organization.[5]

** "In general," Marx wrote in a letter to Engels, "the army is important for economic development. For instance, it was in the army that the ancients first fully developed a wage system. . . . The division of labour *within* one branch was also first carried out in the armies."[6]

surplus labor of an enslaved population, with no end in view but the greater glory of the pharaohs here and in the hereafter. Roads, aqueducts, and canals were built for their military or civilian usefulness, and not generally on a profit-making basis. State-subsidized manufactories produced arms or luxury goods and enjoyed an actual or legal monopoly and large orders from noncommercial buyers, courts, or armies.[8] The management required in such situations remained elementary, and this was all the more true when the labor was that of slaves, and sometimes supervised by slaves as well. The capitalist, however, working with hired labor, which represents a cost for every nonproducing hour, in a setting of rapidly revolutionizing technology to which his own efforts perforce contributed, and goaded by the need to show a surplus and accumulate capital, brought into being a wholly new art of management, which even in its early manifestations was far more complete, self-conscious, painstaking, and calculating than anything that had gone before.

There were more immediate precedents for the early industrial capitalist to draw upon, in the form of mercantile enterprises, plantations, and agricultural estates. Merchant capitalism invented the Italian system of bookkeeping, with its internal checks and controls; and from merchant capital the industrial capitalist also took over the structure of branch organization subdivided among responsible managers. Agricultural estates and colonial plantations offered the experience of a well-developed supervisory routine, particularly since much early mining (and the construction works that attended it) was carried out on the agricultural estates of Great Britain under the supervision of estate agents.

Control without centralization of employment was, if not impossible, certainly very difficult, and so the precondition for management was the gathering of workers under a single roof. The first effect of such a move was to enforce upon the workers regular hours of work, in contrast to the self-imposed pace which included many interruptions, short days and holidays, and in general prevented a prolongation of the working day for the purpose of producing a surplus under then-existing technical conditions. Thus Gras writes in his *Industrial Evolution*:

> It was purely for purposes of discipline, so that the workers could be effectively controlled under the supervision of foremen. Under one roof, or within a narrow compass, they could be started to work at sunrise and kept going till sunset, barring periods for rest and refreshment. And under penalty of loss of all employment they could be kept going almost all throughout the year.[9]

Within the workshops, early management assumed a variety of harsh and despotic forms, since the creation of a "free labor force" required coercive methods to habituate the workers to their tasks and keep them working throughout the day and the year. Pollard notes that "there were few areas of the country in which modern industries, particularly the textiles, if carried on in large buildings, were not associated with prisons, workhouses, and orphanages.

This connection is usually underrated, particularly by those historians who assume that the new works recruited free labour only." So widespread does he find this and other systems of coercion that he concludes that "the modern industrial proletariat was introduced to its role not so much by attraction or monetary reward, but by compulsion, force and fear."[10]

Legal compulsions and a paralegal structure of punishment within factories were often enlarged into an entire social system covering whole townships. Pollard gives the example of the enterprise of Ambrose Crowley, a large mixed ironworks which carried on both primary processes of iron production and fabricating. In the second quarter of the eighteenth century this firm employed more than 1,000 workers, scattered over its central works, warehouses, and company ships. An extraordinary Book of Laws has survived from this enterprise:

> The firm provided a doctor, a clergyman, three schoolmasters and a poor relief, pension and funeral scheme, and by his instructions and exhortations Crowley attempted to dominate the spiritual life of his flock, and to make them into willing and obedient cogs in his machine. It was his express intention that their whole life, including even their sparse spare time (the normal working week being of eighty hours) should revolve around the task of making the works profitable.[11]

In this method of total economic, spiritual, moral, and physical domination, buttressed by the legal and police constraints of a servile administration of justice in a segregated industrial area, we see the forerunner of the company town familiar in the United States in the recent past as one of the most widely used systems of total control before the rise of industrial unionism.

In all these early efforts, the capitalists were groping toward a theory and practice of management. Having created new social relations of production, and having begun to transform the mode of production, they found themselves confronted by problems of management which were different not only in scope but also in kind from those characteristic of earlier production processes. Under the special and new relations of capitalism, which presupposed a "free labor contract," they had to extract from their employees that daily conduct which would best serve their interests, to impose their will upon their workers while operating a labor process on a voluntary contractual basis. This enterprise shared from the first the characterization which Clausewitz assigned to war; it is *movement in a resistant medium* because it involves the control of refractory masses.

The verb *to manage*, from *manus*, the Latin for hand, originally meant to train a horse in his paces, to cause him to do the exercises of the *manège*. As capitalism creates a society in which no one is presumed to consult anything but self-interest, and as the employment contract between parties sharing nothing but the inability to avoid each other becomes prevalent, management becomes a more perfected and subtle instrument. Tradition, sentiment, and pride in workmanship play an ever weaker and more erratic role, and are regarded on both sides as manifestations of a better nature which it would be folly to accommodate. Like a rider who uses reins, bridle, spurs, carrot, whip, and training from birth to impose his will, the capitalist strives, through management, to *control*. And control is indeed the central concept of all management systems, as has been recognized implicitly or explicitly by all theoreticians of management.* Lyndall Urwick, the rhapsodic historian of the scientific management movement and himself a management consultant for many decades, understood the historical nature of the problem clearly:

> In the workshops of the Medieval "master," control was based on the obedience which the customs of the age required the apprentices and journeymen to give to the man whom they had contracted to serve. But in the later phase of domestic economy the industrial family unit was controlled by the clothier only in so far as it had to complete a given quantity of cloth according to a certain pattern. With the advent of the modern industrial group in large factories in urban areas, the whole process of control underwent a fundamental revolution. It was now the owner or manager of a factory, i.e., the "employer" as he came to be called, who had to secure or exact from his "employees" a level of obedience and/or co-operation which would enable him to exercise control. There was no individual interest in the success of the enterprise other than the extent to which it provided a livelihood.[13]

It was not that the new arrangement was "modern," or "large," or "urban" which created the new situation, but rather the new social relations which now frame the production process, and the antagonism between those who carry on the process and those for whose benefit it is carried on, those who manage and those who execute, those who bring to the factory their labor power, and those who undertake to extract from this labor power the maximum advantage for the capitalist.

Notes

1. Sidney Pollard, *The Genesis of Modern Management: A Study of the Industrial Revolution in Great Britain* (Cambridge, Mass., 1965), p. 38.
2. Ibid., pp. 38-47.
3. Katherine Stone, "The Origins of Job Structures in the Steel Industry," *Radical America* (November-December 1973), pp. 19-64.
4. Maurice Dobb, *Studies in the Development of Capitalism* (New York, 1947), pp. 266-67.

---

* For example, Leffingwell: "Effective management implies control. The terms are in a sense interchangeable, as management without control is not conceivable."[12]

5. David S. Landes, *The Unbound Prometheus: Technological Change and Industrial Development in Western Europe from 1750 to the Present* (Cambridge, England and New York, 1969), pp. 58-59.
6. Karl Marx and Frederick Engels, *Selected Works*, vol. I (Moscow, 1969), pp. 529-30.
7. Michael Argyle, *The Social Psychology of Work* (London, 1972), pp. 18-19.
8. Pollard, *The Genesis of Modern Management*, p. 7.
9. N. S. B. Gras, *Industrial Evolution* (1930), p. 77; quoted in ibid., pp. 11-12.
10. Ibid., pp. 163, 207.
11. Ibid., p. 56.
12. William Henry Leffingwell, *Office Management: Principles and Practice* (Chicago, New York, and London, 1925), p. 35.
13. Lyndall Urwick and E. F. L. Brech, *The Making of Scientific Management*, vol. II (London, 1946), pp. 10-11.

Chapter 3

The Division of Labor

The earliest innovative principle of the capitalist mode of production was the manufacturing division of labor, and in one form or another the division of labor has remained the fundamental principle of industrial organization. The division of labor in capitalist industry is not at all identical with the phenomenon of the distribution of tasks, crafts, or specialties of production throughout society, for while all known societies have divided their work into productive specialties, no society before capitalism systematically subdivided the work of each productive specialty into limited operations. This form of the division of labor becomes generalized only with capitalism.

This distinction is made clear, for instance, in Herskovits' description of the division of labor in primitive societies:

> Only rarely is any division of labor within an industry—or, as it might be termed, subdivision of labor—encountered among nonliterate folk. Such intra-industrial specialization would be encountered only in the production of such larger capital goods as houses, canoes, or fish-weirs.* Even here, it is the rule in such cultures that an arrangement of this sort is temporary; moreover, each worker devoting himself to a part of a specific task is most often competent to perform other phases of the work besides that on which he may at the moment be engaged. . . . Thus in groups where the primary division of labor is along sex lines, every man or woman not only will know how to do all those things that men or women habitually do among them, but must be able to do them efficiently. As we move to societies of somewhat greater economic complexity, we find that certain men may spend a larger proportion of their time than others doing wood-carving or iron-working, or certain women making pots or weaving cloth; but all the members of the groups will have some competence in the techniques controlled by those of a given sex. In still other nonliterate societies, certain men and women specialize not only in one technique, but in a certain type of product, as, for instance, where one woman will devote her time to the

---

* Herskovits here performs the customary economic miracle of transforming "houses, canoes, or fish-weirs" into "capital goods," in accordance with the bourgeois-centric view which unself-consciously projects backward and forward throughout history the categories specific to capitalist production, and according to which houses become "capital" even when they were only structures people built as dwellings.

production of pots for everyday use and another make pottery exclusively for religious rites. It must again be stressed that, except under the most unusual circumstances, we do not find the kind of organization where one woman characteristically specializes in gathering the clay, another in fashioning it, and a third in firing the pots; or, where one man devotes himself to getting wood, a second to roughly blocking out the proportions of a stool or figure, and a third to finishing it.[1]

Herskovits gives us here a picture of a division of labor into crafts, a differentiation which in the beginning owes much to sex roles. By and large, however, there is no division of tasks within the crafts. While men or women may habitually be connected with the making of certain products, they do not as a rule divide up the separate operations involved in the making of each product.

This form of division of labor, characteristic of all societies, is, if we follow Marx's terminology, called the *social division of labor*. It is a derivative of the specific character of human work: "An animal forms things in accordance with the standard and the need of the species to which it belongs, whilst man knows how to produce in accordance with the standard of every species."[2] The spider weaves, the bear fishes, the beaver builds dams and houses, but the human is simultaneously weaver, fisherman, builder, and a thousand other things combined in a manner which, because this takes place in, and is possible only through, society, soon compels a social division according to craft. Each individual of the human species cannot alone "produce in accordance with the standard of every species" and invent standards unknown to any animal, but the species as a whole finds it possible to do this, in part through the social division of labor. Thus the social division of labor is apparently inherent in the species character of human labor as soon as it becomes social labor, that is, labor carried on in and through society.

As against this general or social division of labor, there stands the division of labor in detail, the manufacturing division of labor. This is the breakdown of the processes involved in the making of the product into manifold operations performed by different workers.

The practice of regarding the social and the detailed divisions of labor as a single continuum, a single abstract technical principle, is by far the greatest source of confusion in discussions of this subject.* The division of labor in society is characteristic of all known societies; the division of labor in the workshop is the special product of capitalist society. The social division of labor divides society among occupations, each adequate to a branch of

---

* "But, in spite of the numerous analogies and links connecting them," Marx warned, "division of labour in the interior of a society, and that in the interior of a workshop, differ not only in degree, but also in kind."[3]

production; the detailed division of labor destroys occupations considered in this sense, and renders the worker inadequate to carry through any complete production process. In capitalism, the social division of labor is enforced chaotically and anarchically by the market, while the workshop division of labor is imposed by planning and control. Again in capitalism, the products of the social division of labor are exchanged as commodities, while the results of the operation of the detail worker are not exchanged within the factory as within a marketplace, but are all owned by the same capital. While the social division of labor subdivides *society*, the detailed division of labor subdivides *humans*, and while the subdivision of society may enhance the individual and the species, the subdivision of the individual, when carried on without regard to human capabilities and needs, is a crime against the person and against humanity.

The view which ignores the distinction between the social and detailed divisions of labor is given typical expression in the following comments: "Social differentiation and division of labor are universal attributes of human society. Contrary to the view persisting into the recent past that primitive man lives in completely homogeneous and amorphous groups, modern knowledge of primitive and peasant communities reveals much complexity and specialization. . . . Modern specialization cannot therefore be contrasted with an assumed society or period having no division of labor. The difference is one of degree and not of kind."[4] Wilbert Moore here forces us to assume that the division of society among trades, crafts, professions "cannot be contrasted" with the breakup of those occupations, that there is no difference "in kind" between the practice of farming, cabinetmaking, or blacksmithing, and the repeated tightening of a single set of bolts hundreds of times each day or the key punching of thousands of cards each week throughout a lifetime of labor, because *all* are expressions of the "division of labor." On this level of abstraction, obviously, nothing can be learned about the division of labor, except the banal and apologetic conclusion that being "universal," each of its manifestations is probably inevitable. Needless to say, this is precisely the conclusion that bourgeois society prefers.

It is for this reason that the popularity of Emile Durkheim's work, *The Division of Labor in Society*, has grown as its applicability to the modern world has dwindled. Durkheim adopts just such a level of abstraction in his approach: "The only way to succeed in objectively appreciating the division of labor is to study it first in itself, entirely speculatively, to look for its use, and upon what it depends, and finally, to form as adequate a notion as possible of it."[5] He proceeds in this fashion, determinedly avoiding the specific social conditions under which the division of labor develops in our epoch, celebrating throughout his proposition that "the ideal of human fraternity can be realized only in proportion to the progress of the division of labor,"[6] until in the last tenth of his work he discovers the division of labor in the factories and offices of modern capitalism, and dubs them "abnormal forms." But, as has been noted by a recent critic, M. C. Kennedy, "when we inspect these abnormal forms throughout the world, it becomes difficult to find one clear-cut case of the normal division of labor." Kennedy is absolutely right when he calls Durkheim's "normal" form of the division of labor "the ideal of a moralistic sociologist and not a sociologist of morals."[7] *

Our concern at this point, therefore, is not with the division of labor in society at large, but within the enterprise; not with the distribution of labor among various industries and occupations, but with the breakdown of occupations and industrial processes; not with the division of labor in "production in general," but within the capitalist mode of production in particular. It is not "pure technique" that concerns us, but rather the marriage of technique with the special needs of capital.

The division of labor in production begins with the *analysis of the labor process*—that is to say, the separation of the work of production into its constituent elements. But this, in itself, is not what brings into being the detail worker. Such an analysis or separation, in fact, is characteristic in every labor process organized by workers to suit their own needs.

For example, a tinsmith makes a funnel: he draws the elevation view on sheetmetal, and from this develops the outline of an unrolled funnel and its bottom spout. He then cuts out each piece with snips and shears, rolls it to its proper shape, and crimps or rivets the seams. He then rolls the top edge, solders the seams, solders on a hanging ring, washes away the acid used in soldering, and rounds the funnel to its final shape. But when he applies the same process to a quantity of identical funnels, his mode of operation changes. Instead of laying out the work directly on the material, he makes a pattern and uses it to mark off the total quantity of funnels needed; then he cuts them all out, one after the other, rolls them, etc. In this case, instead of making a single funnel in the course of an hour or two, he spends hours or even days on each step of

---

* Georges Friedmann says that had Durkheim lived to see the further development of the division of labor, "he would have been obliged to consider 'abnormal' most of the forms taken by labour in modern society, both in industry and in administration, and even more recently in commerce (I am thinking of the American supermarkets)."[8] The idea that anyone writing several generations after the Industrial Revolution, and after Adam Smith, Babbage, Ure, Marx, and countless others, needed to wait for the "American supermarkets" to learn about the division of labor in capitalism is not convincing. But in general, Friedmann's gingerly handling of Durkheim, whom—despite the fact that in his succeeding pages he finds little of value in the book—he calls "the most vigorous mind that has ever worked on this great problem," testifies to the inflated reputation of Durkheim's contribution.

the process, creating in each case fixtures, clamps, devices, etc. which would not be worth making for a single funnel but which, where a sufficiently large quantity of funnels is to be made, speed each step sufficiently so that the saving justifies the extra outlay of time. Quantities, he has discovered, will be produced with less trouble and greater economy of time in this way than by finishing each funnel individually before starting the next.

In the same way a bookkeeper whose job it is to make out bills and maintain office records against their future collection will, if he or she works for a lawyer who has only a few clients at a time, prepare a bill and post it at once to the proper accounts and the customer statement. But if there are hundreds of bills each month, the bookkeeper will accumulate them and spend a full day or two, from time to time, posting them to the proper accounts. Some of these postings will now be made by daily, weekly, or monthly totals instead of bill by bill, a practice which saves a great deal of labor when large quantities are involved; at the same time, the bookkeeper will now make use of other shortcuts or aids, which become practicable when operations are analyzed or broken up in this way, such as specially prepared ledger cards, or carbon forms which combine into a single operation the posting to the customer's account and the preparation of a monthly statement.

Such methods of analysis of the labor process and its division into constituent elements have always been and are to this day common in all trades and crafts, and represent the first form of the subdivision of labor in detail. It is clear that they satisfy, essentially if not fully, the three advantages of the division of labor given by Adam Smith in his famous discussion in the first chapter of *The Wealth of Nations*:

> This great increase in the quantity of work, which, in consequence of the division of labour, the same number of people are capable of performing, is owing to three different circumstances; first, to the increase of dexterity in every particular workman; secondly, to the saving of the time which is commonly lost in passing from one species of work to another; and lastly, to the invention of a great number of machines which facilitate and abridge labour, and enable one man to do the work of many.[9]

The example which Smith gives is the making of pins, and his description is as follows:

> One man draws out the wire, another straightens it, a third cuts it, a fourth points it, a fifth grinds it at the top for receiving the head; to make the head requires two or three distinct operations; to put it on, is a peculiar business, to whiten the pins is another; it is even a trade by itself to put them into the paper; and the important business of making a pin is, in this manner, divided into about eighteen distinct operations, which, in some manufactories, are all performed

by distinct hands, though in others the same man will sometimes perform two or three of them.[10]

In this example, the division of labor is carried one step further than in the examples of the tinsmith and the bookkeeper. Not only are the operations separated from each other, but *they are assigned to different workers*. Here we have not just the analysis of the labor process but the creation of the detail worker. Both steps depend upon the scale of production: without sufficient quantities they are impracticable. Each step represents a saving in labor time. The greatest saving is embodied in the analysis of the process, and a further saving, the extent varying with the nature of the process, is to be found in the separation of operations among different workers.*

The worker may break the process down, but he never voluntarily converts himself into a lifelong detail worker. This is the contribution of the capitalist, who sees no reason why, if so much is to be gained from the first step—analysis—and something more gained from the second—breakdown among workers—he should not take the second step as well as the first. That the first step breaks up only the process, while the second dismembers the worker as well, means nothing to the capitalist, and all the less since, in destroying the craft as a process under the control of the worker, he reconstitutes it as a process under

---

* The distinction between the analysis of the labor process and the creation of the detail worker may be seen in these lines from a special report presented by George Wallis to the House of Commons about the American worker of the nineteenth century: ". . . the American working boy develops rapidly into the skilled artizan, and having once mastered one part of his business, he is never content until he has mastered all. Doing *one* mechanical operation well, and only that one, does not satisfy him or his employer. He is ambitious to do something more than a set task, and, therefore, he must learn all. The second part of his trade he is allowed to learn as a reward for becoming master of the first, and so on to the end, if he may be said ever to arrive at *that*. The restless activity of mind and body—the anxiety to improve his own department of industry—the facts constantly before him of ingenious men who have solved economic and mechanical problems to their own profit and elevation, are all stimulative and encouraging; and it may be said that there is not a working boy of average ability in the New England States, at least, who has not an idea of some mechanical invention or improvement in manufactures. . . .

". . . Nor does this knowledge of the two or three departments of one trade, or even the pursuit of several trades by one individual, interfere so much with the systematic division of labour as may be supposed. In most instances the change of employment is only made at convenient periods, or as a relief to the workman from the monotony of always doing one thing. . . . There is, however, one drawback to this otherwise successful violation of the economic law of sub-division. It is unfavourable to that perfect skill of hand, and marvellous accuracy, which is always to be found associated with the constant direction of attention and practice of the workman to one thing; and this is often very apparent in most of the manufactured articles of America."[11]

his own control. He can now count his gains in a double sense, not only in productivity but in management control, since that which mortally injures the worker is in this case advantageous to him.*

The effect of these advantages is heightened by still another which, while it is given surprisingly little mention in economic literature, is certainly the most compelling reason of all for the immense popularity of the division of tasks among workers in the capitalist mode of production, and for its rapid spread. It was not formulated clearly nor emphasized strongly until a half-century after Smith, by Charles Babbage.

In "On the Division of Labour," Chapter XIX of his *On the Economy of Machinery and Manufactures*, the first edition of which was published in 1832, Babbage noted that "the most important and influential cause [of savings from the division of labor] has been altogether unnoticed." He recapitulates the classic arguments of William Petty, Adam Smith, and the other political economists, quotes from Smith the passage reproduced above about the "three different circumstances" of the division of labor which add to the productivity of labor, and continues:

> Now, although all these are important causes, and each has its influence on the result; yet it appears to me, that any explanation of the cheapness of manufactured articles, as consequent upon the division of labour, would be incomplete if the following principle were omitted to be stated.
>
> *That the master manufacturer, by dividing the work to be executed into different processes, each requiring different degrees of skill or of force, can purchase exactly that precise quantity of both which is necessary for each process; whereas, if the whole work were executed by one workman, that person must possess sufficient skill to perform the most difficult, and sufficient strength to execute the most laborious, of the operations into which the art is divided.*[13]

To put this all-important principle another way, in a society based upon the purchase and sale of labor power, dividing the craft cheapens its individual

---

* "We have much studied and perfected, of late, the great civilised invention of the division of labour; only we give it a false name. It is not, truly speaking, the labour that is divided; but the men: divided into mere segments of men—broken into small fragments and crumbs of life; so that all the little piece of intelligence that is left in a man is not enough to make a pin, or a nail, but exhausts itself in making the point of a pin, or the head of a nail. Now it is a good and desirable thing, truly, to make many pins in a day; but if we could only see with what crystal sand their points were polished—sand of human soul, much to be magnified before it can be discerned for what it is—we should think there might be some loss in it also. And the great cry that rises from all our manufacturing cities, louder than the furnace blast, is all in very deed for this—that we manufacture everything there except men . . ." Thus Ruskin.[12]

parts. To clarify this point, Babbage gives us an example drawn, like Smith's, from pin manufacture. He presents a table for the labor employed, by type (that is, by age and sex) and by pay, in the English manufacture of those pins known in his day as "Elevens."[14]

Drawing wire	Man	3s. 3d. per day
Straightening wire	Woman	1s. 0d.
	Girl	0s. 6d.
Pointing	Man	5s. 3d.
Twisting and cutting heads	Boy	0s. 4½d.
	Man	5s. 4½d.
Heading	Woman	1s. 3d.
Tinning or whitening	Man	6s. 0d.
	Woman	3s. 0d.
Papering	Woman	1s. 6d.

It is clear from this tabulation, as Babbage points out, that if the minimum pay for a craftsman capable of performing all operations is no more than the highest pay in the above listing, and if such craftsmen are employed exclusively, then the labor costs of manufacture would be more than doubled, *even if the very same division of labor were employed and even if the craftsmen produced pins at the very same speed as the detail workers.**

Let us add another and later example, taken from the first assembly line in American industry, the meatpacking conveyor (actually a *disassembly* line). J. R. Commons has realistically included in this description, along with the usual details, the rates of pay of the workers:

It would be difficult to find another industry where division of labor has been so ingeniously and microscopically worked out. The animal has been surveyed and laid off like a map; and the men have been classified in over thirty specialties and twenty rates of pay, from 16 cents to 50 cents an hour. The 50-cent man is restricted to using the knife on the most delicate parts of the hide (floorman) or to using the ax in splitting the backbone (splitter); and wherever a less-skilled man can be slipped in at 18 cents, 18½ cents, 20 cents, 21 cents, 22½ cents, 24 cents, 25 cents, and so on, a place is made for him, and an occupation mapped out. In working on the hide alone there are nine positions, at eight different rates of pay. A 20-cent man pulls off the tail, a

---

* Not all economists have missed this point. Alfred Marshall called it "Babbage's great principle of economical production."[15] But Marshall, after all, wrote at a time when economists were still interested in the way things worked in the real world.

22½-cent man pounds off another part where good leather is not found, and the knife of the 40-cent man cuts a different texture and has a different "feel" from that of the 50-cent man.[16]

Babbage's principle is fundamental to the evolution of the division of labor in capitalist society. It gives expression not to a technical aspect of the division of labor, but to its social aspect. Insofar as the labor process may be dissociated, it may be separated into elements some of which are simpler than others and each of which is simpler than the whole. Translated into market terms, this means that the labor power capable of performing the process may be purchased more cheaply as dissociated elements than as a capacity integrated in a single worker. Applied first to the handicrafts and then to the mechanical crafts, Babbage's principle eventually becomes the underlying force governing all forms of work in capitalist society, no matter in what setting or at what hierarchical level.

In the mythology of capitalism, the Babbage principle is presented as an effort to "preserve scarce skills" by putting qualified workers to tasks which "only they can perform," and not wasting "social resources." It is presented as a response to "shortages" of skilled workers or technically trained people, whose time is best used "efficiently" for the advantage of "society." But however much this principle may manifest itself at times in the form of a response to the scarcity of skilled labor—for example, during wars or other periods of rapid expansion of production—this apology is on the whole false, The capitalist mode of production systematically destroys all-around skills where they exist, and brings into being skills and occupations that correspond to its needs, Technical capacities are henceforth distributed on a strict "need to know" basis. The generalized distribution of knowledge of the productive process among all its participants becomes, from this point on, not merely "unnecessary," but a positive barrier to the functioning of the capitalist mode of production.

Labor power has become a commodity. Its uses are no longer organized according to the needs and desires of those who sell it, but rather according to the needs of its purchasers, who are, primarily, employers seeking to expand the value of their capital. And it is the special and permanent interest of these purchasers to cheapen this commodity. The most common mode of cheapening labor power is exemplified by the Babbage principle: break it up into its simplest elements. And, as the capitalist mode of production creates a working population suitable to its needs, the Babbage principle is, by the very shape of this "labor market," enforced upon the capitalists themselves.

Every step in the labor process is divorced, so far as possible, from special knowledge and training and reduced to simple labor. Meanwhile, the relatively few persons for whom special knowledge and training are reserved are freed so far as possible from the obligations of simple labor. In this way, a structure is given to all labor processes that at its extremes polarizes those whose time is infinitely valuable and those whose time is worth almost nothing. This might even be called the general law of the capitalist division of labor. It is not the sole force acting upon the organization of work, but it is certainly the most powerful and general. Its results, more or less advanced in every industry and occupation, give massive testimony to its validity. It shapes not only work, but populations as well, because over the long run it creates that mass of simple labor which is the primary feature of populations in developed capitalist countries.

Notes

1. Melville J. Herskovits, *Economic Anthropology: A Study in Comparative Economics* (2nd ed.; New York, 1960), p. 126.
2. Karl Marx, *Economic and Philosophic Manuscripts of 1844*, edited and with an introduction by Dirk J. Struik (New York, 1964), p. 113.
3. Karl Marx, *Capital*, vol. I (Moscow, n.d.), p. 334.
4. Wilbert E. Moore, "The Attributes of an Industrial Order," in S. Nosow and W. H. Form, eds., *Man, Work, and Society* (New York, 1962), pp. 92-93.
5. Emile Durkheim, *The Division of Labor in Society* (Glencoe, Ill., 1947), p. 45.
6. Ibid., p. 406.
7. M. C. Kennedy, "The Division of Labor and the Culture of Capitalism: A Critique" (Ph.D. diss., State University of New York at Buffalo, 1968, pp. 185-86; available from University Microfilms, Ann Arbor, Mich.).
8. Georges Friedmann, *The Anatomy of Work* (London, 1961, and Glencoe, Ill., 1964), p. 75.
9. Adam Smith, *The Wealth of Nations* (New York, 1937), p. 7.
10. Ibid., pp. 4-5.
11. New York Industrial Exhibition, Special Report of Mr. George Wallis, in Nathan Rosenberg, ed., *The American System of Manufactures* (Edinburgh, 1969), pp. 203-204.
12. John Ruskin, *The Stones of Venice*, section II, chapter VI; quoted in Ken Coates, *Essays on Industrial Democracy* (London, 1971), pp. 44-45.
13. Charles Babbage, *On the Economy of Machinery and Manufactures* (London, 1832; reprint ed., New York, 1963), pp. 175-76.
14. Ibid., p. 184.
15. Alfred Marshall, *Industry and Trade* (1919; reprint ed., London, 1932), p. 149.
16. J. R. Commons, *Quarterly Journal of Economics*, vol. XIX, p. 3; quoted in F. W. Taussig, *Principles of Economics* (New York, 1921), p. 42.

Chapter 4

Scientific Management

The classical economists were the first to approach the problems of the organization of labor within capitalist relations of production from a theoretical point of view. They may thus be called the first management experts, and their work was continued in the latter part of the Industrial Revolution by such men as Andrew Ure and Charles Babbage. Between these men and the next step, the comprehensive formulation of management theory in the late nineteenth and early twentieth centuries, there lies a gap of more than half a century during which there was an enormous growth in the size of enterprises, the beginnings of the monopolistic organization of industry, and the purposive and systematic application of science to production. The scientific management movement initiated by Frederick Winslow Taylor in the last decades of the nineteenth century was brought into being by these forces. Logically, Taylorism belongs to the chain of development of management methods and the organization of labor, and not to the development of technology, in which its role was minor.*

Scientific management, so-called, is an attempt to apply the methods of science to the increasingly complex problems of the control of labor in rapidly growing capitalist enterprises. It lacks the characteristics of a true science because its assumptions reflect nothing more than the outlook of the capitalist with regard to the conditions of production. It starts, despite occasional protestations to the contrary, not from the human point of view but from the capitalist point of view, from the point of view of the management of a refractory work force in a setting of antagonistic social relations. It does not attempt to discover and confront the cause of this condition, but accepts it as an inexorable given, a "natural" condition. It investigates not labor in general, but the adaptation of labor to the needs of capital. It enters the workplace not as the representative of science, but as the representative of management masquerading in the trappings of science.

A comprehensive and detailed outline of the principles of Taylorism is essential to our narrative, not because of the things for which it is popularly

---

* It is important to grasp this point, because from it flows the universal application of Taylorism to work in its various forms and stages of development, regardless of the nature of the technology employed. Scientific management, says Peter F. Drucker, "was not concerned with technology. Indeed, it took tools and techniques largely as given."[1]

known—stopwatch, speed-up, etc.—but because behind these commonplaces there lies a theory which is nothing less than the explicit verbalization of the capitalist mode of production. But before I begin this presentation, a number of introductory remarks are required to clarify the role of the Taylor school in the development of management theory.

It is impossible to overestimate the importance of the scientific management movement in the shaping of the modern corporation and indeed all institutions of capitalist society which carry on labor processes. The popular notion that Taylorism has been "superseded" by later schools of industrial psychology or "human relations," that it "failed"—because of Taylor's amateurish and naive views of human motivation or because it brought about a storm of labor opposition or because Taylor and various successors antagonized workers and sometimes management as well—or that it is "outmoded" because certain Taylorian specifics like functional foremanship or his incentive-pay schemes have been discarded for more sophisticated methods: all these represent a woeful misreading of the actual dynamics of the development of management.

Taylor dealt with the fundamentals of the organization of the labor process and of control over it. The later schools of Hugo Münsterberg, Elton Mayo, and others of this type dealt primarily with the adjustment of the worker to the ongoing production process as that process was designed by the industrial engineer. The successors to Taylor are to be found in engineering and work design, and in top management; the successors to Münsterberg and Mayo are to be found in personnel departments and schools of industrial psychology and sociology. Work itself is organized according to Taylorian principles, while personnel departments and academics have busied themselves with the selection, training, manipulation, pacification, and adjustment of "manpower" to suit the work processes so organized. Taylorism dominates the world of production; the practitioners of "human relations" and "industrial psychology" are the maintenance crew for the human machinery. If Taylorism does not exist as a separate school today, that is because, apart from the bad odor of the name, it is no longer the property of a faction, since its fundamental teachings have become the bedrock of all work design.* Peter F. Drucker, who has the advantage of

---

* "As a separate movement," says George Soule, "it virtually disappeared in the great depression of the 1930's, but by that time knowledge of it had become widespread in industry and its methods and philosophy were commonplaces in many schools of engineering and business management."[2] In other words, Taylorism is "outmoded" or "superseded" only in the sense that a sect which has become generalized and broadly accepted disappears as a sect.

considerable direct experience as a management consultant, is emphatic on this score:

> Personnel Administration and Human Relations are the things talked about and written about whenever the management of worker and work is being discussed. They are the things the Personnel Department concerns itself with. But they are not the concepts that underlie the actual management of worker and work in American industry. This concept is Scientific Management. Scientific Management focuses on the work. Its core is the organized study of work, the analysis of work into its simplest elements and the systematic improvement of the worker's performance of each of these elements. Scientific Management has both basic concepts and easily applicable tools and techniques. And it has no difficulty proving the contribution it makes; its results in the form of higher output are visible and readily measurable.
>
> Indeed, Scientific Management is all but a systematic philosophy of worker and work. Altogether it may well be the most powerful as well as the most lasting contribution America has made to Western thought since the Federalist Papers.[3]

The use of experimental methods in the study of work did not begin with Taylor; in fact, the self-use of such methods by the craftsman is part of the very practice of a craft. But the study of work by or on behalf of those who manage it rather than those who perform it seems to have come to the fore only with the capitalist epoch; indeed, very little basis for it could have existed before. The earliest references to the study of work correspond to the beginnings of the capitalist era: such a reference, for example, is found in the *History of the Royal Society of London*, and dates from the middle of the seventeenth century. We have already mentioned the classical economists. Charles Babbage, who not only wrote penetrating discussions of the organization of the labor process in his day, but applied the same concept to the division of mental labor, and who devised an early calculating "engine," was probably the most direct forerunner of Taylor, who must have been familiar with Babbage's work even though he never referred to it. France had a long tradition of attempting the scientific study of work, starting with Louis XIV's minister Colbert; including military engineers like Vauban and Belidor and especially Coulomb, whose physiological studies of exertion in labor are famous, through Marey, who used smoked paper cylinders to make a graphic record of work phenomena; and culminating in Henri Fayol, a contemporary of Taylor, who in his *General and Industrial Management* attempted a set of principles aimed at securing total enterprise control by way of a systematic approach to administrations.[4] The publication of management manuals, the discussions of the problems of management, and the increasingly sophisticated approach taken in practice in the second half of the nineteenth century lend support to the conclusion of the historians of the scientific management movement that Taylor was the culmination of a pre-existing trend: "What Taylor did was not to invent something quite new, but to synthesize and present as a reasonably coherent whole ideas which had been germinating and gathering force in Great Britain and the United States throughout the nineteenth century. He gave to a disconnected series of initiatives and experiments a philosophy and a title."[5]

Taylor has little in common with those physiologists or psychologists who have attempted, before or after him, to gather information about human capacities in a spirit of scientific interest. Such records and estimates as he did produce are crude in the extreme, and this has made it easy for such critics as Georges Friedmann to poke holes in his various "experiments" (most of which were not intended as experiments at all, but as forcible and hyperbolic demonstrations). Friedmann treats Taylorism as though it were a "science of work," where in reality it is intended to be a *science of the management of others' work* under capitalist conditions.[6] It is not the "best way" to do work "in general" that Taylor was seeking, as Friedmann seems to assume, but an answer to the specific problem of how best to control alienated labor—that is to say, labor power that is bought and sold.

The second distinctive feature of Taylor's thought was his concept of control. Control has been the essential feature of management throughout its history, but with Taylor it assumed unprecedented dimensions. The stages of management control over labor before Taylor had included, progressively: the gathering together of the workers in a workshop and the dictation of the length of the working day; the supervision of workers to ensure diligent, intense, or uninterrupted application; the enforcement of rules against distractions (talking, smoking, leaving the workplace, etc.) that were thought to interfere with application; the setting of production minimums; etc. A worker is under management control when subjected to these rules, or to any of their extensions and variations. But Taylor raised the concept of control to an entirely new plane when he asserted as an *absolute necessity for adequate management the dictation to the worker of the precise manner in which work is to be performed.* That management had the right to "control" labor was generally assumed before Taylor, but in practice this right usually meant only the general setting of tasks, with little direct interference in the worker's mode of performing them. Taylor's contribution was to overturn this practice and replace it by its opposite. Management, he insisted, could be only a limited and frustrated undertaking so long as it left to the worker any decision about the work. His "system" was simply a means for management to achieve control of the actual mode of performance of every labor activity, from the simplest to the most complicated. To this end, he pioneered a far greater revolution in the division of labor than any that had gone before.

Taylor created a simple line of reasoning and advanced it with a logic and clarity, a naive openness, and an evangelical zeal which soon won him a strong following among capitalists and managers. His work began in the 1880s but it was not until the 1890s that he began to lecture, read papers, and publish results. His own engineering training was limited, but his grasp of shop practice was superior, since he had served a four-year combination apprenticeship in two trades, those of patternmaker and machinist. The spread of the Taylor approach was not limited to the United States and Britain; within a short time it became popular in all industrial countries. In France it was called, in the absence of a suitable word for management, "l'organisation scientifique du travail" (later changed, when the reaction against Taylorism set in, to "l'organisation rationnelle du travail"). In Germany it was known simply as *rationalization*; the German corporations were probably ahead of everyone else in the practice of this technique, even before World War I.[7]

Taylor was the scion of a well-to-do Philadelphia family. After preparing for Harvard at Exeter he suddenly dropped out, apparently in rebellion against his father, who was directing Taylor toward his own profession, the law. He then took the step, extraordinary for anyone of his class, of starting a craft apprenticeship in a firm whose owners were social acquaintances of his parents. When he had completed his apprenticeship, he took a job at common labor in the Midvale Steel Works, also owned by friends of his family and technologically one of the most advanced companies in the steel industry. Within a few months he had passed through jobs as clerk and journeyman machinist, and was appointed gang boss in charge of the lathe department.

In his psychic makeup, Taylor was an exaggerated example of the obsessive-compulsive personality: from his youth he had counted his steps, measured the time for his various activities, and analyzed his motions in a search for "efficiency." Even when he had risen to importance and fame, he was still something of a figure of fun, and his appearance on the shop floor produced smiles. The picture of his personality that emerges from a study recently done by Sudhir Kakar justifies calling him, at the very least, a neurotic crank.[8] These traits fitted him perfectly for his role as the prophet of modern capitalist management, since that which is neurotic in the individual is, in capitalism, normal and socially desirable for the functioning of society.

Shortly after Taylor became gang boss, he entered upon a struggle with the machinists under him. Because this struggle was a classic instance of the manner in which the antagonistic relations of production express themselves in the workplace, not only in Taylor's time but before and after, and since Taylor drew from this experience the conclusions that were to shape his subsequent thinking, it is necessary to quote at length here from his description of the events.* The following account, one of several he gave of the battle, is taken

---

* Extracts of considerable length from Taylor's several writings will appear in this chapter. This is because Taylor is still the most useful source for any study of scientific management. In the storms of opposition that followed Taylorism, few ventured to put

from his testimony, a quarter-century later, before a Special Committee of the U.S. House of Representatives:

> Now, the machine shop of the Midvale Steel Works was a piecework shop. All the work practically was done on piecework, and it ran night and day—five nights in the week and six days. Two sets of men came on, one to run the machines at night and the other to run them in the daytime.
>
> We who were the workmen of that shop had the quantity output carefully agreed upon for everything that was turned out in the shop. We limited the output to about, I should think, one-third of what we could very well have done. We felt justified in doing this, owing to the piecework system—that is, owing to the necessity for soldiering under the piecework system—which I pointed out yesterday.
>
> As soon as I became gang boss the men who were working under me and who, of course, knew that I was onto the whole game of soldiering or deliberately restricting output, came to me at once and said, "Now, Fred, you are not going to be a damn piecework hog, are you?"
>
> I said, "If you fellows mean you are afraid I am going to try to get a larger output from these lathes," I said, "Yes; I do propose to get more work out." I said, "You must remember I have been square with you fellows up to now and worked with you. I have not broken a single rate. I have been on your side of the fence. But now I have accepted a job under the management of this company and I am on the other side of the fence, and I will tell you perfectly frankly that I am going to try to get a bigger output from those lathes." They answered, "Then, you are going to be a damned hog."
>
> I said, "Well, if you fellows put it that way, all right." They said, "We warn you, Fred, if you try to bust any of these rates, we will have you over the fence in six weeks." I said, "That is all right; I will tell you fellows again frankly that I propose to try to get a bigger output off these machines."
>
> Now, that was the beginning of a piecework fight that lasted for nearly three years, as I remember it—two or three years—in which I was doing everything in my power to increase the output of the shop, while the men were absolutely determined that the output should not be increased. Anyone who has been through such a fight knows and dreads the meanness of it and the bitterness of it. I believe that if I had been an older man—a man of more experience—I

---

the case so baldly as did Taylor, in his naive assumption that all reasonable people, including workers, would see the supreme rationality of his argument and accede to it. What he avows openly are the now-unacknowledged private assumptions of management. On the other hand, most of the academic commentators on Taylor are of limited usefulness, since everything that is so clear in Taylor becomes blurred or misunderstood. Kakar's book is a useful exception, despite his conventional conclusion that "with Taylor's ends there is no quarrel."

should have hardly gone into such a fight as this—deliberately attempting to force the men to do something they did not propose to do.

We fought on the management's side with all the usual methods, and the workmen fought on their side with all their usual methods. I began by going to the management and telling them perfectly plainly, even before I accepted the gang boss-ship, what would happen. I said, "Now these men will show you, and show you conclusively, that, in the first place, I know nothing about my business; and that in the second place, I am a liar, and you are being fooled, and they will bring any amount of evidence to prove these facts beyond a shadow of a doubt." I said to the management, "The only thing I ask you, and I must have your firm promise, is that when I say a thing is so you will take my word against the word of any 20 men or any 50 men in the shop." I said, "If you won't do that, I won't lift my finger toward increasing the output of this shop." They agreed to it and stuck to it, although many times they were on the verge of believing I was both incompetent and untruthful.

Now, I think it perhaps desirable to show the way in which that fight was conducted.

I began, of course, by directing some one man to do more work than he had done before, and then I got on the lathe myself and showed him that it could be done. In spite of this, he went ahead and turned out exactly the same old output and refused to adopt better methods or to work quicker until finally I laid him off and got another man in his place. This new man—I could not blame him in the least under the circumstances—turned right around and joined the other fellows and refused to do any more work than the rest. After trying this policy for a while and failing to get any results I said distinctly to the fellows, "Now, I am a mechanic; I am a machinist. I do not want to take the next step, because it will be contrary to what you and I look upon as our interest as machinists, but I will take it if you fellows won't compromise with me and get more work off of these lathes, but I warn you if I have to take this step it will be a durned mean one." I took it.

I hunted up some especially intelligent laborers who were competent men, but who had not had the opportunity of learning a trade, and I deliberately taught these men how to run a lathe and how to work right and fast. Every one of these laborers promised me, "Now, if you will teach me the machinist's trade, when I learn to run a lathe I will do a fair day's work," and every solitary man, when I had taught them their trade, one after another turned right around and joined the rest of the fellows and refused to work one bit faster.

That looked as if I were up against a stone wall, and for a time I was up against a stone wall. I did not blame even these laborers in my heart, my sympathy was with them all of the time, but I am telling you the facts as they then existed in the machine shops of this country, and in truth, as they still exist.

When I had trained enough of these laborers so that they could run the lathes, I went to them and said, "Now, you men to whom I have taught a trade are in a totally different position from the machinists who were running these lathes before you came here. Every one of you agreed to do a certain thing for me if I taught you a trade, and now not one of you will keep his word. I did not break my word with you, but every one of you has broken his word with me. Now, I have not any mercy on you; I have not the slightest hesitation in treating you entirely differently from the machinists." I said, "I know that very heavy social pressure has been put upon you outside the works to keep you from carrying out your agreement with me, and it is very difficult for you to stand out against this pressure, but you ought not to have made your bargain with me if you did not intend to keep your end of it. Now, I am going to cut your rate in two tomorrow and you are going to work for half price from now on. But all you will have to do is to turn out a fair day's work and you can earn better wages than you have been earning."

These men, of course, went to the management, and protested that I was a tyrant, and a nigger driver, and for a long time they stood right by the rest of the men in the shop and refused to increase their output a particle. Finally, they all of a sudden gave right in and did a fair day's work.

I want to call your attention, gentlemen, to the bitterness that was stirred up in this fight before the men finally gave in, to the meanness of it, and the contemptible conditions that exist under the old piecework system, and to show you what it leads to. In this contest, after my first fighting blood which was stirred up through strenuous opposition had subsided, I did not have any bitterness against any particular man or men. My anger and hard feelings were stirred up against the system; not against the men. Practically all of those men were my friends, and many of them are still my friends.* As soon as I began to be successful in forcing the men to do a fair day's work, they played what is usually the winning card. I knew that it was coming. I had predicted to the owners of the company what would happen when we began to win, and had warned them that they must stand by me; so that I had the backing of the company in taking effective steps to checkmate the final move of the men. Every time I broke a rate or forced one of the new men whom I had trained to work at a reasonable and proper speed, some one of the machinists would deliberately break some part of his machine as an object lesson to demonstrate to the management that a fool foreman was driving the men to overload their machines until they broke. Almost every day ingenious accidents were planned, and these happened to machines in different parts of the shop, and were, of course, always laid to the fool foreman who was driving the men and the machines beyond their proper limit.

---

* This particular bit of mythomania was typical of the man; there was apparently no truth to it. Kakar calls it "characteristic of the obsessional personality."[9]

Fortunately, I had told the management in advance that this would happen, so they backed me up fully. When they began breaking their machines, I said to the men, "All right; from this time on, any accident that happens in this shop, every time you break any part of a machine you will have to pay part of the cost of repairing it or else quit. I don't care if the roof falls in and breaks your machine, you will pay all the same." Every time a man broke anything I fined him and then turned the money over to the mutual benefit association, so that in the end it came back to the men. But I fined them, right or wrong. They could always show every time an accident happened that it was not their fault and that it was an impossible thing for them not to break their machine under the circumstances. Finally, when they found that these tactics did not produce the desired effect on the management, they got sick and tired of being fined, their opposition broke down, and they promised to do a fair day's work.

After that we were good friends, but it took three years of hard fighting to bring this about.[10]

The issue here turned on the work content of a day's labor power, which Taylor defines in the phrase "a fair day's work." To this term he gave a crude physiological interpretation: all the work a worker can do without injury to his health, at a pace that can be sustained throughout a working lifetime. (In practice, he tended to define this level of activity at an extreme limit, choosing a pace that only a few could maintain, and then only under strain.) Why a "fair day's work" should be defined as a physiological maximum is never made clear. In attempting to give concrete meaning to the abstraction "fairness," it would make just as much if not more sense to express a fair day's work as the amount of labor necessary to add to the product a value equal to the worker's pay; under such conditions, of course, profit would be impossible. The phrase "a fair day's work" must therefore be regarded as inherently meaningless, and filled with such content as the adversaries in the purchase-sale relationship try to give it.

Taylor set as his objective the maximum or "optimum" that can be obtained from a day's labor power. "On the part of the men," he said in his first book, "the greatest obstacle to the attainment of this standard is the slow pace which they adopt, or the loafing or 'soldiering,' marking time, as it is called." In each of his later expositions of his system, he begins with this same point, underscoring it heavily.[11] The causes of this soldiering he breaks into two parts: "This loafing or soldiering proceeds from two causes. First, from the natural instinct and tendency of men to take it easy, which may be called *natural soldiering*. Second, from more intricate second thought and reasoning caused by their relations with other men, which may be called *systematic soldiering*." The first of these he quickly puts aside, to concentrate on the second: "The natural laziness of men is serious, but by far the greatest evil from which both workmen and employers are suffering is the *systematic soldiering* which is almost universal under all the ordinary schemes of management and which results from a careful study on the part of the workmen of what they think will promote their best interests."

> The greater part of systematic soldiering . . . is done by the men with the deliberate object of keeping their employers ignorant of how fast work can be done.
>
> So universal is soldiering for this purpose, that hardly a competent workman can be found in a large establishment, whether he works by the day or on piece work, contract work or under any of the ordinary systems of compensating labor, who does not devote a considerable part of his time to studying just how slowly he can work and still convince his employer that he is going at a good pace.
>
> The causes for this are, briefly, that practically all employers determine upon a maximum sum which they feel it is right for each of their classes of employés to earn per day, whether their men work by the day or piece.[12]

That the pay of labor is a socially determined figure, relatively independent of productivity, among employers of similar types of labor power in any given period was thus known to Taylor. Workers who produce twice or three times as much as they did the day before do not thereby double or triple their pay, but may be given a small incremental advantage over their fellows, an advantage which disappears as their level of production becomes generalized. The contest over the size of the portion of the day's labor power to be embodied in each product is thus relatively independent of the level of pay, which responds chiefly to market, social, and historical factors. The worker learns this from repeated experiences, whether working under day or piece rates: "It is, however," says Taylor, "under piece work that the art of systematic soldiering is thoroughly developed. After a workman has had the price per piece of the work he is doing lowered two or three times as a result of his having worked harder and increased his output, he is likely to entirely lose sight of his employer's side of the case and to become imbued with a grim determination to have no more cuts if soldiering can prevent it."[13] To this it should be added that even where a piecework or "incentive" system allows the worker to increase his pay, the contest is not thereby ended but only exacerbated, because the output records now determine the setting and revision of pay rates.

Taylor always took the view that workers, by acting in this fashion, were behaving rationally and with an adequate view of their own best interests. He claimed, in another account of his Midvale battle, that he conceded as much even in the midst of the struggle: "His workman friends came to him [Taylor] continually and asked him, in a personal, friendly way, whether he would advise them, for their own best interest, to turn out more work. And, as a truthful man, he had to tell them that if he were in their place he would fight against turning out any more work, just as they were doing, because under the piece-work system they would be allowed to earn no more wages than they had been earning, and yet they would be made to work harder."[14] *

The conclusions which Taylor drew from the baptism by fire he received in the Midvale struggle may be summarized as follows: Workers who are controlled only by general orders and discipline are not adequately controlled, because they retain their grip on the actual processes of labor. So long as they control the labor process itself, they will thwart efforts to realize to the full the potential inherent in their labor power. To change this situation, control over the labor process must pass into the hands of management, not only in a formal sense but by the control and dictation of each step of the process, including its mode of performance. In pursuit of this end, no pains are too great, no efforts excessive, because the results will repay all efforts and expenses lavished on this demanding and costly endeavor.**

---

* In this respect, the later industrial sociologists took a step backward from Taylor. Rather than face the fact of a conflict of interests, they interpreted the behavior of workers in refusing to work harder and earn more under piece rates as "irrational" and "noneconomic" behavior, in contrast to that of management, which always behaved rationally. And this despite the fact that, in the observations made at the Hawthorne plant of Western Electric from which the "human relations" school emerged, the "lowest producer in the room ranked first in intelligence and third in dexterity; the highest producer in the room was seventh in dexterity and lowest in intelligence."[15]

At least one economist, William M. Leiserson, has given a proper judgment on workers' rationality in this connection: ". . . the same conditions that lead businessmen to curtail production when prices are falling, and to cut wages when labor efficiency is increasing, cause workers to limit output and reduce efficiency when wages are increasing. . . . If the workers' reasoning is wrong, then business economics as it is taught by employers and the business practices of modern industry generally must be equally wrong."[16] The Hawthorne investigators thought, and their followers still think, that the Western Electric workers were "irrational" or motivated by "group" or "social" or other "emotional" considerations in holding their output down, despite the fact that these very Hawthorne investigations were brought to an end by the Western Electric layoffs in the Great Depression of the 1930s, thus demonstrating just how rational the workers' fears were.

One of the most interesting inquiries into this subject was done in the late 1940s by a sociologist at the University of Chicago who took a job in a factory. He studied intensively eighty-four workers, and found among them only nine "rate busters," who were "social isolates" not only on the job but off; eight of the nine were Republicans while the shop was 70 percent Democratic, and all were from farm or middle-class backgrounds while the rest of the shop was predominantly working-class in family history."[17]

** Clearly, this last conclusion depends on Adam Smith's well-known principle that the division of labor is limited by the extent of the market, and Taylorism cannot become generalized in any industry or applicable in particular situations until the scale of production is adequate to support the efforts and costs involved in "rationalizing" it. It is for this reason above all that Taylorism coincides with the growth of production and its concentration in ever larger corporate units in the latter part of the nineteenth and in the twentieth centuries.

The forms of management that existed prior to Taylorism, which Taylor called "ordinary management," he deemed altogether inadequate to meet these demands. His descriptions of ordinary management bear the marks of the propagandist and proselytizer: exaggeration, simplification, and schematization. But his point is clear:

> Now, in the best of the ordinary types of management, the managers recognize frankly that the . . . workmen, included in the twenty or thirty trades, who are under them, possess this mass of traditional knowledge, a large part of which is not in the possession of management. The management, of course, includes foremen and superintendents, who themselves have been first-class workers at their trades. And yet these foremen and superintendents know, better than any one else, that their own knowledge and personal skill falls far short of the combined knowledge and dexterity of all the workmen under them. The most experienced managers frankly place before their workmen the problem of doing the work in the best and most economical way. They recognize the task before them as that of inducing each workman to use his best endeavors, his hardest work, all his traditional knowledge, his skill, his ingenuity, and his good-will—in a word, his "initiative," so as to yield the largest possible return to his employer.[18]

As we have already seen from Taylor's belief in the universal prevalence and in fact inevitability of "soldiering," he did not recommend reliance upon the "initiative" of workers. Such a course, he felt, leads to the surrender of control: "As was usual then, and in fact as is still usual in most of the shops in this country, the shop was really run by the workmen and not by the bosses. The workmen together had carefully planned just how fast each job should be done." In his Midvale battle, Taylor pointed out, he had located the source of the trouble in the "ignorance of the management as to what really constitutes a proper day's work for a workman." He had "fully realized that, although he was foreman of the shop, the combined knowledge and skill of the workmen who were under him was certainly ten times as great as his own."[19] This, then, was the source of the trouble and the starting point of scientific management.

We may illustrate the Taylorian solution to this dilemma in the same manner that Taylor often did: by using his story of his work for the Bethlehem Steel Company in supervising the moving of pig iron by hand. This story has the advantage of being the most detailed and circumstantial he set down, and also of dealing with a type of work so simple that anyone can visualize it without special technical preparation. We extract it here from Taylor's *The Principles of Scientific Management*:

> One of the first pieces of work undertaken by us, when the writer started to introduce scientific management into the Bethlehem Steel Company, was to handle pig iron on task work. The opening of the Spanish War found some

80,000 tons of pig iron placed in small piles in an open field adjoining the works. Prices for pig iron had been so low that it could not be sold at a profit, and therefore had been stored. With the opening of the Spanish War the price of pig iron rose, and this large accumulation of iron was sold. This gave us a good opportunity to show the workmen, as well as the owners and managers of the works, on a fairly large scale the advantages of task work over the old-fashioned day work and piece work, in doing a very elementary class of work.

The Bethlehem Steel Company had five blast furnaces, the product of which had been handled by a pig-iron gang for many years. This gang, at this time, consisted of about 75 men. They were good, average pig-iron handlers, were under an excellent foreman who himself had been a pig-iron handler, and the work was done, on the whole, about as fast and as cheaply as it was anywhere else at that time.

A railroad switch was run out into the field, right along the edge of the piles of pig iron. An inclined plank was placed against the side of a car, and each man picked up from his pile a pig of iron weighing about 92 pounds, walked up the inclined plank and dropped it on the end of the car.

We found that this gang were loading on the average about $12\frac{1}{2}$ long tons per man per day. We were surprised to find, after studying the matter, that a first-class pig-iron handler ought to handle between 47 and 48 long tons per day, instead of $12\frac{1}{2}$ tons. This task seemed to us so very large that we were obliged to go over our work several times before we were absolutely sure that we were right. Once we were sure, however, that 47 tons was a proper day's work for a first-class pig-iron handler, the task which faced us as managers under the modern scientific plan was clearly before us. It was our duty to see that the 80,000 tons of pig iron was loaded on to the cars at the rate of 47 tons per man per day, in place of $12\frac{1}{2}$ tons, at which rate the work was then being done. And it was further our duty to see that this work was done without bringing on a strike among the men, without any quarrel with the men, and to see that the men were happier and better contented when loading at the new rate of 47 tons than they were when loading at the old rate of $12\frac{1}{2}$ tons.

Our first step was the scientific selection of the workman. In dealing with workmen under this type of management, it is an inflexible rule to talk to and deal with only one man at a time, since each workman has his own special abilities and limitations, and since we are not dealing with men in masses, but are trying to develop each individual man to his highest state of efficiency and prosperity. Our first step was to find the proper workman to begin with. We therefore carefully watched and studied these 75 men for three or four days, at the end of which time we had picked out four men who appeared to be physically able to handle pig iron at the rate of 47 tons per day. A careful study was then made of each of these men. We looked up their history as far back as practicable and thorough inquiries were made as to the character, habits, and the ambition of each of them. Finally we selected one from among the four as the most likely man to start with. He was a little Pennsylvania Dutchman who had been observed to trot back home for a mile or so after his work in the evening, about as fresh as he was when he came trotting down to work in the morning. We found that upon wages of $1.15 a day he had succeeded in buying a small plot of ground, and that he was engaged in putting up the walls of a little house for himself in the morning before starting to work and at night after leaving. He also had the reputation of being exceedingly "close," that is, of placing a very high value on a dollar. As one man whom we talked to about him said, "A penny looks about the size of a cart-wheel to him." This man we will call Schmidt.

The task before us, then, narrowed itself down to getting Schmidt to handle 47 tons of pig iron per day and making him glad to do it. This was done as follows. Schmidt was called out from among the gang of pig-iron handlers and talked to somewhat in this way:

"Schmidt, are you a high-priced man?"

"Vell, I don't know vat you mean."

"Oh yes, you do. What I want to know is whether you are a high-priced man or not."

"Vell, I don't know vat you mean."

"Oh, come now, you answer my questions. What I want to find out is whether you are a high-priced man or one of these cheap fellows here. What I want to find out is whether you want to earn $1.85 a day or whether you are satisfied with $1.15, just the same as all those cheap fellows are getting."

"Did I vant $1.85 a day? Vas dot a high-priced man? Vell, yes, I vas a high-priced man."

"Oh, you're aggravating me. Of course you want $1.85 a day—every one wants it! You know perfectly well that that has very little to do with your being a high-priced man. For goodness' sake answer my questions, and don't waste any more of my time. Now come over here. You see that pile of pig iron?"

"Yes."

"You see that car?"

"Yes."

"Well, if you are a high-priced man, you will load that pig iron on that car to-morrow for $1.85. Now do wake up and answer my question. Tell me whether you are a high-priced man or not."

"Vell—did I got $1.85 for loading dot pig iron on dot car to-morrow?"

"Yes, of course you do, and you get $1.85 for loading a pile like that every day right through the year. That is what a high-priced man does, and you know it just as well as I do."

"Vell, dot's all right. I could load dot pig iron on the car to-morrow for $1.85, and I get it every day, don't I?"

"Certainly you do—certainly you do."

"Vell, den, I vas a high-priced man."

"Now, hold on, hold on. You know just as well as I do that a high-priced man has to do exactly as he's told from morning till night. You have seen this man here before, haven't you?"

"No, I never saw him."

"Well, if you are a high-priced man, you will do exactly as this man tells you to-morrow, from morning till night. When he tells you to pick up a pig and walk, you pick it up and you walk, and when he tells you to sit down and rest, you sit down. You do that right straight through the day. And what's more, no back talk. Now a high-priced man does just what he's told to do, and no back talk. Do you understand that? When this man tells you to walk, you walk; when he tells you to sit down, you sit down, and you don't talk back at him. Now you come on to work here to-morrow morning and I'll know before night whether you are really a high-priced man or not."

This seems to be rather rough talk. And indeed it would be if applied to an educated mechanic, or even an intelligent laborer.

With a man of the mentally sluggish type of Schmidt it is appropriate and not unkind, since it is effective in fixing his attention on the high wages which he wants and away from what, if it were called to his attention, he probably would consider impossibly hard work. . . .

Schmidt started to work, and all day long, and at regular intervals, was told by the man who stood over him with a watch, "Now pick up a pig and walk. Now sit down and rest. Now walk—now rest," etc. He worked when he was told to work, and rested when he was told to rest, and at half-past five in the afternoon had his $47\frac{1}{2}$ tons loaded on the car. And he practically never failed to work at this pace and do the task that was set him during the three years that the writer was at Bethlehem. And throughout this time he averaged a little more than $1.85 per day, whereas before he had never received over $1.15 per day, which was the ruling rate of wages at that time in Bethlehem. That is, he received 60 per cent. higher wages than were paid to other men who were not working on task work. One man after another was picked out and trained to handle pig iron at the rate of $47\frac{1}{2}$ tons per day until all of the pig iron was handled at this rate, and the men were receiving 60 per cent. more wages than other workmen around them.[20] *

The merit of this tale is its clarity in illustrating the pivot upon which all modern management turns: the control over work through the control over the

---

* Daniel Bell has recorded this event as follows: "But it was in 1899 that Taylor achieved fame when he taught a Dutchman named Schmidt to shovel forty-seven tons

decisions that are made in the course of work. Since, in the case of pig-iron handling, the only decisions to be made were those having to do with a time sequence, Taylor simply dictated that timing and the results at the end of the day added up to his planned day-task. As to the use of money as motivation, while this element has a usefulness in the first stages of a new mode of work, employers do not, when they have once found a way to compel a more rapid pace of work, continue to pay a 60 percent differential for common labor, or for any other job. Taylor was to discover (and to complain) that management treated his "scientific incentives" like any other piece rate, cutting them mercilessly so long as the labor market permitted, so that workers pushed to the Taylorian intensity found themselves getting little, or nothing, more than the going rate for the area, while other employers—under pressure of this competitive threat—forced their own workers to the higher intensities of labor.*

Taylor liked to pretend that his work standards were not beyond human capabilities exercised without undue strain, but as he himself made clear, this pretense could be maintained only on the understanding that unusual physical specimens were selected for each of his jobs:

---

instead of twelve and a half tons of pig iron a day. Every detail of the man's job was specified: the size of the shovel, the bite into the pile, the weight of the scoop, the distance to walk, the arc of the swing, and the rest periods that Schmidt should take. By systematically varying each factor, Taylor got the optimum amount of barrow load.[21]

In the face of so much circumstantial detail, one hesitates to inquire whether Professor Bell can imagine handling a 92-pound pig of iron on a shovel, let alone what sort of an "arc of the swing" one could manage, or how a "barrow" would handle a whole "scoop" of them. The point here is not that anyone may be tripped up by the use of secondary sources, or get his stories mixed, or have never seen a pig of iron; the point is that sociologists, with few exceptions, deem it proper to write about occupations, work, skills, etc. without even bare familiarity. The result is what one would get from a school of literary critics who never read the novels, plays, poems they write about, but construct their theories entirely on the basis of responses to questionnaires put to "scientifically selected samples" of readers. Bell's error is only the grandfather of a long line of such misapprehensions, which become truly extraordinary as more complex forms of work are dealt with. In this situation, management can—and gleefully does—tell academics anything it pleases about the evolution of work, skills, etc.

* In his classic study of scientific management undertaken in 1915 for the United States Commission on Industrial Relations, Robert F. Hoxie pointed out that most rate cutting in shops which had installed a formal system of scientific management took place indirectly, by creating new job classifications at lower rates, etc. He concludes that under scientific management "what amounts to rate cutting seems to be almost of necessity an essential part of its very nature." [22]

As to the scientific selection of the men, it is a fact that in this gang of 75 pig-iron handlers only about one man in eight was physically capable of handling $47\frac{1}{2}$ tons per day. With the very best of intentions, the other seven out of eight men were physically unable to work at this pace. Now the one man in eight who was able to do this work was in no sense superior to the other men who were working on the gang. He merely happened to be a man of the type of the ox,—no rare specimen of humanity, difficult to find and therefore very highly prized. On the contrary, he was a man so stupid that he was unfitted to do most kinds of laboring work, even. The selection of the man, then, does not involve finding some extraordinary individual, but merely picking out from among very ordinary men the few who are especially suited to this type of work. Although in this particular gang only one man in eight was suited to doing the work, we had not the slightest difficulty in getting all the men who were needed—some of them from inside the works and others from the neighboring country—who were exactly suited to the job.[23] *

Taylor spent his lifetime in expounding the principles of control enunciated here, and in applying them directly to many other tasks: shoveling loose materials, lumbering, inspecting ball bearings, etc., but particularly to the machinist's trade. He believed that the forms of control he advocated could be applied not only to simple labor, but to labor in its most complex forms, without exception, and in fact it was in machine shops, bricklaying, and other such sites for the practice of well-developed crafts that he and his immediate successors achieved their most striking results.

From earliest times to the Industrial Revolution the craft or skilled trade was the basic unit, the elementary cell of the labor process. In each craft, the worker was presumed to be the master of a body of traditional knowledge, and methods and procedures were left to his or her discretion. In each such worker reposed the accumulated knowledge of materials and processes by which production was accomplished in the craft. The potter, tanner, smith, weaver, carpenter, baker, miller, glassmaker, cobbler, etc., each representing a branch of the social division of labor, was a repository of human technique for the

---

* Georges Friedmann reports that in 1927 a German physiologist, reviewing the Schmidt experience, calculated that the level of output set by Taylor could not be accepted as a standard because "most workers will succumb under the pressure of these labors.[24] Yet Taylor persisted in calling it "a pace under which men become happier and thrive."[25] We should also note that although Taylor called Schmidt "a man of the type of the ox," and Schmidt's stupidity has become part of the folklore of industrial sociology, Taylor himself reported that Schmidt was building his own house, presumably without anyone to tell him when to stand and when to squat. But a belief in the original stupidity of the worker is a necessity for management; otherwise it would have to admit that it is engaged in a wholesale enterprise of prizing and fostering stupidity.

labor processes of that branch. The worker combined, in mind and body, the concepts and physical dexterities of the specialty: technique, understood in this way, is, as has often been observed, the predecessor and progenitor of science. The most important and widespread of all crafts was, and throughout the world remains to this day, that of farmer. The farming family combines its craft with the rude practice of a number of others, including those of the smith, mason, carpenter, butcher, miller, and baker, etc. The apprenticeships required in traditional crafts ranged from three to seven years, and for the farmer of course extends beyond this to include most of childhood, adolescence, and young adulthood. In view of the knowledge to be assimilated, the dexterities to be gained, and the fact that the craftsman, like the professional, was required to master a specialty and become the best judge of the manner of its application to specific production problems, the years of apprenticeship were generally needed and were employed in a learning process that extended well into the journeyman decades. Of these trades, that of the machinist was in Taylor's day among the most recent, and certainly the most important to modern industry.

As I have already pointed out, Taylor was not primarily concerned with the advance of technology (which, as we shall see, offers other means for direct control over the labor process). He did make significant contributions to the technical knowledge of machine-shop practice (high-speed tool steel, in particular), but these were chiefly by-products of his effort to study this practice with an eye to systematizing and classifying it. His concern was with the control of labor at any given level of technology, and he tackled his own trade with a boldness and energy which astonished his contemporaries and set the pattern for industrial engineers, work designers, and office managers from that day on. And in tackling machine-shop work, he had set himself a prodigious task.

The machinist of Taylor's day started with the shop drawing, and turned, milled, bored, drilled, planed, shaped, ground, filed, and otherwise machine- and hand-processed the proper stock to the desired shape as specified in the drawing. The range of decisions to be made in the course of the process is—unlike the case of a simple job, such as the handling of pig iron—by its very nature enormous. Even for the lathe alone, disregarding all collateral tasks such as the choice of stock, handling, centering and chucking the work, layout and measuring, order of cuts, and considering only the operation of turning itself, the range of possibilities is huge. Taylor himself worked with twelve variables, including the hardness of the metal, the material of the cutting tool, the thickness of the shaving, the shape of the cutting tool, the use of a coolant during cutting, the depth of the cut, the frequency of regrinding cutting tools as they became dulled, the lip and clearance angles of the tool, the smoothness of cutting or absence of chatter, the diameter of the stock being turned, the pressure of the chip or shaving on the cutting surface of the tool, and the speeds, feeds, and pulling power of the machine.[26] Each of these variables is subject to broad choice, ranging from a few possibilities in the selection and use of a coolant, to a very great number of effective choices in all matters having to do with thickness, shape, depth, duration, speed, etc. Twelve variables, each subject to a large number of choices, will yield in their possible combinations and permutations astronomical figures, as Taylor soon realized. But upon these decisions of the machinist depended not just the accuracy and finish of the product, but also the pace of production. Nothing daunted, Taylor set out to gather into management's hands all the basic information bearing on these processes. He began a series of experiments at the Midvale Steel Company, in the fall of 1880, which lasted twenty-six years, recording the results of between 30,000 and 50,000 tests, and cutting up more than 800,000 pounds of iron and steel on ten different machine tools reserved for his experimental use.* His greatest difficulty, he reported, was not testing the many variations, but holding eleven variables constant while altering the conditions of the twelfth. The data were systematized, correlated, and reduced to practical form in the shape of what he called a "slide rule" which would determine the optimum combination of choices for each step in the machining process.[28] His machinists thenceforth were required to work in accordance with instructions derived from these experimental data, rather than from their own knowledge, experience, or tradition. This was the Taylor approach in its first systematic application to a complex labor process. Since the principles upon which it is based are fundamental to all advanced work design or industrial engineering today, it is important to examine them in detail. And since Taylor has been virtually alone in giving clear expression to principles which are seldom now publicly acknowledged, it is best to examine them with the aid of Taylor's own forthright formulations.

First Principle

"The managers assume . . . the burden of gathering together all of the traditional knowledge which in the past has been possessed by the workmen and then of

---

* Friedmann so far forgets this enormous machine-shop project at one point that he says: "This failure to appreciate the psychological factors in work is at least partially explained by the nature of the jobs to which Taylor exclusively confined his observations: handlers of pig iron, shovel-laborers, and navvies." [27] He was led to this error by his marked tendency to side with the psychological and sociological schools of "human relations" and work adjustment which came after Taylor, and which he always attempts to counterpose to Taylorism, although, as we have pointed out, they operate on different levels. In general, Friedmann, with all his knowledge of work processes, suffers from a confusion of viewpoints, writing sometimes as a socialist concerned about the trends in capitalist work organization, but more often as though the various forms of capitalist management and personnel administration represent scrupulous efforts to find a universal answer to problems of work.

classifying, tabulating, and reducing this knowledge to rules, laws, and formulae. . . ." [29] We have seen the illustrations of this in the cases of the lathe machinist and the pig-iron handler. The great disparity between these activities, and the different orders of knowledge that may be collected about them, illustrate that for Taylor—as for managers today—no task is either so simple or so complex that it may not be studied with the object of collecting in the hands of management at least as much information as is known by the worker who performs it regularly, and very likely more. This brings to an end the situation in which "Employers derive their knowledge of how much of a given class of work can be done in a day from either their own experience, which has frequently grown hazy with age, from casual and unsystematic observation of their men, or at best from records which are kept, showing the quickest time in which each job has been done." [30] It enables management to discover and enforce those speedier methods and shortcuts which workers themselves, in the practice of their trades or tasks, learn or improvise, and use at their own discretion only. Such an experimental approach also brings into being new methods such as can be devised only through the means of systematic study.

This first principle we may call the *dissociation of the labor process from the skills of the workers.* The labor process is to be rendered independent of craft, tradition, and the workers' knowledge. Henceforth it is to depend not at all upon the abilities of workers, but entirely upon the practices of management.

Second Principle

"All possible brain work should be removed from the shop and centered in the planning or laying-out department. . . ." [31] Since this is the key to scientific management, as Taylor well understood, he was especially emphatic on this point and it is important to examine the principle thoroughly.

In the human, as we have seen, the essential feature that makes for a labor capacity superior to that of the animal is the combination of execution with a conception of the thing to be done. But as human labor becomes a social rather than an individual phenomenon, it is possible—unlike in the instance of animals where the motive force, instinct, is inseparable from action—to divorce conception from execution. This dehumanization of the labor process, in which workers are reduced almost to the level of labor in its animal form, while purposeless and unthinkable in the case of the self-organized and self-motivated social labor of a community of producers, becomes crucial for the management of purchased labor. For if the workers' execution is guided by their own conception, it is not possible, as we have seen, to enforce upon them either the methodological efficiency or the working pace desired by capital. The capitalist therefore learns from the start to take advantage of this aspect of human labor power, and to break the unity of the labor process.

This should be called the principle of the *separation of conception from execution*, rather than by its more common name of the separation of mental and manual labor (even though it is similar to the latter, and in practice often identical). This is because mental labor, labor done primarily in the brain, is also subjected to the same principle of separation of conception from execution: mental labor is first separated from manual labor and, as we shall see, is then itself subdivided rigorously according to the same rule.

The first implication of this principle is that Taylor's "science of work" is never to be developed by the worker, always by management. This notion, apparently so "natural" and undebatable today, was in fact vigorously discussed in Taylor's day, a fact which shows how far we have traveled along the road of transforming all ideas about the labor process in less than a century, and how completely Taylor's hotly contested assumptions have entered into the conventional outlook within a short space of time. Taylor confronted this question—why must work be studied by the management and not by the worker himself; why not *scientific workmanship* rather than *scientific management?*—repeatedly, and employed all his ingenuity in devising answers to it, though not always with his customary frankness. In *The Principles of Scientific Management*, he pointed out that the "older system" of management

> makes it necessary for each workman to bear almost the entire responsibility for the general plan as well as for each detail of his work, and in many cases for his implements as well. In addition to this he must do all of the actual physical labor. The development of a science, on the other hand, involves the establishment of many rules, laws, and formulae which replace the judgment of the individual workman and which can be effectively used only after having been systematically recorded, indexed, etc. The practical use of scientific data also calls for a room in which to keep the books, records, etc., and a desk for the planner to work at. Thus all of the planning which under the old system was done by the workman, as a result of his personal experience, must of necessity under the new system be done by the management in accordance with the laws of the science; because even if the workman was well suited to the development and use of scientific data, it would be physically impossible for him to work at his machine and at a desk at the same time. It is also clear that in most cases one type of man is needed to plan ahead and an entirely different type to execute the work.[32]

The objections having to do with physical arrangements in the workplace are clearly of little importance, and represent the deliberate exaggeration of obstacles which, while they may exist as inconveniences, are hardly insuperable. To refer to the "different type" of worker needed for each job is worse than disingenuous, since these "different types" hardly existed until the division of labor created them. As Taylor well understood, the possession of craft knowledge made the worker the best starting point for the development of the science of work; systematization often means, at least at the outset, the gathering of knowledge which *workers already possess*. But Taylor, secure in his obsession with the immense reasonableness of his proposed arrangement, did not stop at this point. In his testimony before the Special Committee of the House of Representatives, pressed and on the defensive, he brought forth still other arguments:

> I want to make it clear, Mr. Chairman, that work of this kind undertaken by the management leads to the development of a science, while it is next to impossible for the workman to develop a science. There are many workmen who are intellectually just as capable of developing a science, who have plenty of brains, and are just as capable of developing a science as those on the managing side. But the science of doing work of any kind cannot be developed by the workman. Why? Because he has neither the time nor the money to do it. The development of the science of doing any kind of work always required the work of two men, one man who actually does the work which is to be studied and another man who observes closely the first man while he works and studies the time problems and the motion problems connected with this work. No workman has either the time or the money to burn in making experiments of this sort. If he is working for himself no one will pay him while he studies the motions of some one else. The management must and ought to pay for all such work. So that for the workman, the development of a science becomes impossible, not because the workman is not intellectually capable of developing it, but he has neither the time nor the money to do it and he realizes that this is a question for the management to handle.[33]

Taylor here argues that the systematic study of work and the fruits of this study belong to management for the very same reason that machines, factory buildings, etc., belong to them; that is, because it costs labor time to conduct such a study, and only the possessors of capital can afford labor time. The possessors of labor time cannot themselves afford to do anything with it but sell it for their means of subsistence. It is true that this is the rule in capitalist relations of production, and Taylor's use of the argument in this case shows with great clarity where the sway of capital leads: Not only is capital the property of the capitalist, but *labor itself has become part of capital*. Not only do the workers lose control over their instruments of production, but they must now lose control over their own labor and the manner of its performance. This control now falls to those who can "afford" to study it in order to know it better than the workers themselves know their own life activity.

But Taylor has not yet completed his argument: "Furthermore," he told the Committee, "if any workman were to find a new and quicker way of doing work, or if he were to develop a new method, you can see at once it becomes to his interest to keep that development to himself, not to teach the other workmen the quicker method. It is to his interest to do what workmen have done in all times, to keep their trade secrets for themselves and their friends. That is the old idea of trade secrets. The workman kept his knowledge to himself instead of developing a science and teaching it to others and making it public property."[34] Behind this hearkening back to old ideas of "guild secrets" is Taylor's persistent and fundamental notion that the improvement of work methods by workers brings few benefits to management. Elsewhere in his testimony, in discussing the work of his associate, Frank Gilbreth, who spent many years studying bricklaying methods, he candidly admits that not only *could* the "science of bricklaying" be developed by workers, but that it undoubtedly *had been*: "Now, I have not the slightest doubt that during the last 4,000 years all the methods that Mr. Gilbreth developed have many, many times suggested themselves to the minds of bricklayers." But because knowledge possessed by workers is not useful to capital, Taylor begins his list of the desiderata of scientific management: "First. The development—by the management, not the workmen—of the science of bricklaying."[35] Workers, he explains, are not going to put into execution any system or any method which harms them and their workmates: "Would they be likely," he says, referring to the pig-iron job, "to get rid of seven men out of eight from their own gang and retain only the eighth man? No!"[36]

Finally, Taylor understood the Babbage principle better than anyone of his time, and it was always uppermost in his calculations. The purpose of work study was never, in his mind, to enhance the ability of the worker, to concentrate in the worker a greater share of scientific knowledge, to ensure that as technique rose, the worker would rise with it. Rather, the purpose was to cheapen the worker by decreasing his training and enlarging his output. In his early book, *Shop Management*, he said frankly that the "full possibilities" of his system "will not have been realized until almost all of the machines in the shop are run by men who are of smaller calibre and attainments, and who are therefore cheaper than those required under the old system."[37]

Therefore, both in order to ensure management control and to cheapen the worker, conception and execution must be rendered separate spheres of work, and for this purpose the study of work processes must be reserved to management and kept from the workers, to whom its results are communicated only in the form of simplified job tasks governed by simplified instructions which it is thenceforth their duty to follow unthinkingly and without comprehension of the underlying technical reasoning or data.

Third Principle

The essential idea of "the ordinary types of management," Taylor said, "is that each workman has become more skilled in his own trade than it is possible for any one in the management to be, and that, therefore, the details of how the work shall best be done must be left to him." But, by contrast: "Perhaps the most prominent single element in modern scientific management is the task idea. The work of every workman is fully planned out by the management at least one day in advance, and each man receives in most cases complete written instructions, describing in detail the task which he is to accomplish, as well as the means to be used in doing the work. . . . This task specifies not only what is to be done, but how it is to be done and the exact time allowed for doing it. . . . Scientific management consists very largely in preparing for and carrying out these tasks."[38]

In this principle it is not the written instruction card that is important.* Taylor had no need for such a card with Schmidt, nor did he use one in many other instances. Rather, the essential element is the systematic pre-planning and pre-calculation of all elements of the labor process, which now no longer exists as a process in the imagination of the worker but only as a process in the imagination of a special management staff. Thus, if the first principle is the gathering and development of knowledge of labor processes, and the second is the concentration of this knowledge as the exclusive province of management—together with its essential converse, the absence of such knowledge among the workers—then the third is the *use of this monopoly over knowledge to control each step of the labor process and its mode of execution.*

As capitalist industrial, office, and market practices developed in accordance with this principle, it eventually became part of accepted routine and custom, all the more so as the increasingly scientific character of most processes, which grew in complexity while the worker was not allowed to partake of this growth, made it ever more difficult for the workers to understand the processes in which they functioned. But in the beginning, as Taylor well

---

* This despite the fact that for a time written instruction cards were a fetish among managers. The vogue for such cards passed as work tasks became so simplified and repetitious as to render the cards in most cases unnecessary. But the concept behind them remains: it is the concept of the direct action of management to determine the process, with the worker functioning as the mediating and closely governed instrument. This is the significance of Lillian Gilbreth's definition of the instruction card as "a self-producer of a predetermined product."[39] The worker as producer is ignored; management becomes the producer, and its plans and instructions bring the product into existence. This same instruction card inspired in Alfred Marshall, however, the curious opinion that from it, workers could learn how production is carried on: such a card, "whenever it comes into the hands of a thoughtful man, may suggest to him something of the purposes and methods of those who have constructed it."[40] The worker, in Marshall's notion, having given up technical knowledge of the craft, is now to pick up the far more complex technical knowledge of modern industry from his task card, as a paleontologist reconstructs the entire animal from a fragment of a bone!

understood, an abrupt psychological wrench was required.* We have seen in the simple Schmidt case the means employed, both in the selection of a single worker as a starting point and in the way in which he was reoriented to the new conditions of work. In the more complex conditions of the machine shop, Taylor gave this part of the responsibility to the foremen. It is essential, he said of the gang bosses, to "nerve and brace them up to the point of insisting that the workmen shall carry out the orders exactly as specified on the instruction cards. This is a difficult task at first, as the workmen have been accustomed for years to do the details of the work to suit themselves, and many of them are intimate friends of the bosses and believe they know quite as much about their business as the latter."[41]

Modern management came into being on the basis of these principles. It arose as theoretical construct and as systematic practice, moreover, in the very period during which the transformation of labor from processes based on skill to processes based upon science was attaining its most rapid tempo. Its role was to render conscious and systematic, the formerly unconscious tendency of capitalist production. It was to ensure that as craft declined, the worker would sink to the level of general and undifferentiated labor power, adaptable to a large range of simple tasks, while as science grew, it would be concentrated in the hands of management.

Notes

1. Peter F. Drucker, "Work and Tools," in Melvin Kranzberg and William H. Davenport, eds., *Technology and Culture* (New York, 1972), pp. 192-93.
2. George Soule, *Economic Forces in American History* (New York, 1952), p. 241.
3. Peter F. Drucker, *The Practice of Management* (New York, 1954), p. 280.
4. See Sudhir Kakar, *Frederick Taylor: A Study in Personality and Innovation* (Cambridge, Mass., 1970), pp. 115-17; and Henri Fayol, *General and Industrial Management* (1916; trans., London, 1949).

---

   * One must not suppose from this that such a psychological shift in relations between worker and manager is entirely a thing of the past. On the contrary, it is constantly being recapitulated in the evolution of new occupations as they are brought into being by the development of industry and trade, and are then routinized and subjugated to management control. As this tendency has attacked office, technical, and "educated" occupations, sociologists have spoken of it as "bureaucratization," an evasive and unfortunate use of Weberian terminology, a terminology which often reflects its users' view that this form of government over work is endemic to "large-scale" or "complex" enterprises, whereas it is better understood as the specific product of the capitalist organization of work, and reflects not primarily scale but social antagonisms.

84 *Labor and Monopoly Capital*

5. Lyndall Urwick and E. F. L. Brech, *The Making of Scientific Management*, 3 vols. (London, 1945, 1946, 1948), vol. I, p. 17.
6. See Georges Friedmann, *Industrial Society* (Glencoe, Ill., 1964), esp. pp. 51-65.
7. Lyndall Urwick, *The Meaning of Rationalisation* (London, 1929), pp. 13-16.
8. Kakar, *Frederick Taylor*, pp. 17-27, 52-54.
9. Ibid., p. 61.
10. *Taylor's Testimony before the Special House Committee*, in Frederick W. Taylor, *Scientific Management* (New York and London, 1947), pp. 79-85; this is a single-volume edition of Taylor's three chief works, *Shop Management* (1903); *Principles of Scientific Management* (1911); and a public document, *Hearings Before Special Committee of the House of Representatives to Investigate the Taylor and Other Systems of Shop Management* (1912), which is given the above title in this volume. Each of the three book-length documents in this volume is paged separately.
11. Frederick W. Taylor, *Shop Management*, in *Scientific Management*, p. 30. See also Taylor's *The Principles of Scientific Management* (New York, 1967), pp. 13-14; and *Taylor's Testimony in Scientific Management*, p. 8.
12. *Shop Management*, pp. 32-33.
13. Ibid., pp. 34-35.
14. *The Principles of Scientific Management*, p. 52.
15. Elton Mayo, *The Social Problems of an Industrial Civilization* (Boston, 1945), p. 42.
16. William M. Leiserson, "The Economics of Restriction of Output"; quoted in Loren Baritz, *The Servants of Power* (New York, 1965), p. 100.
17. William F. Whyte, *Men at Work* (Homewood, Ill., 1961), pp, 98-121; see also Whyte's *Money and Motivation* (New York, 1955), pp. 39-49.
18. *The Principles of Scientific Management*, p. 32.
19. Ibid., pp. 48-49, 53.
20. Ibid., pp. 41-47.
21. Daniel Bell, *Work and Its Discontents*, in *The End of Ideology* (Glencoe, Ill., 1960), p. 227.
22. Robert F. Hoxie, *Scientific Management and Labor* (New York and London, 1918), pp. 85-87.
23. *The Principles of Scientific Management*, pp. 61-62.
24. Friedmann, *Industrial Society*, p. 55.
25. *Shop Management*, p. 25.
26. *The Principles of Scientific Management*, pp. 107-109.
27. Friedmann, *Industrial Society*, p. 63.
28. *The Principles of Scientific Management*, p. 111.
29. Ibid., p. 36.
30. Ibid., p. 22.
31. *Shop Management*, pp. 98-99.

32. *The Principles of Scientific Management*, pp. 37-38.
33. *Taylor's Testimony before the Special House Committee*, pp. 235-236.
34. Loc. cit.
35. Ibid., pp. 75, 77.
36. *The Principles of Scientific Management*, p. 62.
37. *Shop Management*, p. 105.
38. *The Principles of Scientific Management*, pp. 39, 63.
39. Lillian Gilbreth, *The Psychology of Management* (1914), in *The Writings of the Gilbreths*, William R. Spriegel and Clark E. Myers, eds. (Homewood, Ill., 1953), p. 404.
40. Alfred Marshall, *Industry and Trade* (London, 1919, 1932), pp. 391-393.
41. *Shop Management*, p. 108.

Chapter 5

The Primary Effects of Scientific Management

The generalized practice of scientific management, as has been noted, coincides with the scientific-technical revolution. It coincides as well with a number of fundamental changes in the structure and functioning of capitalism and in the composition of the working class. In this chapter, we will discuss, in a preliminary way, some of the effects of scientific management upon the working class; later chapters will return to this discussion after the necessary conditions for understanding it more fully have been established.

The separation of mental work from manual work reduces, at any given level of production, the need for workers engaged directly in production, since it divests them of time-consuming mental functions and assigns these functions elsewhere. This is true regardless of any increase in productivity resulting from the separation. Should productivity increase as well, the need for manual workers to produce a given output is further reduced.

A necessary consequence of the separation of conception and execution is that the labor process is now divided between separate sites and separate bodies of workers. In one location, the physical processes of production are executed. In another are concentrated the design, planning, calculation, and record-keeping. The preconception of the process before it is set in motion, the visualization of each worker's activities before they have actually begun, the definition of each function along with the manner of its performance and the time it will consume, the control and checking of the ongoing process once it is under way, and the assessment of results upon completion of each stage of the process—all of these aspects of production have been removed from the shop floor to the management office. The physical processes of production are now carried out more or less blindly, not only by the workers who perform them, but often by lower ranks of supervisory employees as well. The production units operate like a hand, watched, corrected, and controlled by a distant brain.

The concept of control adopted by modern management requires that every activity in production have its several parallel activities in the management center: each must be devised, precalculated, tested, laid out, assigned and ordered, checked and inspected, and recorded throughout its duration and upon completion. The result is that the process of production is replicated in paper form before, as, and after it takes place in physical form. Just as labor in human beings requires that the labor process take place in the brain of the worker as well as in the worker's physical activity, so now the image of the process, removed from production to a separate location and a separate group, controls the process itself. The novelty of this development during the past century lies not in the separate existence of hand and brain, conception and execution, but the rigor with which they are divided from one another, and then increasingly subdivided, so that conception is concentrated, insofar as possible, in ever more limited groups within management or closely associated with it. Thus, in the setting of antagonistic social relations, of alienated labor, hand and brain become not just separated, but divided and hostile, and the human unity of hand and brain turns into its opposite, something less than human.

This paper replica of production, the shadow form which corresponds to the physical, calls into existence a variety of new occupations, the hallmark of which is that they are found not in the flow of things but in the flow of paper. Production has now been split in two and depends upon the activities of both groups. Inasmuch as the mode of production has been driven by capitalism to this divided condition, it has separated the two aspects of labor; *but both remain necessary to production, and in this the labor process retains its unity.*

The separation of hand and brain is the most decisive single step in the division of labor taken by the capitalist mode of production. It is inherent in that mode of production from its beginnings, and it develops, under capitalist management, throughout the history of capitalism, but it is only during the past century that the scale of production, the resources made available to the modern corporation by the rapid accumulation of capital, and the conceptual apparatus and trained personnel have become available to institutionalize this separation in a systematic and formal fashion.*

The vast industrial engineering and record-keeping divisions of modern corporations have their origins in the planning, estimating, and layout departments, which grew in the wake of the scientific management movement. These early departments had to make their way against the fears of cost-conscious managers, whom Taylor sought to persuade with the following argument: "At first view, the running of a planning department, together with the other innovations, would appear to involve a large amount of additional work and expense, and the most natural question would be is [sic] whether the increased

---

* The Hammonds speak of Boulton, who in the eighteenth century conducted a large-scale machine-tool factory at Soho in England in association with James Watt, as an "adept in scientific management." But the very description they cite of his management method belies this notion, and highlights by contrast the methods of modern management: "While sitting in the midst of his factory, surrounded by the clang of hammers and the noise of engines, he could usually detect when any stoppage occurred, or when the machinery was going too fast or too slow, and issue his orders accordingly."[1] Boulton did, however, have a well-developed supervisory line organization.

efficiency of the shop more than offsets this outlay? It must be borne in mind, however, that, with the exception of the study of unit times, there is hardly a single item of work done in the planning department which is not already being done in the shop. Establishing a planning department merely concentrates the planning and much other brainwork in a few men especially fitted for their task and trained in their especial lines, instead of having it done, as heretofore, in most cases by high priced mechanics, well fitted to work at their trades, but poorly trained for work more or less clerical in its nature."[2] But to this he added the following caution: "There is no question that the cost of production is lowered by separating the work of planning and the brain work as much as possible from the manual labor. Where this is done, however, it is evident that the brain workers must be given sufficient work to keep them fully busy all the time. They must not be allowed to stand around for a considerable part of their time waiting for their particular kind of work to come along, as is so frequently the case."[3] This is by way of serving notice that no part of capitalist employment is exempt from the methods which were first applied on the shop floor.

At first glance, the organization of labor according to simplified tasks, conceived and controlled elsewhere, in place of the previous craft forms of labor, have a clearly degrading effect upon the technical capacity of the worker. In its effects upon the working population as a whole, however, this matter is complicated by the rapid growth of specialized administrative and technical staff work, as well as by the rapid growth of production and the shifting of masses to new industries and within industrial processes to new occupations.

In the discussion of this issue in Taylor's day, a pattern was set which has been followed since. "There are many people who will disapprove of the whole scheme of a planning department to do the thinking for the men,* as well as a number of foremen to assist and lead each man in his work, on the ground that this does not tend to promote independence, self-reliance, and originality in the individual," he wrote in *Shop Management*. "Those holding this view, however, must take exception to the whole trend of modern industrial development."[4] And in *The Principles of Scientific Management*: "Now, when through all of this teaching and this minute instruction the work is apparently made so smooth and easy for the workman, the first impression is that this all tends to make him a mere automaton, a wooden man. As the workmen frequently say when they first come under this system, 'Why, I am not allowed to think or move without someone interfering or doing it for me!' The same criticism and

---

* I ask the reader, in passing, to note the bluntness of the phrase "a planning department to do the thinking for the men." The functions of planning departments have not changed, but in a more sophisticated age, and one in which debates rage about the organization of work, the managers are forewarned, and it is not thought necessary to speak so plainly.

objection, however, can be raised against all other modern subdivision of labor."[5]

These responses, however, clearly did not satisfy Taylor, particularly since they seemed to throw the blame on his own beloved "modern subdivision of labor." And so in both books he went on to further arguments, which in *Shop Management* took this form:

> It is true, for instance, that the planning room, and functional foremanship, render it possible for an intelligent laborer or helper in time to do much of the work now done by a machinist. Is not this a good thing for the laborer and helper? He is given a higher class of work, which tends to develop him and gives him better wages. In the sympathy for the machinist the case of the laborer is overlooked. This sympathy for the machinist is, however, wasted, since the machinist, with the aid of the new system, will rise to a higher class of work which he was unable to do in the past, and in addition, divided or functional foremanship will call for a larger number of men in this class, so that men, who must otherwise have remained machinists all their lives, will have the opportunity of rising to a foremanship.
>
> The demand for men of originality and brains was never so great as it is now, and the modern subdivision of labor, instead of dwarfing men, enables them all along the line to rise to a higher plane of efficiency, involving at the same time more brain work and less monotony. The type of man who was formerly a day laborer and digging dirt is now for instance making shoes in a shoe factory. The dirt handling is done by Italians or Hungarians.[6]

This argument gains force in a period of growth, of the rapid accumulation of capital through production on an ever larger scale, and of the constant opening of new fields of capital accumulation in new industries or the conquest of pre-capitalist production forms by capital. In this context, new drafts of workers are brought into jobs that have already been degraded in comparison with the craft processes of before; but inasmuch as they come from outside the existing working class, chiefly from ruined and dispersed farming and peasant populations, they enter a process unknown to them from previous experience and they take the organization of work as given. Meanwhile, opportunities open up for the advancement of some workers into planning, layout, estimating, or drafting departments, or into foremanships (especially two or three generations ago, when such jobs were customarily still staffed from the shop floors). In this manner, short-term trends opening the way for the advancement of some workers in rapidly growing industries, together with the ever lower skill requirements characteristic at the entry level where large masses of workers are being put to work in industrial, office, and marketing processes for the first time, simply mask the secular trend toward the incessant lowering of the working class as a whole below its previous conditions of skill and labor. As this continues over several generations, the very standards by which the trend is judged become imperceptibly altered, and the meaning of "skill" itself becomes degraded.

Sociologists and economists, nevertheless, continue to repeat Taylor's argument in a world of labor that has become, for the largest portions of the working population, increasingly devoid of any content of either skill or scientific knowledge. Thus Michel Crozier, in *The World of the Office Worker*, concedes that as office work has become an immensely enlarged occupational field, its pay and status advantages over factory work have virtually disappeared: "A mass of unskilled employees assigned a series of simple unchanging operations." "It is this general pattern of evolution," he says, "anticipated by Marxist theoreticians, which constitutes the principal argument in favor of the thesis of proletarization of white-collar employees." His response, strikingly similar to Taylor's, differs from the latter only in that, in place of "Italians and Hungarians" he is pleased to use women as that category of the labor force for which any job is good enough: "The proletarization of white-collar employees does not have the same meaning at all if it is women, and not heads of family, who comprise the majority of the group."[7] As he explains:

> It is true of course, on the other hand, that the 900,000 French office workers of 1920 certainly had a more bourgeois status than the 1,920,000 white-collar employees of 1962. But to the 600,000 male employees of 1920 there now correspond probably 350,000 supervisors and 250,000 highly qualified employees whose status is at least equivalent to that of their predecessors of 1920. As for the 650,000 females newly entered into the profession, thirty years ago they were laborers, seamstresses, or maids. As deadening and as alienating as their assembly-line work may be, for them it may constitute a promotion.
> . . . To be sure, the professions of white-collar employees and minor functionaries are, on the whole, considerably devalued compared to their status only fifty years ago. But this devaluation of the great mass of jobs has been accompanied, we have seen, by a much greater differentiation and a change in recruitment. The majority of white-collar tasks are less interesting, less prestigious, and bring lower remuneration, but they are carried out by women with reduced aspirations. . . .[8]

As craftsmanship is destroyed or increasingly emptied of its traditional content, the remaining ties, already tenuous and weakened, between the working population and science are more or less completely broken. This connection was, in the past, made chiefly through the craftsman or artisan section of the working class, and in the earliest periods of capitalism the connection was quite close. Before the assertion by management of its monopoly over science, craftsmanship was the chief repository of scientific production technique in its then existing form, and historical accounts emphasize the origins of science in craft technique. "Speaking historically," says Elton Mayo, "I think it can be asserted that a science has generally come into being as a product of well-developed technical skill in a given area of activity. Someone, some skilled worker, has in a reflective moment attempted to make explicit the assumptions that are implicit in the skill itself. . . . Science is rooted deep in skill and can only expand by the experimental and systematic development of an achieved skill. The successful sciences consequently are all of humble origin—the cautious development of lowly skills until the point of logical and experimental expansion is clearly gained."[9]

The profession of engineering is a relatively recent development. Before the engineer, the conceptual and design functions were the province of craftsmanship, as were the functions of furthering the industrial arts through innovation. "The appearance of the modern engineer," Bernal says, "was a new social phenomenon. He is not the lineal descendant of the old military engineer but rather of the millwright and the metal-worker of the days of craftsmanship. Bramah (1748-1814), Maudslay (1771-1831), Muir (1806-1888), Whitworth (1803-1887), and the great George Stephenson (1781-1848) were all men of this type."[10] Those even slightly familiar with the history of technology will recognize the importance of the names on this roster, to which can be added James Watt, whose trade was that of mathematical instrument maker; Samuel Crompton, who was himself a spinner from the age of fourteen and continued, in the absence of patent protection, to earn his living as a spinner even after his spinning mule was in widespread use; and many others.* It should also be noted that up to 1824 it was illegal for a British mechanic to accept work abroad, a restriction inconceivable in our own day; the reasons for this were clear so long as the craftsman remained the repository of the technical knowledge of the production process.

---

* Despite the flood of mechanical invention in recent times, it would be impossible to construct such a list for this century. One can think of Frank Whittle, originally a rigger for metal aircraft, who played an important role in the invention of the jet engine, and John Harwood, a watchmaker and watch repairman who invented the self-winding wristwatch, patented in 1923. Hoxie reports that while he was preparing his study of scientific management, during the World War I period, he "saw in one shop an automatic machine invented by a workman which did the work of several hand workers. 'Did he receive any reward?' was the question asked. 'Oh, yes,' came the answer, 'his rate of pay was increased from 17 to 22 cents an hour.' Instances of this kind could be multiplied."[11] But in more recent times such cases are rare. A study of the occupational characteristics of a random sample of persons granted patents in the United States in 1953 showed that "about 60 percent were engineers, chemists, metallurgists, and directors of research and development, and that most of the rest were non-R.&D. executives; almost none were production workers."[12] Here we may pause to give a decent burial to Adam Smith's third argument in favor of the technical division of labor: that the worker, with attention focused upon a single repeated operation, would devise machinery to facilitate that operation. Such truth as it once possessed has long since disappeared in the conditions of capitalist production in which the worker is neither encouraged nor permitted to understand his or her work.

The working craftsman was tied to the technical and scientific knowledge of his time in the daily practice of his craft. Apprenticeship commonly included training in mathematics, including algebra, geometry, and trigonometry, in the properties and provenance of the materials common to the craft, in the physical sciences, and in mechanical drawing. Well-administered apprenticeships provided subscriptions to the trade and technical journals affecting the craft so that apprentices could follow developments.* But more important than formal or informal training was the fact that the craft provided a daily link between science and work, since the craftsman was constantly called upon to use rudimentary scientific knowledge, mathematics, drawing, etc., in his practice.** Such craftsmen were an important part of the scientific public of their time, and as a rule exhibited an interest in science and culture beyond that connected directly to their work. The flourishing Mechanics Institutes of the mid-nineteenth century, which in Britain numbered some 1,200 and had a membership of over 200,000, were in large measure devoted to satisfying this interest through lectures and libraries.[15] The Royal Institution, which existed in England to further the progress of science and its application to industry, was forced, when it became a fashionable place to visit and wished to preserve its exclusivity, to brick up its back door to keep out the mechanics who stole into the gallery.[16] Samuel Gompers, as a cigarmaker living in New York's dense

---

* The effects of the decline of apprenticeship were felt as long ago as the time of the Hoxie report, which says: "It is evident, however, that the native efficiency of the working class must suffer from the neglect of apprenticeship, if no other means of industrial education is forthcoming. Scientific managers, themselves, have complained bitterly of the poor and lawless material from which they must recruit their workers, compared with the efficient and self-respecting craftsmen who applied for employment twenty years ago."[13] These same scientific managers have not ceased to complain bitterly, as is their wont, of the characteristics of a working population which they themselves have shaped to suit their ends, but they have not yet found a way to produce workers who are at one and the same time degraded in their place in the labor process, and also conscientious and proud of their work.

** In a discussion of the craftsmen of the Industrial Revolution, David Landes writes: "Even more striking is the theoretical knowledge of these men. They were not, on the whole, the unlettered tinkerers of historical mythology. Even the ordinary millwright, as Fairbairn notes, was usually 'a fair arithmetician, knew something of geometry, levelling, and mensuration, and in some cases possessed a very competent knowledge of practical mathematics. He could calculate the velocities, strength, and power of machines: could draw in plan and section. . . .' Much of these 'superior attainments and intellectual power' reflected the abundant facilities for technical education in 'villages' like Manchester during this period, ranging from Dissenters' academies and learned societies to local and visiting lecturers, 'mathematical and commercial' private schools with evening classes, and a wide circulation of practical manuals, periodicals, and encyclopaedias."[14]

working-class district on the Lower East Side in the 1860s, saw and experienced this same working-class interest:

> Cooper Union provided opportunities for formal study courses as well as lectures every Saturday evening which were usually attended by from twenty-five hundred to three thousand. Nothing humanly possible ever kept me from attending those Saturday night lectures. I was fairly quivering in my intense desire to know. Mental hunger is just as painful as physical hunger. Every Saturday night some great scholar talked to an open meeting and gave most wonderfully illuminating results of experimentation and study. Sometimes Professor Proctor told us of the wonders of astronomy—of what science had learned of time and distance, light, motion, etc. Truths gleaned in these lectures became a most vital part of me and gave the world marvelously inspiring meaning. Those lectures were treasured opportunities to hear authorities in science tell what they were doing and thinking. I attended these lectures and study classes over a period of twenty years.[17]

We may marvel still at the British silk weavers of Spitalfields, whom Mayhew found, in the middle of the nineteenth century, living in incredible poverty and degradation, and who, but a short time before, when the day of the skilled hand-loom weaver was not yet over, had made their district of London a center of science and culture:

> The weavers were, formerly, almost the only botanists in the metropolis, and their love of flowers to this day is a strongly marked characteristic of the class. Some years back, we are told, they passed their leisure hours, and generally the whole family dined on Sundays, at the little gardens in the environs of London, now mostly built upon. Not very long ago there was an Entomological Society, and they were among the most diligent entomologists, in the kingdom. This taste, though far less general than formerly, still continues to be a type of the class. There was at one time a Floricultural Society, an Historical Society, and a Mathematical Society, all maintained by the operative silk-weavers; and the celebrated Dollond, the inventor of the achromatic telescope, was a weaver; so too were Simpson and Edwards, the mathematicians, before they were taken from the loom into the employ of Government, to teach mathematics to the cadets at Woolwich and Chatham.[18]

The same remarkable history characterized the weavers of Yorkshire and Lancashire, as E. P. Thompson notes: "Every weaving district had its weaver-poets, biologists, mathematicians, musicians, geologists, botanists. . . . There are northern museums and natural history societies which still possess records or collections of lepidoptera built up by weavers; while there are accounts of weavers in isolated villages who taught themselves geometry by chalking on their flagstones, and who were eager to discuss the differential calculus."[19]

The destruction of craftsmanship during the period of the rise of scientific management did not go unnoticed by workers. Indeed, as a rule workers are far more conscious of such a loss while it is being effected than after it has taken place and the new conditions of production have become generalized. Taylorism raised a storm of opposition among the trade unions during the early part of this century; what is most noteworthy about this early opposition is that it was concentrated not upon the trappings of the Taylor system, such as the stopwatch and motion study, but upon its essential effort to strip the workers of craft knowledge and autonomous control and confront them with a fully thought-out labor process in which they function as cogs and levers. In an editorial which appeared in the *International Molders Journal*, we read:

> The one great asset of the wage worker has been his craftsmanship. We think of craftsmanship ordinarily as the ability to manipulate skillfully the tools and materials of a craft or trade. But true craftsmanship is much more than this. The really essential element in it is not manual skill and dexterity but something stored up in the mind of the worker. This something is partly the intimate knowledge of the character and uses of the tools, materials and processes of the craft which tradition and experience have given the worker. But beyond this and above this, it is the knowledge which enables him to understand and overcome the constantly arising difficulties that grow out of variations not only in the tools and materials, but in the conditions under which the work must be done.

The editorial goes on to point to the separation of "craft knowledge" from "craft skill" in "an ever-widening area and with an ever-increasing acceleration," and describes as the most dangerous form of this separation

> the gathering up of all this scattered craft knowledge, systematizing it and concentrating it in the hands of the employer and then doling it out again only in the form of minute instructions, giving to each worker only the knowledge needed for the performance of a particular rela-tively minute task. This process, it is evident, separates skill and knowledge even in their narrow relationship. When it is completed, the worker is no longer a craftsman in any sense, but is an animated tool of the management.[20]

A half-century of commentary on scientific management has not suc-ceeded in producing a better formulation of the matter.*

---

* In this connection, see also Friedmann's *Industrial Society*, where he summarizes "the first reactions of workers" to Taylorism in the United States, England, Germany, and France.[21]

Notes

1. J. L. and Barbara Hammond, *The Rise of Modern Industry* (London, 1925; reprint ed., New York, 1969), p. 119.
2. Frederick W. Taylor, *Shop Management*, in *Scientific Management* (New York and London, 1947), pp. 65-66.
3. Ibid., p. 121.
4. Ibid., p. 146.
5. Frederick W. Taylor, *The Principles of Scientific Management* (New York, 1967), p. 125.
6. Taylor, *Shop Management*, pp. 146-47.
7. Michel Crozier, *The World of the Office Worker* (Chicago and London, 1971), pp. 13-17.
8. Ibid., pp. 18-19.
9. Elton Mayo, *The Social Problems of an Industrial Civilization* (Boston, 1945), pp. 17-18.
10. J. D. Bernal, *Science in History* (London, 1954; revised ed., 1957), p. 389.
11. Robert F. Hoxie, *Scientific Management and Labor* (New York and London, 1918), p. 94.
12. National Commission on Technology, Automation, and Economic Progress, *The Employment Impact of Technological Change*, Appendix Volume II, *Technology and the American Economy* (Washington, D.C., 1966), p. 109.
13. Hoxie, *Scientific Management and Labor*, p. 134.
14. David S. Landes, *The Unbound Prometheus: Technological Change and Industrial Development in Western Europe from 1750 to the Present* (Cambridge and New York, 1969), p. 63.
15. See J. H. Stewart Reid, *The Origins of the British Labour Party* (Minneapolis, Minn., 1955), p. 19; and E. J. Hobsbawm, *The Age of Revolution* (New York, 1962), pp. 213-14.
16. Bernal, *Science in History*, p. 383.
17. Samuel Gompers, *Seventy Years of Life and Labor* (1925; New York, 1957), p. 57.
18. Henry Mayhew, in *The Unknown Mayhew*, Eileen Yeo and E. P. Thompson, eds. (New York, 1971), pp. 105-106.
19. E. P. Thompson, *The Making of the English Working Class* (New York, 1964), pp. 291-92.
20. Hoxie, *Scientific Management and Labor*, pp. 131-32.
21. Georges Friedmann, *Industrial Society* (Glencoe, Ill., 1955), pp, 41-43.

Chapter 6

The Habituation of the Worker
to the Capitalist Mode of Production

The transformation of working humanity into a "labor force," a "factor of production," an instrument of capital, is an incessant and unending process. The condition is repugnant to the victims, whether their pay is high or low, because it violates human conditions of work; and since the workers are not destroyed as human beings but are simply utilized in inhuman ways, their critical, intelligent, conceptual faculties, no matter how deadened or diminished, always remain in some degree a threat to capital. Moreover, the capitalist mode of production is continually extended to new areas of work, including those freshly created by technological advances and the shift of capital to new industries. It is, in addition, continually being refined and perfected, so that its pressure upon the workers is unceasing. At the same time, the habituation of workers to the capitalist mode of production must be renewed with each generation, all the more so as the generations which grow up under capitalism are not formed within the matrix of work life, but are plunged into work from the outside, so to speak, after a prolonged period of adolescence during which they are held in reserve. The necessity for adjusting the worker to work in its capitalist form, for overcoming natural resistance intensified by swiftly changing technology, antagonistic social relations, and the succession of the generations, does not therefore end with the "scientific organization of labor," but becomes a permanent feature of capitalist society.

As a result, there has come into being, within the personnel and labor relations departments of corporations and in the external support organizations such as schools of industrial relations, college departments of sociology, and other academic and para-academic institutions, a complex of practical and academic disciplines devoted to the study of the worker. Shortly after Taylor, industrial psychology and industrial physiology came into existence to perfect methods of selection, training, and motivation of workers, and these were soon broadened into an attempted industrial sociology, the study of the workplace as a social system.

The cardinal feature of these various schools and the currents within them is that, unlike the scientific management movement, they do not by and large concern themselves with the organization of work, but rather with the conditions under which the worker may best be brought to cooperate in the scheme of work organized by the industrial engineer.* The evolving work processes of capitalist society are taken by these schools as inexorable givens, and are accepted as "necessary and inevitable" in any form of "industrial society." The problems addressed are the problems of management: dissatisfaction as expressed in high turnover rates, absenteeism, resistance to the prescribed work pace, indifference, neglect, cooperative group restrictions on output, and overt hostility to management. As it presents itself to most of the sociologists and psychologists concerned with the study of work and workers, the problem is not that of the degradation of men and women, but the difficulties raised by the reactions, conscious and unconscious, to that degradation. It is therefore not at all fortuitous that most orthodox social scientists adhere firmly, indeed desperately, to the dictum that their task is not the study of the objective conditions of work, but only of the subjective phenomena to which these give rise: the degrees of "satisfaction" and "dissatisfaction" elicited by their questionnaires.

The earliest systematic effort in this direction took place in the field of industrial psychology. Its beginnings may be traced back to the experimental psychology taught in nineteenth century Germany, and in particular to the school of psychology at the University of Leipzig. Hugo Münsterberg, after receiving his training in Wilhelm Wundt's "laboratory" at that institution, came to the United States where, at Harvard, he was in a position to observe the development of modern management in its most vigorous and extensive forms, and it became his ambition to marry the methods of the Leipzig school to the

---

* Personnel management, although thought of as that part of the corporate structure concerned with the worker, is usually given short shrift when a reorganization of actual work is under way. In a recent book, two prominent industrial engineers accord to almost every management level a greater role in the change in work methods than the role which they prescribe for the personnel department. They say flatly, in their recommendations for an overall "operations improvement program": "In the beginning, in most organizations, the personnel director will have no active role in the conduct of an operations improvement program." They restrict the place of this official to his value "as a sounding board for employee reactions," and to orienting new employees to the program and to answering questions and complaints.[1] As with personnel directors, so also with their academic counterparts in labor sociology. Charles Rumford Walker, one of the more experienced and sophisticated, as well as more "humane," of these stresses this in a section of one of his papers devoted to the "Strategic Role of the Engineer," in which he recognizes that the direction of the evolution of work is determined by "managers and engineers, as architects of the future," while the role of sociologists is that of trying to importune, press upon, and persuade the real designers of the work process to take into account the "neglected human dimension" in order to reduce discontent and increase productivity, to "seize the opportunity" offered by swift technological change, etc.[2]

new practice of scientific management. His *Psychology and Industrial Efficiency* (published in German in 1912, with an English version following the next year) may be called the first systematic outline of industrial psychology.[3] Like Taylor, Münsterberg disdained to conceal his views and aims:

> Our aim is to sketch the outlines of a new science which is intermediate between the modern laboratory psychology and the problems of economics: the psychological experiment is systematically to be placed at the service of commerce and industry.[4]

But what are the ends of commerce and industry? Münsterberg leaves that to others: "Economic psychotechnics may serve certain ends of commerce and industry, but whether these ends are the best ones is not a care with which the psychologist has to be burdened."[5] Having relieved his "science" of this burden, and having turned the task of setting the parameters of his investigations over to those who control "commerce and industry," he returns to this subject only when it is suggested that perhaps the point of view of the workers, who are also part of "commerce and industry," should be taken into consideration. So crass and vulgar an appeal to special interests arouses his horror, and he rejects it sternly:

> The inquiry into the possible psychological contributions to the question of reinforced achievement must not be deterred by the superficial objection that in one or another industrial concern a dismissal of wage-earners might at first result. Psychotechnics does not stand in the service of a party, but exclusively in the service of civilization.[6]

Having identified the interests of "civilization" not with the immense majority of workers but with those who manage them, he can now face without blanching the everyday effects of "scientific work design" upon the worker: ". . . the development of scientific management has shown clearly that the most important improvements are just those which are deduced from scientific researches, without at first giving satisfaction to the laborers themselves, until a new habit has been formed."[7] He sees the role of psychological science in industry as the selection of workers from among the pool offered on the labor market, and their acclimatization to the work routines devised by "civilization," the formation of the "new habit":

> . . . we select three chief purposes of business life, purposes which are important in commerce and industry and every economic endeavor. We ask how we can find the men whose mental qualities make them best fitted for the work which they have to do; secondly, under what psychological conditions we can secure the greatest and most satisfactory output of work from every man; and finally, how we can produce most completely the influence on human minds which are desired in the interests of business.[8]

In this definition we have the aims—although rarely so flatly stated—of the subsequent schools of psychological, physiological, and social investigation of the worker and work. By and large, they have sought a model of workers and work groups which would produce the results desired by management: habituation to the terms of employment offered in the capitalist firm and satisfactory performance on that basis. These schools and theories have succeeded one another in a dazzling proliferation of approaches and theories, a proliferation which is more than anything else testimony to their failure.

The spread of industrial psychology in the United States was in the beginning largely due to the efforts of Walter Dill Scott, a psychologist at Northwestern University who took his doctorate at Leipzig and came to the new field by way of a prior career in advertising. During and after World War I, psychological testing was used by a number of major corporations (American Tobacco, National Lead, Western Electric, Loose-Wiles Biscuit, Metropolitan Life), and the first psychological consulting service for industry was established at the Carnegie Institute of Technology in 1915, where Scott assumed the first chair of applied psychology in an American academic institution. During the war such testing was conducted on a grand scale in the United States armed forces, also under Scott, and the popularity this gave to the new device encouraged its spread throughout industry after the war. In England and Germany the trend was similar, with Germany perhaps ahead of all others in the field.[9]

The premise of industrial psychology was that, using aptitude tests, it was possible to determine in advance the suitability of workers for various positions by classifying them according to degrees of "intelligence," "manual dexterity," "accident proneness," and general conformability to the "profile" desired by management. The vanity of this attempt to calibrate individuals and anticipate their behavior in the complex and antagonistic dynamics of social life was soon exposed by practice. The prolonged and exhaustive experiments conducted at the Western Electric plant on the west side of Chicago—the so-called Hawthorne experiments—during the last years of the 1920s crystallized the dissatisfaction with industrial psychology. In those experiments, a Harvard Business School team under the leadership of Elton Mayo arrived at chiefly negative conclusions—conclusions, moreover, which were remarkably similar to those with which Taylor had begun his investigations almost a half-century earlier. They learned that the performance of workers had little relation to "ability"—and in fact often bore an *inverse* relation to test scores, with those scoring best producing at lower levels and vice-versa—and that workers acted collectively to resist management work-pace standards and demands. "The belief," said Mayo, "that the behavior of an individual within the factory can be predicted before employment upon the basis of a laborious and minute examination by tests of his mechanical and other capacities is mainly, if not wholly mistaken."[10]

The chief conclusion of the Mayo school was that the workers' motivations could not be understood on a purely individual basis, and that the key to their behavior lay in the social groups of the factory. With this, the study of the habituation of workers to their work moved from the plane of psychology to that of sociology. The "human relations" approach, first of a series of behavioral sociological schools, focused on personnel counseling and on ingratiating or nonirritating styles of "face to face" supervision. But these schools have yielded little to management in the way of solid and tangible results. Moreover, the birth of the "human relations" idea coincided with the Depression of the 1930s and the massive wave of working-class revolt that culminated in the unionization of the basic industries of the United States. In the illumination cast by these events, the workplace suddenly appeared not as a system of bureaucratic formal organization on the Weberian model, nor as a system of informal group relations as in the interpretation of Mayo and his followers, but rather as a system of power, of class antagonisms. Industrial psychology and sociology have never recovered from this blow. From their confident beginnings as "sciences" devoted to discovering the springs of human behavior the better to manipulate them in the interests of management, they have broken up into a welter of confused and confusing approaches pursuing psychological, sociological, economic, mathematical, or "systems" interpretations of the realities of the workplace, with little real impact upon the management of worker or work.*

If the adaptation of the worker to the capitalist mode of production owes little to the efforts of practical and ideological manipulators, how is it in fact accomplished? Much of the economic and political history of the capitalist world during the last century and a half is bound up with this process of adjustment and the conflicts and revolts which attended it, and this is not the place to attempt a summary. A single illustration, that of the first comprehensive conveyor assembly line, will have to suffice as an indication that the wrenching of the workers out of their prior conditions and their adjustment to the forms of work engineered by capital is a fundamental process in which the

---

* The actual place of industrial psychology and sociology in corporate policies was succinctly expressed by three specialists in industrial engineering at the end of an article called "Current Job Design Criteria": "It can be concluded that company policies and practices [this refers to the companies studied in the article] in job design are inconsistent with programs and policies in human relations and personnel administration. On the one hand, specific steps are taken to minimize the contribution of the individual, and on the other hand he is propagandized about his importance and value to the organization."[11] But this is more than an "inconsistency," since job design represents *reality* while personnel administration represents only *mythology*. From the point of view of the corporation, there is no inconsistency, since the latter represents a manipulation to habituate the worker to the former.

principal roles are played not by manipulation or cajolery but by socioeconomic conditions and forces.

In 1903, when the Ford Motor Company was founded, building automobiles was a task reserved for craftsmen who had received their training in the bicycle and carriage shops of Michigan and Ohio, then the centers of those industries. "Final assembly, for example," writes Eli Chinoy, "had originally been a highly skilled job. Each car was put together in one spot by a number of all-around mechanics."[12] By 1908, when Ford launched the Model T, procedures had been changed somewhat, but the changes were slight compared with what was soon to come. The organization of assembly labor at that time is described as follows by Keith Sward:

> At Ford's and in all the other shops in Detroit, the process of putting an automobile together still revolved around the versatile mechanic, who was compelled to move about in order to do his work. Ford's assemblers were still all-around men. Their work was largely stationary, yet they had to move on to their next job on foot as soon as the car-in-the-making at their particular station had been taken the whole distance—from bare frame to finished product. To be sure, time had added some refinements. In 1908 it was no longer necessary for the assembler to leave his place of work for trips to the tool crib or the parts bin. Stock-runners had been set aside to perform this function. Nor was the Ford mechanic himself in 1908 quite the man he had been in 1903. In the intervening years the job of final assembly had been split up ever so little. In place of the jack-of-all-trades who formerly "did it all," there were now several assemblers who worked over a particular car side by side, each one responsible for a somewhat limited set of operations."[13]

The demand for the Model T was so great that special engineering talent was engaged to revise the production methods of the company. The key element of the new organization of labor was the endless conveyor chain upon which car assemblies were carried past fixed stations where men performed simple operations as they passed. This system was first put into operation for various subassemblies, beginning around the same time that the Model T was launched, and developed through the next half-dozen years until it culminated in January 1914 with the inauguration of the first endless-chain conveyor for final assembly at Ford's Highland Park plant. Within three months, the assembly time for the Model T had been reduced to one-tenth the time formerly needed, and by 1925 an organization had been created which produced almost as many cars in a single day as had been produced, early in the history of the Model T, in an entire year.

The quickening rate of production in this case depended not only upon the change in the organization of labor, but upon the control which management, at a single stroke, attained over the pace of assembly, so that it could now double and triple the rate at which operations had to be performed and thus subject its workers to an extraordinary intensity of labor. Having achieved this, Ford then moved to flatten the pay structure as a further cost-cutting measure:

> Before the advent of the assembly line, the company had made a general practice of dispensing more or less liberal bonuses in order to stimulate production and individual initiative. But the moment moving belt lines came into being, Ford did away with incentive pay. He reverted to the payment of a flat hourly rate of wages. The company had decided, said *Iron Age* in July 1913, to abandon its graduated pay scale in favor of "more strenuous supervision." Once the new wage policy had been put into effect, the run-of-the-mine Ford employe could expect no more variation in his earnings than in the operations which he was called upon to perform. His maximum pay was frozen, seemingly for good, at $2.34 per day, the rate of pay which was standard for the area.[14]

In this way the new conditions of employment that were to become characteristic of the automobile industry, and thereafter of an increasing number of industries, were established first at the Ford Motor Company. Craftsmanship gave way to a repeated detail operation, and wage rates were standardized at uniform levels. The reaction to this change was powerful, as Sward relates:

> As a consequence, the new technology at Ford's proved to be increasingly unpopular; more and more it went against the grain. And the men who were exposed to it began to rebel. They registered their dissatisfaction by walking out in droves. They could afford to pick and choose. Other jobs were plentiful in the community; they were easier to get to; they paid as well; and they were less mechanized and more to labor's liking.
>
> Ford's men had begun to desert him in large numbers as early as 1910. With the coming of the assembly line, their ranks almost literally fell apart; the company soon found it next to impossible to keep its working force intact, let alone expand it. It was apparent that the Ford Motor Co. had reached the point of owning a great factory without having enough workers to keep it humming. Ford admitted later that his startling factory innovations had ushered in the outstanding labor crisis of his career. The turnover of his working force had run, he was to write, to 380 percent for the year 1913 alone. So great was labor's distaste for the new machine system that toward the close of 1913 every time the company wanted to add 100 men to its factory personnel, it was necessary to hire 963.[15]

In this initial reaction to the assembly line we see the natural revulsion of the worker against the new kind of work. What makes it possible to see it so clearly is the fact that Ford, as a pioneer in the new mode of production, was competing with prior modes of the organization of labor which still characterized the rest of the automobile industry and other industries in the area. In this microcosm, there is an illustration of the rule that the working class is progressively subjected to the capitalist mode of production, and to the successive forms which it takes, *only as the capitalist mode of production conquers and destroys all other forms of the organization of labor, and with them, all alternatives for the working population.* As Ford, by the competitive advantage which he gained, forced the assembly line upon the rest of the automobile industry, in the same degree workers were forced to submit to it by the disappearance of other forms of work in that industry.

The crisis Ford faced was intensified by the unionization drive begun by the Industrial Workers of the World among Ford workers in the summer of 1913. Ford's response to the double threat of unionization and the flight of workers from his plants was the announcement, made with great fanfare early in 1914, of the $5.00 day. Although this dramatic increase in wages was not so strictly adhered to as Ford would have had the public believe when he launched it, it did raise pay at the Ford plant so much above the prevailing rate in the area that it solved both threats for the moment. It gave the company a large pool of labor from which to choose and at the same time opened up new possibilities for the intensification of labor within the plants, where workers were now anxious to keep their jobs. "The payment of five dollars a day for an eight-hour day," Ford was to write in his autobiography, "was one of the finest cost-cutting moves we ever made."[16]

In this move can be seen a second element in the adjustment of workers to increasingly unpopular jobs. Conceding higher relative wages for a shrinking proportion of workers in order to guarantee uninterrupted production was to become, particularly after the Second World War, a widespread feature of corporate labor policy, especially after it was adopted by union leaderships. John L. Lewis resolved upon this course of action shortly after the war: in return for encouraging the mechanization of the coal-mining industry and the reduction of employment, he insisted upon an increasing scale of compensation for the ever smaller and ever more hard-driven miners remaining in the pits. The bulk of the organized labor movement in production industries followed his lead, either openly or implicitly, in the decades thereafter. And these policies were greatly facilitated by the monopolistic structure of the industries in question. The workers who were sloughed off, or the workers who never entered manufacturing industries because of the proportional shrinkage of those industries, furnished the masses for new branches of industry at lower rates of pay.

If the petty manipulations of personnel departments and industrial psychology and sociology have not played a major role in the habituation of worker to work, therefore, this does not mean that the "adjustment" of the worker is free of manipulative elements. On the contrary, as in all of the functionings of the capitalist system, manipulation is primary and coercion is held in reserve—except that this manipulation is the product of powerful economic forces, major corporate employment and bargaining policies, and the inner workings and evolution of the system of capitalism itself, and not primarily of the clever schemes of labor relations experts. The apparent acclimatization of the worker to the new modes of production grows out of the destruction of all other ways of living, the striking of wage bargains that permit a certain enlargement of the customary bounds of subsistence for the working class, the weaving of the net of modern capitalist life that finally makes all other modes of living impossible. But beneath this apparent habituation, the hostility of workers to the degenerated forms of work which are forced upon them continues as a subterranean stream that makes its way to the surface when employment conditions permit, or when the capitalist drive for a greater intensity of labor oversteps the bounds of physical and mental capacity. It renews itself in new generations, expresses itself in the unbounded cynicism and revulsion which large numbers of workers feel about their work, and comes to the fore repeatedly as a social issue demanding solution.

Notes

1. Bruce Payne and David D. Swett, *Office Operations Improvement* (New York, 1967), pp. 41-42.
2. National Commission on Technology, Automation, and Economic Progress, *The Employment Impact of Technological Change*, Appendix Volume II, *Technology and the American Economy* (Washington, D.C., 1966), pp. 288-315, esp. section IV.
3. Loren Baritz, *The Servants of Power: A History of the Use of Social Science in American Industry* (Middletown, Conn., 1960; paperback ed., New York, 1965), pp. 26-36.
4. Hugo Münsterberg, *Psychology and Industrial Efficiency* (Boston and New York, 1913), p. 3.
5. Ibid., p. 19.
6. Ibid., p. 144.
7. Ibid., p. 178.
8. Ibid., pp. 23-24.
9. For a brief history of industrial psychology, see Baritz, *The Servants of Power*.
10. Quoted in ibid., p. 95.
11. Louis E. Davis, Ralph R. Canter, and John Hoffman, "Current Job Design Criteria," *Journal of Industrial Engineering*, vol. 6, no. 2 (1955); reprinted in Louis E. Davis and James C. Taylor, eds., *Design of Jobs* (London, 1972), p. 81.
12. Eli Chinoy, "Manning the Machine—The Assembly-Line Worker," in Peter L. Berger, ed., *The Human Shape of Work: Studies in the Sociology of Occupations* (New York, 1964), p. 53.
13. Keith Sward, *The Legend of Henry Ford* (New York and Toronto, 1948), p. 32.
14. Ibid., p. 48.
15. Ibid., pp. 48-49.
16. Ibid., p. 56.

Part II

Science and Mechanization

Chapter 7

The Scientific-Technical Revolution

Considered from a technical point of view, all production depends upon the physical, chemical, and biological properties of materials and the processes which can be based upon them. Management, in its activities as an organizer of labor, does not deal directly with this aspect of production; it merely provides the formal structure for the production process. But the process is not complete without its content, which is a matter of technique. This technique, as has been noted, is at first that of skill, of craft, and later assumes an increasingly scientific character as knowledge of natural laws grows and displaces the scrappy knowledge and fixed tradition of craftsmanship. The transformation of labor from a basis of skill to a basis of science may thus be said to incorporate a content supplied by a scientific and engineering revolution within a form supplied by the rigorous division and subdivision of labor favored by capitalist management.

With the rise of modern industry, Marx wrote, the "varied, apparently unconnected, and petrified forms of the industrial processes now resolved themselves into so many conscious and systematic applications of natural science to the attainment of given useful effects."[1] But, like many of Marx's most illuminating observations, this was in his own day more an anticipatory and prophetic insight than a description of reality. The age of "conscious and systematic applications of natural science" had barely announced its arrival when these words were published in 1867. The last two decades of the nineteenth century form a watershed marking so great a change in the role of science in production that the contrast—despite similarities which connect both periods of capitalism—can hardly be exaggerated.

Science is the last—and after labor the most important—social property to be turned into an adjunct of capital. The story of its conversion from the province of amateurs, "philosophers," tinkerers, and seekers after knowledge to its present highly organized and lavishly financed state is largely the story of its incorporation into the capitalist firm and subsidiary organizations. At first science costs the capitalist nothing, since he merely exploits the accumulated knowledge of the physical sciences, but later the capitalist systematically organizes and harnesses science, paying for scientific education, research, laboratories, etc., out of the huge surplus social product which either belongs directly to him or which the capitalist class as a whole controls in the form of tax revenues. A formerly relatively free-floating social endeavor is integrated into production and the market.

The contrast between science as a generalized social property incidental to production and science as capitalist property at the very center of production is the contrast between the Industrial Revolution, which occupied the last half of the eighteenth and the first third of the nineteenth centuries, and the scientific-technical revolution, which began in the last decades of the nineteenth century and is still going on. The role of science in the Industrial Revolution was unquestionably great. Before the rise of capitalism—that is, until the sixteenth and seventeenth centuries in Europe—the body of fundamental scientific knowledge in the West was essentially that of classical antiquity, that of the ancient Greeks as preserved by Arab scholarship and in medieval monasteries. The era of scientific advance during the sixteenth and seventeenth centuries supplied some of the conditions for the Industrial Revolution, but the connection was indirect, general, and diffuse—not only because science itself was as yet unstructured by capitalism and not directly dominated by capitalist institutions, but also because of the important historical fact that technique developed in advance of, and as a prerequisite for, science. Thus, in contrast with modern practice, science did not systematically lead the way for industry, but often lagged behind and grew out of the industrial arts. Instead of formulating significantly fresh insights into natural conditions in a way that makes possible new techniques, science in its beginnings under capitalism more often formulated its generalizations side by side with, or as a result of, technological development.* If we choose as a prime example the steam engine—because of the significant scientific principles it exemplified and because it was the central working mechanism of the Industrial Revolution— we can see this clearly. One historian of science has written of the process by which the steam engine came into being:

> How much of this development was owing to the science of heat? All the available evidence indicates that it was very little. This point of view was expressed emphatically by a writer on the history of the invention of the steam engine, Robert Stuart Meikleham. In the preface to his book *Descriptive History of the Steam Engine*, of 1824, he wrote, "We know not who gave

---

* Of the technical skill that existed in Britain in the eighteenth century, Landes writes: "This should not be confused with scientific knowledge; in spite of some efforts to tie the Industrial Revolution to the Scientific Revolution of the sixteenth and seventeenth centuries, the link would seem to have been an extremely diffuse one: both reflected a heightened interest in natural and material phenomena and a more systematic application of empirical searching. Indeed, if anything, the growth of scientific knowledge owed much to the concerns and achievements of technology; there was far less flow of ideas or methods the other way; and this was to continue to be the case well into the nineteenth century."[2]

currency to the phrase of the invention being one of the noblest gifts that science ever made to mankind. The fact is that science, or scientific men, never had anything to do in the matter. Indeed there is no machine or mechanism in which the little that theorists have done is more useless. It arose, was improved and perfected by working mechanics—and by them only."[3]

This view is buttressed by the fact that in the early days of the development of steam power the prevailing scientific theory of heat was the caloric theory, from which, as Lindsay points out, "few really significant deductions about the properties of steam could be drawn."[4] Landes concludes that the development of steam technology probably contributed much more to the physical sciences than the other way around:

> It is often stated that the Newcomen machine and its forerunners would have been unthinkable without the theoretical ideas of Boyle, Torricelli, and others; and that Watt derived much of his technical competence and imagination from his work with scientists and scientific instruments at Glasgow. There is no doubt some truth in this, though how much is impossible to say. One thing is clear, however: once the principle of the separate condenser was established, subsequent advances owed little or nothing to theory. On the contrary, an entire branch of physics, thermodynamics, developed in part as a result of empirical observations of engineering methods and performance.[5]

To contrast this with the manner in which science has been employed as the cutting edge of industrial change during the past three-quarters of a century is to contrast science in two very different modes of existence. The organized scientific professions as we know them today hardly existed before the second half of the nineteenth century. At the beginning of the century, the universities were still oriented toward classical learning, scientific societies were in their infancy, and scientific patronage was principally a private affair. Scientists were "typically 'amateurs,' or men for whom science was often an avocation, however passionate their interest in it. . . . Not until the late nineteenth century . . . is there a firmly established social basis for large numbers of scientists in the universities, industries, and governments of Western society."[6] Even as late as 1880, Thomas Huxley could speak of those "ranged around the banners of physical science" as "somewhat of a guerrilla force, composed largely of irregulars."

The old epoch of industry gave way to the new during the last decades of the nineteenth century primarily as a result of advances in four fields: electricity, steel, coal-petroleum, and the internal combustion engine. Scientific research along theoretical lines played enough of a role in these areas to demonstrate to the capitalist class, and especially to the giant corporate entities then coming into being as a result of the concentration and centralization of capital, its importance as a means of furthering the accumulation of capital.

This was particularly true in the electrical industries, which were entirely the product of nineteenth-century science, and in the chemistry of the synthetic products of coal and oil.

The story of the incorporation of science into the capitalist firm properly begins in Germany. The early symbiosis between science and industry which was developed by the capitalist class of that country proved to be one of the most important facts of world history in the twentieth century, furnished the capability for two world wars, and offered to the other capitalist nations an example which they learned to emulate only when they were forced to do so many decades later. The role of science in German industry was the product of the weakness of German capitalism in its initial stages, together with the advanced state of German theoretical science.

It would be well for those who still do not understand the importance of German speculative philosophy to ponder, if not the example of Marx, of which they are so mistrustful, the concrete instance of modern science and its sharply contrasting careers in Germany on the one hand and in the United States and Britain on the other. "If much in contemporary Britain is to be explained in terms of Bentham's philosophy," writes P. W. Musgrave in his study of technical change in Britain and Germany, "so did Hegel have a great influence in Germany."[7] Hegel's influence on the development of science was, as Musgrave points out, both direct and indirect. In the first instance, there was his role in the reform of Prussian education in the second decade of the nineteenth century. And next, there was the pervasive influence of German speculative philosophy, of which Hegel was the culminating thinker, in giving to German scientific education a fundamental and theoretical cast. Thus while Britain and the United States were still in the grip of that common-sense empiricism which stunts and discourages reflective thought and basic scientific research, in Germany it was these very habits of mind that were being developed in the scientific community.[8] It was for this reason more than any other that the primacy in European science passed from France to Germany in the middle of the nineteenth century, while Britain in the same period remained mired in "what J. S. Mill called 'the dogmatism of common sense' backed by rule of thumb."[9]

By 1870, the German university system could boast a considerable number of professors and lecturers, especially in the sciences, who, favored by light duties and well-equipped laboratories, could pursue basic research. Industrial research laboratories such as that maintained by Krupp at Essen were to become models for corporate research everywhere. The polytechnic institutes which had arisen during the 1830s and 1840s as an alternative to university education, and were to evolve into the celebrated Technische Hochschulen, attracted students from all over the world. And the apprenticeship system, stronger than elsewhere, was producing higher grades of mechanics in large quantities in those crafts required by the new industries.

The manner in which Germany anticipated the modern era is nowhere better illustrated than in the story of the German chemical industry: "It was Germany which showed the rest of the world how to make critical raw materials out of a sandbox and a pile of coal. And it was IG Farben which led the way for Germany. IG changed chemistry from pure research and commercial pill-rolling into a mammoth industry affecting every phase of civilization."[10]

The leadership in chemistry and its industrial applications first belonged to France, especially after the cutting off of supplies of soda, sugar, and other products during the Napoleonic wars "promoted the French chemical industry and helped to give France chemical predominance for thirty years."[11] Thus Germans and others learned their chemistry in France in the first half of the nineteenth century; one of these students was Justus von Liebig, who, after studying with Gay-Lussac and other French chemists, returned to Germany to lay the foundations for modern organic, and especially agricultural, chemistry. One of Liebig's students, August Wilhelm von Hofmann, found his first teaching job in England, where in 1845 he became the first director of the Royal College of Chemistry. Hofmann had a particular interest in the chemistry of coal tar, a subject into which he led his best British pupils, among them William Henry Perkin. The earliest efforts of chemists had been merely to get rid of coal tar by boiling it off, but since it boiled in stages and at different temperatures, the result was a variety of tars which could, by chemical processing, be made to yield useful substances. Perkin, in 1856 (at the age of eighteen), derived the first true synthetic dye from aniline, a coal tar derivative; it could color fabrics and hold its color against washing, time, and sunlight. The importance of this discovery was the juncture it established between the older textile industry and the new steel industry which produced coal tar as a by-product of the use of coal in reducing iron.

Britain was, of course, the greatest textile and steel manufacturing country in the world, but British manufacturers turned a deaf ear to Perkin. They imported dyes from all over: indigo from the Far East, alizarin red from madder root, scarlets from cochineal and tin solutions. Germany, on the other hand, had coal but, having entered the race for colonies late, no access to the world's dyestuffs. Perkin turned to the German capitalists, and in so doing helped lay the foundation for the long German supremacy in the chemical industries. By the turn of the century, the six largest German chemical works employed more than 650 chemists and engineers, while the entire British coal tar industry had no more than thirty or forty.[12]* Thus at a time when British and American

---

* James B. Conant tells this story: "At the time of our entry into World War I, a representative of the American Chemical Society called on the Secretary of War, Newton Baker, and offered the service of the chemists in the conflict. He was thanked

industry used university-trained scientists only sporadically, for help on specific problems, the German capitalist class had already created that total and integrated effort which organized, in the universities, industrial laboratories, professional societies and trade associations, and in government-sponsored research a continuous scientific-technological effort as the new basis for modern industry. This was soon recognized by the more far sighted economists of that day (notably by Marshall and Veblen). Henry L. Gantt, after Taylor probably the foremost advocate and practitioner of scientific management of his time, wrote in 1910:

> It is an economic law that large profits can be permanently assured only by efficient operation. . . . The supreme importance of efficiency as an economic factor was first realized by the Germans, and it is this fact that has enabled them to advance their industrial condition, which twenty years ago was a jest, to the first place in Europe, if not in the world. We naturally want to know in detail the methods they have used; and the reply is that they have recognized the value of the scientifically trained engineer as an economic factor.
>
> In the United States, superb natural resources have enabled us to make phenomenal progress without much regard to the teachings of science, and in many cases in spite of our neglect of them. The progress of Germany warns us that we have now reached the point where we must recognize that the proper application of science to industry is of vital importance to the future prosperity of this country. . . . Our universities and schools of higher learning are still dominated by those whose training was largely literary or classical, and they utterly fail to realize the difference between a *classical* and an *industrial* age. This difference is not sentimental, but real; for that nation which is industrially most efficient will soon become the richest and most powerful.[14]

Thus, early in the era of monopoly capitalism, the borrowings from Germany left a trail through American higher education and industry. It was not only the brewing industry which imported scientifically trained specialists (in its case brewmasters) from Germany: Carnegie put a German chemist to work at the start of the 1870s and in part through his efforts dispelled much of the uncertainty that had previously surrounded the manufacture of pig iron; and General Electric enlisted C. P. Steinmetz, the German physicist, chiefly to help design alternating current equipment.[15]

The corporate research laboratories of the United States begin more or less with the beginnings of the era of monopoly capitalism. The first research organization established for the specific purpose of systematic invention was set up by Thomas Edison at Menlo Park, New Jersey, in 1876, and the first

---

and asked to come back the next day. On so doing, he was told by the Secretary of War that while he appreciated the offer of the chemists, he found that it was unnecessary as he had looked into the matter and found the War Department already had *a* chemist."[13]

government laboratories were established by the Department of Agriculture under the Hatch Act of 1887. Arthur D. Little began his independent research laboratory in 1886. These were the forerunners of the corporate research organizations: Eastman Kodak (1893), B. F. Goodrich (1895), and most important, General Electric (1900). General Motors did a great deal of its research through Charles F. Kettering's Dayton Engineering Laboratories Company (DELCO), organized in 1909, and acquired by GM in 1919, although at the same time the corporation set up other laboratories, such as the one organized for it by the Arthur D. Little Company in 1911 to do materials testings and analysis; in 1920, all GM research activities were combined to form the General Motors Research Corporation at Moraine, Ohio. Frank B. Jewett began research for Bell Telephone Laboratories in 1904. The Westinghouse Research Laboratories were begun in Pittsburgh in 1917. By 1920 there were perhaps 300 such corporate laboratories, and by 1940, over 2,200. By then, corporations with a tangible net worth of over $100 million averaged research staffs of 170, and those with a net worth exceeding a billion dollars averaged research staffs of 1,250. The Bell Telephone laboratories, employing over 5,000, was by far the largest research organization in the world.[16]

Along with these research laboratories came the increase of scientific and engineering education in new or expanded university departments in the physical sciences, through learned journals and societies, and at trade association research facilities, as well as a growing government role in research. For a long time, however, imitation of the German example was imitation of manner rather than matter. The tradition of a thin and facile empiricism did not offer favorable soil for the development of basic science, and the corporate magnates, still impatient of free and undirected research and anxious for nuts-and-bolts engineering innovations, hardly bothered to conceal beneath their new commitment to science a contempt for its most fundamental forms. The most important of the corporate research laboratories, that organized by General Electric at Schenectady eight years after the merger of Edison General Electric and Thomson-Houston, was typical in this regard. "It was soon recognized by the directors of this new company that the amount of technological development which could be drawn out of the scientific knowledge already accumulated, though large, was finite and that there would be a greater chance of ingenious developments if there were more science to work with."[17] But the directors of the new company, and those of many others as well, were slow to understand the importance of the work of such pioneer scientists in the United States as Willard Gibbs, who helped establish a basis for physical chemistry by his use of thermodynamics in the study of chemical reactions. The general characteristic of the work required of scientists in these corporate laboratories remained Edisonian, with the modification that in place of Edison's laborious trial and error, scientific calculation was to lead to quicker solutions. Thus General Electric put Irving Langmuir to work studying the effect of various gases in lamp bulbs on the radiation of thermal energy from the filament, and on the rate of evaporation of the filament material.[18] In other corporate laboratories, particularly those of the automotive industry, interest in "science" was confined to trouble-shooting (gear noise, vibration, etc.) and product engineering (transmission fluids, paints, fuels, compression problems, etc.). The guiding principle seems to have been almost entirely fast payoff; it was this motivation which led to the disaster of the early 1920s when the entire operating force of several divisions of General Motors awaited, from day to day, the outcome of Kettering's attempts to get his so-called copper-cooled (air-cooled) engine ready for production.

It was not until the rise of Nazism in Germany and World War II, as a result of which a great deal of scientific talent was either driven from Germany by Hitler's racial and political policies or was appropriated by the victorious allies, that the United States acquired a scientific base equal to its industrial power, which had prior to this development depended largely upon the engineering exploitation of foreign science. Thus it has been only since World War II that scientific research in the United States, heavily financed by corporations and government, and buttressed by further drafts of scientific talent from all over the world, has systematically furnished the scientific knowledge utilized in industry.*

By the last quarter of the nineteenth century, what Landes called "the exhaustion of the technological possibilities of the Industrial Revolution" had set in.[20] The new scientific-technical revolution which replenished the stock of technological possibilities had a conscious and purposive character largely absent from the old. In place of spontaneous innovation indirectly evoked by the social processes of production came the planned progress of technology and product design. This was accomplished by means of the transformation of science itself into a commodity bought and sold like the other implements and labors of production. From an "external economy," scientific knowledge has become a balance-sheet item.[21] Like all commodities, its supply is called forth by demand, with the result that the development of materials, power sources, and processes has become less fortuitous and more responsive to the immediate needs of capital. The scientific-technical revolution, for this reason, cannot be understood in terms of specific innovations—as in the case of the Industrial Revolution, which may be adequately characterized by a handful of key

---

* As spending for research and development has grown, a characteristic pattern of financing and control has appeared. Most such research is financed by federal expenditures and controlled by private industry. Thus in the early 1960s, three-fourths of such research, concentrated chiefly in the areas of engineering and the physical sciences, was carried on by corporations, while the federal government paid for some three-fifths of the cost directly and most of the rest indirectly, through tax write-offs.[19]

inventions—but must be understood rather in its totality as a mode of production into which science and exhaustive engineering investigations have been integrated as part of ordinary functioning. The key innovation is not to be found in chemistry, electronics, automatic machinery, aeronautics, atomic physics, or any of the products of these science-technologies, but rather in the transformation of science itself into capital.*

Notes

1. Karl Marx, *Capital*, vol. I (Moscow, n.d.), pp. 456-57.
2. David S. Landes, *The Unbound Prometheus: Technological Change and Industrial Development in Western Europe from 1750 to the Present* (Cambridge and New York, 1969), p. 61.
3. Robert B. Lindsay, *The Role of Science in Civilization* (New York and London, 1963), pp. 209-10.
4. Ibid.
5. Landes, *The Unbound Prometheus*, p. 104.
6. Bernard Barber, *Science and the Social Order* (Glencoe, Ill., 1952), p. 69.
7. P. W. Musgrave, *Technical Change, the Labour Force and Education: A Study of the British and German Iron and Steel Industries, 1860-1964* (London and New York, 1967), p. 45. See especially the chapter entitled "The Roots of Germany's Advantage."
8. Ibid., pp. 62 *et seq.*
9. Ibid., pp. 50-51.
10. Richard Sasuly, *IG Farben* (New York, 1947), p. 19.
11. J. D. Bernal, *Science in History* (1954; revised ed., London, 1957), p. 381.
12. Sasuly, *IG Farben*, p. 25.
13. James B. Conant, *Modern Science and Modern Man* (New York, 1952), p. 9.
14. H. L. Gantt, *Work, Wages, and Profits* (New York, 1910), pp. 179-80.
15. Edward C. Kirkland, *Industry Comes of Age; Business, Labor, and Public Policy, 1860-1897* (New York, 1962), pp. 175-77.
16. Lindsay, *The Role of Science in Civilization*, pp. 215-22; Barber, *Science and the Social Order*, pp. 157 *et seq.*; Spencer Klaw, *The New Brahmins: Scientific Life in America* (New York, 1968), pp. 169-70; Leonard Silk, *The Research*

---

* A pamphlet published in 1957 by the New York Stock Exchange firm of Modell, Roland, and Stone under the title "The Scientific-Industrial Revolution" notes that while the steam engine was the prime mover of the Industrial Revolution, no single innovation of recent times occupies the same position. The advances made in a large number of fields "are tightly interrelated in a veritable seamless web of technological change," so as to constitute "mere branches of one master technology" based upon an "elaborate apparatus of scientific research and testing." "Science," it concludes, "is the 'steam engine' we have been seeking, and the collective scientist is the master technologist."

Revolution (New York, Toronto and London, 1960), p. 54; Alfred P. Sloan, Jr., *My Years With General Motors* (New York, 1965), pp. 248-50.

17. Lindsay, ibid., p. 216.
18. Ibid., pp. 216-17.
19. National Commission on Technology, Automation, and Economic Progress, *The Employment Impact of Technological Change*, Appendix Volume II, *Technology and the American Economy* (Washington, D.C., 1966), pp. 109-19, esp. Table 8, p. 112.
20. Landes, *The Unbound Prometheus*, p. 237.
21. See Shigeto Tsuru, "Marx and the Analysis of Capitalism," in *Marx and Contemporary Scientific Thought* (The Hague and Paris, 1969), pp. 322-30.

Chapter 8

The Scientific-Technical Revolution and the Worker

"In manufacture," wrote Marx, referring to the hand workshops that preceded the Industrial Revolution, "the revolution in the mode of production begins with the labour-power, in modern industry it begins with the instruments of labour."[1] In other words, in the first stage of capitalism the traditional work of the craftsman is subdivided into its constituent tasks and performed in series by a chain of detail workers, so that the process is little changed; what has changed is the *organization of labor*. But in the next stage, machinofacture, the instrument of labor is removed from the worker's hand and placed in the grip of a mechanism and the forces of nature are enlisted to supply power which, transmitted to the tool, acts upon the materials to yield the desired result; thus the change in the mode of production in this case comes from a change in the *instruments of labor*.

To the next question—how is the labor process transformed by the scientific-technical revolution?—no such unitary answer may be given. This is because the scientific and managerial attack upon the labor process over the past century embraces all its aspects: labor power, the instruments of labor, the materials of labor, and the products of labor. We have seen how labor is reorganized and subdivided according to rigorous principles which were only anticipated a century ago. The materials used in production are now so freely synthesized, adapted, and substituted according to need that an increasing number of industries practice substantially altered manufacturing processes as a result of this fact alone. The instruments used in production, including those used in transport and communications, have been revolutionized not only in respect to the power, speed, and accuracy with which they accomplish their tasks, but often act to gain the desired result by way of entirely different physical principles from those traditionally employed. And the products of production have themselves been freely transformed and invented in accordance with marketing and manufacturing needs. Taking nothing for granted and nothing as permanent, modern production constantly overhauls all aspects of its performance, and in some industries has completely reconstituted itself more than once in the space of a hundred years. Thus modern electronic circuitry, to cite only a single example, would be completely incomprehensible in its mode of operation, in the manner of its production, and even in the very materials used, to those who, only a couple of generations ago, designed and made the first examples of this genre.

Insofar as these changes have been governed by manufacturing rather than marketing considerations (and the two are by no means independent), they have been brought about by the drive for greater productivity: that is, the effort to find ways to incorporate ever smaller quantities of labor time into ever greater quantities of product. This leads to faster and more efficient methods and machinery. But in the capitalist mode of production, new methods and new machinery are incorporated within a management effort to dissolve the labor process as a process conducted by the worker and reconstitute it as a process conducted by management. In the first form of the division of labor, the capitalist disassembles the craft and returns it to the workers piecemeal, so that the process as a whole is no longer the province of any individual worker. Then, as we have seen, the capitalist conducts an analysis of each of the tasks distributed among the workers, with an eye toward getting a grip on the individual operations. It is in the age of the scientific-technical revolution that management sets itself the problem of grasping the process as a whole and controlling every element of it, without exception. "Improving the system of management," wrote H. L. Gantt, "means the elimination of elements of chance or accident, and the accomplishment of all the ends desired in accordance with knowledge derived from a scientific investigation of everything down to the smallest detail of labor. . . ."[2] And it is the scientific-technical revolution which furnishes the means for the partial realization of this theoretical ideal.

Thus, after a million years of labor, during which humans created not only a complex social culture but in a very real sense created themselves as well, the very cultural-biological trait upon which this entire evolution is founded has been brought, within the last two hundred years, to a crisis, a crisis which Marcuse aptly calls the threat of a "catastrophe of the human essence."[3] The unity of thought and action, conception and execution, hand and mind, which capitalism threatened from its beginnings, is now attacked by a systematic dissolution employing all the resources of science and the various engineering disciplines based upon it. The subjective factor of the labor process is removed to a place among its inanimate objective factors. To the materials and instruments of production are added a "labor force," another "factor of production," and the process is henceforth carried on by management as the sole subjective element.* This is the ideal toward which management tends, and in pursuit of which it uses and shapes every productive innovation furnished by science.

---

* When the conditions are fully realized through an automatic machine system, wrote Marx in the *Grundrisse der Kritik der politischen Ökonomie*, then: "The production process has ceased to be a labour process in the sense of a process dominated by

This displacement of labor as the subjective element of the process, and its subordination as an objective element in a productive process now conducted by management, is an ideal realized by capital only within definite limits, and unevenly among industries. The principle is itself restrained in its application by the nature of the various specific and determinate processes of production. Moreover, its very application brings into being new crafts and skills and technical specialties which are at first the province of labor rather than management. Thus in industry all forms of labor coexist: the craft, the hand or machine detail worker, the automatic machine or flow process. But far more important than this relative restraint on the operation of the principle is the resulting continual shifting of employment. The very success of management in increasing productivity in some industries leads to the displacement of labor into other fields, where it accumulates in large quantities because the processes employed have not yet been subjected—and in some cases cannot be subjected to the same degree—to the mechanizing tendency of modern industry. The result therefore is not the *elimination* of labor, but its *displacement* to other occupations and industries, a matter which will be discussed more fully in later chapters.

The reduction of the worker to the level of an instrument in the production process is by no means exclusively associated with machinery. We must also note the attempt, either in the absence of machinery or in conjunction with individually operated machines, *to treat the workers themselves as machines.* This aspect of scientific management was developed by Taylor's immediate successors.

Taylor popularized time study as part of his effort to gain control over the job. Time study may be defined as the measurement of elapsed time for each component operation of a work process; its prime instrument is the stopwatch, calibrated in fractions of an hour, minute, or second. But this kind of time study was found too gross to satisfy the increasingly demanding standards pursued by managers and their engineers. From their point of view, Taylor's approach had two major defects. First, the various activities of labor could by this means be analyzed only in their actual daily practice, and in relatively gross increments. And second, the method remained tied to particular forms of concrete

labour as its governing unity."[4] The *Grundrisse* consists of monographs written by Marx for his own clarification and served as a preparatory manuscript for *Capital*. Here Marx allowed himself to speculate further, to revolve his subject under his eye more freely, than in the writings he prepared for publication. The sections on labor and production are thus extraordinarily interesting, although substantially everything in them appears in a more fully worked out and final form in *Capital*; the bold formulation quoted above is one of the more suggestive remarks which did not find a place, to my knowledge, in the writings he published.

labor. In other words, the universality of the approach Taylor had taken was not matched by an equally universal methodology.

A new line of development was opened by Frank B. Gilbreth, one of Taylor's most prominent followers. He added to time study the concept of motion study: that is, the investigation and classification of the basic motions of the body, regardless of the particular and concrete form of the labor in which these motions are used. In *motion and time study*, the elementary movements were visualized as the building blocks of every work activity; they were called, in a variant of Gilbreth's name spelled backward, *therbligs*. To the stopwatch were added the chronocyclegraph (a photograph of the workplace with motion paths superimposed), stroboscopic pictures (made by keeping the camera lens open to show changing positions assumed by the worker), and the motion picture; these were to be supplemented by more advanced means. In its first form, motion study catalogs the various movements of the body as standard data, with the aim of determining time requirements and making the procedure "primarily a statistical problem rather than a problem of observation and measurement of particular workers."[5]

Therblig charts used by industrial engineers, work designers, and office managers give to each motion a name, a symbol, a color code, and a time in ten-thousandths of a minute. The basic motion symbols are given in a recent textbook by the chairman of the Industrial Engineering Division at the University of Wisconsin as follows:[6]

G	Grasp	UD	Unavoidable Delay
RL	Release Load	AD	Avoidable Delay
P	Position	H	Hold
PP	Pre-position	R	Rest
A	Assemble	PN	Plan
DA	Disassemble	I	Inspect
U	Use	W	Walk
SH	Search	B	Bending
ST	Select	SI	Sit
TL	Transport Loaded	SD	Stand Up
TE	Transport Empty	K	Kneel

Each of these motions is described in machine terms. For example, *Bending*, we are told, is "trunk movement with hips as hinge." These defined motions are in fact classifications of motion types, for each is in turn broken down into finer motion types. Thus G, *Grasp*, has four basic subclassifications:

G1 *Contact Grasp* (pick up wafer by touching with fingertip).
G2 *Pinch Grasp* (thumb opposes finger).
G3 *Wrap Grasp* (hand wraps around).
G4 *Regrasp* (shift object to gain new control).

Transport Empty is further defined according to the distance the hand must extend, and *Transport Loaded* is broken down not only according to distance but also to the weight of the load. To pick up a pencil, therefore, would involve the proper categories of *Transport Empty, Pinch Grasp,* and *Transport Loaded,* each with a standard time value, and the sum of the time categories for these three therbligs, given in ten-thousandths of a minute, constitutes the time for the complete motion.

The combination of motions required to perform each operation is worked out on a therblig chart: "The therblig chart (Therb CH) is the *detailed* symbolic and systematic presentation of the method of work performed by the body members."[7] As a rule, the therblig chart is a two-column affair, representing separately the activities of each hand, whether in motion or at rest, during any part of the time sequence.

The therblig was only the first of a series of standard data systems, which are now constructed by many large corporations for their internal use (see Chapter 15, "Clerical Workers"), or provided by research organizations. Of these various systems of "predetermined work time," the most popular is Methods-Time Measurement, put out by the MTM Association for Standards and Research in Ann Arbor, Michigan. This association publishes "Application Data" in booklet form.* In this system, the time standard used is the TMU, which is defined as one hundred-thousandth of an hour, equal to six ten-thousandths of a minute or thirty-six thousandths of a second. It offers refinements of the therblig to apply to many conditions. *Reach,* for instance, is tabulated separately for objects in fixed or varying locations, for objects jumbled with others, for very small objects, and so forth, and for distances varying from three-fourths of an inch up to thirty inches. For example, to reach a single object the location of which may vary slightly from cycle to cycle, twenty inches away, consumes according to the MTM chart 18.6 TMU, or .6696 second (not, we ask the reader to note, two-thirds of a second, which would be .6666 second; a difference which, in an operation repeated a thousand times a day, would add up to three seconds).

Move is defined for objects from 2.5 to 47.5 lbs.: to either hand or against stop; to approximate or indefinite location; to exact location.

Turn and apply pressure is given for pressures up to 35 lbs., and for vectors of 30 degrees to 180 degrees, in increments of 15 degrees.

Position: loosely, closely, or exactly; for easy-to-handle and difficult-to-handle objects (its opposite, *Disengage,* is also given for the same conditions).

---

* The front cover of the booklet bears the boxed legend: "Do not attempt to use this chart or apply Methods-Time Measurement in any way unless you understand the proper application of the data. This statement is included as a word of caution to prevent difficulties resulting from misapplication of the data."

Release is given not only for normal release (by opening fingers), but for contact release (releasing typewriter key).

Body, leg, and foot motions are set forth for the various movements of Bend, Sit, Stop, Walk, etc., for varying distances. And finally, a formula is given for Eye Travel Time:

$$ET = 15.2 \times \frac{T}{D} \, TMU$$

with a maximum of 20 TMU. Eye Focus is defined as occupying 7.3 TMU.*

More recent research has attempted to overcome the defects inherent in standard data, which, in breaking down motions into elementary components, neglect the factors of velocity and acceleration in human motions—motions which take place as a flow rather than as a series of disjunctive movements. Efforts have been made to find a means of gaining a continuous, uninterrupted view of human motion, and to measure it on that basis. In the course of this research, the use of radar, accelerometers, photoelectric waves, air pressure, magnetic fields, capacitive effects, motion pictures, radioactivity, etc., have been investigated, and in the end, sound waves, using the Doppler shift, have been chosen as the most suitable. An inaudible sound source (20,000 cycles per second) given off by a transducer is attached to the body member under consideration. Three microphones, each ten feet from an assumed one cubic yard of work area, are placed in such a way that each represents one of the three spatial dimensions, and they pick up the increased or decreased number of cycles per second as the sound source moves toward or away from each of them. These changes in cycles are converted into changes in voltage, the output of which is therefore proportional to the velocity of motion. The three veloci-ties are recorded on magnetic tape (or plotted on oscillographic paper) and can then be combined into a total velocity by vector summation. Total acceleration and total distance can be derived, and can then be handled mathematically, and by computer, for analysis and prediction. This device goes by the name Universal Operator Performance Analyzer and Recorder (UNOPAR), and is said to be, if nothing else, an excellent timing device accurate to .000066 minutes, though not to be compared in this respect to electronic timing devices, which are accurate to a millionth of a second. (But these last, we are told ruefully, are useful only for experimental purposes, and not in the workplace.)[9]

Physiological models are also used for the measurement of energy expen-diture, for which oxygen consumption and heart rate are the most usual indicators; these are charted by means of oxygen-supply measuring devices

---

* These last are instances of the charting approach to human sensory activity, visual, auditory, and tactile, which have been developed since the early 1950s and which aim at comprehending a larger range of work activities outside the purely manual, in order to apply them not only to clerical work but also to professional and semi-profes-sional specialties.[8]

and electrocardiograms. Forces applied by the body (as well as to it) are measured on a force platform, using piezo-electric crystals in the mountings. In another variant, we read, in an article entitled "The Quantification of Human Effort and Motion for the Upper Limbs," about a framework called "the exoskeletal kinematometer," which is described as "a device which mounts *externally* upon the human subject for the purpose of *measuring* the *kinematic* characteristics of his limbs during the performance of a task."[10] The measurement of eye movements is done through photographic techniques and also by electro-oculography, which uses electrodes placed near the eye.

The data derived from all these systems, from the crudest to the most refined, are used as the basis for engineering the "human factor" in work design. Since the accumulation of data does away with the need to time each operation, management is spared the friction that arises in such a procedure, and the worker is spared the knowledge that the motions, time, and labor cost for his or her job have been precalculated, with "humane" allowances for rest, toilet, and coffee time, before anyone was hired and perhaps even before the building was erected.* By eliminating the need for repeated experiments, they make available to any user, at low cost, figures which may be combined and recombined in any desired fashion, merely by the use of pencil and paper, to bring into being predetermined time standards for any engineering or office purpose. The time values of given motion patterns are respected in management circles as "objective" and "scientific," and bear the authority such values are presumed to carry. In recent years, motion-time study or therblig systems have had their logic and arithmetic assigned to computers, so that the time allowance for various job elements is worked out by the computer on the basis of standard data, perhaps supplemented by time study observations.**

---

* A management team with the Dickensian name of Payne and Swett see in this the very first advantage of standard data: its "favorable impact on employee relations," which is their euphemism for the above.[11]

** This was the mode used by the General Motors Assembly Division in its reorganization, begun in 1968, of the jobs of both clerical and production workers, in which the number of jobs was reduced and the number of operations assigned to each worker was increased, the number of repair or inspection workers reduced, and the number of supervisors to enforce the new standards was increased. It was this reorganization which led to the 1972 strikes in the General Motors plants at Norwood, Ohio, lasting 174 days, and Lordstown, Ohio, lasting three weeks (although the Lordstown strike got all the journalistic attention because it was attributed largely to the youthful composition of the work force at that plant, while the Norwood strike was susceptible of no such interpretation).[12] A vice-president of General Motors pointed out that in ten plant reorganizations conducted by the General Motors Assembly Division after 1968, eight of them produced strikes. "I'm not boasting," he added, "I'm just relating relevant history."[13]

The animating principle of all such work investigations is the view of human beings in machine terms. Since management is not interested in the person of the worker, but in the worker as he or she is used in office, factory, warehouse, store, or transport processes, this view is from the management point of view not only eminently rational but the basis of all calculation. The human being is here regarded as a mechanism articulated by hinges, ball-and-socket joints, etc. Thus an article in the *British Journal of Psychiatry* aptly entitled "Theory of the Human Operator in Control Systems" says: ". . . as an element in a control system, a man may be regarded as a chain consisting of the following items: (1) sensory devices . . . (2) a computing system which responds . . . on the basis of previous experience . . . (3) an amplifying system—the motor-nerve endings and muscles . . . (4) mechanical linkages . . . whereby the muscular work produces externally observable effects."[14] In this we see not merely the terms of a machine analogy used for experimental purposes, nor merely a teaching metaphor or didactic device, but in the context of the capitalist mode of production the operating theory by which people of one class set into motion people of another class. It is the reductive formula that expresses both how capital employs labor and what it makes of humanity.

This attempt to conceive of the worker as a general-purpose machine operated by management is one of many paths taken toward the same goal: the displacement of labor as the subjective element of the labor process and its transformation into an object. Here the entire work operation, down to its smallest motion, is conceptualized by the management and engineering staffs, laid out, measured, fitted with training and performance standards—all entirely in advance. The human instruments are adapted to the machinery of production according to specifications that resemble nothing so much as machine-capacity specifications. Just as the engineer knows the rated revolutions per minute, electrical current demand, lubrication requirements, etc. of a motor according to a manufacturer's specification sheet, he tries to know the motions-of-a-given-variety of the human operator from standard data. In the system as a whole little is left to chance, just as in a machine the motion of the components is rigidly governed; results are precalculated before the system has been set in motion. In this, the manager counts not only upon the physiological characteristics of the human body as codified in his data, but also upon the tendency of the cooperative working mass, of which each worker is, along with the machines, one of the limbs, to enforce upon the individual the average pace upon which his calculations are based.*

---

* This is a description of a "theoretical ideal" system from management's point of view, and not an attempt to describe the actual course of events. We are here omitting for the moment the fact that workers are rebellious, and that the average pace of production is decided in a practice which largely assumes the form of a struggle, whether organized or not. Thus the machinery operated by management has internal frictions,

It is, finally, worthy of note that in management's eyes as well as in the practice it dictates, the more labor is governed by classified motions which extend across the boundaries of trades and occupations, the more it dissolves its concrete forms into the general types of work motions. This mechanical exercise of human faculties according to motion types which are studied independently of the particular kind of work being done, brings to life the Marxist conception of "abstract labor." We see that this abstraction from the concrete forms of labor—the simple "expenditure of human labor in general," in Marx's phrase—which Marx employed as a means of clarifying the value of commodities (according to the share of such general human labor they embodied), is not something that exists only in the pages of the first chapter of *Capital*, but exists as well in the mind of the capitalist, the manager, the industrial engineer. It is precisely their effort and métier to visualize labor not as a total human endeavor, but to abstract from all its concrete qualities in order to comprehend it as universal and endlessly repeated motions, the sum of which, when merged with the other things that capital buys—machines, materials, etc.—results in the production of a larger sum of capital than that which was "invested" at the outset of the process. Labor in the form of standardized motion patterns is labor used as an interchangeable part, and in this form comes ever closer to corresponding, in life, to the abstraction employed by Marx in analysis of the capitalist mode of production.

---

and this is true of human machinery as well as mechanical. The problem as it presents itself to management is well summarized by James R. Bright of the Harvard Business School: "Meanwhile, refinement toward mechanical ends has gone on—or has attempted to go on—with people. Many past efforts to gain precision in manufacturing have been to subdivide and apportion human effort to minute parts of the task and thus to increase reliability by facilitating machine-like action. Managers and engineers have tried to obtain this by arbitrary rule of quotas and standard tasks, by mechanistic devices such as the indexing machine or pacing by conveyor, and by motivating devices such as incentive systems, profit-sharing plans, or even music in the shop. In the abstract, these are nothing more than efforts to constrain people to perform consistently in the desired manner at points on the production line where machines are not available or not economical. In other words, this is 'force-closure' applied to the human element of the manufacturing system. The attempt has been to create timed, predictable, consistent production action on the part of human beings. Yet, such an approach inevitably must be short of perfection. As links or 'resistant bodies' in the supermachine, human beings are not mechanically reliable. They do not consistently 'respond in the desired manner,' nor can they be constrained to do so. . . . Thinking of the factory in these terms enables one to appreciate why the so-called automatic factory is far from automatic: only a portion of the economic task of the factory has been adequately constrained. People are needed to fill in many of the gaps in mechanization and to provide control on levels as yet beyond mechanical or economic feasibility."[15]

Notes

1. Karl Marx, *Capital*, vol. I (Moscow, n.d.), p. 351.
2. H. L. Gantt, *Work, Wages, and Profits* (New York, 1910), p. 29.
3. Herbert Marcuse, "Neue Quellen zur Grundlegung des historischen Materialismus," in *Philosophie und Revolution: Aufsätze von Herbert Marcuse* (Berlin, 1967), pp. 96-97; quoted by Bruce Brown, *Marx, Freud and the Critique of Everyday Life* (New York and London, 1973), p. 14.
4. Karl Marx, *Grundrisse: Foundation of the Critique of Political Economy* (London and New York, 1973), p. 693.
5. William Foote Whyte, *Money and Motivation* (New York, 1955), p. 203.
6. Gerald Nadler, *Work Design* (Homewood, Ill., 1963), see pp. 298-308.
7. Ibid., P. 290.
8. Ibid., pp. 348-51.
9. Ibid., chapters 18 and 19.
10. J. D. Ramsey, "The Quantification of Human Effort and Motion for the Upper Limbs," *International Journal of Production Research*, vol. 7, no. 1 (1968).
11. Bruce Payne and David D. Swett, *Office Operations Improvement* (American Management Association, Inc., New York, 1967), p. 28.
12. *Wall Street Journal*, December 6, 1972.
13. Emma Rothschild, *Paradise Lost: The Decline of the Auto-Industrial Age* (New York, 1973), pp. 121-22.
14. K. J. W. Kraik, *British Journal of Psychiatry*, vol. XXXVIII, pp. 56-61, 142-48; quoted in Nadler, *Work Design*, p. 371.
15. James R. Bright, *Automation and Management* (Boston, 1958), pp. 16-17.

Chapter 9

Machinery

Machines may be defined, classified, and studied in their evolution according to any criteria one wishes to select: their motive power, their complexity, their use of physical principles, etc. But one is forced at the outset to choose between two essentially different modes of thought. The first is the engineering approach, which views technology primarily in its internal connections and tends to define the machine in relation to itself, as a technical fact. The other is the social approach, which views technology in its connections with humanity and defines the machine in relation to human labor, and as a social artifact.

As an illustration of the first approach, we may take the work of Abbott Payson Usher. In *A History of Mechanical Inventions*, Usher began with the nineteenth-century classifiers, Robert Willis and Franz Reuleaux, whose definitions he quotes. First from Willis:

> Every machine will be found to consist of a train of pieces connected together in various ways, so that if one be made to move, they all receive a motion, the relation of which to that of the first is governed by the nature of the connection.

And Reuleaux:

> A machine is a combination of resistant bodies so arranged that by their means the mechanical forces of nature can be compelled to do work accompanied by certain determinate motions.

Following this approach, Usher himself describes the evolution of machinery in the following way:

> The parts of the machine are more and more elaborately connected so that the possibility of any but the desired motion is progressively eliminated. As the process of constraint becomes more complete, the machine becomes more perfect mechanically. . . . Such a transformation results in the complete and continuous control of motion. . . . The completeness of the constraint of motion becomes in Reuleaux's analysis the criterion of mechanical perfection. Loosely adjusted and ill-controlled machines are supplanted by closely adjusted machines that can be controlled minutely.[1]

From a technical standpoint, the value of such a definition is apparent. The precision of the mechanism, and the degree of its automatic or self-acting character, are determined by the success of the designer in eliminating "any but the desired motion" and achieving "the complete and continuous control of motion."* But what is missing from this definition, or present only by implication, is a view of machinery in relation to the labor process and to the worker. We may contrast the approach taken by Marx, who singles out from among a great many possible criteria this very aspect of machinery:

> The machine proper is therefore a mechanism that, after being set in motion, performs with its tools the same operations that were formerly done by the workman with similar tools. Whether the motive power is derived from man, or from some other machine, makes no difference in this respect. From the moment that the tool proper is taken from man, and fitted into a mechanism, a machine takes the place of a mere implement. The difference strikes one at once, even in those cases where man himself continues to be the prime mover.[2]

This initial step, removing the tool from the hands of the worker and fitting it into a mechanism, is for Marx the starting point of that evolution which begins with simple machinery and continues to the automatic system of machinery. Like all starting points in Marx, it is not fortuitous. Marx selects from among a host of technical characteristics the specific feature which forms the juncture between humanity and the machine: its effect upon the labor process. The technical is never considered purely in its internal relations, but in relation to the worker.**

The analysis of the machine by means of purely technical characteristics, such as its power source, the scientific principles it employs, etc., may yield much information of value to engineers, but this study of the machine "in itself" has little direct value for a comprehension of its social role. The moment we begin to assess its evolution from the point of view of the labor process,

---

* This same definition is often used by management analysis as an overall picture of the workplace, for which they recommend the development of constraint and the elimination of all but the desired motion; and this definition may be, as we have seen, applied to the workers themselves as *they* are subjected to criteria of mechanical perfection.

** In engineering literature, by contrast, the worker tends to disappear, which accounts for the fact that this literature is written almost entirely in the awkward grammar of the passive voice, in which operations seem to perform themselves, without human agency.

It is also worth noting that Usher, when he wishes to quote from Marx a "definition" of machinery, seizes upon a descriptive passage where Marx, before tackling the analysis of machinery, indicates that "fully developed machinery consists of three essentially different parts, the motor mechanism, the transmitting mechanism, and finally the tool or working machine."[3] It is typical of the engineering mind that it is drawn by this, the technical description, while that which for the labor process is truly definitive escapes attention.

however, its technical characteristics group themselves around this axis and lines of development begin to emerge. Such a "critical history of technology," which Marx noted had not been written in his day, is no more in evidence in ours. But if it existed it would furnish the basis for a taxonomy of machines as they are used in production, as well as a classification according to the technical features that are utilized by capital as the basis for the organization and control of labor.

Some sociologists have attempted to sketch broad "production systems" or "varieties of technology." Joan Woodward has divided production into the making of "integral products" (in single units, small batches, large batches, and by mass production); "dimensional products" (in batches and by continuous flow processes, as in chemical plants); and "combined systems" (in which standardized components are made in large batches and subsequently assembled in a continuous flow process, or, conversely, a flow process is used to prepare a product which is subsequently broken down into smaller units for packaging and sale).[4] Robert Blauner divides production technologies into four varieties: craft, machine tending, assembly line, and continuous process.[5] As distinguished from these scattergun approaches, James R. Bright of the Graduate School of Business Administration at Harvard has taken a much closer look at the characteristics of machines in association with labor.[6] He has outlined a "mechanization profile" of seventeen levels (to be described more fully later in this chapter), which he applies to a large number of production processes and to the way they utilize varying levels of mechanization as they take their course from start to finish. The "degrees of mechanical accomplishment in machinery" are judged on the basis of the question: "In what way does a machine supplement man's muscles, mental processes, judgment, and degree of control?"[7] Bright comments (in 1966): "To my knowledge, this is still the only theory interlinking machine evolution and worker contribution."[8] It is worthy of note that just as Bright has apparently been alone in the academic world in this kind of detailed study of what machines actually do as they become more automatic, and what the worker is called upon to know and to do, so also are his conclusions strikingly different from those who let themselves be guided only by vague impressions.

From this point of view, the key element in the evolution of machinery is not its size, complexity, or speed of operation, but the manner in which its operations are controlled. Between the first typewriter and the electrically driven ball-type machine of the present there lies a whole epoch of mechanical development, but nothing that has been changed affects the manner in which the typewriter is guided through its activities and hence there is little essential difference in the relation between typist and machine. The labor process remains more or less as it was, despite all refinements. The application of power to various hand tools such as drills, saws, grindstones, wrenches, chisels, rivet hammers, staplers, sanders, buffers, etc. has not changed the relation between worker and machine—for all that they belong to a recent branch of machinery because they had to wait upon the development of specialized electrical or pneumatic power systems before they became possible. In all these forms, the guidance of the tool remains entirely in the hands of the worker, whatever other properties or capacities may have been added.

It is only when the tool and/or the work are given a fixed motion path by the structure of the machine itself that machinery in the modern sense begins to develop. The drill press, the lathe fitted with a slide rest, and the sewing or knitting machine all move cutting tools or needles along grooves cut into the machine frame or parts. The grindstone turns in a path determined by its axle and bearings; the moving blade of the shears descends, and the head of the trip-hammer or piledriver falls in accord with the structure of each device.

But this is only the first step in the development of machinery. The laying-down of these fixed motion paths opens the way for further control of the motion of the tool or the work, by internal gearing, cams, etc. At first, as Bright points out, this takes the form of a fixed or single cycle. The cutting tool of a lathe, for instance, or the bit of a drill press, may be connected to the power source in such a way that when the connection is locked the tool will be brought against the work at a fixed rate of approach and to a predetermined depth, after which it will retract to its original position. This single cycle may also be a repeated one, as in the case of the planer which draws the full length of the work against the cutting tool, removes a shaving from the surface, and returns to repeat the process; the cutting tool is meanwhile shifted so that the next shaving may be removed, and this continues without outside intervention until the entire surface has been planed.

Once this type of cycle has been mastered, it is only a further mechanical step to the construction of multiple function machines in which the mechanism indexes its way, according to a preset pattern, through a sequence of operations. This is the principle of the automatic turret lathe, which carries its series of tools in a turret that revolves to the next tool as the previous one completes its cycle. In such machines the sequence of operations is either built once and for all into the mechanism and cannot be altered (this is the case with the home washing machine, for instance, which follows a sequence of operations that may be changed as to duration, or some of which may be skipped, but which can, basically, do only that which it was designed and built to do), or the machine may be adapted to a limited variety of functions by changing its internal (cam or gearing) arrangements. It is characteristic of all machinery, up to this stage in its evolution, that the pattern of its action is fixed within the mechanism and has no links to either external controls or its own working results. Its movements are not so much *automatic* as *predetermined*.*

Between the stage represented by machines constructed according to this concept and the next stage of machine development, there is a significant difference: control over the machine in accordance with *information coming from outside the direct working mechanism*. This may take the form of measurements of the machine output itself. It is a simple step from installing on a printing press a counter to record the number of sheets that have passed through the press, to arranging this counter so that it shuts off the press, or rings a bell, when the selected number has been reached. The classic example of the flyball governor, which uses the motion of the weights, as they are flung outward by increasing speed or fall inward as speed reduces, to control the throttle of the engine is a perfect instance of a machine which regulates its own pace by measuring its own output. In checking the results of its own work, the machine may simply stop, signal, or reject, as in the case of the key punch verifier, which signals and marks any difference between the holes already punched in the card and the keys struck by the operator. Or, in its furthest refinements, the machine may measure the results of its work while that work is in progress, compare these results with an image of the desired product, and make continual adjustments throughout the course of the operation so that the result conforms to the plan.

This capacity to draw upon information from external sources, or from the progress of its own operation, brings about a certain reversal in the trend of machine development. Prior to this, the evolution of machinery had been from the universal to the special purpose machine. The broad range of earlier machinery had been general purpose equipment, adapted not to a particular product or to a specialized operation, but to a range of operations. Lathes existed for metal-turning, not for the manufacture of a particular size and class of screw or shaft; presses were adaptable to a variety of forming operations, not to a particular part. As machinery underwent its first phase of progress toward increase in control, this took the form of fixed arrangements adapting the machine to a particular product or operation. In an advanced state, such as the machining of an automobile engine block, a single machine drills scores of holes from various angles, mills surfaces to final finish, counterbores, taps threads, etc., performing these operations simultaneously or in rapid sequence.

---

* Bright includes the possibility of reducing the need for human intervention in such a machine still further by putting the actuation of the machine under remote control, so that many machines may be set in motion or stopped from a single control site; there is also the possibility of doing away with the need to start and stop the machine if the introduction of the workpiece itself actuates the mechanism, and the completion and ejection of the workpiece stops the machine until the next piece is introduced. But this and other such refinements do not change the internally fixed character of the machine cycle.

Such machines can be used for no other purpose, and they come into existence when the continuous volume of production can repay the cost of elaborate equipment. Thus one finds on many production lines carefully engineered devices—powered assembly jigs, single purpose stamping presses, rigidly positioned cutting tools adapted to a single motion, welding or riveting heads, etc.—which would have no useful function away from that particular production line. But the ability to guide the machine from an external source of control in many cases restores the universality of the machine. It can now regain its adaptability to many purposes without loss of control, since that control is no longer dependent upon its specialized internal construction. A lathe can be controlled even more efficiently by a punched-paper or magnetic tape, and be immediately adaptable to work of every kind suitable to its size and power.

As important in its way as the refinements of control in separate machines has been the process of adapting machines to one another. This process begins as a problem of plant layout of individual machines, in an arrangement that follows the sequence of operations so that each machine can deliver the work in process to the subsequent operation. The next step is the provision of chutes, conveyors, etc. for moving the work from machine to machine; in their most developed form these are the transfer machines used in the production lines for engines in the automobile industry. When such a system includes arrangements for the actuation of the machine by the workpiece, so that the need for direct labor diminishes still further, the production line has become "automatic." But when a production line has reached this continuous and automatic state, it is close to the point where it becomes a single machine instead of a system of connected machinery. Thus the machine which prints, folds, gathers, covers, and binds the sheets of a paperback book would hardly be recognizable to an outsider as a combination of the several machines it has brought together in such a process of evolution. For this to take place, all that need be done is for the production system of linked machines to be conceived and redesigned as a single, massive, integrated whole. In this fashion, the control over machine processes grows until they can be rendered more nearly automatic within the compass of a system of interlocked machines or a single machine which embraces an entire production process and conducts it with greatly reduced human intervention.

The evolution of machinery from its primitive forms, in which simple rigid frames replace the hand as guides for the motion of the tool, to those modern complexes in which the *entire process* is guided from start to finish by not only mechanical but also electrical, chemical, and other physical forces—this evolution may thus be described as an increase in human control over the action of tools. These tools are controlled, in their activities, as extensions of the human organs of work, including the sensory organs, and this feat is accomplished by an increasing human understanding of the properties of matter—in other words, by the growth of the scientific command of physical principles. The study and understanding of nature has, as its primary manifestation in human civilization, the increasing control by humans over labor processes by means of machines and machine systems.

But the control of humans over the labor process, thus far understood, is nothing more than an abstraction. This abstraction must acquire concrete form in the social setting in which machinery is being developed. And this social setting is, and has been from the beginnings of the development of machinery in its modern forms, one in which humanity is sharply divided, and nowhere more sharply divided than in the labor process itself. The mass of humanity is subjected to the labor process for the purposes of those who control it rather than for any general purposes of "humanity" as such. In thus acquiring concrete form, the control of humans over the labor process turns into its opposite and becomes the control of the labor process over the mass of humans. Machinery comes into the world not as the servant of "humanity," but as the instrument of those to whom the accumulation of capital gives the *ownership* of the machines. The capacity of humans to control the labor process through machinery is seized upon by management from the beginning of capitalism as the *prime means whereby production may be controlled not by the direct producer but by the owners and representatives of capital.* Thus, in addition to its technical function of increasing the productivity of labor—which would be a mark of machinery under any social system—machinery also has in the capitalist system the function of divesting the mass of workers of their control over their own labor. It is ironic that this feat is accomplished by taking advantage of that great human advance represented by the technical and scientific developments that increase human control over the labor process. It is even more ironic that this appears perfectly "natural" to the minds of those who, subjected to two centuries of this fetishism of capital, actually see the machine as an alien force which subjugates humanity!

The evolution of machinery represents an expansion of human capacities, an increase cf human control over environment through the ability to elicit from instruments of production an increasing range and exactitude of response. But it is in the nature of machinery, and a corollary of technical development, that the control over the machine need no longer be vested in its immediate operator. This possibility is seized upon by the capitalist mode of production and utilized to the fullest extent. What was mere *technical possibility* has become, since the Industrial Revolution, an *inevitability* that devastates with the force of a natural calamity, although there is nothing more "natural" about it than any other form of the organization of labor. Before the human capacity to control machinery can be transformed into its opposite, a series of special conditions must be met which have nothing to do with the physical character of the machine. The machine must be the property not of the producer, nor of the associated producers, but of an alien power. The interests of the two must be antagonistic. The manner in which labor is deployed around the machinery—from the labor required to design, build, repair, and control it to the labor required to feed and operate it—must be dictated not by the human needs of the producers but by the special needs of those who own both the machine and the labor power, and whose interest it is to bring these two together in a special way. Along with these conditions, a social evolution must take place which parallels the physical evolution of machinery: a step-by-step creation of a "labor force" in place of self-directed human labor; that is to say, a working population conforming to the needs of this social organization of labor, in which knowledge of the machine becomes a specialized and segregated trait, while among the mass of the working population there grows only ignorance, incapacity, and thus a fitness for machine servitude. In this way the remarkable development of machinery becomes, for most of the working population, the source not of freedom but of enslavement, not of mastery but of helplessness, and not of the broadening of the horizon of labor but of the confinement of the worker within a blind round of servile duties in which the machine appears as the embodiment of science and the worker as little or nothing. But this is no more a technical necessity of machinery than appetite is, in the ironic words of Ambrose Bierce, "an instinct thoughtfully implanted by Providence as a solution to the labor question."

Machinery offers to management the opportunity to do by wholly mechanical means that which it had previously attempted to do by organizational and disciplinary means. The fact that many machines may be paced and controlled according to centralized decisions, and that these controls may thus be in the hands of management, removed from the site of production to the office—these technical possibilities are of just as great interest to management as the fact that the machine multiplies the productivity of labor.* It is not always necessary, for this purpose, that the machine be a well-developed or sophisticated example of its kind. The moving conveyor, when used for an assembly line, though it is an exceedingly primitive piece of machinery, answers perfectly to the needs of capital in the organization of work which may not be otherwise mechanized. Its pace is in the hands of management, and is determined by a mechanical device the construction of which could hardly be simpler but one which enables management to seize upon the single essential control element of the process.

To explore this subject in somewhat greater detail by means of a very recent instance, let us take as an example the work of the machine shop. This

---

* "One great advantage which we may derive from machinery," wrote Babbage, "is from the check which it affords against the inattention, the idleness, or the dishonesty of human agents."[9]

remains the fundamental branch of all industry, not only because of the great role which machine tools play in a great many areas of production, but also because it is in machine shops that the machinery of industry is itself fabricated. It is also particularly important because of the recent innovations in machine control which are revolutionizing production methods in machine shops, and which have initiated control systems that are spreading into many quite different industries. It has a further interest for this discussion because in this industry one may see how machinery is utilized to tackle the very machine-shop problems with which Taylor wrestled for so many years.

The problem of controlling machine tools presents itself to management largely as a problem of unit or small-batch production. Highly automatic machine systems adapted to mass production or continuous flow processes are of little help in this respect, since they represent huge fixed investments which can return their cost only when applied to a large volume. And it has been estimated that three-fourths of all production in the metal-working industries of the United States takes place in batches of fifty units or less.[10] Quantities as small as these must be manufactured on universal or general purpose machine tools, and the tooling, fixtures, and setup costs that may be distributed among these short runs are necessarily limited. Thus this vast area of metal cutting has until recently remained the province of the skilled machinist. Insofar as management has found an answer to the problems of cheapening labor and controlling production, it has taken the form, on the one hand, of breaking down the machinist's craft among machine operators specializing in the lathe, milling machine, and other individual machines, and making machine setup itself a specialty; and, on the other hand, of predetermining operations according to management standards in the Taylor tradition.

The mechanical solution to the problem has taken the form of *numerical control*,* which has been called "probably the most significant new development in manufacturing technology since Henry Ford introduced the concept of the moving assembly line."[11] In application to machine tools alone, this concept is working a revolution in industry, but its applications are spreading beyond machine tools and potentially embrace a great variety of machine and hand operations. It is therefore worth considering in detail, as a prime instance of the managerial use of machinery in the capitalist mode of production, and how this affects the worker and the labor process.

The concept of this form of control over machinery has been traced back to two French inventions: that of Falcon in 1725, a knitting machine controlled by a perforated card, and that of Jacquard in 1804, a knitting and weaving

---

* The term comes from the control (usually by a punched-tape reading device) over the movements of the tool or the work by means of numbers (for instance, 2.375 inches) which represent distances along three axes, and by means of which the tool may be guided to any point in a three-dimensional solid.

machine controlled in the same way. The principle is like that of the player piano, which is actuated by holes in a paper roll. It was picked up again by an American inventor who in 1916 patented a continuous-path machine for cutting cloth in the garment industry. An application of this method to the control of machine tools was patented in 1930, but the development and application of the concept did not really begin, despite this long history, until after the Second World War. Financing for the research was made available by the United States Air Force and was carried on by the John Parsons Corporation and later by the Massachusetts Institute of Technology, which demonstrated in 1952 a prototype in the form of a vertical milling machine operated under numerical control.[12]

The possibility of widespread industrial application of this as well as many other control systems materialized with the electronics revolution of the 1950s and 1960s, which furnished cheap and reliable circuitry for the control instruments. This began with the transistor, which at first simply replaced the vacuum tube on a one-for-one basis. By the early 1960s, however, integrated circuits combined transistors and other components on tiny chips of silicon crystal, so that eventually large-scale integrated circuits offering the functions of hundreds of expensive and bulkier parts were combined on a single chip. As the yield of batch production processes climbed, the cost fell from an average price per circuit function (one transistor) of $2 in 1965 to under three cents in 1971. The reliability of operation and ease of repair through modular replacement, combined with this cheapening of increasingly complex circuitry, are the basis for the revolution in control technology, and it is here rather than in earlier experiments that the source of this new industrial technique and its broad use must be sought.*

By 1968, no more than 1 percent of machine tools in industrial use were numerically controlled, but the shape of the future could be seen in the fact that 20 percent of all new machine tools shipped in that year were equipped with this attachment. And in trade showings of machinery, as well as in industry journals, the big majority of machines displayed or advertised are now tools of this type.

With numerical control, the machine process is subjected to the control of a separate unit, which receives instructions from two sources: in numerical form from an external source, and in the form of signals from monitoring devices which check the ongoing process at the point of contact between tool and work. Using this information, the control unit originates signals which activate power drives controlling the work, tool, coolant, etc.

From a technical point of view, the system offers several advantages. Complex metal cutting—for example, the machining of surfaces to compound

---

* On this, see *Business Week*'s recent special issue on productivity, which characterizes the goals of increased productivity through solid-state electronic controls as "fewer parts, less-skilled, low-cost labor, and fewer manufacturing steps."[13]

curves—slow and demanding when the calculations are made in the course of cutting, may be coded with relative ease and cut with assurance; this was one of the features which, because of its applicability to the shaping of dies and other parts used in aircraft production, interested the air force in the method. The coding of any job is quickly completed when separated from machine execution, and once coded a job need never be analyzed again: the tape may be kept on file and used whenever a remake is called for. The processes of metal cutting are virtually automatic, relieving the worker of the need for close control of the machine while cutting is in progress. The separation of conceptualization and calculation from the machine means that the tool itself is in more constant use for metal cutting; at the same time, it goes through its continuous cutting path without interruption, which also makes for more efficient use of these expensive pieces of equipment.

The unity of this process in the hands of the skilled machinist is perfectly feasible, and indeed has much to recommend it, since the knowledge of metal-cutting practices which is required for programming is already mastered by the machinist. Thus there is no question that from a practical standpoint there is nothing to prevent the machining process under numerical control from remaining the province of the total craftsman. That this almost never happens is due, of course, to the opportunities the process offers for the destruction of craft and the cheapening of the resulting pieces of labor into which it is broken. Thus, as the process takes shape in the minds of engineers, the labor configuration to operate it takes shape simultaneously in the minds of its designers, and in part shapes the design itself. The equipment is made to be *operated*; operating costs involve, apart from the cost of the machine itself, the *hourly cost of labor*, and this is part of the calculation involved in machine design. The design which will enable the operation to be broken down among cheaper operators is the design which is sought by management and engineers who have so internalized this value that it appears to them to have the force of natural law or scientific necessity.*

---

* That engineers think in this fashion, or are guided in this direction by all the circumstances of their work, will not appear strange to anyone with the slightest familiarity with engineering as it has developed from its nineteenth-century beginnings. "The monogram of our national initials, which is the symbol for our monetary unit, the dollar, is almost as frequently conjoined to the figures of an engineer's calculations as are the symbols indicating feet, minutes, pounds, or gallons," said Henry R. Towne, the industrialist and pioneer of shop management, in a paper read to the American Society of Mechanical Engineers in 1886. "The *dollar*," he said on a later occasion, "is the final term in almost every equation which arises in the practice of engineering. . . ."[14] Or, in the words of a chemist in more recent years: "I'm no longer really interested in problems that don't involve economic considerations. I've come to see economics as another variable to be dealt with in studying a reaction—there's pressure, there's temperature, and there's the dollar."[15]

Numerical control is thus used to divide the process among *separate* operatives, each representing far less in terms of training, abilities, and hourly labor costs than does the competent machinist. Here we see once more the Babbage principle, but now in a setting of technical revolution. The process has become more complex, but this is lost to the workers, who do not rise with the process but sink beneath it. Each of these workers is required to know and understand not *more* than did the single worker of before, but much *less*. The skilled machinist is, by this innovation, deliberately rendered as obsolete as the glassblower or Morse code telegrapher, and as a rule is replaced by three sorts of operatives.

First, there is the parts programmer. The process of taking the specifications of an engineering drawing and recording them on a planning sheet is essentially the same work as that previously done by the machinist when, drawing in hand, he approached a given job. But the parts programmer is not required to know everything else the machinist knew: that is to say, the actual craft of cutting metals in its execution on the machine. He learns instead merely the shadow of the process in tabulated and standardized form, and with that his learning ceases. He is taught to work this information up in a manner suitable for coding.

"The planner," in the words of one description, "simulates the machining done in the shop. . . . He goes through every step in very much detail, leaving no decision to be made later at the machine. The planner determines the feeds and speeds, the cutters required, and even the miscellaneous functions such as when coolant is to be on or off. Importantly, he determines the feed rates and the depths of cut to be taken."[16] To convert the specifications on the drawing into a planning sheet requires, in the case of much of the equipment used for numerical control, only a knowledge of blueprint reading such as the craftsman acquires in his first months of apprenticeship, plus the basic arithmetic of adding and subtracting, plus the use of standard data on machine capabilities. This may be made more or less difficult by the type of equipment used and the complexity of the job in hand. In a recent development, the machining specifications are themselves stored on computer tape and the programmer need only make a description of the part (both rough form and finished form) by simply converting the engineering drawing into a listing of dimensions, using nothing but simple machine-shop terms. The computer delivers a machine control tape, a printout of what is on the tape, a tool list, and the computed job cycle time. This system, it is claimed, reduces program time for a part that once required four or five hours to only twenty or thirty minutes. One company advertises another programming system that uses a "10-word program vocabulary" and says: "Within a week a shop man can program effectively."[17] An article in *Monthly Labor Review* says: "Most of the functions of the skilled machinist have been shifted to the parts programmer. Consequently, skilled machinists often staff these positions."[18] This may have been so at the outset, but the job of parts programmer now increasingly falls to the technical college graduate (often from the two-year junior college) who fits the "labor profile" of this desk job more closely than the machinist, especially in being cheaper.

The next job is that of converting the planning sheet into machine-readable form—usually a paper tape punched on a simple coding machine. Here the candidate is immediately selected by unanimous choice: the "girl" machine operator who learns her job in a few days, attains optimum efficiency in a few weeks or months, and is drawn from a large pool at hardly more than half the pay of the machinist.

So far as the machine operator is concerned, it is now possible to remove from his area of competence whatever skills still remain after three-quarters of a century of "rationalization." He is now definitively relieved of all the decisions, judgment, and knowledge which Taylor attempted to abstract from him by organizational means. The true "instruction card"—Lillian Gilbreth's "self-producer of a predetermined product"—is at last fully revealed in the program tape. "Numerically controlled machines," we are told by one authority, "are fundamentally easier to operate. The skills required of an operator are less than with conventional machines, where he must often be a trained machinist. With numerical control equipment, the operator must, of course, know his equipment. He must have the training and intelligence required to perform several rather straightforward prescribed routines, but he does not possess the technical skills of the experienced machinist. The intelligence corresponding to these latter skills is on the tape in numerical control."[19]

The difference between the trained machinist—even one so limited in craftsmanship that he can operate only a single machine—and the operator of a numerically controlled machine is often understated, both by managers, who are prepared (in public at least) to conceal the downgrading in the interest of a smoother transition and for public relations reasons, and also unions, for whom the exaggeration of the "demanding nature" and "increased responsibility" of the new process is a routine part of contract bargaining. But some idea of the manner in which managers view this difference can be seen in the following response to a University of Michigan survey of companies using numerical control: "Cost of developing and training an operator to produce identical parts by conventional methods and machines compared with NC machining system is approximately 12 to 1."[20] This would mean that if it takes four years to give a machinist his basic training, an operator of the sort required by numerically controlled machine tools may be trained in four months. Experience bears this out.*

---

* This is not to say that, in unionized situations, the pay of machinists is immediately reduced to operator levels the moment numerical control is introduced. In some exceptional instances, where very few numerically controlled machine tools have

Control in this form, and in other forms that are developing out of it, is by no means limited to metal-cutting machinery; the principle has general applicability in many crafts. In this connection, the evolution of boiler shop and other heavy plate construction work is of interest. In these trades the best-paid craft has long been that of layout. The layout man takes off the blueprint the specifications of each part and inscribes them on the plate stock, along with directions for flame-cutting or shearing, punching or drilling, bending or rolling, etc. It was at one point noted that the layout man spent a certain amount of his time simply marking his layout with close-spaced center-punched marks. In those shops that had enough work to warrant a subdivision of tasks in the layout department, this task was taken from the layout mechanic and vested in "markers," at a far lower pay rate. Then, in the 1950s, a method was devised for drawing each piece, in the drafting room, to accurate scale on a transparency which could be projected on the steel from a slide projector mounted high above the layout trestles. Now the layout man became nothing more than a marker himself; after he had adjusted the focus so that a single dimension was correct, he had no more to do than mark. But with numerical control, the steel can go straight to the flame-cutting tables, where the cutting torch is guided by the control tape, so that not only is the work of layout eliminated—or rather transferred to the office—but so is the so-called semi-skill of the flame cutter.

In the same way, in sheetmetal shops numerically controlled machines are now used for cutting required shapes (with "nibbling" tools, multiple-tool turrets, etc.) without the necessity of shop layout or skilled sheetmetal workers. One furniture manufacturer makes kitchen cabinets and bedroom furniture out of vinyl-clad particle board by numerical control, using a so-called mitre-fold process. The boards are cut in such a way that they fold to make complete units and are held together by the "wood-grained vinyl covering"; folded and glued, each "unit" is complete. It takes just one hour of labor to assemble each piece of this furniture, one-third the time taken by woodworkers (our source leaves to the imagination of the reader the quality and appearance of these surpassingly modern products).[21] And it remains only to be noted that the process of

---

been brought into a shop, the union has been able successfully to insist that the entire job, including programming and coding, be handled by the machinist. In many other cases, the pay scale of the machinist has been maintained or even increased by the union after the introduction of numerical control, even though he has become no more than an operator. But such pay maintenance is bound to have a temporary character, and is really an agreement, whether formal or not, to "red circle" these jobs, as this is known in negotiating language; that is, to safeguard the pay of the incumbents. Management is thus sometimes forced to be content to wait until the historical process of devaluation of the worker's skill takes effect over the long run, and the relative pay scale falls to its expected level, since the only alternative to such patience is, in many cases, a bitter battle with the union.

making an engineering drawing has itself been found to be readily susceptible to the same attack, so that there now exist drafting machines which draw plans from tape under numerical control. In each of these cases, the public unveiling of the new devices is accompanied by much self-congratulation and by philanthropic phrases about the lightening of the toil of the worker, the ease with which laborious tasks are accomplished, and so forth. Few write so plainly about the way in which functions are distributed, and the effect this is having upon the world of work, as did Thilliez, the engineer who introduced numerical control into the Renault plants, in his 1967 technical book, *La Commande numérique des machines*:

> But in addition the technique of numerical control implies an effect which might be called extraordinary, on the level of the philosophy of the organization of the enterprise. It separates the intellectual work from the work of execution, just as has for a long time been the case with the fabrication of long runs on special purpose machines, and this separation allows the execution of both functions under the technical conditions best adapted to a superior organization, thus in the final accounting most profitable.[22]

Such a separation of "intellectual work from the work of execution" is indeed a "technical condition" best adapted to a hierarchical organization, best adapted to control of both the hand and the brain worker, best adapted to profitability, best adapted to everything but the needs of the people. These needs, however, are, in the word of the economists, "externalities," a notion that is absolutely incomprehensible from the human point of view, but from the capitalist point of view is perfectly clear and precise, since it simply means external to the balance sheet.

While the forms of utilization of machinery—the manner in which labor is organized and deployed around it—are dictated by the tendencies of the capitalist mode of production, the drive to mechanize is itself dictated by the effort to increase the productivity of labor. But the increasing productivity of labor is neither sought nor utilized by capitalism from the point of view of the satisfaction of human needs. Rather, powered by the needs of the capital accumulation process, it becomes a frenzied drive which approaches the level of a generalized social insanity. Never is any level of productivity regarded as sufficient. In the automobile industry, a constantly diminishing number of workers produces, decade by decade, a growing number of increasingly degraded products which, as they are placed upon the streets and highways, poison and disrupt the entire social atmosphere—while at the same time the cities where motor vehicles are produced become centers of degraded labor on the one hand and permanent unemployment on the other. It is a measure of the manner in which capitalist standards have diverged from human standards that this situation is seen as representing a high degree of "economic efficiency."

The most advanced methods of science and rational calculation in the hands of a social system that is at odds with human needs produce nothing but irrationality; the more advanced the science and the more rational the calculations, the more swiftly and calamitously is this irrationality engendered. Like Captain Ahab, the capitalist can say, "All my means are sane, my motives and object mad."

The drive for increased productivity inheres in each capitalist firm by virtue of its purpose as an organization for the expansion of capital; it is moreover enforced upon laggards by the threats of national and international competition. In this setting, the development of technology takes the form of a headlong rush in which social effects are largely disregarded, priorities are set only by the criteria of profitability, and the equitable spread, reasonable assimilation, and selective appropriation of the fruits of science, considered from the social point of view, remain the visions of helpless idealists.* Each advance in productivity shrinks the number of truly productive workers, enlarges the number of workers who are available to be utilized in the struggles between corporations over the distribution of the surplus, expands the use of labor in wasteful employment or no employment at all, and gives to all society the form of an inverted pyramid resting upon an ever narrower base of useful labor. Yet no matter how rapidly productivity may grow, no matter how miraculous the contributions of science to this development, no satisfactory level can ever be attained. Thus, a century after the beginning of the scientific-technical revolution and almost two centuries after the Industrial Revolution, the problem for capitalism which towers over all others, and which takes the form of a crisis threatening survival itself, remains: *more productivity*. In *Business Week* we read: "Five years of inflation, recession, and uncertain recovery have forced the men who manage U.S. business and the men who make U.S. economic policy to a painful conclusion: Somehow the nation must make a quantum jump in efficiency. It must get more output from its men and

---

* The occasional dream that flickers in the minds of those who have assimilated the capitalist way of looking at all problems is quickly extinguished by "practical" considerations. Thus Alfred Marshall, early in the present epoch: "In fact, if all the world were a single people, with one purpose and that the highest, it might be well to put some check on this rapid supersession of human skill; even at the expense of delaying the increase of material comforts and luxuries. But Britain can exist only by obtaining her necessary supplies of food and raw products in return for the exportation of manufactures: and her hold on external markets can be maintained only by her use of the most effective processes known."[23] The impulse to view society from a human standpoint, "a single people, with one purpose and that the highest," does Marshall credit, but he can entertain it no longer than is necessary to dismiss it from the standpoint of British capitalism, whose single impulse, and that the lowest, requires first of all the sacrifice of the British people.

machines."[24] The very "efficiency" which produced the crises is here seen as the only answer to it. The machine which, working at top speed, threatens to fly apart is to be preserved from that threat by running it even faster. Each capitalist nation will further degrade its own working population and social life in an attempt to save a social system which, like the very planets in their orbits, will fall to its destruction if it slows in its velocity. Here we have the *reductio ad absurdum* of capitalist efficiency, and the expression in concrete terms of the insoluble contradiction that exists between the development of the means of production and the social relations of production that characterize capitalism.

In pursuit of this "solution," industry, trade, and offices rationalize, mechanize, innovate, and revolutionize the labor process to a truly astonishing degree. The methods used are as various as the resources of science itself. And since these resources are so vast, where they cannot accomplish a large saving of labor by a revolution in production they achieve the same effect by a degradation of the product.

The construction industry, for example, divides its efforts between the destruction of sound buildings and their replacement with shoddy structures whose total life span will not equal the useful life remaining to the demolished buildings. This industry, which because of the nature of its processes is still largely in the era of hand craftsmanship supplemented by powered hand tools, the lowest level of mechanization, makes continual and determined efforts to climb out of this disadvantageous position. It favors new materials, especially plastics, painting and plastering with spray guns (a single spray plasterer keeps a number of workers busy smoothing), and the pre-assembly of as many elements as possible on a factory basis (a carpenter can install six to ten prefabricated door assemblies, pre-hung in the frames with hardware already in place, in the time it takes to hang a single door by conventional methods; and in the process becomes a doorhanger and ceases to be a carpenter). The trend of dwelling construction is best exemplified by the rapidly growing "mobile home" segment of the industry. The "mobile home" is a mass-produced factory product; of the three parties involved—the workers, the manufacturers, and the residents—only the middle one has any advantage to show from the transaction. Yet mobile homes are spreading over the landscape triumphantly, and one may easily predict for them a still greater future because of the high degree of "efficiency" with which they allocate labor and capital.

A quarter-century ago, Siegfried Giedion described the transformation of the crusty, wholesome loaf of bread into a "product" with the "resiliency of a rubber sponge."[25] But the production process for the manufacture of this bread is a triumph of the factory arts. Continuous mixing, reduction of brew fermentation time, dough which is metered, extruded, divided, and panned to the accuracy of a gram in the pound, conveyorized baking and automatic depan-ning, cooling, slicing, wrapping, and labelling have effectively rid the bakery of the troublesome and unprofitable arts of the baker, and have replaced the baker himself with engineers on the one hand and factory operatives on the other. The speed with which the operation is conducted is a marvel of effi-ciency, and, apart from its effects on the worker, if only it were not necessary for the people to consume the "product" the whole thing could be considered a resounding success.

Furniture production is being remade in the image of the automobile industry. It has increasingly become a mass-production process in which the skills and effects of woodworking and cabinetmaking are disappearing. Shap-ing is done on automatic contour-profilers operated by unskilled labor. Routers for grooving and cutouts are done by template-controlled machines with a cam and sensing system of programming. "Unskilled operators need only to feed material to the machine; in some applications, even feeding is automatic."[26] "The use of pneumatic power clamps and assembly machines is speeding the assembly of frames, case ends, drawers, and chairs, while requiring fewer and less-skilled workers. One machine takes parts directly from a tenoner, feeds metal parts from hoppers, inserts these parts, drives pins or nails, and ejects a completed shelving onto a conveyor at a rate of 7 to 10 per minute, and only one operative is required to load the hoppers and pinners. Another machine takes panels, aligns and joins them perfectly square, drives staples to hold the assembly true while the glue dries, and permits the assembly of a kitchen cabinet by one man every 60 seconds."[27] Painting has been mechanized, using automatic spray and flow-coating techniques. Upholstery work is now done with precut, preformed, and stretch materials, thus putting an end to the traditional skills of that trade.

In meatpacking, the industry which was the first in the United States to introduce conveyor lines, the on-the-rail dressing system has displaced the older conveyor. "In rail systems, stunned cattle are hoisted to a high conveyor rail, on which they are slaughtered and then moved through all dressing operations to the chill cooler. Workers, stationed on mechanized platforms which move vertically and horizontally according to the requirements of each task, use power knives and saws. Mechanical hide strippers, which grasp and peel the hide from the carcass, substantially reduce the skilled hand-cutting operations once necessary to remove a high-quality hide without damage. Labor savings per unit may be between 25 and 60 percent on the kill line. These savings are in reduction of waiting time between performance of individual tasks, which are now machine-paced and synchronized, and elimination of constant repositioning of the carcass necessary in the older 'bed' system."[28] There is a machine which permits an image of each carcass to be projected on a screen so that workers can be guided in making major cuts by a pointer which indicates them; far fewer workers need to know how and where to cut a carcass. Machines emulsify, form, smoke, cook, chill, peel, wash, and package frankfurters. Electronic machines that weigh and package poultry along with mechanical pluckers process up to 9,000 chickens an hour, although, we are told, the prevalence of "low wage rates in poultry packing plants" is among the factors which "tend to retard technological change" in that branch of the industry.[29]

In the manufacture of wearing apparel, every aspect of the production process is being energetically attacked. Since this is an industry which is characterized by the existence of many shops, most of them relatively small, a great many are still in the stage of traditional "rationalization," breaking down operations into a large number of smaller and simpler steps. At the same time these steps are being speeded up by the introduction of a variety of devices, chiefly attachments to sewing machines such as needle positioners, automatic thread cutters, pleaters, and hemmers. The use of two- or three-layer bonded materials, which eliminate separate linings, and synthetic fabrics, which may be processed by novel methods such as the electronic fusing of seams in place of sewing, opens up new vistas for cheapening and transforming mass-produced clothing. Advanced production methods are copied from sheet-metal and boiler-shop techniques: die-cutting to replace hand cutting, pattern-grading equipment which produces different size copies of a master pattern, etc. There is a photoline tracer which guides a sewing head along the path of a pattern placed in a control unit. Improving on this, a photoelectric control is used to guide a sewing head along the edge of the fabric. In these latter innovations we see the manner in which science and technology apply similar principles to dissimilar processes, since the same control principles may be applied to complex contours, whether on steel or cloth.

In typesetting, the printing industry first took the path of eliminating the linotyper's skill through the use of tape-controlled linecasting, the essence of which was the separation of the keyboard from the casting of lead slugs. The operator prepares a control tape on a machine much more rapid and simpler to operate than the linotype. But the use of photocomposition in tandem with the electronic computer has enabled the industry to begin the elimination of metal type altogether, and along with it the need for the operator to justify lines and hyphenate words, since these functions can be performed by a computer which utilizes a record of the syllabification of almost every word in the language. That this rids the typesetter of one more load of useless knowledge has already been amply pointed out, but no one has yet pointed to the knowledge acquired in its place.

Despite the variety of means used in all the innovations we have been describing, their unifying feature is the same as that which we noted at the outset of this discussion: the progressive elimination of the control functions of the worker, insofar as possible, and their transfer to a device which is controlled, again insofar as possible, by management from outside the direct process. It is this which dominates the new place of the worker in production processes, and it is this above all which is slighted or entirely neglected in conventional assessments. The knowledge of labor and production processes which the outsider may gain from a study of nontechnical sources is limited by the vague and imprecise impressions which pass for information, and from which sociologists and journalists, already too eager to achieve optimistic conclusions, glean their notions about the trend of labor in modern society. Morris A. Horowitz and Irwin L. Herrenstadt did an exhaustive survey of such materials in the course of their attempt to study changes in skill requirements of various occupations, and they report the following:

> Limiting our focus to the past 15 years, we examined various bibliographies and indexes in an effort to pull together the literature relevant to our field of interest. Over 500 bibliographic titles were selected for careful scrutiny and analysis. The overwhelming majority of these speculated about the effects of automation based upon general impressions, discussions with a few industrialists or union leaders, or a few very limited case studies conducted by others. If an article or book discussed automation and manpower, it typically referred to employment opportunities resulting from technological change, the effects on the occupational structure of the plant or industry, or the effects on the skill composition of the labor force. Only a small number of studies made any effort to investigate and analyze the effects of automation on job content and the worker characteristics required of the changing jobs.*

This very paucity of systematic information and analysis makes all the more important James R. Bright's unique study, referred to earlier in this chapter. In 1954, research was begun at the Harvard Business School on the "managerial implications" of "automation." In 1958, Bright published a volume entitled *Automation and Management*, which begins with a survey of the

---

* Horowitz and Herrenstadt are to be thanked for this survey, but unfortunately the remainder of their article is just as useless as the literature they criticize. It is an attempt to assess "worker characteristics required of the changing jobs" entirely on the basis of the descriptions of "job content" in the second and third editions, 1949 and 1965 respectively, of the *Dictionary of Occupational Titles* published by the Department of Labor. A more arid and unrewarding exercise can hardly be imagined, and the result is that after scores of pages of meticulous tabulation and statistics, the authors conclude that "the overall or net change in the skill requirements" during these fifteen years was "remarkably small"; that the "small net change" was "the product of numerous offsetting changes"; and that the result "on balance" is "either inconsequential or inconclusive with respect to overall skill levels."[30]

evolution of mechanization in manufacturing (with special attention to the electric lamp and shoe industries) and then analyzes in great detail thirteen of the most advanced production systems in operation at the time of the study. These included the Ford Cleveland Engine Plant; a highly automated bread bakery; a small integrated oil refinery with the reputation of being an outstanding example of automatic control; a new automatic production line for the manufacture of oil seals; the foam rubber mattress department of a rubber company, in which the entire process, from raw material stores to finished product warehouse had been integrated into a single radically new system; a chemical plant making commercial fertilizer; a feed and grain plant with a high degree of automaticity; a small coal mine which attempted extensive use of automatic equipment; a plating plant in which a complex production sequence was subjected to a highly automatic handling system; an instrument manufacturer with a unique work-feeding system; an electrical parts manufacturer who applied automatic methods to assembly operations; another plating plant with a differing system of work organization; and a V-8 engine plant. Bright later wrote several articles (see, for example, the July-August 1958 issue of *Harvard Business Review*) and, most important, a summary of his conclusions with regard to skill written in 1966 for the National Commission on Technology, Automation, and Economic Progress.

While the Bright studies dealt in general with the "management" aspects of automation, the principal focus was the "skill requirements" of increasingly mechanized industries. It must be pointed out that Bright nowhere indicates a concern with this aspect of his subject from the point of view of the worker, but views the problem entirely from the management standpoint. His approach is detached and rigidly factual, and his concern is expressed in his final conclusion: "I suggest that excessive educational and skill specification is a serious mistake and potential hazard to our economic and social system. We will hurt individuals, raise labor costs improperly, create disillusion and resentment, and destroy valid job standards by setting standards that are not truly needed for a given task. . . ."[31]

In the preface to his book, Bright notes: "A controversial area of this study will lie, no doubt, in my conclusions regarding the skill required of the work force in the automated plant. The relationship of skill requirements to the degree of automaticity as a declining rather than increasing ratio is not commonly accepted, or even considered." Nevertheless, after exploring his tentative conclusions with three to four hundred industrialists, and in presenting his findings to "at least a dozen industrial audiences totaling perhaps three thousand persons," he notes that "in general, these conclusions have not been strongly challenged" except with regard to plant maintenance skills, and even these challenges he attributes to "intense personal experiences" peculiar to special situations.[32]

Bright's work is not only informative but especially useful for the analytical framework it provides, since he sets up a "mechanization profile" of seventeen levels (see Bright's chart of mechanization levels, p. 149). Apart from the first two—work with the hand and with a hand tool—each level deals with a specific machine function and its operating characteristics. With this "profile," Bright was able to chart the entire series of operations in every production system he studied, thus affording a far more realistic glimpse of so-called automatic production systems than that furnished by the glowing self-tributes of managers or the breathless prose of journalists.

On mechanization levels 1 to 4 Bright concludes that since control is entirely up to the worker, skill is increasing (see Bright's chart, "Changing Contribution Required of Operators," pp. 151-52). On levels 5 to 8, where control is mechanical but still dependent upon the worker, some skills are increasing but a number have turned downward, resulting, in Bright's opinion, in an overall decrease in total skill required. In levels 9 to 11, where the machine has been put under external control at least to the extent of signalling its own needs, most skills turn downward. And finally, in the top six levels, which are characterized by self-modifications of machine action and therefore correspond to advanced methods of automatic production, *every* indicator of skill used by Bright, from knowledge and experience through decision-making, plunges downward sharply, and the indicators of "Worker contribution" all read either "Decreasing-nil," or flatly, "Nil" (with vague exceptions only for "Responsibility" and "Education").[33] The result is summarized by a curve which Bright calls the "Hump in Skill Requirements." (See Bright's curve of "Skill versus Automation," p. 154.)[34] It describes a "suggested average experience as mechanization increases," and shows an increase only through the first four levels, a decrease thereafter, and a plunge into the nether regions with the installation of those elements of mechanization which are associated with the popular term "automation." He outlines the idea as follows:

> Consider a metalworker. Using hand tools, such as a file, he requires considerable dexterity. As power is added but the tool guidance is left in the operator's hands, he needs new levels of dexterity and decision-making to control the machine action, and these grow in importance. A high degree of attention is required. Knowledge requirement, hence training and/or experience requirement, grows with the introduction of the power tool, for he must know how to adjust and direct the more complex machine of Level 4. He must become a "machinist."
>
> When the mechanically controlled machines of levels 5 and 6 are encountered, job knowledge may not be reduced but attention, decision-making, and machine control requirements are partially or largely reduced. In many instances, the technical knowledge requirement of machine functioning and adjustment is reduced tremendously. This is why "machine operators," rather

*Levels of Mechanization and Their Relationship
to Power and Control Sources
(as charted by James R. Bright)*

Initiating control source		Type of machine response			Power source	Level number	Level of mechanization
From a variable in the environment		Responds with action	Modifies own action over a wide range of variation		Mechanical (nonmanual)	17	Anticipates action required and adjusts to provide it
						16	Corrects performance while operating
						15	Corrects performance after operating
			Selects from a limited range of possible prefixed actions			14	Identifies and selects appropriate set of actions
						13	Segregates or rejects according to measurement
						12	Changes speed, position, direction according to measurement signal
		Responds with signal				11	Records performance
						10	Signals preselected values of measurement (includes error detection)
						9	Measures characteristic of work
From a control mechanism that directs a predetermined pattern of action		Fixed within the machine				8	Actuated by introduction of work piece or material
						7	Power-tool system, remote controlled
						6	Power tool, program control (sequence of fixed functions)
						5	Power tool, fixed cycle (single function)
From man	Variable					4	Power tool, hand control
						3	Powered hand tool
					Manual	2	Hand tool
						1	Hand

than machinists are so frequently quite adequate. The job becomes more nearly one of simple machine actuation, workfeeding, patrolling, and inspecting.

In moving to higher levels of mechanization where the machines supply control signals there is a further reduction in the attention-judgment-decision-action activity demanded of the worker. Of course, this *may* be offset by increasing technical complexity of the equipment and its adjustment, which requires additional knowledge by the worker. Yet the reverse seems more common.

When the variable control levels (Levels 11-17) are reached, we find that the worker contributes little or no physical or mental effort to the production activity. More of the functions are mechanized. The inspecting devices feed corrective information into the machine and thus relieve the operator of mental effort, decision-making, judgment, and even the need to adjust the machine. By its very definition the truly automatic machine needs no human assistance for its normal functioning. "Patrolling" becomes the main human contribution. The "operator," if he is still there, becomes a sort of watchman, a monitor, a helper. We might think of him as a liaison man between machine and operating management.[35]

That this conclusion is not simply the result of an abstract schematization of the problem, but corresponds to real conditions, is made clear by Bright through numerous examples: "During the several years that I spent in field research on managerial problems in so-called automated plants and in exploring automation with industrialists, government personnel, social scientists, and other researchers, I was startled to find that the upgrading effect had not occurred to anywhere near the extent that is often assumed. On the contrary, there was more evidence that automation had reduced the skill requirements of the operating work force, and occasionally of the entire factory force, including the maintenance organization."[36]

Bright's reference to the maintenance organization reflects a considerable study he made of maintenance and repair work in the plants he analyzed. He found that the effect of increased mechanization, particularly in its more developed stages, upon the need for skilled maintenance mechanics is not so simple as is usually supposed. On the one side, it is certainly true that the mechanization of a larger span of the production process, the novelty of the equipment used, the electronic circuitry and electro-hydraulic-pneumatic actuating mechanisms, and other such factors tend to increase the need for maintenance and for new skills. But on the other side, he points to a great many factors which tend in the other direction. For example: "One of the effects of automation is to compress the production line and literally to reduce the total physical amount of machinery for a given output, even though that machinery may be more complex. Hence, in several instances the maintenance force was reduced simply because the total volume of machinery was reduced. This reduction more than compensated for the increase in the complexity of the equipment."[37] This tendency is reinforced by the mechanization of trouble prevention itself with monitoring devices that anticipate difficulties, by the simplification and standardization of control mechanisms, and so on.

At the same time, the novelty of the control equipment affects only small parts of the maintenance staff. "I found no evidence," says Bright, "that tinsmiths, pipefitters, welders, and carpenters required increased skill, some evidence that hydraulic and pneumatic repairmen need better training because of the increased complexity of the control circuitry, and much evidence that a significant proportion of electricians need extensive additional training." But even in the last instance, Bright points out, the need for electronic maintenance skills requires retraining a very limited number of mechanics. In one plant, in a maintenance crew of seven hundred, eighty were electricians, and the plant engineer found that he needed only three or four competent electronic repairmen per shift. "In other words, only about 10 percent of his electricians needed specialized skill—and these amounted to only 1 percent of his total maintenance force."[38] Overall, while Bright found a number of plants that increased their maintenance staffs substantially, he also found contrasting instances, such as the following:

> The most automatic small refinery in the U.S. in 1954 had a maintenance force amounting to 21 percent of the total work force. Conventional refineries show a 50 to 60 percent ratio.
>
> Two major parts-manufacturing plants, each employing over 10,000, have devoted their attention to automatic production since 1946. Both are well known in engineering circles for outstanding automation accomplishments and use literally hundreds of highly automatic machines. Both maintenance forces are characterized by one peculiarity—lack of change. The maintenance force has remained a steady 3.5 to 5 percent of the work force in one firm, and 6 to 8 percent in the other, over the last dozen years of aggressive mechanization with automatic machinery.[39]*

The entire evolution is marked by the very same design characteristic that the consumer sees in home appliances or automobiles: the modular construction of equipment for easy replacement of entire assemblies. While the consumer finds it expensive to buy an entire new assembly in order to replace a part worth a few cents, and also finds the consequent deterioration

---

* John I. Snyder, Jr., president and chairman of U.S. Industries, Inc., manufacturers of automatic machinery and controls, writes: "Another myth is that automation will create jobs, not only in the running of machines, but in the building and maintenance of them. Of course this is true to a degree, but not nearly to the degree that some would have us believe. Experience has shown that after the initial 'debugging' of automated machines, they require relatively very little maintenance." [40]

Changing Contribution Required of Operators with Advances in Levels of Mechanization
(as charted by James R. Bright)

Worker contribution[1] or sacrifice traditionally receiving compensation	Mechanization levels				
	1–4	5–8	9–11	12–17
	Hand control	Mechanical control	Variable control, signal response	Variable control, action response
Physical effort	Increasing-decreasing	Decreasing	Decreasing-nil	Nil
Mental effort	Increasing	Increasing-decreasing	Increasing-decreasing	Decreasing-nil
Manipulative skill (dexterity)	Increasing	Decreasing	Decreasing-nil	Nil
General skill	Increasing	Increasing	Increasing-decreasing	Decreasing-nil
Education	Increasing	Increasing	Increasing or decreasing	Increasing or decreasing
Experience	Increasing	Increasing-decreasing	Increasing-decreasing	Decreasing-nil

Exposure to hazards	Increasing	Decreasing	Decreasing	Nil
Acceptance of undesirable job conditions	Increasing	Decreasing	Decreasing-nil	Decreasing-nil
Responsibility[2]	Increasing	Increasing	Increasing-decreasing	Increasing, decreasing, or nil
Decision-making	Increasing	Increasing-decreasing	Decreasing	Decreasing-nil
Influence on productivity[3]	Increasing	Increasing-decreasing, or nil	Decreasing-nil	Nil
Seniority	Not affected	Not affected	Not affected	Not affected

1. Refers to operators and not to setup men, maintenance men, engineers, or supervisors.
2. Safety of equipment, of the product, of other people.
3. Refers to opportunity for the worker to increase output through extra effort, skill, or judgment.

Why Advances in Automation Can Have
Contrary Effects on Skill Requirements
(as charted by James R. Bright)

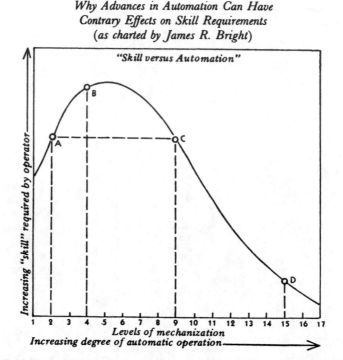

of repair skills among servicemen exasperating, in industry, where the length of time the production system is shut down for repairs is the most important and expensive factor, replacing entire assemblies is by far the cheapest way. But this tendency further reduces the number of mechanics who are able to do anything but replace the entire module after the source of the malfunction has been located—and this is something advanced electronic machinery increasingly does for itself. Moreover, even the work of the repair mechanic is now being studied and standardized in much the same fashion as that of the production worker. One such system is called Universal Maintenance Standards:

> UMS uses a number of selected jobs or types of work whose work content is known and divides them into ranges of time. . . . One national organization had by the end of 1960 almost finished establishing universal standard data elements for all plants. Anyone in any plant could use the same standard for the jobs in his department. Fifty-two thousand universal elements had been isolated and studied. The data are placed on punch cards and magnetic tape to utilize a computer with a large memory. Plans will allow each foreman anywhere in the country to call into a central unit, to get a standard time for the job in which he is interested. . . . A foreman can, for example, get a standard

time for a job that may only be running a couple of hours. These jobs were not studied previously because it took too long to make the studies.[41]

The picture of mechanization and skill cannot be completed without reference to those industries where mechanization has made the process so automatic that the worker takes virtually no physical part in it whatsoever. This theoretical ideal can be but seldom realized, and most plants considered "automatic" still require a great deal of direct labor of all sorts. But in the chemical industry it very often comes closer to realization than elsewhere, because of the nature of the continuous processes employed and the possibility of moving the entire product-in-preparation within enclosed vessels and piping. Thus the chemical operator is singled out, time and again, as the outstanding beneficiary of "automation," and the praises of this job are sung in countless variations. The work of the chemical operator is generally clean, and it has to do with "reading instruments" and "keeping charts." These characteristics already endear him to all middle-class observers, who readily confuse them with skill, technical knowledge, etc. Yet few have stopped to think whether it is harder to learn to read a dial than to tell time. Even Blauner, who selected this work as his example of the tendency of modern industry to bring the total process of production back within the ken of the worker, admits that chemical operators need know nothing about chemical processes.[42] He cites one oil refinery personnel executive who has placed a limit on the I.Q.'s of workers hired for operating jobs, another who calls them "only watchmen," and reports this outburst by a chemical operator:

> It takes skill to be an operator. Maybe you've heard of this job-evaluation program that's been going on. Well, our supervisor thinks there's not much skill in our work. The way he described our jobs for the job-evaluation program, it's like he thinks you could train a bunch of chimps and they could do the job. He thinks we're a bunch of idiots. That has caused unhappy feelings.[43]

Transfers from operations to maintenance are common, Blauner says, but there are virtually no transfers in the other direction. This may also have something to do with pay rates, since, as reported by the Bureau of Labor Statistics for June 1971, the *highest* average pay rate among chemical operators (Class A) is lower than the *lowest* average classification among maintenance mechanics. Class B chemical operators are paid on the level of stock clerks.[44]

What happens in such an industry is comparable to what happens in other production systems: the automation of processes places them under the control of management engineers and destroys the need for knowledge or training. "In the chemical industry, although the division of labour does not as a rule take the form of the assembly line, the modernization of equipment has considerably lessened the time needed to train 'experienced' workers. In a factory for distilling coal-tar (Lyons, 1949), the training of a 'good distiller,' which previously took about six months, to-day takes three weeks. This is due particularly to the process of continuous distillation, resulting from more numerous and more sensitive measuring devices."[45]

Those who have tried to see in continuous-process industry (as it is organized in the capitalist mode of production) the method, at last discovered, whereby the worker is restored to his human birthright, but who at the same time are aware of the low pay and undemanding duties in these occupations, wrestle with the dilemma to no avail. Thus Joan Woodward:

> The main problem in this type of industry appeared to be establishing the occupational status of the plant operators; these men, although often highly skilled, were not formally recognized as skilled outside their own firm. The traditional differentiation between the skilled and the semi-skilled worker does not allow for a situation in which the manual and motor elements of skill have been taken out of the main production task, while the conceptual and perceptual elements remain.
>
> The skill of a plant operator is of the perceptual and conceptual kind in that over a period of time he has to learn to absorb a great deal of information and to act on it continuously. But, this skill not being recognized formally, the plant operator has to be recruited as a semi-skilled worker at a comparatively low rate of pay. Several firms felt that this created difficulties for them, as in the competitive labour situation of the area it was very difficult to find and keep men of sufficiently high calibre at this low figure. A job in which the emphasis is laid more on the intellectual elements of skill, and which calls for articulation in both speech and writing, can attract only those with the minimum educational qualifications.[46]

Here we are told that the chemical process operator is not formally credited with a high degree of skill because the nature of that skill is chiefly intellectual, conceptual, requires education, etc. But in capitalist society, it is these very elements which are always accorded a higher degree of recognition than manual skills; why not in this case? We are further told that this problem exists only outside the firm; within the firm the skill is presumably recognized and appreciated. But despite this, "the plant operator has to be recruited as a semi-skilled worker at a comparatively low rate of pay." The exact nature of the constraint is not specified, and so we must take leave to doubt it. Is not the matter better understood as being exactly what it seems, without resort to convoluted theorizing? Those who, unlike Joan Woodward, are not even aware of the low pay, the low "occupational status," and the limited training of the chemical operator in their ignorance manage much more smoothly the feat of seeing him as the worker who now controls entire factories, needs much "technical knowledge," and represents a reversal of the trend of modern industry.

Considered only in their physical aspect, machines are nothing but developed instruments of production whereby humankind increases the effectiveness of its labor. Just as in producing a simple tool the worker fashions, preparatory to the direct production process itself, an aid for that process, in the same way the production of modern means of production, no matter how complex or developed, represents the expenditure of labor time not for the direct making of the product but for the making of instruments to help in the making of the product or service. This past labor, incorporated into instruments of production, imparts its value to the product piecemeal, as it is used up in productions—a fact which the capitalist recognizes in the depreciation allowance.

Once labor has been embodied in instruments of production and enters the further processes of labor to play its role there, it may be called, following Marx, *dead labor*, to distinguish it from the *living labor* which takes part directly in production. Now, as a material process, production which makes use of tools, instruments, machinery, buildings, etc. is an ordinary and easily comprehensible activity: living labor making use of its own past stored-up labor to carry on production. As such a purely physical process, its terms are as clear as the relation between the first axes or potter's wheels and the men and women who used them.

But within the framework of capitalist social relations, all this is reversed. The means of production become the property of the capitalist, and thus past or dead labor takes the form of capital. The purely physical relationship assumes the social form given to it by capitalism and itself begins to be altered. The ideal toward which capitalism strives is the domination of dead labor over living labor. In the beginning this ideal is seldom realized, but as capitalism develops machinery and makes use of its every suitable technical peculiarity for its own ends, it brings into being this system of the domination of living by dead labor not just as an allegorical expression, not just as the domination of wealth over poverty, of employer over employed, or of capital over labor in the sense of financial or power relationships, but as a *physical fact*. And this is brought about, as we have seen, by the incessant drive to enlarge and perfect machinery on the one hand, and to diminish the worker on the other. The expression Marx gave to this process at a time when it was just beginning cannot be improved upon even from the present vantage point of another century of its further development:

> Every kind of capitalist production, in so far as it is not only a labour-process, but also a process of creating surplus-value, has this in common, that it is not the workman that employs the instruments of labour, but the instruments of labour that employ the workman. But it is only in the factory system that this inversion for the first time acquires technical and palpable reality. By means of its conversion into an automaton, the instrument of labour confronts the labourer, during the labour-process, in the shape of capital, of dead labour, that

dominates, and pumps dry, living labour-power. The separation of the intellectual powers of production from the manual labour, and the conversion of those powers into the might of capital over labour, is, as we have already shown, finally completed by modern industry erected on the foundation of machinery. The special skill of each individual insignificant factory operative vanishes as an infinitesimal quantity before the science, the gigantic physical forces, and the mass of labour that are embodied in the factory mechanism and, together with that mechanism, constitute the power of the "master." [47]

It is of course this "master," standing behind the machine, who dominates, pumps dry, the living labor power; it is not the productive strength of machinery that weakens the human race, but the manner in which it is employed in capitalist social relations. It has become fashionable, however, to attribute to machinery the powers over humanity which arise in fact from social relations. Society, in this view, is nothing but an extrapolation of science and technology, and the machine itself is the enemy. The machine, the mere product of human labor and ingenuity, designed and constructed by humans and alterable by them at will, is viewed as an independent participant in human social arrangements. It is given life, enters into "relations" with the workers, relations fixed by its own nature, is endowed with the power to shape the life of mankind, and is sometimes even invested with designs upon the human race.* This is the reification of a social relation; it is, as we have already noted earlier in this chapter, nothing but *fetishism*, in Marx's sense of the term. "In order . . . to find an analogy, we must have recourse to the mist-enveloped regions of the religious world. In that world the productions of the human brain appear as independent beings endowed with life, and entering into relation both with one another and the human race. So it is in the world of commodities with the products of men's hands. This I call the Fetishism which attaches itself to the

---

* It is characteristic of bourgeois ideologists that although many of them take a positive view of the effects of machinery and some others adopt an attitude of horror at its effects, both attribute the results, whether hopefully or pessimistically interpreted, to "the machine." Thus Jacques Ellul, today a leader of the pessimists, waits no longer than the fifth page of his book on this subject before making his standpoint perfectly clear: "It is useless to rail against capitalism. Capitalism did not create our world; the machine did." A few lines further he says: "The machine took its place in a social milieu that was not made for it, and for that reason created the inhuman society in which we live." But what was that "social milieu" if not capitalism? And was it just by chance that the machine "took its place" in this social milieu? Was it an accidental confluence, or was it the whole course of its history which made capitalism create the machine and use it as it does? The arbitrariness of this starting point is of a piece with Ellul's artificial view throughout, which is constructed on every level to exonerate capitalism; perhaps this accounts for its being so fashionable in liberal circles.[48]

products of labour, so soon as they are produced as commodities."[49] This fetishism achieves its greatest force when it attaches to those products of men's hands which, in the form of machinery, become capital. Acting for the master in a way which he plans with inexhaustible care and precision, they seem in human eyes to act *for themselves and out of their own inner necessities*. These necessities are called "technical needs," "machine characteristics," "the requirements of efficiency," but by and large they are the exigencies of capital and not of technique. For the machine, they are only the expression of that side of its possibilities which capital tends to develop most energetically: the technical ability to separate control from execution.

In reality, machinery embraces a host of possibilities, many of which are systematically thwarted, rather than developed, by capital. An automatic system of machinery opens up the possibility of the true control over a highly productive factory by a relatively small corps of workers, providing these workers attain the level of mastery over the machinery offered by engineering knowledge, and providing they then share out among themselves the routines of the operation, from the most technically advanced to the most routine. This tendency to socialize labor, and to make of it an engineering enterprise on a high level of technical accomplishment, is, considered abstractly, a far more striking characteristic of machinery in its fully developed state than any other. Yet this promise, which has been repeatedly held out with every technical advance since the Industrial Revolution, is frustrated by the capitalist effort to reconstitute and even deepen the division of labor in all of its worst aspects, despite the fact that this division of labor becomes more archaic with every passing day.* This observation may easily be verified by the fact that workers in each industry today are far less capable of operating that industry than were the workers of a half-century ago, and even less than those of a hundred years ago. The "progress" of capitalism seems only to deepen the gulf between worker and machine and to subordinate the worker ever more decisively to the yoke of the machine.**

---

* As Georges Friedmann says, for once clearly and unambiguously: "The theory of automation gives hope of the total disappearance of unpleasant work, the relocating of workers driven from industry by technical progress in other skilled occupations, and the transformation of the man at work into a sort of demiurge or creator, making and minding machines. But these are technicians' abstractions which the actual evolution of capitalist societies since the beginning of this century has cruelly contradicted."[50]

** One of Marx's comments on this score has so often been subjected to a flat misreading in recent years that it is necessary to comment on it. The passage: ". . . Modern Industry . . . imposes the necessity of recognising, as a fundamental law of production, variation of work, consequently fitness of the labourer for varied work, consequently the greatest possible development of his varied aptitudes. It becomes a question of life and death for society to adapt the mode of production to the normal functioning of this

If the machine is fetishized, the division of labor in its present form is the subject of a veritable religion. Consider this from the author of a book on modern science and society:

> The industrial assembly line, for instance, is an important social invention in the division of labor, and modern machine technology is impossible without it no matter how much scientific knowledge we have. Therefore, since science and technology are now extremely interdependent and fructifying for each other, both are fundamentally dependent upon the maintenance of that great division of labor which is so essential a characteristic of modern industrial society."[53]

The chief advantage of the industrial assembly line is the control it affords over the pace of labor, and as such it is supremely useful to owners and managers whose interests are at loggerheads with those of their workers. From a technological point of view, it is extraordinarily primitive and has little to do with "modern machine technology." Nevertheless, in such barbarous relics is found the seat of "scientific knowledge" and the basis for technology. Apologists for chattel slavery, from Greece to the American South, used to argue that the labors of their fieldhands and domestic slaves were necessary so that they could preserve and develop art, science, and culture. Modern apologists go

---

law. Modern Industry, indeed, compels society, under penalty of death, to replace the detail-worker of to-day, crippled by life-long repetition of one and the same trivial operation, and thus reduced to the mere fragment of a man, by the fully developed individual, fit for a variety of labours, ready to face any change of production, and to whom the different social functions he performs, are but so many modes of giving free scope to his own natural and acquired powers."[51] This, extracted from its context, has been understood to mean that Marx was predicting that with the further development of capitalism an "educated" and "technical" working class would be created by modern industry. In fact, that was not his thought at all, as a reading of the section in question makes clear. He saw capitalism as being in direct contradiction to the tendency of modern industry to call into being a new type of worker, a "fully developed individual," and what he is saying here is that society itself is threatened with extinction unless it rids itself of the capitalist system which, the more modern scientific industry makes it obsolete, the more tenaciously it holds on to and even deepens an outmoded division of labor. "Although then," he says in another place, "technically speaking, the old system of division of labour is thrown overboard by machinery, it hangs on in the factory, as a traditional habit handed down from Manufacture [that is, hand industry], and is afterwards systematically re-moulded and established in far more hideous form by capital, as a means of exploiting labour-power." And at this point he has a footnote assailing Proudhon for interpreting machinery as a synthesis of detail operations for the benefit of the worker.[52] Every line Marx wrote on this subject makes it clear that he did not expect from capitalism or from science and machinery as used by capitalism, no matter how complex they become, any general increase in the technical scope, scientific knowledge, or broadening of the competence of the worker, and that in fact he expected the opposite.

further and instruct the workers that they must keep to their places on the "industrial assembly line" as a precondition for the development of a science and technology *which will then devise for them still better examples of the division of labor*. And it is truly in this way that workers, so long as they remain servants of capital instead of freely associated producers who control their own labor and their own destinies, work every day to build for themselves more "modern," more "scientific," more dehumanized prisons of labor.

Notes

1. Abbott Payson Usher, *A History of Mechanical Inventions* (1929; Boston, 1959), pp. 117-18.
2. Karl Marx, *Capital*, vol. I (Moscow, n.d.), pp. 353-54.
3. Usher, *A History of Mechanical Inventions*, p. 116; quoting Marx, ibid., p. 352.
4. Joan Woodward, *Industrial Organization: Theory and Practice* (London, 1965), chapter 3, esp. pp. 37-42. See also William L. Zwerman, *New Perspectives on Organization Theory* (Westport, Conn., 1970), pp. 5-9.
5. Robert Blauner, *Alienation and Freedom: The Factory Worker and His Industry* (Chicago, 1964), p. 8.
6. James R. Bright, *Automation and Management* (Boston, 1958); and "The Relationship of Increasing Automation and Skill Requirements," in National Commission on Technology, Automation, and Economic Progress, *The Employment Impact of Technological Change*, Appendix Volume II, *Technology and the American Economy* (Washington, D.C., 1966), pp. 201-21.
7. Ibid., p. 210.
8. Ibid., p. 207n.
9. Charles Babbage, *On the Economy of Machinery and Manufactures* (1832; rept. ed., New York, 1963), p. 54.
10. Frank Lynn, Thomas Roseberry, and Victor Babich, "A History of Recent Technological Innovations," in National Commission, *The Employment Impact of Technological Change*, p. 88.
11. Ibid., p. 89.
12. *Loc. cit.*
13. *Business Week*, September 9, 1972, pp. 93-94.
14. Henry R. Towne, Foreword to *Shop Management*; in Frederick Taylor, *Scientific Management* (New York and London, 1947), pp. 5-6.
15. Spencer Klaw, *The New Brahmins: Scientific Life in America* (New York, 1968), p. 192.
16. William C. Leone, *Production Automation and Numerical Control* (New York, 1967), pp. 71-73.
17. Advertisement by Computer Machining Technology in *American Machinist*, November 13, 1972, p. 33.
18. Lloyd T. O'Carroll, "Technology and Manpower in Nonelectrical Machinery," *Monthly Labor Review* (June 1971), p. 61.

19. Leone, *Production Automation and Numerical Control*, p. 81.
20. Donald N. Smith, "NC for Profit and Productivity," *American Machinist*, October 16, 1972, p. 71.
21. *Business Week*, September 9, 1972, p. 94.
22. Quoted in *Cahiers du Mai*, no. 38 (November 1972), p. 15.
23. Alfred Marshall, *Industry and Trade* (London, 1919), p. 212.
24. *Business Week*, September 9, 1972, p. 80.
25. Siegfried Giedion, *Mechanization Takes Command* (New York, 1948), p. 198.
26. U.S. Dept. of Labor, *Technological Trends in Major American Industries*, Bulletin No. 1474 (Washington, 1966), pp. 45-46.
27. *Loc. cit.*
28. Ibid., p. 114.
29. Ibid., p. 117.
30. Morris A. Horowitz and Irwin L. Herrenstadt, "Changes in the Skill Requirements of Occupations, in Selected Industries," in National Commission, *The Employment Impact of Technological Change*, pp. 227, 287.
31. Bright, "Automation and Skill Requirements," in ibid., p. 220.
32. James R. Bright, *Automation and Management* (Boston, 1958), pp. vii, 9, 9n.
33. Ibid., pp. 186-87.
34. The three charts are reproduced from Bright, "Automation and Skill Requirements," pp. 210, 214, and 217, with the permission of the *Harvard Business Review* where they appeared originally.
35. Bright, *Automation and Management*, p. 188.
36. Bright, "Automation and Skill Requirements." p. 208.
37. Ibid., p. 216.
38. *Loc. cit.*
39. *Loc. cit.*
40. John I. Snyder, Jr., "The Myths of Automation," *American Child* (January 1964), p. 2.
41. Gerald Nadler, *Work Design* (Homewood, Ill., 1963), pp. 485-87.
42. Blauner, *Alienation and Freedom*, pp. 144-45.
43. Ibid., pp. 158, 160.
44. *Monthly Labor Review* (October 1972), p. 57.
45. Georges Friedmann, *The Anatomy of Work* (London, 1961, and New York, 1964), pp. 5-6.
46. Woodward, *Industrial Organization*, pp. 63-64.
47. Marx, *Capital*, vol. I, pp. 393-99.
48. Jacques Ellul, *The Technological Society* (New York, 1964), p. 5.
49. *Capital*, vol. I, p. 77.
50. Georges Friedmann, *Industrial Society* (Glencoe, Ill., 1955), p. 384.
51. *Capital*, vol. I, p. 458.
52. Ibid., p. 398.
53. Bernard Barber, *Science and the Social Order* (Glencoe, Ill., 1952), p. 70.

Chapter 10

Further Effects of Management and Technology on the Distribution of Labor

Marx has pointed out that unlike generals, who win their wars by recruiting armies, captains of industry win their wars by discharging armies. A necessary consequence of management and technology is a reduction in the demand for labor. The constant raising of the productivity of labor through the organizational and technical means that have been described herein must, in itself, produce this tendency. The application of modern methods of management and machine technology, however, become practical only with the rapid increase in the scale of production. Thus the rapid increase in the productivity of labor tends to be counterbalanced by the growth in production. Chiefly as a consequence of this, employment in those industries concerned with the production of goods has not declined in absolute terms. Statistics which estimate the numbers of workers in those industrial divisions which are directly concerned with the fabrication of goods (including manufacturing, contract construction, mining, lumbering, fishing, and the so-called mechanical industries—the latter being a term used in early censuses) show a constant rise since the earliest occupational census of 1820 (see table, page 164 below). The enormous size of the working population still concentrated in these industries, and the fact that, despite all mechanization, this total has continued to grow until the present, reflects, besides the growth of output, the limits mechanization itself places on the process of labor displacement. The point at which the worker is cheaper than the machinery which replaces him or her is determined by more than a mere technical relationship: it depends as well upon the level of wages, which in turn is affected by the supply of labor as measured against the demand. And the supply of labor, including the size of the reserve army of workers hunting for jobs, depends in part upon the mechanization of industry, which transforms employed workers into surplus workers. Thus the very rapidity of mechanization, insofar as it makes available a supply of cheap labor by discharging workers from some industries or putting an end to the expansion of employment in others, acts as a check upon further mechanization.*

---

* It has been pointed out that the transfer machines which characterize so-called Detroit automation were first used by Morris Motors in 1927 but were not considered economical, in view of the relative price of labor power at the time.[1]

If the displacement of labor cannot be seen in the figures for the absolute size of the working population occupied in the making of goods, it can be seen in the measures of its *relative* size. If we convert the tabulation to the form of percentages of total nonagricultural employment for each census year, the trend emerges with some clarity (see percentage column of table, below).

*Non-Agricultural Workers, 1820-1970**

	Total number in thousands	Workers in manufacturing, construction, and other "goods producing" industries	
		number in thousands	percent
1820	810	369	45.6
1830	1,167	550	47.1
1840	1,702	828	48.6
1850	2,732	1,375	50.3
1860	4,244	2,153	50.7
1870	6,023	2,979	49.5
1880	8,885	4,539	51.1
1890	13,549	6,549	48.3
1900	18,374	8,641	47.0
1910	25,750	11,836	46.0
1920	30,931	14,179	45.8
1870	6,075	2,890	47.6
1880	8,807	4,237	48.1
1890	13,380	6,155	46.0
1900	18,161	8,103	44.6
1910	25,779	11,864	46.0
1920	30,985	14,221	45.9
1930	38,658	15,345	40.0
1920	27,350	12,745	46.6
1930	29,424	11,943	40.6
1940	32,376	13,204	40.8
1950	45,222	18,475	40.9
1960	54,234	20,393	37.6
1970	70,616	23,336	33.0

* This table is constructed in three parts because there is no single continuous series covering the entire 150 years since the first occupational census. Nor is it possible to splice the three series together, since they were each constructed on somewhat different principles. The first two sections of the table (by, respectively, P. K. Whelpton in 1926 and Alba Edwards in 1943) are attempts at reconstruction of census data; the final portion is from Bureau of Labor Statistics figures as gathered in their monthly payroll surveys. Despite the lack of a continuous series constructed on a single set of principles for the entire period, and despite the unreliability of early occupational statistics, the trends are clear, both as to numbers and percentages.[2]

In view of the untrustworthy nature of nineteenth-century statistics, it would perhaps be wrong to draw from them any other conclusion than that the percentage of those gainfully occupied who were to be found in these goods-producing industries fluctuated in a fairly narrow range, between 45 and 50 percent of nonagricultural employment. And this situation, strikingly enough, continued until 1920; thereafter, the percentage moved consistently downward to the 33 percent figure of the 1970 census. The balance between the growth of production on the one side and the growth of productivity on the other held for a century and was, it would appear, finally broken in the decade of the 1920s, when employment in these manufacturing, extractive, and construction industries began for the first time to fall off as a proportion of all nonfarm employment.

But the more striking tendency is the marked change in occupational composition *within* these industries. As has already been pointed out, the separation of conceptualization from execution—the removal of all possible work from the shop floor, the point of execution, to the office—and the further necessity of maintaining a shadow replica of the entire process of production in paper form, brings into being large technical and office staffs. Statistics from all the principal capitalist countries indicate that there has been a rapid rise, starting before the turn of the century, in the proportion of those not employed directly in production. Characteristically, there were in manufacturing industries around the start of this century somewhere between five and ten nonproduction employees for every hundred employed in production, and by the post-World War II period this had risen to more than twenty per hundred. The figures given for United States manufacturing industries are as follows:[3] *

	Administrative	Production	Admin./prod. ratio
1899	348,000	4,496,000	7.7 percent
1909	750,000	6,256,000	12.0
1923	1,280,000	8,187,000	15.6
1929	1,496,000	8,361,000	17.9
1937	1,518,000	8,553,000	17.7
1947	2,578,000	11,916,000	21.6

* The United States Census data for the ratio of nonproduction to production workers in manufacturing shows "a secular trend upward, beginning in 1899, with some variation in slope but unmistakable in direction. This means that if one is looking for causal forces, the place to look is the whole twentieth century." This is the conclusion of George E. Delehanty, who has done one of the most thorough investigations of this subject. Delehanty points out that the series maintained by the Bureau of Labor Statistics on a different basis gives a different picture, showing a constancy in the ratio up to 1952, and then an upward trend. After reviewing the evidence for both series, Delehanty is forced to conclude that it is impossible to choose between them on the basis of

It is most important to note, however, that not all of this increase is attributable to the tendencies that have concerned us thus far: the reorganization of production and the use of large-scale machine systems. The category of nonproduction employment used in all these figures is a mélange; it is, as Delehanty notes, a *residual* category, including all those employed in manufacturing apart from production, maintenance, and auxiliary workers. This means it includes not only engineers, technicians, and the clerical workers associated with production tasks, but all administrative, financial, marketing, and other such employment. Available figures do not permit a ready separation of the two types of nonproduction employment into those associated with the production process and those associated with other aspects of the corporation's activity, but there are ample indications that the *technical* portion of nonproduction employment is the smaller.

For example, Emil Lederer, an early investigator of this subject, noted that in Germany between 1895 and 1907, technical personnel in manufacturing, mining, and construction increased by 153 percent, while commercial personnel increased by 206 percent.[5] And Delehanty points out that in 1961, in United States manufacturing, while there were 35 nonproduction workers for every 100 production workers, only 7.9 of these were engineers, scientists, or technicians.[6]

It is probably better to turn from these industrial statistics to the occupational figures for technical people if we are to attempt to estimate the size of the grouping created by the new industrial revolution to bear responsibility for the conceptualization and planning of production. According to these figures, there were in 1970 some 1.2 million technical engineers in the United States, employed chiefly in the goods-producing industries but also in transportation and communications, as independent consultants, by government, etc. At the same time, there were about a million technicians, including draftsmen, as well as some 365,000 natural scientists of all kinds. Since this total of close to 2.5 million in these occupations may be compared with a total of no more than 80,000 in the same occupations in 1900, it is clear that these are virtually new occupational groupings, produced by the revolution in production of the past century.

But despite this rapid growth, what is remarkable is the concentration of the technical expertise of United States industries in a relatively small grouping. Taken together, the technical engineers, chemists, scientists, architects, draftsmen, designers, and technicians represented not much more than 3 percent of the total labor force in 1970. Of course, this must be enlarged by the addition of some number, impossible to estimate, of managers serving as

available statistical evidence.[4] But whatever the cause of this statistical quirk, it seems clear enough that the increase in the proportion of nonproduction workers began, in the United States as elsewhere, long before 1952.

primarily technical superiors; but it should also be lowered by the large numbers of natural scientists in fields remote from production in any form, and also by the large numbers of draftsmen (including tracers and detailers) and technicians whose jobs are confined to the repetition of simple activities that are rapidly learned and do not encompass any true conceptualization or planning functions. On balance, it is probably proper to say that the technical knowledge required to operate the various industries of the United States is concentrated in a grouping in the neighborhood of only 3 percent of the entire working population—although this percentage is higher in some industries and lower in others.

The profession of technical engineer is at the present time almost completely restricted to those who have taken at least a four-year degree in engineering. Alongside the traditional specialties within this field and such recent arrivals as aeronautical engineering, industrial engineering, which was a small specialty as recently as the 1930s, has grown most rapidly. This is the aspect of engineering concerned most directly with the design of the production process. In the early part of the nineteenth century, the engineering professions scarcely existed; it has been estimated that there were no more than some 30 engineers or quasi-engineers in the United States in 1816. The first census which enumerated the profession separately, that of 1850, showed about 2,000 civil engineers, few of whom had gained their titles through academic training and most of whom were engaged in canal and railroad construction. It was only with the rise of manufacturing industry that the other categories of engineering came into significant existence, and between 1880 and 1920 the number of engineers of all sorts increased by nearly 2000 percent, from 7,000 to 136,000; now the civil engineer was overshadowed by mining, metallurgical, mechanical, electrical, and chemical engineers. Where, in 1870, only 866 engineering degrees had been granted in the United States, more than that number were enrolled in engineering colleges in the single year 1890, and by 1910 enrollment had risen to 30,000.[7]

The enormous and continuous growth in demand for engineers has created a new mass occupation. On the one hand, this has, along with other new professions such as accounting, given a place to those thrust out of the old middle class by the relative decline of the petty entrepreneurial occupations in trade and other erstwhile arenas of small business. But on the other hand, having become a mass occupation engineering has begun to exhibit, even if faintly, some of the characteristics of other mass employments: rationalization and division of labor, simplification of duties, application of mechanization, a downward drift in relative pay, some unemployment, and some unionization.

In a study done for the National Bureau of Economic Research, *The Demand and Supply of Scientific Personnel*, David M. Blank and George J. Stigler point out that "in the United States since 1890: demand has grown quite rapidly but supply has grown even more rapidly so salaries have drifted downward relative to those for the entire working population." Their index of the ratio of median engineering salaries to those of the full time manufacturing wage earner shows that, if the 1929 ratio is taken as 100, by 1954 the ratio was only 66.6.[8]

The engineer's job is chiefly one of design, but even design, where a project has grown large enough, may be subjected to the traditional rules of the division of labor. An example of how this is done may be seen from the manner in which the A. O. Smith Company went about the engineering of its new automobile frame plant in the 1950s. The design work was broken down into segments, both of the design task to be done and of various technical specialties:

> First we developed a rating chart for all the engineers available. Technical specialties, attitudes, type of work were included. For instance, some might be draftsmen, capable designers, or medium designers, etc. This rating was developed by the group leaders who best knew these people.
>
> We even had a psychological evaluation of every man. . . .
>
> Then we brought the engineers together and told them what our objective was. . . . We laid down certain rules of operation. We said that we would brook absolutely no interference with the rules but would follow them religiously. Anyone who did not so operate would have to move aside. We said that eight hours a day they were to follow the rules. We wanted all complaints to come to us formally and we would consider them and amend the rules, but we wanted no one to make changes or alter procedure from the operating pattern we had established.
>
> We asked each of our group leaders to put on blinders and absolutely not to worry about the other fellow's job. That was engineering management's business to handle.[9]

Admittedly, this procedure was adopted under the pressure of time, but many large engineering projects are handled in a similar way, to the point where many engineers are restricted to a design specialty or an engineering routine, while the conception to which they have been subordinated remains "engineering management's business." At the same time, so-called computer-aided design and computer-aided engineering encourage the translation of the traditional graphic language of the engineer into numerical form so that it may be handled by computers and numerical control instrumentation.[10] This opens the way for the transfer of part of the engineer's function to electronic equipment. Much of the design process, which consists of the recall of standard information, from handbooks, files, etc., together with calculations based upon this information, can then be stored in computer records and the calculations done much more rapidly by the computer.

Some objects, like mechanical cams, can be designed by programmed computations, skipping the use of drawings either as input specifications or as directions for production. The present practice is chiefly to produce numerical tables and text printouts, but the increased use of numerical control of machine tools encourages a trend toward computer outputs of magnetic tapes which then operate production machinery directly.

Small electric motors are examples of much more complicated products which are designed today in a completely automatic way. For a given specification, the computer chooses standardized iron cores for stator and rotor design, as well as rotor axles and casings. It also makes some engineering computations for the wire dimensions and the windings. The input for such an automatic design procedure is simply a table form in which the desired performance data are filled in by an engineer. The computer output is a list of standard parts and data on the wire, the configuration of the windings, and the turns to be wound.[11]

These methods are also being applied to stress analysis for the intricate patterns of flush rivets in aircraft, to bridge design, hospital planning, and other engineering problems. Apart from the labor-saving aspects of the technique, it alters the occupational composition in the same manner as does numerical control. Since such techniques are used in accord with the management-favored division of labor, they replace engineers and draftsmen with data-entry clerks and machine operators, and further intensify the concentration of conceptual and design knowledge. Thus the very process which brought into being a mass engineering profession is being applied to that profession itself when it has grown to a large size, is occupied with duties which may be routinized, and when the advance of solid-state electronic technology makes it feasible to do so.

Outside of the medical and dental fields, there were approximately a million technicians in employment in 1970. Of these, some 310,000 were draftsmen and another 90,000 were surveyors, air traffic controllers, and radio operators, leaving about 600,000 as the total of all others, including engineering and physical science technicians. There is no generally accepted definition of the term, but the distinguishing characteristic of the technician is that he or she functions as "support" for the engineer or scientist; the routine which can be passed to a lower-paid and slightly trained person goes to the technician.* Most have no special training or education apart from what they learned on their jobs; but with the growth of attendance in higher educational institutions,

---

* It should be noted that there is a considerable discrepancy between European and American engineering practices insofar as the use of engineering technicians is concerned. "Overall British industry," says a recent study, "employs 4.7 technicians per professional as against the American ratio of 0.62 technicians per professional." The French and German ratios, while not so high as the British, are still very high compared to the American; in the neighborhood of 2.5 technicians per professional engineer. This means that this occupational classification, important in these European countries, is relatively small in the United States. It also means that whatever the importance given to the classification in Europe, that significance cannot be automatically transferred to the United States.[12]

employers are increasingly using graduates of two-year technical institutes and even holders of four-year degrees. Pay is not much above that received by craftsmen; for example, in early 1971 the average weekly pay of draftsmen was $170, while the average weekly earnings of all craftsmen and foremen were $167.[13]

If in these groups, and particularly among engineers and scientists, is concentrated the technical expertise required by management in modern production processes, this does not exhaust the changes wrought by the revolution in management and technique. A mass of clerical workers has come into existence whose work embraces all that was formerly handled on an informal basis in the shop itself, or on a minimal basis in the small shop offices of the past. Since management now carries on the production process from its desktops, conducting on paper a parallel process that follows and anticipates everything that happens in production itself, an enormous mass of recordkeeping and calculation comes into being. Materials, work in progress, finished inventory, labor, machinery, are subjected to meticulous time and cost accounting. Each step is detailed, recorded, and controlled from afar, and worked up into reports that offer a cross-sectional picture at a given moment, often on a daily basis, of the physical processes of production, maintenance, shipment, storage, etc. This work is attended by armies of clerks, data-processing equipment, and an office management dedicated to its accomplishment. Since there is no way to separate this work from the other administrative work of the corporation—both because work auxiliary to production is not classified and enumerated separately, and also because it is in fact so intermingled with the rest of the administrative work that it probably cannot be subjected to separate statistical accounting—work of this sort must be left for later discussion. It must await the description of other forces in monopoly capitalism, apart from the technical ones we have been discussing, which have caused shifts in the occupations of the working population.

Notes

1. Edwin Mansfield, "Technological Change: Measurement, Determinants, and Diffusion," in National Commission on Technology, Automation, and Economic Progress, *The Employment Impact of Technological Change*, Appendix Volume II, *Technology and the American Economy* (Washington, D.C., 1966), p. 100.
2. P. K. Whelpton, "Occupational Groups in the United States, 1820-1920," *Journal of the American Statistical Association* (September 1926), p. 335; Alba M. Edwards, Sixteenth Census Reports, *Comparative Occupation Statistics for the United States, 1870-1940* (Washington, 1943), chapter XIII; U.S. Bureau of Labor Statistics, *Handbook of Labor Statistics 1972*, Bulletin 1735 (Washington, 1972), p. 89.
3. Reinhard Bendix, *Work and Authority in Industry* (New York, 1956, 1963), p. 214 (as computed from Seymour Melman, "The Rise of Administrative

Overhead in the Manufacturing Industries of the United States, 1899-1947," *Oxford Economic Papers*, vol. III [1951], p. 66).

4. George E. Delehanty, *Nonproduction Workers in U.S. Manufacturing* (Amsterdam, 1968), pp. 50-55.
5. Ibid., p. 66.
6. Ibid., p. 142.
7. Robert Perrucci and Joel E. Gerstl, *The Engineers and the Social System* (New York and London, 1969), p. 53.
8. David M. Blank and George J. Stigler, *The Demand and Supply of Scientific Personnel* (New York, 1957), pp. 21, 25.
9. James R. Bright, *Automation and Management* (Boston, 1958), p. 96.
10. Robert H. Cushman, "Using Computer Aided Design to Talk to Machines in the Factory," *EDN (Electrical Design News)*, August 15, 1972, pp. 28-32.
11. Börje Langefors, "Automated Design," in Robert Colborn, ed., *Modern Science and Technology* (Princeton, N.J., 1965), p. 699.
12. B. C. Roberts, Ray Loveridge, John Gennard, J. V. Eason, et al., *Reluctant Militants: A Study of Industrial Technicians* (London, 1972), p. 7; William M. Evan, "On the Margin—The Engineering Technicians," in Peter L. Berger, ed., *The Human Shape of Work: Studies in the Sociology of Occupations* (New York, 1964), Table I, p. 104.
13. *Occupational Outlook Quarterly* (Fall 1973), p. 28; Paul O. Flaim and Nicholas I. Peters, "Usual Weekly Earnings of American Workers," *Monthly Labor Review* (March 1972), p. 33.

Part III

Monopoly Capital

Chapter 11

Surplus Value and Surplus Labor

The atomized and competitive model of capitalism, in which the individual owner of capital (or family group, or small group of partners) and the capitalist firm were identical, and production in each industry was distributed among a reasonably large number of firms, is no longer the model of capitalism today. Economists and social observers of a variety of persuasions are in general agreement that it has been displaced by a substantially different structure, although they may disagree in their descriptions and analyses of the new structure. Marxists have used various names for this new stage of capitalism since it made its appearance: *finance capitalism, imperialism, neocapitalism, late capitalism.* But since it has been generally recognized that, as Lenin put it in one of the pioneer treatments of the subject, "the economic quintessence of imperialism is monopoly capitalism," it is the latter term that has proved most acceptable.[1] The most substantial recent discussion of this new stage from the Marxist point of view is found in *Monopoly Capital*, by Paul Baran and Paul M. Sweezy.[2]

Monopoly capital had its beginnings, it is generally agreed, in the last two or three decades of the nineteenth century. It was then that the concentration and centralization of capital, in the form of the early trusts, cartels, and other forms of combination, began to assert itself; it was consequently then that the modern structure of capitalist industry and finance began to take shape. At the same time, the rapid completion of the colonization of the world and the international rivalries and armed clashes over the division of the globe into spheres of economic influence or dominance opened the modern imperialist era. Monopoly capitalism thus embraces the increase of monopolistic organizations within each capitalist country, the internationalization of capital, the international division of labor, imperialism, the world market and the world movement of capital, and changes in the structure of state power.

It will already have been noticed that the crucial developments in the processes of production date from precisely the same period as monopoly capitalism. Scientific management and the whole "movement" for the organization of production on its modern basis have their beginnings in the last two decades of the last century. And the scientific-technical revolution, based on the systematic use of science for the more rapid transformation of labor power into capital, also begins, as we have indicated, at the same time. In describing these two facets of the activity of capital, we have therefore been describing two of the prime aspects of monopoly capital. Both chronologically and functionally, they are part of the new stage of capitalist development, and they grow out of monopoly capitalism and make it possible.

It is unnecessary either to repeat or to attempt to summarize the description of the changes in capitalism to be found in *Monopoly Capital*, for obvious reasons, but also because not all the aspects which Baran and Sweezy analyze are of direct interest to us in this discussion. The angle of vision adopted in that work was the view of capitalist society as the producer of a gigantic and growing economic surplus, and the authors were concerned with the way that surplus is used, or "absorbed," in monopoly capitalism. And at the outset, they point out:

> We do not claim that directing attention to the generation and absorption of surplus gives a complete picture of this or any other society. And we are particularly conscious of the fact that this approach, as we have used it, has resulted in almost total neglect of a subject which occupies a central place in Marx's study of capitalism: the labor process. We stress the crucial role of technological change in the development of monopoly capitalism but make no attempt to inquire systematically into the consequences which the particular kinds of technological change characteristic of the monopoly capitalist period have had for the nature of work, the composition (and differentiation) of the working class, the psychology of workers, the forms of working-class organization and struggle, and so on. These are all obviously important subjects which would have to be dealt with in any comprehensive study of monopoly capitalism.[3]

As this makes clear, Baran and Sweezy deal less with the movements of production than with the movements of its outcome, the product. But, as they point out, not only technological change but also a *changing product* bring about new and different processes of labor, a new occupational distribution of the employed population, and thus a changed working class. It is thus clear that the investigation of the movements of *labor* undertaken here are but another form of the investigation of the movements of *value* undertaken in *Monopoly Capital*.

The process by which the movement of value and the movement of labor go hand in hand was described by Marx in his exposition of the general law of capitalist accumulation:

> With accumulation, and the development of the productiveness of labor that accompanies it, the power of sudden expansion of capital grows also. . . . The mass of social wealth, overflowing with the advance of accumulation, and transformable into additional capital, thrusts itself frantically into old branches of production, whose market suddenly expands, or into newly formed

branches. . . . In all such cases, there must be the possibility of throwing great masses of men* suddenly on the decisive points without injury to the scale of production in other spheres. . . . This increase is effected by the simple process that constantly "sets free" a part of the labourers; by methods which lessen the number of labourers employed in proportion to the increased production.[4]

Considered on the scale of the century that has passed since Marx, the "methods which lessen the number of labourers employed in proportion to the increased production" have "set free" workers in vast numbers. The figures for the United States, which are by no means untypical of the major capitalist countries, indicate, as we have already pointed out, that employment in the nonfarm industries devoted to the production of goods began in the 1920s to drop from its traditional 45 to 50 percent of urban employment, and had fallen to 33 percent by 1970. But at the same time the proportion of the working population occupied in agriculture, which amounted to approximately 50 percent in 1880, had by 1970 sunk to less than 4 percent of total employment. Since agriculture, together with manufacturing, construction, and their accompanying extractive industries, occupied three-fourths of the population in 1880 and by 1970 had fallen to only about three-eighths, the mass of labor to be traced is indeed huge; millions of jobs for those who, "freed" from agriculture and "freed" from manufacturing industries, are nevertheless occupied in some way in the social division of labor. In tracing this mass of labor, we will be led not only to "newly formed branches of production" in Marx's sense, but also, as were Baran and Sweezy, into branches of *non*production, entire industries and large sectors of existing industries whose only function is the struggle over the allocation of the social surplus among the various sectors of the capitalist class and its dependents. In this process, capital which "thrusts itself frantically" into every possible new area of investment has totally reorganized society, and in creating the new distribution of labor has created a social life vastly different from that of only seventy or eighty years ago. And this restless and insatiable activity of capital continues to transform social life almost daily before our eyes, without heed that by doing so it is creating a situation in which social life becomes increasingly impossible.

The surplus we seek, because it is a surplus of labor rather than of value, is somewhat different from the surplus Baran and Sweezy sought to trace. For example, for their purpose it was perfectly proper to include in the economic surplus the enormous and apparently irreducible military establishment

---

* Marx here uses the word *Menschenmassen,* which in this context would more properly translate as "human masses" or "masses of people." Since the masses dragooned for the new branches of capitalist industry are now more often *women* than *men,* it is all the more necessary to call attention to the male linguistic bias which in this case, as in others, has affected the translation of Marx.

maintained by capital at great social expense. This is of course one of the chief ways in which the abundance created by modern production is absorbed, drained off, wasted, beneficially for capital though with great injury to society. But insofar as this military establishment involves the bolstering up of demand for the products of manufacturing industry, the labor so utilized is already accounted for in the manufacturing sector of the economy. The fact that labor is used in the making of useless or harmful products does not for the moment concern us. It is the surplus of labor that has been drawn into new forms of production or of nonproduction that concerns us, since it is in this way that the occupational structure and thus the working class have been transformed.

We have already described the manner in which occupations within the manufacturing industries are rearranged and the balance is shifted toward indirect labor so that labor in the mass, as it is applied directly in production, may be lessened in numbers and controlled in its activities. This shift creates a small proportion of technical jobs, most of them closely linked to management, and a larger proportion of lower-grade routinized technical or unskilled clerical jobs. It is now necessary to focus not on the occupational shifts within these traditional industries but rather on the industrial shifts, the movements that change the entire social division of labor. In doing this we are following the course of capital, and the paths along which it has drawn labor. And for this we must attempt to sketch some of the broad social forces at work, and the social changes which are themselves nothing but the results of the rapid accumulation of capital in the monopoly era, as well as the conditions of further accumulation.

Notes

1. V. I. Lenin, *Imperialism, the Highest Stage of Capitalism*, in *Selected Works*, vol. V (New York, n.d.), p. 114.
2. Paul A. Baran and Paul M. Sweezy, *Monopoly Capital* (New York, 1966).
3. Ibid., pp. 8-9.
4. Karl Marx, *Capital*, vol. I (Moscow, n.d.), pp. 592-93.

Chapter 12

The Modern Corporation

The first of these forces is to be found in the changed structure of the capitalist enterprise. The foundations for the theory of the monopolistic corporation were laid by Marx when he described the tendency of capital to agglomerate in huge units. This comes about in the first instance by the *concentration* of capital, which Marx defined as the natural result of the accumulation process: each capital grows and with it grows the scale of production it carries on. The *centralization* of capital, on the other hand, changes the distribution of existing capitals, bringing together "capitals already formed," by means of "destruction of their individual independence, expropriation of capitalist by capitalist, transformation of many small into few large capitals. . . . Capital grows in one place to a huge mass in a single hand, because it has in another place been lost by many."[1] This centralization may be accomplished, as Marx points out, either through competition or through the credit system, whereby many owners make their capital available to a single control.

The scale of capitalist enterprise, prior to the development of the modern corporation, was limited by both the availability of capital and the management capacities of the capitalist or group of partners. These are the limits set by personal fortunes and personal capabilities. It is only in the monopoly period that these limits are overcome, or at least immensely broadened and detached from the personal wealth and capacities of individuals. The corporation as a form severs the direct link between capital and its individual owner, and monopoly capitalism builds upon this form. Huge aggregates of capital may be assembled that far transcend the sum of the wealth of those immediately associated with the enterprise. And operating control is vested increasingly in a specialized management staff for each enterprise. Since both capital and professional management—at its top levels—are drawn, by and large, from the same class, it may be said that the two sides of the capitalist, owner and manager, formerly united in one person, now become aspects of the class. It is true that ownership of capital and the management of enterprises are never totally divorced from each other in the individuals of the class, since both remain concentrated in a social grouping of extremely limited size: therefore, as a rule, top managers are not capital-less individuals, nor are owners of capital necessarily inactive in management. But in each enterprise the direct and personal unity between the two is ruptured. Capital has now transcended its limited and limiting personal form and has entered into an institutional form. This remains true even though claims to ownership remain, in the last resort, largely personal or familial in accordance with the rationale and juridical structure of capitalism.

To belong to the capitalist class by virtue of ownership of capital, one must simply possess adequate wealth; that is the only requirement for membership in that sense. To belong to the capitalist class in its aspect as the direct organizer and manager of a capitalist enterprise is another matter. Here, a process of selection goes on having to do with such qualities as aggressiveness and ruthlessness, organizational proficiency and drive, technical insight, and especially marketing talent. Thus while the managerial stratum continues to be drawn from among those endowed with capital, family, connections, and other ties within the network of the class as a whole, it is not closed to some who may rise from other social classes, not through the acquisition of wealth on their part but through the co-optation of their talent on the part of the capitalist organization which they serve. In this case the ownership of capital later follows from the managerial position, rather than the other way around. But this is exceptional, not just because top management is drawn as a rule from within the class, but also because the stratum as a whole is not a large one.

While the title of "manager" is bestowed in various statistical classifications upon a great variety of jobs, the possession of this title has, for most, nothing to do with the capitalist management of the substantial corporations of the country. For example, the Bureau of the Census classified almost six and one-half million persons, out of some 80 million, as "managers and administrators, except farm," in the census of 1970. But this included perhaps a million managers of retail and service outlets, and as much as another million self-employed petty proprietors in these same fields. It included buyers and purchasing agents, officials and administrators at the various levels of government, school administration, hospitals and other such institutions; postmasters and mail superintendents; ships' officers, pilots, and pursers; building managers and superintendents; railroad conductors; union officials; and funeral directors. Since such categories consume almost half of the entire classification, it is clear without further analysis of the rest that the managerial stratum of true operating executives of the corporate world is quite a small group.

But though proportionately small in the total population, this stratum has become very large in comparison with the pre-monopoly situation. Speaking of the early part of the nineteenth century, Pollard says: "The large-scale entrepreneur of the day began with very limited managerial, clerical or administrative staff: he wrote his own letters, visited his own customers, and belaboured his men with his own walking stick." The small number of clerks employed even in large establishments did not only bookkeeping but timekeeping, quality control, traveling, and draftsmanship. For years, says Pollard, Watt made all his drawings himself, and he gives this remarkable statistic: "The Arkwrights, in 1801-4, employed only three clerks to look after 1,063 workers, nearly all of whom, again, were paid by complicated piece rates."[2] In the United States, Alfred D. Chandler points out: "Before 1850 very few American businesses needed the services of a full-time administrator or required a clearly defined administrative structure. Industrial enterprises were very small, in comparison with those of today. And they were usually family affairs. The two or three men responsible for the destiny of a single enterprise handled all its basic activities—economic and administrative, operational and entrepreneurial."[3]

The institutionalization of capital and the vesting of control in a specialized stratum of the capitalist class corresponds chronologically to an immense growth in the scale of management operations. Not only is the size of enterprises growing at a great pace—to the point where a few enterprises begin to dominate the productive activity of each major industry—but at the same time the functions undertaken by management are broadened very rapidly. We have already traced this development in the sphere of production. When fully reorganized in the modern corporation, the producing activities are subdivided among functional departments, each having a specific aspect of the process for its domain: design, styling, research and development; planning; production control; inspection or quality control; manufacturing cost accounting; work study, methods study, and industrial engineering; routing and traffic; materials purchasing and control; maintenance of plant and machinery, and power; personnel management and training; and so on.

But if the engineering organization was the first requirement, it was soon outstripped in functional importance by the marketing apparatus. The first great integrated corporations, which began to appear in the United States in the 1880s and 1890s, were constructed on the basis of a new approach to the marketing problem, and it is not too much to say that after the assurance of basic engineering requirements it was this revolutionary marketing approach that served as the basis for the monopolistic corporation. The earlier pattern had been one of buying and selling through commission agents, wholesalers, and the like. The growing scope of the market, based upon improvements in transport and communications as well as upon the rapid increase in the size of cities created by the growth of industry, showed itself not only through increases in volume but also in geographical dispersion. The fundamental corporate innovation in this area was the national marketing organizations they established as part of their own structures, organizations which were soon to become international.[4]

The transportation network was the first arena for the giant corporation. The railroads and shipping organizations, by virtue of their demand for steel rails, plate, and structural shapes, drew in their wake the steel industry which had just begun to become proficient in the manufacture of steel at a price and quantity that made these developments possible.

Special adaptations of the means of transport to food shipping, in the form of insulated and refrigerated compartments (at first iced, later mechanically cooled), made possible the long-distance movement of the most essential commodities required by the rapidly growing urban centers. The cities were released from their dependence on local supplies and made part of an international market. Gustavus Swift began in the mid-1870s to market Western meat in the Eastern region, and by the end of the century his organization had become a giant vertically integrated manufacturing, shipping, and marketing empire. This lead was soon followed by a number of other meatpackers, as well as by Andrew Preston who, beginning with bananas in the 1890s, had laid the foundation for the United Fruit Company by the end of the decade.

In general, the industrialization of the food industry provided the indispensable basis of the type of urban life that was being created; and it was in the food industry that the marketing structure of the corporation—embracing sales, distribution, and intensive consumer promotion and advertising—became fully developed. The canning industry had come into being in the 1840s with the development of stamping and forming machinery for producing tin cans on a mass basis. The expansion of this industry to embrace national and international markets did not come, however, until the 1870s, when further technical developments, including rotary pressure cookers and automatic soldering of cans—not to speak of the development of rail and sea transport—made it possible.[5] And soon thereafter, in the 1890s, the automatic-roller process for milling grain formed the basis for the international marketing of centrally produced flour.

Apart from food, various other industries based themselves upon the urban pattern of life that was coming into being. Steel-frame construction in the cities brought about a demand which supplemented and soon replaced the railroads as the prime market for steel. The production of petroleum was perforce localized, while its use was international, and the marketing apparatus of the oil industry corresponded to this. The tobacco industry is another example: cigarettes were smoked almost entirely in the cities. The cigarette rolling machine devised in 1881 furnished the technical basis upon which Duke raised a national and international sales organization.

Cyrus McCormick's vast agricultural-machinery enterprise was built upon his own worldwide marketing and distribution organization, as was William Clark's Singer Sewing Machine Company. In these cases, as in the cases of the many machine-building and electrical-equipment companies that came into existence in the early period of monopoly capitalism, the need for a self-operated marketing organization was imposed, in addition to those factors we have already discussed, by two further reasons. First, the orders, specifications, and uses of the products became more technical and complicated, and demanded a specially trained sales organization which could work closely with the engineering division. And second, the new machines could not be sold without the provision of maintenance, service, and in many cases installation. This made it difficult for the manufacturer to be represented on the spot by existing trade facilities. Factors such as the need to provide service and replacement parts virtually dictated to the new automobile industry the construction of its own marketing network.

Thus marketing became the second major subdivision of the corporation, subdivided in its turn among sales, advertising, promotion, correspondence, orders, commissions, sales analysis, and other such sections. At the same time, other functions of management were separated out to form entire divisions. Finance, for example, although not as a rule large in size, became the brain center of the entire organism, because here was centralized the function of watching over capital, of checking and controlling the progress of its enlargement; for this purpose, the finance division has its own subdivisions for borrowing, extending credit, collections, supervising cash flow, stockholder relations, and overall supervision of the financial condition of the corporation. And so on, throughout the various functions and activities of the corporation, including construction and real estate, legal, public relations, personnel and labor relations, etc.

Each of these corporate subdivisions also requires, for its own smooth functioning, internal departments which reflect and imitate the subdivisions of the entire corporation. Each requires its own accounting section, ranging from the complex cost accounting of the manufacturing divisions to the simpler budgeting functions required of even the smallest divisions. Each often controls its own hiring through its own personnel department; many require separate maintenance and cleaning sections, as well as traffic and routing, office management, purchasing, planning, correspondence, and so forth. Thus each corporate division takes on the characteristics of a separate enterprise, with its own management staff.

The picture is rendered still more complex by the tendency of the modern corporation to integrate, vertically as well as horizontally. Thus, by growth and by combination, the manufacturing corporation acquires facilities for the production of raw materials, for transportation, semi-banking institutions for the raising of capital or extending of credit, etc. At the same time, horizontal integration brings together a variety of products under the aegis of a single aggregate of capital, sometimes assembling under one overall financial control products and services bearing no discernible relation to each other except in their function as sources of profit. Each of these massive sub-corporations requires a complete management structure, with all of its divisions and subdivisions.

As Chandler has related, the eventual outcome of this pyramiding was the need for decentralization, and the result was the modern decentralized corporate structure pioneered by Du Pont, General Motors, Standard Oil of New Jersey, and Sears Roebuck in the 1920s, and much imitated since. The essence of the policy has been best explained, in brief form, by Alfred P. Sloan, long-time operating head of General Motors and the person responsible, more than any other, for the adaptation of this method to that corporation. It places, he said, "each operation on its own foundation . . . assuming its own responsibility and contributing its share to the final result." The final result is of course the accumulation of capital. Each section "develops statistics correctly reflecting the relation between the net return and the invested capital of each operating division—the true measure of efficiency. . . ." This "enables the Corporation to direct the placing of additional capital where it will result in the greatest benefit to the Corporation as a whole."[6]

From this brief sketch of the development of the modern corporation, three important aspects may be singled out as having great consequences for the occupational structure. The first has to do with *marketing*, the second with the *structure of management*, and the third with the *function of social coordination* now exercised by the corporation.

The overall purpose of all administrative controls is, as in the case of production controls, the elimination of uncertainty and the exercise of constraint to achieve the desired result.* Since markets must remain the prime area of uncertainty, the effort of the corporation is therefore to reduce the *autonomous character* of the demand for its products and to increase its *induced* character. For this purpose, the marketing organization becomes second in size only to the production organization in manufacturing corporations, and other types of corporations come into existence whose entire purpose and activity is marketing.

These marketing organizations take as their responsibility what Veblen called "a quantity-production of customers." His description of this task, while couched in his customarily sardonic language, is nevertheless a precise expression of the modern theory of marketing: "There is, of course, no actual

---

* Seymour Melman says: "The explanation of the rather homogeneous increase in the administrative type of overhead will be found, we suggest, in the growing variety of business activities which are being subjected to controls, both private and public. As administrators have sought to lessen the uncertainty of their prospects, by controlling more and more of the factors which determine the advantage of their plants and firms, they have attempted to control, in ever greater detail, production costs, intensity of work, market demands for products, and other aspects of firm operation. Following this hypothesis, the evolution of the business process towards the expansion of controlled areas of activity by management comprises the basis for the additions to administrative functions, and, thereby, the enlarged administration personnel."[7]

fabrication of persons endowed with purchasing power *ad hoc* . . . ; nor is there even any importation of an unused supply of such customers from abroad,—the law does not allow it." Rather, as he points out, there is "a diversion of customers from one to another of the competing sellers." But, from the point of view of each seller, this appears as "a production of new customers or the upkeep of customers already in use by the given concern. So that this acquisition and repair of customers may fairly be reckoned at a stated production-cost per unit; and this operation lends itself to quantity production." Veblen goes on to point out that "the fabrication of customers can now be carried on as a routine operation, quite in the spirit of the mechanical industries and with much the same degree of assurance as regards the quality, rate and volume of output; the mechanical equipment as well as its complement of man-power employed in such production of customers being held to its work under the surveillance of technically trained persons who might fairly be called publicity engineers."[8]

Moreover, within the manufacturing organization, marketing considerations become so dominant that the structure of the engineering division is itself permeated by and often subordinated to it. Styling, design, and packaging, although effectuated by the producing part of the organization, represent the imposition of marketing demands upon the engineering division. The planning of product obsolescence, both through styling and the impermanence of construction, is a marketing demand exercised through the engineering division, as is the concept of the *product cycle*: the attempt to gear consumer needs to the needs of production instead of the other way around. Thus through the direct structure of the marketing organization, and through the predominance of marketing in all areas of the corporation's functioning, a large amount of labor is channeled into marketing.

Second, the change in the overall structure of management: We have already described the specialization of the management function, and the reorganization of management from a simple *line* organization—a direct chain of command over operations from executive head through superintendent and foreman—into a complex of *staff organizations* suited to a subdivision of authority by various specialized functions. It must now be noted that this represents the dismemberment of the functions of the enterprise head. Corresponding to the managing functions of the capitalist of the past, there is now a complex of departments, each of which has taken over in greatly expanded form a single duty which he exercised with very little assistance in the past. Corresponding to each of these duties there is not just a single manager, but an entire operating department which imitates in its organization and its functioning the factory out of which it grew. The particular management function is exercised not just by a manager, nor even by a staff of managers, but by an *organization of workers under the control of managers, assistant managers, supervisors, etc. Thus the relations of purchase and sale of labor power, and*

hence of alienated labor, have become part of the management apparatus itself.
Taken all together, this becomes the administrative apparatus of the corporation. Management has become *administration, which is a labor process
conducted for the purpose of control within the corporation*, and conducted
moreover as a labor process exactly analogous to the process of production,
although it produces no product other than the operation and coordination of
the corporation. From this point on, to examine management means also to
examine this labor process, which contains the same antagonistic relations as
are contained in the process of production.* The effects of this will become
clearer when we examine the evolution of clerical work.

Finally, there is the corporate function of social coordination. The complexity of the social division of labor which capitalism has developed over the
past century, and the concentrated urban society which attempts to hold huge
masses in delicate balance, call for an immense amount of social coordination
that was not previously required. Since capitalist society resists and in fact has
no way of developing an overall planning mechanism for providing this social
coordination, much of this public function becomes the internal affair of the
corporation. This has no juridical basis or administrative concept behind it; it
simply comes into being by virtue of the giant size and power of the corporations, whose internal planning becomes, in effect, a crude substitute for
necessary social planning. Apart from the federal government, for example,
corporations are the largest employing and administrative units in the United
States. Thus the five hundred largest industrial corporations employ almost 15
million persons, or three-quarters of the persons employed by all industrial
corporations. The *internal* planning of such corporations becomes in effect
social planning, even though, as Alfred P. Sloan explained, it is based upon the

---

* In the words of one observer: "The corporation is a society which accomplishes
its work through division of labor—a proposition now so much taken for granted that
it is surprising to think it once represented a discovery. In the modern industrial
corporation, division of labor has been carried to great lengths. Not only are there
broadly separate functions tied to classes of individuals—marketing, production,
finance, law, accounting, technology, management—but within each of these there are
many subdivisions, any one of which may constitute a career. This functionalism rests
on the clear description of the varied, interrelated tasks that make up the corporation's
work. The 'job description' is a statement of task meant to be independent of the
individual who fills the job. Individuals become 'personnel' or 'manpower' in relation
to such job descriptions. . . .

"In the twentieth century we have become increasingly aware of the tendency of
this industrial functionalism to take on the characteristics of the production process
itself. Not only is the complex work of the corporation divided into many discrete tasks
performed by discrete individuals, but there has been a strong tendency to make these
tasks consist of simple, uniform, repeatable elements capable of at least partial
mechanization."[9]

"net return" on "invested capital," which he calls "the true measure of efficiency." The rapid growth of administrative employment in the corporations thus reflects the urgency of the need for social coordination, the general absence of such coordination, and the partial filling of the gap by the corporation operating on a capitalist basis and out of purely capitalist motivations. The expansion of governmental functions of social coordination in recent decades is another expression of this urgent need, and the fact that such government activities are highly visible, in comparison with those of the corporation, has led to the notion that the prime exercise of social control is done by government. On the contrary, so long as investment decisions are made by the corporations, the locus of social control and coordination must be sought among them; government fills the interstices left by these prime decisions.

Notes

1. Karl Marx, *Capital*, vol. I (Moscow, n.d.), p. 586.
2. Sidney Pollard, *The Genesis of Modern Management* (Cambridge, Mass., 1965), pp. 198, 230-31.
3. Alfred D. Chandler, Jr., *Strategy and Structure: Chapters in the History of the Industrial Enterprise* (Cambridge, Mass., 1962), p. 19.
4. Ibid. On this, and for what follows, I am indebted to the first chapter of Chandler's book.
5. Lewis Corey, *Meat and Man: A Study of Monopoly, Unionism, and Food Policy* (New York, 1950), pp. 38-39.
6. Alfred P. Sloan, Jr., *My Years With General Motors* (New York, 1965), p. 50.
7. Seymour Melman, "The Rise in Administrative Overhead in the Manufacturing Industries of the United States, 1899-1947," *Oxford Economic Papers*, new series, no. 3 (1951), P. 92; quoted in George E. Delehanty, *Nonproduction Workers in U.S. Manufacturing* (Amsterdam, 1968), p. 75.
8. Thorstein Veblen, *Absentee Ownership and Business Enterprise in Recent Times* (New York, 1923), pp. 305-306.
9. Donald L. Schon, *Technology and Change: The New Heraclitus* (New York, 1967), pp. 60-61.

Chapter 13

The Universal Market

It is only in its era of monopoly that the capitalist mode of production takes over the totality of individual, family, and social needs and, in subordinating them to the market, also reshapes them to serve the needs of capital. It is impossible to understand the new occupational structure—and hence the modern working class—without understanding this development. How capitalism transformed all of society into a gigantic marketplace is a process that has been little investigated, although it is one of the keys to all recent social history.

Industrial capitalism began with a limited range of commodities in common circulation. On the household level these included the basic foodstuffs in more or less unprocessed form, such as grains and meals, fish and meats, dairy products, vegetables, distilled and fermented liquors, bread and biscuits, and molasses. Other regular household needs included tobacco, coal and candles, lamp oils and soap, tallow and beeswax, paper and printed matter. Clothing production was in its infancy, but the market in the early part of the nineteenth century was already well developed for thread and textiles, including knit goods, and boots and shoes. Household items also included the lumber products of sawmills and planing mills, iron hardware, bricks and stone, clay and glass products, furniture, furnishings, china and utensils, musical instruments, tinware and silverware, cutlery, clocks and watches, apothecary chemicals and drugs.

Behind these were the commodities required as raw materials for the manufacture of such articles: iron and nonferrous ores and metals, raw lumber, tar, pitch, turpentine, potash, furs, hemp, quarry products, and so forth. Transportation required the manufacture of carts, wagons, coaches and carriages, ships and boats, casks and barrels. And the industries which produced tools and implements, such as scythes, plows, axes, and hammers, had just begun to produce machinery in the form of pumps, steam engines, spinning and weaving equipment, and the early machine tools.

In this earliest stage of industrial capitalism, the role of the family remained central in the productive processes of society. While capitalism was preparing the destruction of that role, it had not yet penetrated into the daily life of the family and the community; so much was this the case that one student of United States industrial history described this as the "family stage, in which household manufacturing was supreme. Practically all of the family's needs were supplied by its members. The producer and consumer were virtually identical. The family was the economic unit, and the whole system of production was based upon it. Before 1810 this stage was common throughout many sections of the country; after this date it became more or less localized."[1]

So long as the bulk of the population lived on farms or in small towns, commodity production confronted a barrier that limited its expansion. On the United States farm, for example, much of the construction work (apart from basic framing, as a rule) was accomplished without recourse to the market, as was a good deal of house furnishing. Food production, including the raising of crops and livestock and the processing of these products for table use was of course the daily activity of the farm family, and in large measure so also was the home production of clothing. The farmer and his wife and their children divided among them such tasks as making brooms, mattresses, and soap, carpentry and small smith work, tanning, brewing and distilling, harness making, churning and cheese making, pressing and boiling sorghum for molasses, cutting posts and splitting rails for fencing, baking, preserving, and sometimes even spinning and weaving. Many of these farm activities continued as the natural mode of life of the family even after the beginnings of urbanization and the transfer of employment from the farm to the factory or other city job. Here is a description of the life of workers around the turn of the century which indicates the extent of the transformation that has taken place in the last seventy or eighty years:

> Except in the crowded tenement districts of the large cities—which housed a small fraction of the total urban population—town and city dwellers often produced some of their own food. Especially in the coal and steel regions, the grounds around the urban and suburban house sometimes looked much like a rural farmyard. Many families kept chickens or rabbits, sometimes pigs or goats, and even a cow or two, and raised vegetables and fruits in their own garden plots. A study of 2,500 families living in the principal coal, iron, and steel regions in 1890 suggests that about half of them had livestock, poultry, vegetable gardens, or all three. Nearly 30 percent purchased no vegetables other than potatoes during the course of a year. Describing the anthracite coal region of Pennsylvania in 1904, Peter Roberts wrote that "it is interesting to pass along the Schuylkill and Tremont valleys and see the many little farms which are cultivated by mine employees of the Philadelphia and Reading Coal and Iron Company. In the strike of 1902, hundreds of mine employees' families could not have carried on the fight were it not for the small farms and large gardens they cultivate."
>
> Though only a few miles from the center of the greatest metropolis in the land, Queens County and much of Brooklyn were still semirural in 1890, and many families were as dependent on small-scale agriculture as on the industrial

or commercial employment of the men in the family. North of what is now the midtown area, Manhattan itself was more bucolic than urban, and pigs and goats were often seen along the East River as far south as Forty-second Street. At a time when men worked ten or twelve hours a day, six days a week, much of the care of urban livestock and gardens inevitably fell to women—quite apart from the fact that such tasks were theirs by tradition.

Most purchased foods came into the urban home in their natural, unprocessed, uncanned, unpackaged state. Perhaps the majority of wives undertook a strenuous annual bout of preserving, pickling, canning, and jelly-making, and most baking was done in the family kitchen. Among 7,000 working-class families investigated by the U. S. Bureau of Labor between 1889 and 1892, less than half purchased any bread, and almost all bought huge amounts of flour, an average of more than 1,000 pounds per family per year. Even among the families of skilled craftsmen, who earned more than most other workingmen, one fourth bought no bread, and flour consumption averaged over two pounds per family per day.

No respectable home in 1890 was without a well-used sewing machine—one of the first items widely sold on the installment plan. Most men's clothing was bought, but most of the clothing of women and children was still made at home. In addition, there were curtains and sheets to be hemmed, caps and sweaters and stockings to be knitted and darned. Every prospective mother was expected to knit and sew a complete wardrobe for her first child, and to replenish it thereafter as needed.[2]

Before the present stage of capitalism, food processing was the province on the one side of the farm family, and on the other of the household. The role of industrial capital was minimal, except in transportation. But during the last hundred years industrial capital has thrust itself between farm and household, and appropriated all the processing functions of both, thus extending the commodity form to food in its semi-prepared or even fully prepared forms. For example, almost all butter was produced on farms in 1879; by 1899 this had been reduced to well under three-fourths, and by 1939 little more than one-fifth of butter was being made on farms. Livestock slaughter moved away from the farm both earlier and more rapidly. The proportion of flour used by commercial bakeries climbed rapidly from only one-seventh in 1899 to more than two-fifths by 1939. And during the same period, the per capita production of canned vegetables multiplied fivefold, and of canned fruits twelve times over.[3] As with food, so with clothing, shelter, household articles of all sorts: the range of commodity production extended itself rapidly.

This conquest of the labor processes formerly carried on by farm families, or in homes of every variety, naturally gave fresh energy to capital by increasing the scope of its operations and the size of the "labor force" subjected to its exploitation. The workers for the new processing and manufacturing industries were drawn from the previous sites of these labor processes: from the farms and from the homes, in great part in the form of women progressively transformed in ever larger numbers from housewives into workers. And with the industrialization of farm and home tasks came the subjugation of these new workers to all the conditions of the capitalist mode of production, the chief of which is that they now pay tribute to capital and thus serve to enlarge it.

The manner in which this transition was accomplished includes a host of interrelated factors, not one of which can be separated from the others. In the first place, the tighter packing of urbanization destroys the conditions under which it is possible to carry on the old life. The urban rings close around the worker, and around the farmer driven from the land, and confine them within circumstances that preclude the former self-provisioning practices of the home. At the same time, the income offered by the job makes available the wherewithal to purchase the means of subsistence from industry, and thus, except in times of unemployment, the constraint of necessity which compelled home crafts is much weakened. Often, home labor is rendered uneconomic as compared with wage labor by the cheapening of manufactured goods, and this, together with all the other pressures bearing on the working-class family, helps to drive the woman out of the home and into industry. But many other factors contribute: the pressure of social custom as exercised, especially upon each younger generation in turn, by style, fashion, advertising, and the educational process (all of which turn "homemade" into a derogation and "factory made" or "store bought" into a boast); the deterioration of skills (along with the availability of materials); and the powerful urge in each family member toward an independent income, which is one of the strongest feelings instilled by the transformation of society into a giant market for labor and goods, since the source of status is no longer the ability to make many things but simply the ability to purchase them.

But the industrialization of food and other elementary home provisions is only the first step in a process which eventually leads to the dependence of all social life, and indeed of all the interrelatedness of humankind, upon the marketplace. The population of cities, more or less completely cut off from a natural environment by the division between town and country, becomes totally dependent upon social artifice for its every need. But social artifice has been destroyed in all but its marketable forms. Thus the population no longer relies upon social organization in the form of family, friends, neighbors, community, elders, children, but with few exceptions must go to market and only to market, not only for food, clothing, and shelter, but also for recreation, amusement, security, for the care of the young, the old, the sick, the handicapped. In time not only the material and service needs but even the emotional patterns of life are channeled through the market.

It thereby comes to pass that while population is packed ever more closely together in the urban environment, the atomization of social life proceeds apace. In its most fundamental aspect, this often noticed phenomenon can be explained only by the development of market relations as the substitute for individual and community relations. The social structure, built upon the market, is such that relations between individuals and social groups do not take place directly, as cooperative human encounters, but through the market as relations of purchase and sale. Thus the more social life becomes a dense and close network of interlocked activities in which people are totally interdependent, the more atomized they become and the more their contacts with one another separate them instead of bringing them closer. This is true, for related reasons, also of family life. Apart from its biological functions, the family has served as a key institution of *social life*, *production*, and *consumption*. Of these three, capitalism leaves only the last, and that in attenuated form, since even as a consuming unit the family tends to break up into component parts that carry on consumption separately. The function of the family as a cooperative enterprise pursuing the joint production of a way of life is brought to an end, and with this its other functions are progressively weakened.

This process is but one side of a more complex equation: As the social and family life of the community are weakened, new branches of production are brought into being to fill the resulting gap; and as new services and commodities provide substitutes for human relations in the form of market relations, social and family life are further weakened. Thus it is a process that involves economic and social changes on the one side, and profound changes in psychological and affective patterns on the other.

The movement of capitalist society in this direction is bound up, on the economic side, with the capitalist drive to innovate new products, new services, new industries. The surplus produced first of all in the manufacturing industries in the form of concentrations of wealth is matched on the side of labor by the relative decline in demand for workers in those same industries as they are mechanized. The ample streams of capital meet the "freed" labor in the marketplace upon the ground of new products and industries. This results first of all in the conversion into a commodity of every product of human labor, so that goods-producing labor is carried on in none but its capitalist form. Then new commodities are brought into being that match the conditions of life of the urban dweller, and are put into circulation in the forms dictated by the capitalist organization of society. Thus a plentiful supply of printed matter becomes a vehicle for corporate marketing, as do scientific marvels of the twentieth century such as radio and television. The automobile is developed as an immensely profitable form of transportation which in the end destroys the more practical forms of transportation in the interest of profit. Like machinery in the factory, the machinery of society becomes a pillory instead of a convenience, and a substitute for, instead of an aid to, competence.

In a society where labor power is purchased and sold, working time becomes sharply and antagonistically divided from nonworking time, and the worker places an extraordinary value upon this "free" time, while on-the-job time is regarded as lost or wasted. Work ceases to be a natural function and becomes an extorted activity, and the antagonism to it expresses itself in a drive for the shortening of hours on the one side, and the popularity of labor-saving devices for the home, which the market hastens to supply, on the other. But the atrophy of community and the sharp division from the natural environment leaves a void when it comes to the "free" hours. Thus the filling of the time away from the job also becomes dependent upon the market, which develops to an enormous degree those passive amusements, entertainments, and spectacles that suit the restricted circumstances of the city and are offered as substitutes for life itself. Since they become the means of filling all the hours of "free" time, they flow profusely from corporate institutions which have transformed every means of entertainment and "sport" into a production process for the enlargement of capital.* By their very profusion, they cannot help but tend to a standard of mediocrity and vulgarity which debases popular taste, a result which is further guaranteed by the fact that the mass market has a powerful lowest-common-denominator effect because of the search for maximum profit. So enterprising is capital that even where the effort is made by one or another section of the population to find a way to nature, sport, or art through personal activity and amateur or "underground" innovation, these activities are rapidly incorporated into the market so far as is possible.

The ebbing of family facilities, and of family, community, and neighborly feelings upon which the performance of many social functions formerly depended, leaves a void. As the family members, more of them now at work away from the home, become less and less able to care for each other in time of need, and as the ties of neighborhood, community, and friendship are reinterpreted on a narrower scale to exclude onerous responsibilities, the care of humans for each other becomes increasingly institutionalized. At the same

---

* A story datelined Los Angeles in the *New York Times* of February 20, 1973, tells of a car-smashing derby attended by almost 24,000 persons: "Around a centerpiece of wrecked automobiles, a Cadillac Eldorado bearing a red sign: 'See Parnelli Jones destroy this car,' a Rolls Royce Silver Shadow, a Lincoln Continental Mark IV and some $50,000 worth of other late-model cars bashed each other into junk here yesterday. Billed as the 'world's richest demolition derby,' it ended in a limping, sputtering confrontation between a battered Ford LTD and a Mercury station wagon. . . .

" 'I figure it's a little like the last of the Roman Empire,' George Daines said as he bought tickets (at $8 for adults and $4 for children) for himself and his son. 'I wanted to be here to watch the last of the American empire.' "

time, the human detritus of the urban civilization increases, not just because the aged population, its life prolonged by the progress of medicine, grows ever larger; those who need care include children—not only those who cannot "function" smoothly but even the "normal" ones whose only defect is their tender age. Whole new strata of the helpless and dependent are created, or familiar old ones enlarged enormously: the proportion of "mentally ill" or "deficient," the "criminals," the pauperized layers at the bottom of society, all representing varieties of crumbling under the pressures of capitalist urbanism and the conditions of capitalist employment or unemployment. In addition, the pressures of urban life grow more intense and it becomes harder to care for any who need care in the conditions of the jungle of the cities. Since no care is forthcoming from an atomized community, and since the family cannot bear all such encumbrances if it is to strip for action in order to survive and "succeed" in the market society, the care of all these layers becomes institutionalized, often in the most barbarous and oppressive forms. Thus understood, the massive growth of institutions stretching all the way from schools and hospitals on the one side to prisons and madhouses on the other represents not just the progress of medicine, education, or crime prevention, but the clearing of the marketplace of all but the "economically active" and "functioning" members of society, generally at public expense and at a handsome profit to the manufacturing and service corporations who sometimes own and invariably supply these institutions.

The growth of such institutions calls forth a very large "service" employment, which is further swelled by the reorganization of hospitality on a market basis in the form of motels, hotels, restaurants, etc. The growth not only of such institutions but of immense amounts of floor space devoted to wholesaling and retailing, offices, and also multiple-dwelling units, brings into being a huge specialized personnel whose function is nothing but cleaning, again made up in good part of women who, in accord with the precepts of the division of labor, perform one of the functions they formerly exercised in the home, but now in the service of capital which profits from each day's labor.

In the period of monopoly capitalism, the first step in the creation of the universal market is the conquest of all goods production by the commodity form, the second step is the conquest of an increasing range of services and their conversion into commodities, and the third step is a "product cycle" which invents new products and services, some of which become indispensable as the conditions of modern life change to destroy alternatives. In this way the inhabitant of capitalist society is enmeshed in a web made up of commodity goods and commodity services from which there is little possibility of escape except through partial or total abstention from social life as it now exists. This is reinforced from the other side by a development which is analogous to that which proceeds in the worker's work: the atrophy of competence. In the end, the population finds itself willy-nilly in the position of being able to do little or nothing itself as easily as it can be hired, done in the marketplace, by one of the multifarious new branches of social labor. And while from the point of view of consumption this means total dependence on the market, from the point of view of labor it means that all work is carried on under the aegis of capital and is subject to its tribute of profit to expand capital still further.

The universal market is widely celebrated as a bountiful "service economy," and praised for its "convenience," "cultural opportunities," "modern facilities for care of the handicapped," etc. We need not emphasize how badly this urban civilization works and how much misery it embraces. For purposes of our discussion, it is the other side of the universal market, its dehumanizing aspects, its confinement of a large portion of the population to degraded labor, that is chiefly of interest. Just as in the factory it is not the machines that are at fault but the conditions of the capitalist mode of production under which they are used, so here it is not the necessary provision of social services that is at fault, but the effects of an all-powerful marketplace which, governed by capital and its profitable investment, is both chaotic and profoundly hostile to all feelings of community. Thus the very social services which should facilitate social life and social solidarity have the opposite effect. As the advances of modern household and service industries lighten the family labor, they increase the futility of family life; as they remove the burdens of personal relations, they strip away its affections; as they create an intricate social life, they rob it of every vestige of community and leave in its place the cash nexus.

It is characteristic of most of the jobs created in this "service sector" that, by the nature of the labor processes they incorporate, they are less susceptible to technological change than the processes of most goods-producing industries. Thus while labor tends to stagnate or shrink in the manufacturing sector, it piles up in these services and meets a renewal of the traditional forms of pre-monopoly competition among the many firms that proliferate in fields with lower capital-entry requirements. Largely nonunion and drawing on the pool of pauperized labor at the bottom of the working-class population, these industries create new low-wage sectors of the working class, more intensely exploited and oppressed than those in the mechanized fields of production.

This is the field of employment, along with clerical work, into which women in large numbers are drawn out of the household. According to the statistical conventions of economics, the conversion of much household labor into labor in factories, offices, hospitals, canneries, laundries, clothing shops, retail stores, restaurants, and so forth, represents a vast enlargement of the national product. The goods and services produced by unpaid labor in the home are not reckoned at all, but when the same goods and services are produced by paid labor outside the home they are counted. From a capitalist point of view, which is the only viewpoint recognized for national accounting purposes, such reckoning makes sense. The work of the housewife, though it has the same material or service effect as that of the chambermaid, restaurant worker, cleaner, porter, or laundry worker, is outside the purview of capital; but when she takes one of these jobs outside the home she becomes a productive worker. Her labor now enriches capital and thus deserves a place in the national product. This is the logic of the universal market. Its effect upon the patterns of employment and the composition of the working class will later be treated in greater detail.

Notes

1. Rolla Milton Tryon, *Household Manufactures in the United States: 1640-1860* (Chicago, 1917), pp. 243-44.
2. Robert W. Smuts, *Women and Work in America* (1959; paperback ed., New York, 1971) pp. 11-13.
3. George J. Stigler, *Trends in Output and Employment* (New York, 1947), pp. 14, 24.

Chapter 14

The Role of the State

The use of the power of the state to foster the development of capitalism is not a new phenomenon peculiar to the monopoly stage of the past hundred years. The governments of capitalist countries have played this role from the beginnings of capitalism. In the most elementary sense, the state is guarantor of the conditions, the social relations, of capitalism, and the protector of the ever more unequal distribution of property which this system brings about. But in a further sense state power has everywhere been used by governments to enrich the capitalist class, and by groups or individuals to enrich themselves. The powers of the state having to do with taxation, the regulation of foreign trade, public lands, commerce and transportation, the maintenance of armed forces, and the discharge of the functions of public administration have served as an engine to siphon wealth into the hands of special groups, by both legal and illegal means.

But with monopoly capitalism this role is greatly expanded and takes on a more complex and sophisticated form. In some countries, particularly Germany and Japan, monopoly capitalism both created and was created by a new state power; thus the modern role of the state appears in these countries from the very beginning of the epoch. In other countries, principally the United States and Britain, the capitalist class had marked off for the government a more circumscribed sphere of operations, and for this and other reasons the growth of social and economic interventionism on the part of the state assumed, for a time, the peculiar shape of a movement for reform and appeared to develop as a *struggle against capital*, although this proved illusory. At any rate, in the end and in all places the maturing of the various tendencies of monopoly capitalism created a situation in which the expansion of direct state activities in the economy could not be avoided. This can be clearly seen if we consider some of the reasons for this development under four general headings:

1. Monopoly capitalism tends to generate a greater economic surplus than it can absorb. As a result it becomes increasingly vulnerable to disorders in its overall functioning, in the forms of stagnation and/or severe depression, marked by unemployment and idle plant capacity.* With the diagnosis pointing

---

* It is far beyond our scope to try to deal with this subject here. I recommend to the reader the excellent exposition in Baran and Sweezy, *Monopoly Capital*. While the entire work is devoted to the generation and absorption of the surplus, see especially Chapters 3 and 8.

to a shortage in "effective demand," it has finally been accepted by the policy-makers of capitalist societies that government spending will, to the extent that it is enlarged, fill this gap—the effect of an increase in government spending being merely proportional if taxes are increased a like amount, but greater than proportional if spending outruns tax revenues.[1] But this policy, which has in one form or another been adopted by all capitalist countries, did not become universally accepted doctrine until a half-century after the beginnings of monopoly capitalism, and then only because of the prolonged depression of the 1930s, a crisis which found no spontaneous resolution and which threatened the existence of capitalism on a world scale.

2. The internationalization of capital—with respect to markets, materials, and investments—rapidly created a situation of economic competition which brought in its wake military clashes among capitalist countries. At the same time the spread of revolutionary movements in the countries dominated by foreign capital gave to all capitalist countries an interest in policing the world structure of imperialism. In this situation, the traditional concept of a peacetime military establishment supplemented by war mobilization in time of need eventually gave way, because of the unremitting crisis nature of military needs, to a *permanent war mobilization* as the ordinary posture. This meshed with the need for a government guarantee of "effective demand," and provided a form of absorption of the economic surplus acceptable to the capitalist class.* Like other aspects of monopoly capitalism, this one too was pioneered by Germany (during the Nazi era in the 1930s) and has been practiced on a grand scale by the United States since World War II.

3. Within capitalist nations, poverty and insecurity have become more or less permanent features of social life, and have grown beyond the ability of private philanthropies to cope with them. Since these and other sources of discontent are concentrated in great cities and, if allowed to persist without amelioration, threaten the very existence of the social structure, the government intervenes to sustain life and relieve insecurity. Characteristically, the disputes within the capitalist class over this issue, including disagreements over the scale, scope, and auspices of the welfare measures to be adopted, offer an arena for political agitation which engages the working population as well, and offers a substitute for the revolutionary movements which would soon gain ground if the rulers followed a more traditional laissez-faire course.

---

* *Business Week* once explained this as follows: "There's a tremendous social and economic difference between welfare pump priming and military pump priming. . . . Military spending doesn't really alter the structure of the economy. It goes through the regular channels. As far as a business man is concerned, a munitions order from the government is much like an order from a private customer." Spending for public works and public welfare, on the other hand, "makes new channels of its own. It creates new institutions. It redistributes income. It shifts demand from one industry to another. It changes the whole economic pattern. . . ."[2]

4. With the rapid urbanization of society, and the acceleration of the pace of economic and social life, the need for other government-provided services has increased and the number and variety of these has thereby multiplied. Foremost among these services is education, which has assumed a much enlarged role in the era of monopoly capitalism. The place of educational services in catering to the occupational needs of capitalist society will be treated in a later section of this book, but here we must mention another important function of the educational structure: with the disappearance of farm and small-town life as the major arenas of child-rearing, the responsibility for the care and socialization of children has become increasingly institutionalized. The minimum requirements for "functioning" in a modern urban environment—both as workers and as consumers—are imparted to children in an institutional setting rather than in the family or the community. At the same time, what the child must learn is no longer adaptation to the slow round of seasonal labor in an immediately natural environment, but rather adaptation to a speedy and intricate social machinery which is not adjusted to social humanity in general, let alone to the individual, but dictates the rounds of production, consumption, survival, and amusement. Whatever the formal educational content of the curriculum, it is in this respect not so much what the child *learns* that is important as what he or she *becomes wise to*. In school, the child and the adolescent practice what they will later be called upon to do as adults: the conformity to routines, the manner in which they will be expected to snatch from the fast-moving machinery their needs and wants.*

The school system which provides this as well as other forms of training is only one of the services which are necessarily expanded in the industrialization and urbanization of society and in the specifically capitalist form taken by these transformations. Public health, postal, and many other government functions are similarly expanded by the needs of an intricate and delicately balanced social structure which has no means of social coordination or planning other than the internal corporate planning of the monopolies that provide the skeletal structure of the economy. And many of these "services," such as

---

* This is a way of life that has seldom been expressed more exactly than by Veblen: ". . . 'the consumer,' as the denizens of these machine-made communities are called, is required to conform to this network of standardisations in his demand and uses of them. . . . To take effectual advantage of what is offered as the wheels of routine go round, in the way of work and play, livelihood and recreation, he must know by facile habituation what is going on and how and in what quantities and at what price and where and when, and for the best effect he must adapt his movements with skilled exactitude and a cool mechanical insight to the nicely balanced moving equilibrium of the mechanical processes engaged. To live—not to say at ease—under the exigencies of this machine-made routine requires a measure of consistent training in the mechanical apprehension of things. The mere mechanics of conformity to the schedule of living implies a degree of trained insight and facile strategy in all manner of quantitative adjustments and adaptations, particularly at the larger centres of population, where the routine is more comprehensive and elaborate."[3]

	Gross National Product (GNP) (in billions of dollars)	Total government spending	Government spending as percent of GNP
1903	23.0	1.7	7.4
1913	40.0	3.1	7.7
1929	104.4	10.2	9.8
1939	91.1	17.5	19.2
1949	258.1	59.5	23.1
1959	482.1	131.6	27.3
1961	518.7	149.3	28.8

prisons, police, and "social work," expand extraordinarily because of the embittered and antagonistic social life of the cities.

The growth of government spending, relatively slow in the first half-century of monopoly capitalism, becomes extremely rapid thereafter. The following tabulation made by Baran and Sweezy illustrates this, in terms both of spending figures and the percentage of Gross National Product passing through government in the United States.[4]

It must not be supposed, however, that the impact of government spending upon the occupational structure is proportional to these figures. Much of government spending is channeled through the existing structure of the market rather than through direct government employment: it takes the form of military orders, the letting of contracts for highway and building construction, transfer payments to individuals and businesses, etc. Thus in 1961, when the federal, state, and local governments were spending almost 29 percent of the Gross National Product, the combined civilian employment of all three types of government was 13 percent of total civilian employment. But even this percentage is large, and it has been growing. In federal employment, it is concentrated heavily in the civilian establishment for administering the military; in state and local governments, it is concentrated in education.

Notes

1. Paul A. Baran and Paul M. Sweezy, *Monopoly Capital* (New York, 1966), pp. 143-45.
2. *Business Week*, February 12, 1949.
3. Thorstein Veblen, *The Instinct of Workmanship and the State of the Industrial Arts* (New York, 1914), pp. 313-14.
4. Baran and Sweezy, *Monopoly Capital*, p. 146.

Part IV

The Growing Working-Class Occupations

Chapter 15

Clerical Workers

If we view the evolution of those occupations called "clerical" over a long time span, from the Industrial Revolution to the present, we are soon led to doubt that we are dealing with the continuous evolution of a single stratum. The clerical employees of the early nineteenth-century enterprise may, on the whole, more properly appear as the ancestors of modern professional management than of the present classification of clerical workers. While it is probable that some of the clerks of that time corresponded roughly to the modern clerical worker in function and status, it is for various reasons more accurate to see the clerical workers of the present monopoly capitalist era as virtually a new stratum, created in the last decades of the nineteenth century and tremendously enlarged since then. It is very important that this be understood, because if it is not, and if one ascribes to the millions of present-day clerical workers the "middle class" or semi-managerial functions of that tiny and long-vanished clerical stratum of early capitalism, the result can only be a drastic misconception of modern society. Yet this is exactly the practice of academic sociology and popular journalism.

The place of the handful of clerks in the early industrial enterprise—and there were generally fewer than a half-dozen in even the largest firms—was semi-managerial in terms of the present distribution of functions. Lockwood says of the mid-nineteenth century in his book on British clerical labor that "many of the clerks mentioned at the earlier period were probably performing duties which would nowadays be classified as 'managerial.' "[1] And, in fact, in the eighteenth and early nineteenth centuries, "clerk" or "chief clerk" was the title of the manager in some British industries, railways, and public services. It was not uncommon for clerks to be paid by the manager out of his own salary, thus attesting to their position as assistant managers or at least assistants to the manager, and some would be favored with annuities upon the closing of a works or inheritances upon the death of the owner (Matthew Boulton, the pioneer machine builder, included such a provision in his will). Managers and owners filled clerical posts with their relatives, since clerks often rose into managerships or partnerships.[2] Klingender, writing of the period 1840 to 1860 in Britain, says: "As long as the requirements of banking, commerce, or industry did not exceed the resources of family concerns or small partnerships, there could not be an extensive development of clerical labour. In this early stage there was an almost feudal relationship between the small number of clerks to be found in such offices and their employers. The clerk was more a family servant than a wage labourer."[3] Lewis Corey, writing about the United States, says: "The clerk was an honored employee 150 years ago, and still more so in earlier times. His position was a confidential one, the employer discussed affairs with him and relied on his judgment; he might, and often did, become a partner and marry the employer's daughter. The clerk was measurably a professional and undeniably a member of the middle class."[4]

This picture of the clerk as assistant manager, retainer, confidant, management trainee, and prospective son-in-law can of course be overdrawn. There were clerks—hard-driven copyists in law offices, for example—whose condition and prospects in life were little better than those of dock workers. But by and large, in terms of function, authority, pay, tenure of employment (a clerical position was usually a lifetime post), prospects, not to mention status and even dress, the clerks stood much closer to the employer than to factory labor.

This is underlined by the tiny size of the nineteenth-century clerical groups. The census of 1870 in the United States classified only 82,000—or six-tenths of 1 percent of all "gainful workers"—in clerical occupations.* In Great Britain, the census of 1851 counted some 70,000 to 80,000 clerks, or eight-tenths of 1 percent of the gainfully occupied. By the turn of the century the proportion of clerks in the working population had risen to 4 percent in Great Britain and 3 percent in the United States; in the intervening decades, the clerical working class had begun to be born. By the census of 1961, there were in Britain about 3 million clerks, almost 13 percent of the occupied population; and in the United States in 1970, the clerical classification had risen to more than 14 million workers, almost 18 percent of the gainfully occupied, making this equal in size, among the gross classifications of the occupational scale, to that of operatives of all sorts.

It must be emphasized, for the sake of avoiding confusion with the common but absolutely meaningless term "white-collar worker," that the clerical classification to which these figures refer and which is discussed in this section includes only such occupations as bookkeeper (generally speaking the highest occupation in this group), secretary, stenographer, cashier, bank teller, file clerk, telephone operator, office machine operator, payroll and timekeeping clerk, postal clerk, receptionist, stock clerk, typist, and the like—

---

* Occupational statistics more than a half-century old must be viewed with skepticism, since the methods of counting and of classification, apart from their crudity, were often not comparable to those used at present. They must be taken as estimates rather than precise statistics (even modern statistics fall far short of precision, especially when they involve counts and classifications of the low-wage strata). In the present discussion they are used as indicators of relative orders of magnitude, and they are adequate for that purpose.

and it includes these clerical workers no matter where they are employed, in private or in government offices, in manufacturing, trade, banking, insurance, etc.

The creation of a new class of workers, having little continuity with the small and privileged clerical stratum of the past, is emphasized by fundamental changes in two other respects: composition by sex, and relative pay.

The British census of 1851 counted 19 women under the heading of "commercial clerks," and altogether it is estimated that no more than one-tenth of 1 percent of clerks were women—in other words, fewer than 100 of all clerks in the British Isles. In the United States as late as 1900, the clerical classification of under 900,000 persons was still more than three-quarters male. By the censuses of 1961 in Great Britain and 1960 in the United States, the percentage of women had risen in both countries to about two-thirds. And within only another decade in the United States, three-fourths were women: this represented an increase from a little over 200,000 female clerical workers in 1900 to more than 10 million only seventy years later! Male clerical workers, a rapidly declining proportion, are increasingly confined to occupations such as postal clerks and mail carriers, stock clerks and storekeepers, and shipping and receiving clerks.[5]

If we consider the pay scales for clerical labor as compared with the pay of production labor, the change is just as emphatic. According to Lockwood, the lower grades of British clerks in the period 1850 to 1880 were in the per annum range of £75 to £150. Only some 10 to 15 percent of the working class of the time was in that same range, the portion which Lockwood calls a "highly select superaristocracy."[6] We may conclude from this that the pay of clerks began at about the point where the pay of production and transportation workers left off. In the United States, in 1900, clerical employees of steam railroads and in manufacturing establishments had average annual earnings of $1,011; in the same year, the average annual earnings of workers in these industries was $435 for manufacturing and $548 for steam railroads.[7] And there are other indications that the average pay of the clerical classification was about double the production and transportation workers' average; in 1899, for example, the average pay of all full-time postal employees was $955.[8]

The extent of the change in relative pay scales that has taken place since that time is made clear in a Special Labor Force Report on weekly earnings of full-time workers in the United States, which groups workers by occupation and which was based upon data gathered by the Bureau of Labor Statistics in May 1971.[9] According to this report, the median usual weekly wage for full-time clerical work *was lower than that in every type of so-called blue-collar work*. In fact, it was lower than the median in all urban occupational classifications except service employment:

Occupational group	Median usual weekly earnings of full-time workers
Craftsmen and foremen	$167
Operatives and kindred workers	120
Nonfarm laborers	117
Clerical workers	**115**
Service workers (except private household)	96

Nor does the fact that these medians are a form of averaging distort the picture of relative pay. In fact, the earnings distribution simply bears out the impression conveyed by the medians:

	Percent Distribution by Earnings				
	Under $60	$60-$99	$100-$149	$150-$199	$200 or more
Craftsmen and foremen	1.3	8.6	29.3	31.6	29.2
Operatives and kindred workers	4.2	29.0	36.5	20.8	9.4
Nonfarm laborers	6.9	28.6	38.3	18.6	7.6
Clerical workers	**5.2**	**29.8**	**42.2**	**16.4**	**6.3**
Service workers (except private household)	16.4	35.9	28.2	12.4	7.2

From this tabulation it is clear how similar the pay scales and distributions are in the clerical and operative categories, the differences between the two—both in overall medians and in distribution—favoring the operatives.*

Clerical work in its earlier stages has been likened to a craft.[12] The similarities are indeed apparent. Although the tools of the craft consisted only of pen, ink, other desk appurtenances, and writing paper, envelopes, and ledgers, it represented a total occupation, the object of which was to keep current the records

---

* In Great Britain the trend has been similar. Writing in 1958 and basing himself upon data up to 1956, Lockwood says: ". . . the gross change in income relativities is unmistakable. The main result of this change is that the average clerk is now very roughly on the same income level as the average manual worker, or perhaps even slightly below."[10] And the same conclusion was reached by David M. Gordon on the basis of 1959 data for the United States: "The full distributions of clerical and sales jobs and blue-collar manual jobs were almost exactly comparable," so far as earnings are concerned.[11] But within only a decade, the rapidly worsening relative pay position of clerical workers brought them, on the average, *below* all forms of so-called blue-collar jobs.

of the financial and operating condition of the enterprise, as well as its relations with the external world. Master craftsmen, such as bookkeepers or chief clerks, maintained control over the process in its totality, and apprentices or journeymen craftsmen—ordinary clerks, copying clerks, office boys—learned their crafts in office apprenticeships, and in the ordinary course of events advanced through the levels by promotion. The work involved, in addition to ordinary bookkeeping on the double-entry or Italian model (to which was added the rudiments of cost as well as profit-and-loss accounting at the beginning of the nineteenth century), such tasks as timekeeping and payroll, quality control, commercial traveling, drafting, copying duplicates by hand, preparing accounts in several copies, etc.

In its most general aspects, office work entails accounting and recordkeeping, planning and scheduling, correspondence and interviewing, filing and copying, and the like. But with the development of the modern corporation these functions assume the particular forms of the various departments and branches of the enterprise.

The factory office, which began with its first and original functionary, the timekeeper, usually added as its second functionary a foreman's clerk, whose task was to assist the foreman by keeping track of the work in process and its stages of completion. These clerks had as their responsibility the records of workers, materials, and tasks. Out of these rudimentary functions grew the modern cost, planning and scheduling, purchasing, and engineering and design sections.

Sales, previously handled chiefly by the owner himself, perhaps assisted by a clerk who doubled as traveler, became the function of a marketing division, subdivided into sections to handle sales traveling, correspondence with customers, salesmen, and manufacturers, order processing, commissions, sales analyses, advertising, promotion, and publicity. A separate financial office takes care of financial statements, borrowing, extending credit, ensuring collections, assessing and regulating cash flow, etc. And so on for other office divisions, among which the most important is an administration office where corporate policy is made and enforced upon all divisions.

The offices so described are those of a producing corporation, in which commodities in the form of goods or services are made and sold; these offices are thus subsidiary and complementary to the productive labor processes carried on elsewhere within the same corporation. But with the development of monopoly capitalism came the extraordinary enlargement of those types of enterprises which, entirely separated from the process of production, carry on their activities either chiefly or entirely through clerical labor.

Commercial concerns which deal only with the purchase and resale of commodities generally require three types of labor in large masses: distributive (for warehousing, packing, shipping), sales, and clerical. This is particularly true on the wholesale level, in which the clerks are the largest category of workers, outnumbering even sales workers. But even in retail trade, some kinds of enterprises, such as general merchandising and mail order houses, show a very large percentage of clerical labor.

In the pure *clerical industries*, this tendency is carried much further. Banks and credit agencies conduct only one mode of labor, the clerical, and below the managerial level the labor employed consists almost entirely of clerks who work in offices and service workers who clean the offices. The only thing that prevents this from being the case with brokerage and investment houses and insurance companies is the need for a large number of salespeople. To a lesser degree, the same heavily clerical character of the labor process is true of law offices and the offices of other institutionalized professions, advertising agencies, the publishers of books and periodicals insofar as they do not themselves do the work of manufacture, philanthropic and religious organizations, correspondence schools, agencies for travel, employment, etc., and government offices for public administration.

In all these industries, the development of capital has transformed the operating function of the capitalist from a personal activity into the work of a mass of people. The function of the capitalist is to represent capital and to enlarge it. This is done either by controlling the production of surplus value in the productive industries and activities, or by appropriating it from outside those industries and activities. The industrial capitalist, the manufacturer, is an example of the first; the banker of the second.* These management functions of control and appropriation have in themselves become labor processes. They are conducted by capital in the same way that it carries on the labor processes of production: with wage labor purchased on a large scale in a labor market and organized into huge "production" machines according to the same principles that govern the organization of factory labor. Here the productive processes of society disappear into a stream of paper—a stream of paper, moreover, which is processed in a continuous flow like that of the cannery, the meatpacking line, the car assembly conveyor, by workers organized in much the same way.

----

* The fact that banking corporations produce nothing, but merely profit from the mass of capital in money form at their disposal through activities which once went by the name "usury," no longer subjects them to discredit in monopoly capitalist society as it once did in feudal and in early capitalist society. In fact, financial institutions are accorded a place at the pinnacle of the social division of labor. This is because they have mastered the art of expanding capital without the necessity of passing it through any production process whatsoever. (The magical appearance of the feat merely conceals the fact that such corporations are appropriating a share in the values produced elsewhere.) The cleanliness and economy of the procedure, its absolute purity as a form of the accumulation of capital, now elicit nothing but admiration from those who are still tied to production.

This ghostly form of the production process assumes an ever greater importance in capitalist society, not only because of the requirements of the new way in which production is organized, and not only because of the growing need for coordination and control, but for another and more significant reason as well. In the social forms of capitalism all products of labor carry, apart from their physical characteristics, the invisible marks of *ownership*. Apart from their physical form, there is their social form as *value*. From the point of view of capital, the representation of value is more important than the physical form or useful properties of the labor product. The particular kind of commodity being sold means little; the net gain is everything. A portion of the labor of society must therefore be devoted to the accounting of value. As capitalism becomes more complex and develops into its monopoly stage, the accounting of value becomes infinitely more complex. The number of intermediaries between production and consumption increases, so that the value accounting of the single commodity is duplicated through a number of stages. The battle to realize values, to turn them into cash, calls for a special accounting of its own. Just as in some industries the labor expended upon marketing begins to approach the amount expended upon the production of the commodities being sold, so in some industries the labor expended upon the mere transformation of the form of value (from the commodity form into the form of money or credit)—including the policing, the cashiers and collection work, the record-keeping, the accounting, etc.—begins to approach or surpass the labor used in producing the underlying commodity or service. And finally, as we have already noted, entire "industries" come into existence whose activity is concerned with nothing but the transfer of values and the accounting entailed by this.

Since the work of recording the movement of values is generally accomplished by a capitalist agency for its particular ends, its own accounting has no standing with other organizations. This leads to an immense amount of duplication. The normal presumption in intercorporate dealings is not one of honesty but of dishonesty; unverified records are not considered adequate or trustworthy for any purposes but those of the institution which keeps them. Thus each pair of corporations, in their dealings with each other in the transactions of purchase and sale, credit and payment, etc., maintain a complete set of records, each the mirror image of those kept by the other. That which appears on the books of one as a credit shows in the books of the other as a debit. Since, when disputes arise, the burden of proof is shuffled back and forth between the parties in accordance with the available documentation, each set of records is as a rule a private affair to be used not for helpful coordination but as a weapon.

The internal recordkeeping of each corporate institution is, moreover, constructed in a way which assumes the possible dishonesty, disloyalty, or laxity of every human agency which it employs; this, in fact, is the first principle of modern accounting. It is for this reason, among others, that double-entry bookkeeping proved so suitable to capitalist accounting. Under this system, every transaction is recorded at birth in two places, and the entire movement of the values that pass through the enterprise is reflected in an interlocking set of accounts which check and verify each other. The falsification of only one single account will usually lead directly to the falsifier, and as a rule the work of falsifying many accounts so that they continue in balance with each other is possible only through the collaboration of a number of people. This system of dovetailing accounts is supplemented by a variety of independent checks and controls. In total, a modern financial system, although not impervious to falsification or error, is a well-guarded structure a large part of which exists for purposes of self-security, and as a rule such falsifications as are found in it appear not by accident but by the policy of the management.

Nor is this all. Since corporations must exhibit financial statements to the outside world for the purpose of raising capital, and since various other needs for such public disclosure exist—such as bank credit, settlement of accounts with outside parties as required under contracts with them, etc.—still another means of establishing the truth of records is provided. This is the independent audit by an accounting firm which makes it a "profession" to investigate records either when called upon or on a continuing basis, and to "certify" their results. The dishonesty presumed of all corporations is offset by the special function of such auditors, who are supposed to *make a profession of honesty*, although this is not usually the case either. At any rate, this brings into existence still another set of records and another species of duplicatory clerical work. And to this may be added much of the work of government regulatory and tax offices which deal with the same material from still other standpoints.

Thus the value-form of commodities separates itself out from the physical form as a vast paper empire which under capitalism becomes as real as the physical world, and which swallows ever increasing amounts of labor. This is the world in which value is kept track of, and in which surplus value is transferred, struggled over, and allocated. A society which is based upon the value-form surrenders more and more of its working population to the complex ramifications of the claims to ownership of value. Although there is no way of calculating it or testing the proposition, it is likely that the greatest part of the rapid increase of clerical labor is due to this; certainly there is no doubt that the demands of marketing, together with the demands of value accounting, consume the bulk of clerical time.

With the rapid growth of offices in the last decades of the nineteenth century, and the change of office work from something merely incidental to management into a labor process in its own right, the need to systematize and control it began to be felt. When this work was carried on in offices which contained only a few desks separated by a railing from the proprietor, it was, in effect, self-supervising, and required only the usual prudent safeguards against embezzlement, etc. In industrial enterprises, clerical expenses were small and incidental to production expenses. In commercial and financial offices, these expenses were also small and incidental before the era of mass merchandising, "consumer" banking, and group insurance. None of these enterprises could yet feel that its success was significantly dependent upon the efficiency of the clerical labor process.

As this situation changed, the intimate associations, the atmosphere of mutual obligation, and the degree of loyalty which characterized the small office became transformed from a prime desideratum into a positive liability, and management began to cut those ties and substitute the impersonal discipline of a so-called modern organization. To be sure, in doing so it was careful throughout this transitional period to retain as long as it could the feelings of obligation and loyalty it had traditionally fostered; but its own special commitments to its office staff were severed, one by one, as the office grew. The characteristic feature of this era was the ending of the reign of the bookkeeper and the rise of the office manager as the prime functionary and representative of higher management. Office managership, a product of the monopoly period of capitalism, developed as a specialized branch of management, with its own schools, professional associations, textbooks and manuals, periodicals, standards, and methods.

In the context of the times in which it took place, this naturally meant the application of scientific management methods to the office. By the first decades of the present century, the effort was well under way. In 1917, a volume entitled *Scientific Office Management*, and subtitled *A report on the results of applications of the Taylor System of Scientific Management to offices, supplemented with a discussion of how to obtain the most important of these results*, was published in New York, Chicago, and London. Its author, William Henry Leffingwell, had begun to use the Taylor system ten years earlier, and had accumulated considerable experience in offices like those of the Curtis Publishing Company. The following year Lee Galloway, for many years professor at New York University, published his standard work, *Office Management: Its Principles and Practice*. In these volumes, among others, the program of office management is clearly set forth: the purpose of the office is control over the enterprise, and the purpose of office management is control over the office. Thus Galloway:

> The larger . . . business offices grow, the more difficult and important become the problems of management. Orders must be given to employees by the managers, and reports of work performed must be recorded. Inspectors, superintendents, foremen, senior clerks, and office managers increase in

number—their function being to keep the employees and machines working harmoniously. At first one of these supervisors can give instructions verbally and keep the details in his memory, but as the subdivisions of work increase the necessity grows for continual communication between the various ranks of authority. Letters and memos, production orders and work tickets, speaking tubes and telautographs, cost statistics and controlling accounts, time clocks and messenger boys, multiply to keep pace with the growing complexity of business and to save the time of executives and workmen alike.[13]

The emphasis in this passage is upon the increase in clerical work in the processes of production. But Galloway soon extends the idea to cover the total office function in the capitalist enterprise:

Execution implies *control*—control of the factory organization—control of the financial organization—control of the marketing organization. It is the work of the office organization, under the supervision of the office manager, to devise records, methods, and systems for carrying out the function of control and for co-ordinating the activities of one department with those of another.[14]

With the growth of the control function, and with the consequent transformation of these functions of management into independent labor processes, comes the need to control the new labor processes, according to the same principles as those applied to the factory. Leffingwell thus says at the opening of his work:

Time and motion study reveal just as startling results in the ordinary details of clerical work as they do in the factory. And after all, since every motion of the hand or body, every thought, no matter how simple, involves the consumption of physical energy, why should not the study and analysis of these motions result in the discovery of a mass of useless effort in clerical work just as it does in the factory?[15]

These early practitioners of scientific management applied to the office the basic concepts of the Taylor system, beginning with the breakup of the arrangement under which each clerk did his or her own work according to traditional methods, independent judgment, and light general supervision, usually on the part of the bookkeeper. Work was henceforth to be carried on as prescribed by the office manager, and its methods and time durations were to be verified and controlled by management on the basis of its own studies of each job. Thus Leffingwell instances the installation of the Taylor system in the offices of the Curtis Publishing Company, which conducted a large mail order operation. The opening of mail was reorganized, with the result that five hundred pieces per hour were handled by one clerk, as against the previous one hundred; the same efforts were applied to the standardization of over five hundred other clerical operations.

Stenographic output and other forms of typing were studied most carefully. "Some typewriter concerns equip their machines with a mechanical contrivance which automatically counts the strokes made on the typewriter and records them on a dial." This meter was used in conjunction with a time clock, which the typist punched at the start and finish of each job. Metering of this kind was used as the basis for piecework payments (it took some time before management experts discovered that under such a regimen typists never used the tabulator key, always the space bar, in order to increase their count). Companies using typewriters without such advanced equipment made use of the square-inch method described in many textbooks down to the present day. A celluloid sheet ruled in square inches is placed over the typed page, and the number of characters within the area of type is shown at the end of the last line. "If the letter is double-spaced," Galloway adds with the meticulous scientific spirit that characterizes his school, "the number of square inches is of course divided by two." The same result is obtained with a line gauge which measures length and number of lines. But these devices are merely preliminaries to the elaborate systems for recording output, typist by typist, by day and by week, so that the number of lines transcribed from dictation, copied from other documents, etc., is subject to continuous check.[16] Dictation time is also recorded, at first by the page and later, with the spread of dictation machines, by mechanical means. The object is a report which accounts for the time of every stenographer. The entire charting system resembles a factory production record, and is used in the same way for setting minimum standards and raising average standards of production.

As in the case of the factory, the system of production records is in itself a way of increasing output, apart from any changes in office methods. "As a means of knowing the capacity of every clerk," wrote Leffingwell, "and also as a means of spurring him to even better efforts, the planning department keeps daily records of the amount of work performed by each clerk and his relative efficiency. The keeping of such records alone has been known to greatly increase the efficiency of many offices." A great many of the effects obtained by scientific management came from this alone, despite the pretense that the studies were being conducted for purposes of methods improvement. When Leffingwell says, for example, that "the output of one clerk was doubled merely by the re-arrangement of the work on the desk," we may understand this was an effect of close and frightening supervision rather than a miracle of efficiency; this was understood by the managers as well, although concealed beneath a "scientific" mystique.[17]

From the beginning, office managers held that all forms of clerical work, not just routine or repetitive ones, could be standardized and "rationalized." For this purpose they undertook elaborate studies of even those occupations which involved little routine, scores of different operations each day, and the exercise of judgment. The essential feature of this effort was to make the clerical worker, of whatever sort, account for the entire working day. Its effect was to make the work of every office employee, no matter how experienced, the subject of management interference. In this way, management began to assert in the office its hitherto unused or sporadically exercised right of control over the labor process.

The introduction of piecework systems in their various forms—straight piece rates, incentives, or the Taylor differential system—followed naturally on the heels of the other innovations. "One of the great changes which forced business men to revise their opinions about the wages system was the enormous growth of the operating side of business. It became necessary to employ hundreds of clerks, typists, and bookkeepers instead of a half-dozen or so. The management was confronted with a new condition in which it was impossible to determine whether or not the employees were living up to the standard of a fair day's work."[18]

The early "scientific" office managers were primarily concerned with the theory of existing procedures rather than with the mechanization of the office; like Taylor, they took the existing level of technical development as given. Although the basic instrument of office labor, the typewriter, was in universal use, and the instruments for adding, dictating, and ledger posting by mechanical means had already been devised, the mechanization of the office still lay far in the future. Insofar as office managers dealt with the tools and materials of office labor, they concerned themselves chiefly with the trivia of arranging, and selecting among, existing possibilities. Office layout was given an inordinate amount of attention, and the use of pneumatic tubes for communication between desks and offices, and of endless conveyor belts for the movement of work in process, became quite fashionable. The economies sought in the organization of masses of labor can be seen, to take a single instance, from the following: Leffingwell calculated that the placement of water fountains so that each clerk walked, on the average, a mere hundred feet for a drink would cause the clerical workers in one office to walk an aggregate of fifty thousand miles each year just to drink an adequate amount of water, with a corresponding loss of time for the employer. (This represents the walking time of a thousand clerks, each of whom walked only a few hundred yards a day.) The care with which arrangements are made to avoid this "waste" gives birth to the sedentary tradition which shackles the clerical worker as the factory worker is shackled—by placing everything within easy reach so that the clerk not only need not, but dare not, be too long away from the desk.*

---

* "Save ten steps a day for each of 12,000 employees," said Henry Ford of his system of having stock-chasers bring materials to the worker instead of having the worker move around freely, "and you will have saved fifty miles of wasted motion and misspent energy."[19] All motions or energies not directed to the increase of capital are

"If the paper upon which the writing is done is of good hard quality and a fine pen is used instead of a stub pen, the use of a blotter, and the thousands of useless motions caused by it, may be dispensed with. It is a saving far exceeding the pen supply for years. The size and shape of the penholder should also be carefully studied and standardized." One manager made a "time study" of the evaporation of inks and found that nonevaporating inkwells would save a dollar a year on each inkwell. This is reported in all seriousness, along with the observation that the "rate of evaporation, of course, varies with the humidity, and the results would not be constant." A time study of the removal of pins or paper clips from correspondence before filing or destroying "showed that it required ten minutes to remove one pound of clips and pins. . . . It is true that the pins have to be put in the pin cushion, but this work can be done by the office messenger between trips. A thousand pins can be put in a pin cushion," Leffingwell adds, with uncharacteristic inexactitude, "in fifteen to twenty minutes." He concludes this discussion on a hortatory note:

> This brief outline of how the physical office may be standardized will give you an idea of the amount of detail to be considered. Under scientific management, however, the work of standardization is never quite complete. New and improved methods are constantly being evolved and tried out in order to keep up to date. The standards of today may be entirely revolutionized tomorrow. This is no excuse for not standardizing but is an argument for it. Some managers of steel companies, for example, were willing to let well enough alone, thinking that the investment they had in equipment was sufficient for all purposes and that it was folly to be continually remodeling. Carnegie, on the other hand, junked all his old equipment and installed modern machinery and methods. The result is well known. The office manager who has the courage of a Carnegie will win just as surely as the ironmaster did.[20]

By later standards, the equipment and methods of the early Carnegies of office management were crude, and represented merely the first response to the problem of the large-scale office. As in the factory, the solution to the problem was found first in the technical division of labor and second in mechanization. Although these are today aspects of the same process, historically they came about in stages, and it is preferable to separate them and deal first with the division of labor in office processes.

---

of course "wasted" or "misspent." That every individual needs a variety of movements and changes of routine in order to maintain a state of physical health and mental freshness, and that from this point of view such motion is *not* wasted, does not enter into the case. The solicitude that brings everything to the worker's hand is of a piece with the fattening arrangements of a cattle feed-lot or poultry plant, in that the end sought is the same in each case: the fattening of the corporate balance sheet. The accompanying degenerative effects on the physique and well-being of the worker are not counted at all.

The work processes of most offices are readily recognizable, in industrial terms, as continuous flow processes. In the main they consist of the flow of documents required to effect and record commercial transactions, contractual arrangements, etc. While the processes are punctuated by personal interviews and correspondence, these serve merely to facilitate the flow of documentation. We may take as our example the most common form of transaction, the sale of commodities; it will be understood that everything that takes place in this process has as its mirror image a corresponding process on the part of the firms on the other side, with the signs reversed.

The *customer order* is the cell of the process. It moves through a stream of records and calculations which begin with its appearance in the salesman's order book, or in the mail, or over the telephone, until it reaches its final resting place as an infinitesimal portion of the corporation's statement of financial condition. The order must be opened and examined. The customer must be clearly identified as to firm name, address for billing, separate address, if any, for shipping, and, most important, credit standing. (If the order comes with payment already attached, it becomes part of a tributary which subsequently rejoins the main stream.) The items ordered must be clearly and properly interpreted as to type and quantity. The correct discount must be chosen for each order in accordance with corporate sales policy, which is more or less complex and is stratified according to quantities ordered, type of customer, special arrangements, etc. An invoice or bill must be prepared listing the merchandise for shipment and extending quantities by unit price; this invoice must be totaled, discounted, and supplementary charges such as shipping or tax added. Now the invoice moves on to another stage: On the one side, some of its copies provide shipping documents for the shipping division and packing slips for the customer. On the other side, further copies provide the raw materials of the accounting procedure. In the latter process, the invoice totals are posted to accounts for sales on the one side and the customer's account (or cash) on the other. Customer accounts are further posted, in controlled batch totals, to an overall accounts-receivable account. At the same time, tabulations must be made from the invoice to record the depletion of inventory, to keep sales records on each stock item, as well as sales records by salesman and territory for the calculation of sales commission due, for charting sales trends, etc. Finally, the summaries of these various accounts, tested for internal consistency and balance with each other, form the raw materials for the monthly summary accounts and the statements of financial condition of the division or corporation.

In traditional form, this entire process was the province of the bookkeeper, with the assistance of other clerical help such as the order biller, junior clerk for posting, etc. But as soon as the flow of work becomes large enough, and the methods of office management are applied, the process is subdivided into minute operations. Characteristically, separate clerks open the mail, date and route the orders, interpret customer information, clear credit, check the items ordered for clarity and to see if they are in inventory, type an invoice, add prices to it, extend, discount, calculate shipping charges, post to the customer account, etc., etc. just as in manufacturing processes—in fact, even more easily than in manufacturing processes—the work of the office is analyzed and parcelled out among a great many detail workers, who now lose all comprehension of the process as a whole and the policies which underlie it. The special privilege of the clerk of old, that of being witness to the operation of the enterprise as a whole and gaining a view of its progress toward its ends and its condition at any given moment, disappears. Each of the activities requiring interpretation of policy or contact beyond the department or section becomes the province of a higher functionary.

Needless to say, this conception is all the more readily applicable to those transactions which reflect no movement of physical commodities, such as banking and other financial transactions, the payment of insurance premiums and claims, and so on. But even those processes which, in an outsider's view, would appear to be difficult to subdivide in this way become, with sufficient volume, susceptible to the same treatment. Correspondence, for example, may be sorted into a variety of standard inquiries and problems and then answered with preformulated responses—either duplicated by machine or repetitiously typed (nowadays on automatic, tape-controlled typewriters). That smaller portion which requires individual treatment can be set aside for the attention of a higher grade of correspondence clerk while all the rest is classified, batched, and counted. On the basis of batch totals, the higher echelons of the office will then be able to see the type of inquiry or error which has caused the correspondence and use this as a check against other departments, or weigh these figures against past experience and against the experience of the trade as a whole. At the same time, the batch totals can be correlated with the time taken for dealing with correspondence of a particular sort, so that the expenditure of labor time may be kept under constant scrutiny and control.

In general, the rationalization of most office work and the replacement of the all-around clerical worker by the subdivided detail worker proceeds easily because of the nature of the process itself. In the first place, clerical operations are conducted almost entirely on paper, and paper is far easier than industrial products to rearrange, move from station to station, combine and recombine according to the needs of the process, etc. Second and more important, much of the "raw material" of clerical work is numerical in form, and so the process may itself be structured according to the rules of mathematics, an advantage which the managers of physical production processes often strive after but can seldom achieve. As flows subject to mathematical rules, clerical processes can be checked at various points by mathematical controls. Thus, contrary to the past opinion of many that office work was unlike factory work in that its complexities rendered it more difficult to rationalize, it proved easier to do so once the volume of work grew large enough and once a search for methods of rationalization was seriously undertaken.

Mental and Manual Labor

In the beginning, the office was the site of mental labor and the shop the site of manual labor. This was even true, as we have seen, *after* Taylor and in part *because* of Taylor: scientific management gave the office a monopoly over conception, planning, judgment, and the appraisal of results, while in the shop nothing was to take place other than the physical execution of all that was thought up in the office. Insofar as this was true, the identification of office work with thinking and educated labor, and of the production process proper with unthinking and uneducated labor, retained some validity. But once the office was itself subjected to the rationalization process, this contrast lost its force. The functions of thought and planning became concentrated in an ever smaller group within the office, and for the mass of those employed there the office became just as much a site of manual labor as the factory floor.* With the transformation of management into an administrative labor process, manual work spreads to the office and soon becomes characteristic of the tasks of the mass of clerical workers.

Labor in general is a process whose determinate forms are shaped by the end result, the product. The materials and instruments used by the shoemaker, tailor, butcher, carpenter, machinist, or farmer may vary with the state of technology, but they must be adapted to the production of footwear, apparel, meat, wooden structures, metal shapes, or grain. The typical, although not exclusive, product of mental labor consists of markings on paper. Mental labor is carried on in the brain, but since it takes form in an external product—symbols in linguistic, numeric, or other representational forms—it involves manual operations such as writing, drawing, operating writing machines, etc.—for the purpose of bringing this product into being. It is therefore possible to separate the functions of conception and execution: all that is required is that the scale of the work be large enough to make this subdivision economical for the corporation.

Among the first to recognize this was Charles Babbage. Babbage was not only responsible for the design of one of the first calculating engines

---

* In Lockwood's words: "One of the main changes in the division of labour has been the appearance of the specialized, semi-skilled office employee who is responsible for the 'processing' of data. The actual division of tasks very often preceded mechanization, but machinery has speeded up the trend by which a small group of executives, who make decisions about the selection and analysis of data, are separated from a mass of subordinates whose functions less and less justify their classification as brain workers."[21]

("computers"), but in his *On the Economy of Machinery and Manufactures*, written in the 1830s, he included a prophetic chapter called "On the Division of Mental Labour," in which he subjected the matter to one of its earliest and most trenchant analyses. "We have already mentioned," he begins, "what may, perhaps, appear paradoxical to some of our readers,—that the division of labour can be applied with equal success to mental as to mechanical operations, and that it ensures in both the same economy of time."[22] This he demonstrates by the following example.

During the French Revolution, the adoption of the decimal system made it necessary that mathematical tables adapted to that system be produced. This task was given to a certain M. Prony, who soon found that even with the help of several associates he could not expect to complete the job during his lifetime. While pondering the problem, he happened to pass a bookseller's shop where Adam Smith's recently published *Wealth of Nations* was displayed, and opened it to the first chapter. He decided to put his logarithms and trigonometric functions into manufacture, like pins, and set up two separate workshops—the product of each to serve as verification for that of the other—for this purpose.

He divided the task among three sections. The first section, consisting of five or six eminent French mathematicians, was charged with the work of devising the formulas best adapted for use by the other sections. The second group, made up of seven or eight persons with a good knowledge of mathematics, undertook the problem of converting these formulas into numerical values and devising means of checking the calculations. The third section, varying in number from sixty to eighty persons, used nothing more than simple addition or subtraction and returned the results to the second section for checking. Babbage describes the process and its requirements as follows:

> When it is stated that the tables thus completed occupy seventeen large folio volumes, some idea may perhaps be formed of the labour. From that part executed by the third class, which may almost be termed mechanical, requiring the least knowledge and by far the greatest exertions, the first class were entirely exempt. Such labour can always be purchased at an easy rate. The duties of the second class, although requiring considerable skill in arithmetical operations, were yet in some measure relieved by the higher interest naturally felt in those more difficult operations.[23]

Of the third section, Babbage says: "It is remarkable that nine-tenths of this class had no knowledge of arithmetic beyond the first two rules which they were thus called upon to exercise, and that these persons were usually found more correct in their calculations, than those who possessed a more extensive knowledge of the subject." The way is thereby opened for two conclusions which capitalism finds irresistible, regardless of their consequences for humanity. The first is that the labor of educated or better-paid persons should never be "wasted" on matters that can be accomplished for them by others of lesser training. The second is that those of little or no special training are superior for the performance of routine work, in the first place because they "can always be purchased at an easy rate," and in the second place because, undistracted by too much in their brains, they will perform routine work more correctly and faithfully. It remains only to add to this story that Babbage foresaw the time when the "completion of a calculating engine" would eliminate the necessity for the operations of addition and subtraction performed by the third section, and that thereafter it would prove possible to find ways to simplify the work of the second section. In Babbage's vision we can see the conversion of the entire process into a mechanical routine supervised by the "first section" which, at that point, would be the only group required to understand either mathematical science or the process itself The work of all others would be converted into the "preparation of data" and the operation of machinery.

The progressive elimination of thought from the work of the office worker thus takes the form, at first, of reducing mental labor to a repetitious perform-ance of the same small set of functions. The work is still performed in the brain, but the brain is used as the equivalent of the hand of the detail worker in production, grasping and releasing a single piece of "data" over and over again. The next step is the elimination of the thought process completely—or at least insofar as it is ever removed from human labor—and the increase of clerical categories in which nothing but manual labor is performed.

Office Work as Manual Labor

The management experts of the second and third generation after Taylor erased the distinction between work in factories and work in offices, and analyzed work into simple motion components. This reduction of work to *abstract labor*, to finite motions of hands, feet, eyes, etc., along with the absorption of sense impressions by the brain, all of which is measured and analyzed without regard to the form of the product or process, naturally has the effect of bringing together as a single field of management study the work in offices and in factories. The modern "science" of motion study treats office and factory work according to the same rules of analysis, as aspects of the unvarying motions of human "operators." A typical handbook by a management engineer thus begins with a section headed "The Concept of the Universal Process," and in discuss-ing work "in a shop, warehouse, store, office, or any other area," first takes pains to establish the *general applicability* of work measurement and produc-tion control systems to work of every kind: "Each situation presents a different surface appearance, and so the work which is performed in each of these diverse areas is ordinarily assumed to be very different. But a very marked similarity of basic purpose exists in all of these areas. . . . The universality of the process may be seen by analyzing that which goes to make up the process. To say that wherever humans labor they are performing the same types of work certainly seems to be a ridiculous statement. This seems to be even more inaccurate when it is remembered that much work is mental in nature, and not physical. But the statement is true."[24] "Universal standard data," the collection of which began with an eye principally toward factory work, are now applied at least as frequently to work in the office.

In addition, standard data have been collected specifically for office purposes, in the form of studies of particularly common office motions that are offered as interchangeable parts from which office managers may assemble their own complete operations. The Systems and Procedures Association of America, for instance, has assembled in compact form such a manual, entitled *A Guide to Office Clerical Time Standards: A Compilation of Standard Data Used by Large American Companies* (Detroit, 1960). The organizations which contributed their materials to this handbook are the General Electric Company, Stanford University, the General Tire and Rubber Company, Kerr-McGee Oil Industries, Inc., Owens-Illinois, Harris Trust and Savings Bank of Chicago, and the Chicago Chapter of the Systems and Procedures Association.*

The clerical standards maintained by these organizations begin with unit time values for the various elements of motion, as we have described above in Chapter 8, but they go on to agglomerate elemental motions into office tasks, and to offer the office manager the standards by which labor processes may be organized and calibrated. For example:

Open and close	*Minutes*
File drawer, open and close, no selection	.04
Folder, open or close flaps	.04
Desk drawer, open side drawer of standard desk	.014
Open center drawer	.026
Close side	.015
Close center	.027
Chair activity	
Get up from chair	.033
Sit down in chair	.033
Turn in swivel chair	.009
Move in chair to adjoining desk or file (4 ft. maximum)	.050

* The tables in the *Guide* are published without direct identification of the source corporation, but the information given makes identification clear in most cases. Thus "Company A," from whose data most of the examples used here are taken, is identified only as a "large manufacturer of electrical appliances and allied products," but of the cooperating parties, the only organization that fits this description is General Electric, which contributed the office standards used in its Distribution Transformer Department, manufacturer of heavy power-processing equipment. In what follows, we manage to catch a glimpse of the office standards and analyses under which modern office workers are actually supervised, whether they know it or not, and this is superior to looking at textbook standards.

Walking time is tabulated for distances from one foot to a thousand feet, but since walking within the office requires many turns, "Walking (confined)" adds .01 minute for each turn. The reading of a one- to three-digit number is presumed to take .005 minutes, and of a seven- to nine-digit number, .015 minutes. To make comparison checks, going from one paper to another, is rated at .0026 minutes per character. To read typed copy, per inch: .008 minutes. And to write, not including "get" or "release" of pencil or pen:

Numerals, per number	.01 minute
Print characters, each	.01 minute
Normal longhand, per letter	.015 minute

For some reason, the operation called "jogging" is a favorite of office management experts, and is charted, analyzed, and timed in scores of studies. In this instance, the time for "jog" ("basic times, paper in hand") is given as follows:

1st jog	.006 minute
2nd or subsequent	.009 minute
Pat following jog	.004 minute
Pat following pat	.007 minute

In this table, the time for jogs from one to ten is given, and we are told to "add .01 for each jog over 10."

The time value for "Cut with scissors" is given as .44 minute, with ".30 for each additional snip."* "A snip," we are told, "includes opening, moving forward and closing the scissors." Tabulations are given for unit time values for rubber stamping, including the time for getting the stamp, checking the date setting, and putting it aside, and for stamping a series of sheets and putting them aside, with allowance for inking the stamp at every fourth impression. Also for the time required to collate, gather, lay aside, handle, punch, staple (or remove staples), rubber band (or remove), move material between stations, count, fold or unfold, open mail container (envelope) and remove contents, insert mail in container. Unit times are given for locating a single item in a drawer file, Kardex file, Linedex file, Speed-O-Matic file, binder or folder, log sheet, planning card, or at a specific position on a form. Times are given to file random items, to start a new file, to do numerical and miscellaneous filing, to enter or write, and at this point, still another chart for jogging.

---

* Why it is that, when one is "jogging" or rapping a stack of papers to align them, the second jog takes longer than the first is not made clear. Nor is it clear why it should take almost half a minute to make the first snip with a scissors, and almost a third of a minute for each additional snip, unless these are misprints.

Typing times are subjected to a stringent analysis. The conventional standards for words per minute are charted against minutes per inch; but beyond this, time values are assigned to the steps of handling the paper, inserting it in the typewriter, aligning (for various numbers of sheets and carbons), erasing, making strike-over corrections, and "handling material after." We are given such intelligence as the "fact" that back spacing (per space) requires .0060 minutes on a manual machine and .0025 on an electric model. Further tables cover the time required for various duplicating processes, by offset, spirit, and mimeograph. A tabulation covering the operation of a key-driven calculator includes time values for clearing the machine and turning over each sheet between calculations (.0120 minute).*

The charts used by Company B, which is described as a large manufacturer of rubber products, plastics, etc.—and is therefore presumably the General Tire and Rubber Company—offer a similar array of detailed tabulations. In addition to charts which duplicate, in other forms, the kinds of materials we have already described, there are charts for pinning, clipping, counting cash, operating Pitney Bowes postage meters, matching papers, xeroxing, working bookkeeping machines, and an extraordinary table as follows:

Punch Time Clock

Identify card	.0156
Get from rack	.0246
Insert in clock	.0222
Remove from clock	.0138
Identify position	.0126
Put card in rack	.0270
	.1158

For the rest, tabulations supplied by other companies include, in addition to more of the same, time information for the operation of a great many office machines, including key punch and billing machines, and also for such bookkeeping functions as posting entries to ledgers by pen.

With the growing use of keyboard machines in offices, the analysis of the time requirements of operating them has become ever more intensive. For an example of this type of analysis, we turn to a 1963 volume called *Work Measurement in Machine Accounting*, two of the three authors of which were at the time of writing associated with the Ætna Life Insurance Co. In their

---

* All the charts taken from the standards of Company A bear the legend: "Bare standards—no allowances included for rest or personal needs." These are to be added, since modern capital is nothing if not meticulous and considerate.

treatment of key punching (the operation of the machine which punches holes in the eighty-column standard data-processing card), the authors arrive at the following breakdown of the time needed to punch a numeric character:*

	Unit time (TMUs)	Frequency	Standard time ((TMUs)
Reach to key	1.6	1	1.6
Contact key	0.0	1	0.0
Depress key	1.7	1	1.7
Release key	1.7	1	1.7
Release contact with key	0.0	1	0.0
			5.0

Since a TMU is defined as one one-hundred-thousandth (.00001) of an hour, and there are thus 28 TMUs in each second, this means that a key punch machine is to be operated at the rate of $5\frac{3}{5}$ strokes per second when purely numeric punching is being done. For the punching of alphabetical characters, however, one additional TMU per stroke is allowed for "mental time." In this way, the Ætna specialists calculated that to punch numeric values in 26 columns, and alphabetic characters in 24, skipping over the other 30 columns, allowing for automatic duplication and allowing 20 TMUs ($\frac{3}{7}$ of a second), for consulting the information source, as well as 17.2 TMUs for additional handling, it should take .2295 minutes to punch the card and .2017 minutes for another operator to verify it on a second machine. Under 15 seconds per card is allowed, in other words, for key punching or for verification, including a 5 percent allowance for error. But since key punch operators have to handle work before and after punching, a further set of calculations is made in order to account for all the operator's time: a tabulation of 31 motions, including time for "stand," "sit," "get pencil," "initial cards," "open and close card clip," "open and close drawer," "get rubber band," "band cards," etc.[25]

In the clerical routine of offices, the use of the brain is never entirely done away with—any more than it is entirely done away with in any form of manual work. The mental processes are rendered repetitious and routine, or they are reduced to so small a factor in the work process that the speed and dexterity with which the manual portion of the operation can be performed dominates

---

* It is worth noting that this simple list of three unit times, with their total, is made into a "table" by the addition of two useless lines and two useless columns. This is typical of the manner in which management "experts" dress their presentations in the trappings of mathematics in order to give them the appearance of "science"; whether the sociologists have learned this from the schools of business administration or the other way around would make a nice study.

the labor process as a whole. More than this cannot be said of any manual labor process, and once it is true of clerical labor, labor in that form is placed on an equal footing with the simpler forms of so-called blue-collar manual labor. For this reason, the traditional distinctions between "manual" and "white-collar" labor, which are so thoughtlessly and widely used in the literature on this subject, represent echoes of a past situation which has virtually ceased to have meaning in the modern world of work. And with the rapid progress of mechanization in offices it becomes all the more important to grasp this.

The Mechanization of the Office

Machinery that is used to multiply the useful effects of labor in production may be classified, as we have seen, according to the degree of its control over motion. Insofar as control over motion rests with the operator, the machine falls short of automatic operation; insofar as it is rendered automatic, direct control has been transferred to the machine itself. In office machinery, however, the control over *motion* is generally incidental to the purpose of the machine. Thus the rapidity and precision of the high-speed printer are not required in order to print rapidly—there are other and faster ways to ink characters onto paper—but in order to record a controlled flow of information as it is processed in the computer. It is one part of a machine system designed to control not motion but *information*.

Information exists, in the main, in the form of a record of symbolic characters: the alphabet, numbers, and other conventional symbols. Until recently, the processing of these characters—that is to say, assembling and reassembling them in required forms and combining or analyzing them according to the rules of mathematics—was directly dependent upon the human brain. While various mechanical means for recording or combining them were in daily office use, such as the typewriter, the adding or calculating machine, and the bookkeeping machine, each of these machines could only carry or process information through a very short part of its total cycle before it again had to involve the human brain to move it into its next position. In this sense, the office process resembled a pipeline that required a great many pumping stations at very close intervals. The difficulty lay in the form in which information was recorded: so long as it took the form of a notation which could be apprehended only by the human senses, humans were required to seize it and move or manipulate it. Thus every key-driven mechanical adding or calculating machine depended on the line-by-line keyboard work of the operator, and its storage and processing facilities were limited to the capacities of a few mechanical registers. While this situation continued, every office machine remained on the primitive level of the hand tool, or power-assisted hand tool.

The change began with the machine for counting punched cards invented by Dr. Herman Hollerith in 1885 and used to tabulate the United States census of 1890. The importance of this invention lay not in any technical advance, but entirely in the concept it embodied. In recording bits of data, each on its own card, by means of a system that gave to each column and rank of the card a specific meaning, the punched-card system made available a means of "reading" and "interpreting" simple data without direct human participation. Now, through one means or another of sensing the holes, machines could sort and classify, combine and tabulate, the bits of data on the cards. The significance of the method lay in the recasting of the form of the information so that it could be picked up by a machine.

This revolutionary conception passed through a series of purely technical improvements in the years that followed, first electromechanical, in which electrical impulses were made to control mechanical registers, and then electronic, in which information is handled and stored by means of the electrical impulses themselves and the mechanical elements virtually disappear. The effect upon the storage and handling capacities of computing systems has been enormous. In contrast to the punched card, which in its standard form stores eighty characters on a surface slightly larger than two playing cards, the common type of magnetic disk pack, which consists of eleven fourteen-inch disks mounted a half-inch apart, will hold up to 29 million characters. And these can be transferred at the rate of 156,000 characters per second to or from the computer processing unit, within which they may be manipulated in operations that are measured in millionths or even billionths of a second each. Thus once the information is recorded, bit by bit, by means of key-driven machines, it may be summoned, brought together from diverse sources, arranged, combined mathematically, etc., in very short periods of time, and the results displayed on a screen, or more commonly recorded by the high-speed printer which is itself a typewriter that puts to shame the combined efforts of scores of typists.

The computer system working on these principles is the chief, though not the only, instrument of mechanization of the office. Its first applications were for large-scale routine and repetitive operations which to some extent were already performed mechanically: payrolls, billing, accounts payable and accounts receivable, mortgage accounting, inventory control, actuarial and dividend calculations, etc. But it was soon applied in new tasks, such as for elaborate sales reports, production-cost accounting, market research information, sales commissions, and so forth, all the way up to general accounting, at which point the corporation's books of record are put into computerized form.

This automatic system for data-processing resembles automatic systems of production machinery in that it re-unifies the labor process, eliminating the many steps that had previously been assigned to detail workers. But, as in manufacturing, the office computer does not become, in the capitalist mode of production, the giant step that it could be toward the dismantling and scaling down of the technical division of labor. Instead, capitalism goes against the grain of the technological trend and stubbornly reproduces the outmoded division of labor in a new and more pernicious form. The development of computer work has been so recent and so swift that here we can see reproduced in compressed form the evolution of labor processes in accord with this tendency.

For a short time in the 1940s and early 1950s, the data-processing occupations displayed the characteristics of a craft. This was during the period when tabulating equipment based on the punched card dominated the industry. Installations were small and the tabulating craftsman worked on all machines: the sorter, collator, tabulator, calculator, etc.* These machines were programmed by wiring a panel board for each machine, and this operation was learned as the worker gained a general familiarity with all the machines. Thus the equivalent of an apprenticeship was a period of learning the use of all the equipment, and the programming done at that time was simply the highest skill of an all-around trade.

The development of a data-processing craft was abortive, however, since along with the computer a new division of labor was introduced and the destruction of the craft greatly hastened. Each aspect of computer operations was graded to a different level of pay frozen into a hierarchy: systems managers, systems analysts, programmers, computer console operators, key punch operators, tape librarians, stock room attendants, etc. It soon became characteristic that entry into the higher jobs was at the higher level of the hierarchy, rather than through an all-around training. And the concentration of knowledge and control in a very small portion of the hierarchy became the key here, as with automatic machines in the factory, to control over the process.

The upper level of the computer hierarchy is occupied by the systems analyst and the programmer. The systems analyst is the office equivalent of the industrial engineer, and it is his or her job to develop a comprehensive view of the processing of data in the office and to work out a machine system which will satisfy the processing requirements. The programmer converts this system into a set of instructions for the computer. In early computer installations, the programmer was generally a systems analyst as well, and combined the two functions of devising and writing the system. But with the encroachment of the division of labor, these functions were increasingly separated as it became clear that a great deal of the work of programming was routine and could be delegated to cheaper employees. Thus the designation of "programmer" has by this time become somewhat ambiguous, and can be applied to expert

---

* Except for the key punch machine; being a keyboard machine, this was immediately recognized as a job for "girls."

program analysts who grasp the rationale of the systems they work on, as well as to program coders who take as their materials the pre-digested instructions for the system or subsystem and simply translate them mechanically into specialized terminology. The training for this latter work occupies no more than a few months, and peak performance is realized within a one- to two-year period. In accordance with the logic of the capitalist division of labor, most programmers have been reduced to this level of work.

Below this level, computer work leaves the arena of specialized or technical skills and enters the realm of working-class occupations. The computer operator runs the computer in accordance with a set of rigid and specific instructions set down for each routine. The training and education required for this job may perhaps best be estimated from the pay scales, which in the case of a Class A operator are on about the level of the craftsman in the factory, and for Class C operators on about the level of the factory operative.

The largest single occupation created by computerization is that of the key punch operator. Since it in many ways typifies the direction being taken by office work, it is worth examining in some detail.

The extraordinary swiftness with which computers process information depends in the first instance upon the careful preparation of a data base for the computer's use. While all other office functions dwindle in the face of the computer, this one tends to grow. First, everything which the computer digests must be translated into uniform codes. Second, the pre-calculated operation of the entire system depends upon the provision of adequate coding to cover every requirement at the time of entering the original data; nothing can be left for later recognition, apprehension, and action by the human brain if it is to be done by the computer in the course of its operations. Third, every preassigned code must be prepared for the computer in accordance with a strict and undeviating form so that it can have the desired effect. And fourth, this must be done in a relatively error-free way, since the computer does not recognize errors (except insofar as they transcend the parameters set in the program) but acts upon all the information it is given.

This requires the preparation of data according to rigid forms because no matter how ingeniously the matter is approached, the computer cannot interpret any symbols but those that derive their meaning from their form and position. The computer card, punched as desired by a key-driven machine and verified by a repetition on another such machine, is still the most common such form. It is not the only one, however, and a variety of other devices that record data on a magnetic tape, or print out symbols that can be "read" by an optical scanner, are now in use. Their advantage is not that they "eliminate key punching," as some hasty publicists have rushed to announce, but that they simplify the operation still further so that it may be performed on keyboards similar to that of the typewriter, and so divest the coding operation of even the very limited amount of training it now requires. Although the manner of coding may be varied, it cannot be eliminated; and while there are some ways in which the volume of coding may be held in check, in general it tends to grow with the growth of computerization. To describe key punching, therefore, is to describe the sort of work which, in this form or another, is growing rapidly in offices.

The training required for this sort of work has been described in one sociological study as follows:

> Card punching can be a rather monotonous job when it involves large masses of homogeneous data, pre-sorted and prepared in ready-to-copy columnar format. The job can be learned in a matter of a week or two, and satisfactory production skills can be attained within some six months. Despite most employers' stated preference, a high-school diploma is not essential for satisfactory performance. Some training officials estimated that a ninth-grade reading level and equivalent proficiency in arithmetic provide a good starting base.
>
> For all these reasons, a highly knowledgeable personnel man, in the course of one interview, described keypunch operating as a "semi-blue-collar" job. He considered the term descriptive not only of the nature of the job, but also of the entry requirements, both formal and informal. In many instances girls who lack formal education or the "social graces of the office" can be placed in keypunching, whereas they would probably be rejected for other purely white-collar work.[26]

The authors of this study, who like most of their colleagues in the social sciences prefer to look on the bright side, profess themselves "intrigued" by the view expressed by this personnel manager. They are quick to theorize that key punching can become a handy substitute for unskilled manufacturing jobs which in the past "served as the first step on the ladder." But within a page they themselves are forced to characterize key punching as a "dead-end" occupation: "Whereas messengers are frequently promoted to file clerks, file clerks to typists, and typists to secretaries, keypunch operators tend to remain keypunch operators."[27]

The work itself is described by key punch department managers themselves as "extremely boring" with "no intelligence looked for" and a very high turnover rate.[28] Here is a description, reported on the occasion of the change-over from a pre-computer tabulating machine system (which also required punched cards) to a computer system:

> One key-puncher reported that before the installation of the computer, her work had been somewhat varied and had occasionally called for the exercise of judgment. This had made it bearable. Every three or four weeks, as the conversion to automation proceeds, several of her associates are transferred

from the original group of key-punchers and assigned to the new work, which is more monotonous and repetitious. Since there is no variation in job content, the pace is continuous, steady, and "pressured." The most frequent comment among the girls is, "We are working for the machine now."

Mrs. Duncan described all key-punch girls as "nervous wrecks." "If you happen to speak to an operator while she is working, she will jump a mile. You can't help being tense. The machine makes you that way. Even though the supervisor does not keep an official production count on our work, she certainly knows how much each of us is turning out—by the number of boxes of cards we do." Mrs. Calvin, a former operator for a different company, reported the same kind of tension: "If you just tap one of them on the shoulder when she is working, she'll fly through the ceiling."

Both women reported that absenteeism was very high among their group. Mrs. Duncan remarked, "Someone is always saying, 'I don't think I'll come in tomorrow. I just can't stand this any longer.' " Although the girls do not quit, they stay home frequently and keep supplies of tranquilizers and aspirin at their desks. The key-punchers felt that they were really doing a factory job and that they were "frozen" to their desk as though it were a spot on the assembly-line.[29]

As in the factory, the machine-pacing of work becomes increasingly available to office management as a weapon of control. The reduction of office information to standardized "bits" and their processing by computer systems and other office equipment provides management with an automatic accounting of the size of the work load and the amount done by each operator, section, or division:

Precise measurement of clerical output is one of the aspects of the production room approach heightened by if not exclusively new to automated offices. Simplification and routinization of office tasks by automation makes the work much more amenable to objective count and measurement. The American Management Association has published numerous studies reporting the experience of various large firms in developing clerical cost programs by means of time measurement of office operations. These articles refer only indirectly to employee irritation and resistance. In the Standard Oil Company of Ohio, for example, a special name was coined to avoid such terms as "work measurement," which was considered to be "irritating to the employees and made it difficult to secure their participation."

The Seventh Annual Conference on Systems and Procedures in 1958 stressed that the systems profession is devoted to methods improvement or "working smarter." Implicit in this was the job of motivating the office worker to greater productivity. Henry Gunders, associate director, Management Advisory Services, Price Waterhouse and Company, Houston, Texas, maintained that in the unmeasured office the rate of clerical output is low. He estimates that such an office is operating on 50 to 60% efficiency, and that with clerical output measured, even unaccompanied by incentives, there would be a 20 to 30% increase in output. It is stated that incentives are most applicable to already mechanized jobs. When an office machine is used, various devices such as stroke counters, automatic sequential numbering, and the like simplify counting. Similarly, prenumbered documents, processed in sequence, facilitate production counting.

Most of the firms included in this study quantify the operations associated with data-processing. Key-punching, in particular, lends itself to objective count. Government agencies and private business firms reported that this type of work measurement was standard procedure. In some instances, the girls fill out a daily tally form indicating how many inches they have punched, and the verifiers keep count of the errors. An executive of one large insurance company commented that, although it is not generally mentioned, an objective record of productivity is kept, and the operator whose output lags is fired. Many firms rely on the supervisor to keep a visual check which can be objective because she would know the total number of trays of cards processed during any period. One official explained that the careful tally of key-punch output in his firm was made necessary because all service functions must be allocated as to cost, and that check on operators' speed was a secondary consideration. Serial checking on other types of office equipment is the method used by many firms, and is applicable to calculators, check sorters and various machines besides key-punches. "Industrialization" of clerical work is evident not only in the work count, but also in the use of a moving belt to carry the work from one station to the next. Several companies studied use this method of carrying orders from the point of origin through the various stages of processing to the computer.

The factory atmosphere is unmistakably present. Not only are the office machine operators often required to punch a time clock, but they are not permitted to converse while at work. They are subject to dismissal with as little notice as a week or at most a month. There are few distinguishing marks between the employee in the electronic office and the factory worker in light manufacturing.[30]

As work has been simplified, routinized, and measured, the drive for speed has come to the fore. "Everything is speed in the work now," said a woman who found herself near a nervous breakdown, and the pace is "terrific." And with the economies furnished by the computer system and the forcing of the intensity of labor come layoffs which selectively increase the tendency toward factory-like work: "With each reduction in force, the remaining workers are told to increase their output. Automation has reduced the staff in that office by more than one-third, and more mechanization is in prospect. The union spokesman said that the categories of jobs which have disappeared are those which require some skill and judgment. Those remaining are the tabulating and key-punch operations, which become even simpler, less varied, and more routinized as work is geared to the computer." The vice-president of an insurance company, pointing to a room filled with key punch operators, remarked: "All they lack is a chain," and explained himself by adding that the machines kept the "girls" at their desks, punching monotonously and without cease.* And the workers themselves are under no illusions about their "white-collar" jobs: "This job is no different from a factory job except that I don't get paid as much," one operator in a large farm-equipment office said.[31]

The educational requirements for this new kind of office work are subject to confusion, some of it deliberate, between the needs of the work itself and other considerations. Thus the authors of a recent study of electronic data-processing in New York write:

> We have already noted the general tendency of employers to specify a high-school diploma as a prerequisite to employment for keypunch operators. It is also true, however, that many successful** operators are hired without the diploma, particularly in a period when the labor market is tight. Our interviews convinced us that a high-school diploma is viewed as something other than a certification of academic or intellectual proficiency.
>
> Some firms, admittedly, relish their ability to state that "all our employees are high-school graduates," as an indication of status or prestige. The great majority, however, view the diploma as a certification of responsibility, motivation, and reliability.... "Sure, we can find out quickly if a girl can really punch cards. But will she come in every Monday? Will she stay after 5 o'clock when we're pushed for overtime? Will she drift to another job after three weeks?" These are the kinds of questions that were repeatedly raised by employers.[32]

Earlier in the computer era, various managements not yet oriented in the field and perhaps somewhat deceived by their own glowing estimates of the mass "upgrading of the labor force" that would take place, hired the "wrong kind of labor." This was particularly true in banking, where the snobbish tradition of "superior" employees had not yet been overcome by managers. Thus in one study of bank computerization it was decided that personnel managers were "recruiting girls of too high an intellectual calibre for the new simple machine jobs." [33] Experience soon showed, in the words of another

---

* This vice-president gives us a clear illustration of the fetishism which puts the blame for the situation on the "machines" rather than on the social relations within which they are employed. He knew when he made this remark that it was not the "machines" but he himself who chained the workers to their desks, for in his next breath he pointed out that a count of production was kept for the workers in that machine room.

** This term in itself is quite remarkable, and can only be understood if taken to mean key punch operators who turn out to be "successful" hiring strokes for the personnel manager.

study of technological change in banking, that "it would be misleading to assume that a massive upgrading will take place, for a large proportion of jobs created up to this point are relatively low rated. Encoders are a case in point: Encoding 'is a low-grade job which is easily and quickly learned, requiring only the ability to operate a 10-key keyboard.' At one bank, 'Due to the simplicity of operator training for single pocket proof encoders, the job, as related to our job evaluation scale, has been downgraded three grades and reduced from an average base of $68 to $53 per week.'* An EDP clerk is only 'a slightly higher grade position than that of encoder. . . .' At the large branch bank referred to above, approximately 70 percent of the jobs created were low rated, while at the small branch bank they comprised around 50 percent of the new jobs."[35] And it is in the nature of the organization of work around the computer system that, like factory work, it does not have the advancement ladder characteristic of the bank and office of several generations ago. This was recognized early in the computer era by the American Management Association, which, in a special report designed to help employers set up data-processing operations, said: "To be honest—we don't want people to take data-processing jobs as stepping stones to other jobs. We want permanent employees capable of doing good work and satisfied to stay and do it. To promise rapid advancement is to falsify the facts. The only rapid advancement for the bulk of nonsupervisory data-processing staff is *out of data-processing!*"[36]

So far as the traditional grades of office labor are concerned, the computerization of office accounting procedures further weakens the position of those skilled in the system as a whole, particularly bookkeepers. The decline of the bookkeeper, which had begun, as we have seen, with the rise of the office manager, was helped along by the rise of the bookkeeping or posting machine, which converted a certain amount of skilled ledger work into a mechanical operation. The decline was continued, especially in banking, by the development of electronic bookkeeping machines, which complete the conversion of bookkeepers into machine operators and at the same time reduce the demand for them sharply. Thus one multi-branch bank reported that within eighteen months after installing electronic bookkeeping machines, the bookkeeping staff of 600 had been reduced to 150, and the data-processing staff had grown to 122. This is in line with the experience of most banks, which achieve a reduction in overall labor requirements of 40 to 50 percent for the same volume of work, and in the process cut down the bookkeeping people sharply and replace them with machine operators.[37]

Not only bookkeepers, but even the lower grades of management, feel the effects in a similar way. The computer presents management with an enormous

---

* These pay figures refer to 1963. Elsewhere, the job of coder is characterized thus by a data-processing executive: "The only gal who will stick with this work has to have a husband with two broken legs and five hungry kids. No one else could stand it."[34]

temptation to save management time as well as labor time by "mechanizing" many choices and decisions. It is probably for this reason that Howard C. Carlson, a psychologist employed by General Motors, has said: "The computer may be to middle management what the assembly line is to the hourly worker."[38]

The tendency of the labor process exemplified in the various machine jobs is not confined to the workers grouped immediately around the computer. On the contrary, with the exception of a specialized minority whose technical and "systems" skills are expanded, this tendency increasingly affects all clerical workers. The reasons for this may be separated into two parts.

First, the formal demands of computerization extend far beyond those machine operators who work with the raw materials or finished products of the computer. Since coding operations are performed mechanically according to fixed layouts, the materials prepared by others for the machine rooms must also follow strict rules of form. Thus the clerk who uses nothing but paper and writing instruments, and who apprehends the information in the first instance from original source documents, is governed by the same rules of form. This has led to the possibility of transferring the work of the key punch operator to the other grades of clerk, a change which is now under way and which will undoubtedly accelerate. Under this system, the work of transcribing information into a form that can be used by the computer is spread throughout the office instead of being localized in machine rooms, by means of terminals or other simple keyboard machines that can be operated by any clerk. In this way, machine operation is generalized throughout the office. If, in the first instance, this involves a combination of jobs—that of interpreting being combined with that of keyboard operation—the next step is the simplification and even elimination of the judgmental steps involved in interpretation by tying the new keyboard machine to the computer and utilizing its storage and swift-search capacities. Thus, in a variety of ways, the reduction of data to symbolic form with accurate positional attributes becomes, increasingly, the business of the office as a whole, as a measure to economize on labor costs.

Second, a variety of other machines and systems are applied to other work processes not within the immediate orbit of the computer. For example, file clerks serve elaborate and semiautomatic machine systems which eliminate the need to know the sequence of the alphabet, or even the sequence of numbers; everything is eliminated but the task of placing under the photographic apparatus of the machine, as swiftly as possible, one document after another. Typists, mail sorters, telephone operators, stock clerks, receptionists, payroll and timekeeping clerks, shipping and receiving clerks are subjected to routines, more or less mechanized according to current possibilities, that strip them of their former grasp of even a limited amount of office information, divest them of the need or ability to understand and decide, and make of them so many mechanical eyes, fingers, and voices whose functioning is, insofar as possible, predetermined by both rules and machinery. As an important instance of this, we may note the changes in the work of the bank teller, once an important functionary upon whose honesty, judgment, and personality much of the public operation and relations of the bank used to depend. Attached to mechanical and electronic equipment, these employees have been transformed into checkout clerks at a money supermarket counter, their labor power purchased at the lowest rates in the mass labor market, their activities prescribed, checked, and controlled in such a way that they have become so many interchangeable parts. And it should be added that the teller's function, limited as it now is, will gradually be replaced by new mechanical-electronic equipment that originated in England and has been spreading in the United States. A cash machine which, activated by a customer card, supplies cash from the customer's account is no more than the first tentative step in this direction. So-called automated tellers are able, on the same principle, to transact any of a number of banking functions, including deposits to or withdrawals from savings or checking accounts, transfers between accounts, and loan repayments.[39] Such equipment requires not so much a revolution in banking technology as the modification of existing equipment so that it may be used directly by the customer, with minimal opportunity for error or fraud. The fact that this is becoming increasingly common in trade and service areas indicates that much automated equipment is so simple to operate that it requires *no training whatsoever*; it also foreshadows the weakening of the demand for labor in fields of employment that have been expanding rapidly.

The trend in what is known as "secretarial work" assumes great importance in this transformation of clerical labor, for two reasons. First, it is an occupational category of enormous size. Some 2.75 million persons were employed as secretaries in the United States in 1970, according to the census for that year, almost all of them women. This is the largest single category of clerical labor. And second, we are at the beginning of a revolution in this field which will transform the office almost to the same extent as it is now being transformed by the computer. To understand this incipient upheaval, we must review this occupation and its fundamental rationale.

From a functional standpoint, the secretary came into existence as a device to extend the administrative scope of the entrepreneur and proprietor. Later, as the managerial structure grew, the secretary, from this same functional standpoint, came to represent a pure expression of the Babbage principle: it was thought "wasteful," from the capitalist point of view, to have a manager spend time typing letters, opening mail, sending parcels, making travel arrangements, answering the telephone, etc., when these duties could be performed by labor power hired at anywhere from one-third to one-fiftieth of the remuneration of the manager. But here the operation of the Babbage principle is further stimulated by the fact that the managers are organizing not the distant labor processes of subordinates, but *their own* labor. Since they tend to place an exaggerated value upon their own time, and a minimal value upon the time of others as compared with their own, the Babbage principle goes to work in the offices of managing executives with particular force, all the more so as it is intensified by the prestige attaching to managers with large staffs, the usefulness of a retinue of office servants for the transacting of personal matters, and other career, social, and personal considerations.

Thereafter this system of secretarial assistance spreads to lower ranks as well, as the numbers of managerial and semi-managerial employees increase. Since the Babbage principle operates wherever a mass of work may be subdivided and its "lower" portions separated out and delegated, it invades all the realms of paper work performed by "executives," assistants to executives, heads of small departments sometimes consisting of no more than the "head" and a secretary, professional and even semi-professional employees. The Babbage principle has here transcended its own limits, especially as social and prestige factors come into play and the personal secretary becomes a perquisite of the privileged job as one of its chief privileges. Top managers watched this multiplication of secretaries with nothing more than amusement, until it grew to dimensions which threatened the balance sheet.

For management to tackle this monstrosity in order to reduce the drain on the corporate pocketbook is by no means simple. It is not just a matter of attacking a traditional and entrenched privilege, but one which is enjoyed by the lower reaches of the managerial structure itself, those whose loyalty and interest in the corporation is guaranteed by, among other things, these very trappings and pretenses of managerial status. Corporate managements confront the danger, in any such attack, of alienating their own instruments of control over the administrative structure. True, some managements have not allowed such a situation to develop, or have destroyed it at an earlier stage—stenographic pools as a substitute for personal secretaries, for example, are hardly unknown—but many others have shrunk from the task. There is ample evidence, however, that this situation is ending, and that management is now nerving itself for major surgery upon its own lower limbs.

The reasons for this new attitude are various. The most important has already been mentioned: the extent to which this expensive practice has burgeoned, and the immense amounts of payroll it devours, not just through the multiplication of secretaries but through the effect of this arrangement upon the entire functioning of the office. But there are other factors: the completion of the basic work of rationalization in the factory, so far as it can be carried through, freeing management to turn to the office; the maturation of "systems thinking" among managers to the point where they have reconceptualized the entire problem; the spread of the methods of close calculation throughout smaller firms that might otherwise escape them for a while longer, through the purchase of such firms by conglomerates whose first step is to send in systems engineers (and here the fact that the blame for the changes can be assigned to distant proprietors makes the installation of new systems by corporate management somewhat easier); the perfection of various cheap systems of centralized communications and recording; even the new attitudes of women, who dispute and scorn the body-servant role and make it more difficult to recruit tractable secretaries—all of these are among the factors which both encourage and facilitate the ending of the secretarial explosion.

Office managements have thus entered upon a sweeping campaign to destroy what they call the "social office," to use a phrase which has recently gained popularity.[40] It is only necessary to follow the periodicals published for top office managers, such as *Administrative Management*, to see that they are attacking on this front not only with a newly systematized armamentarium of ideas and procedures, but with a fresh determination, and that the object of this attack is no longer just the clerk but the comfortable arrangements made by their own lower managers.

There is of course no disposition on the part of office managements to reject the Babbage principle and to have those functionaries who are now assisted by secretaries begin to do their own typing and other chores. This would contradict the basic tenet of management that each task must be performed at the lowest possible rate of pay. Rather, they feel that the time has come to end a system which makes of each functionary a supervisor over the labor of one assistant, because the labor time of secretaries is used wastefully and inefficiently, is subject only to relaxed and friendly supervision by a superior who is more interested in personal convenience than in office efficiency, and because such functionaries often cannot delegate enough work to fully occupy the time of another person.

Secretarial work is analyzed into two parts: typing and administrative routine (sometimes reception and telephone answering are separated from the latter as a distinct function). The first is being made the business of what has been named the "word processing center." This center is a modernized version of the stenographic pool; it does not send stenographers to take dictation from executives, but rather gives each executive a link with the stenographic process through the telephone on his end and recording equipment on the other. These recordings are then "processed" by typists, and the finished letter, document, brief, contract, script, or any other form requiring typing is brought by messenger for checking and signature. As distinguished from a stenographic pool, which merely held and dispatched labor power to departments as required, this system visualizes the construction of a separate production department whose business it is to manufacture to order all the correspondence and other documentary work required anywhere throughout the offices of the enterprise. Thus this major portion of the secretarial job now becomes the province of production workers, assisted by electronic equipment. Not unexpectedly, this concept and its application have made the furthest strides in Germany, and an article in *Administrative Management* describes the stress given there to the use of canned texts and automatic typewriters. Word processing is

> a process of having word originators (executives, sales correspondents, lawyers, and the like) select formula clauses from pre-coded, pre-organized clause books. For example, an administrator who would normally dictate the same kind of reply to a letter several times a day, instead selects the appropriate clauses (by code number) from the clause book—or from memory if he's used them often enough. Once selected, clause codes plus individual names, addresses and other variable inserts (such as dates or prices) are either dictated into recorders or jotted down on "to-be-typed" forms. This source dictation or form is then used by the typist to prepare a final letter. Automatic typewriters repetitively type the "canned" clauses, and the typist manually keyboards in the new or variable data. . . . Benefits are word originator and typist efficiency, and more work produced from the same number of hours on the job. In addition, less training is required of all the people involved.[41]

This last "benefit," the reduction of training for "all," indicates the sensitivity of management to the proliferation of correspondents and other such "word originators," each of whom is required to know how to formulate a passable paragraph so that it may be understood by the recipient; under the new system, this requirement disappears, leaving only the ability to *select the proper paragraph.*

The other functions of the secretary are taken over by an "administrative support center." The superior who formerly had a secretary is known, in relation to this center, not as a "word originator" but as a "principal," and it is considered that a ratio of four to eight principals to each "administrative support secretary" will prove adequate. This support center handles all the nontyping chores formerly required of the secretary, foremost among them being filing, phone answering, and mail handling. "Filing," we are told, "should be performed in the support center—not in the principal's office." The clear objective of such arrangements is to prevent the renewal of the previous situation by imperceptible degrees, and to ensure that all secretarial work is performed under centralized production supervision and not under the supervision of the "principal." Moreover, "principals should answer their own phone, but the phone should also ring in the center so if the principal doesn't pick it up by the third ring the secretary can get it." Like the "word processing center," the "administrative support center" is connected to the various offices by phone and messenger service.[42]

Thus, under the new arrangement, the secretarial function is replaced by an integrated system which aims at centralized management, the breakdown of secretarial jobs into detail operations subdivided among production workers, and the reduction of the number of secretarial workers to one-half, one-quarter, or even smaller fractions of their former number. Among the subsidiary benefits management expects to derive from this arrangement is the reduction and thus cheapening of the skills of administrative employees, and, not the least, the squeezing out of the minutes and hours of labor power lost in the personal relations and contacts among secretaries and between secretaries and their "principals"—which is what they mean when they speak of the "end of the social office." The force and seriousness of this campaign, which has begun in this form only in the past few years, can be seen not only from its conception as a total system with its own jargon, technology, and specialists, and from the space now being devoted to it in office management periodicals, but also from the launching of new periodicals and organizations devoted entirely to this subject (for instance, *Word Processing Report* and the Word Processing Institute). The total system has been installed in a great variety of corporations, including sophisticated publishing offices in New York, where systems analysts have shown themselves to be sturdy of purpose and impervious to the barbed comments of editors who are being deprived of their secretaries.

We have now described, in its major facets, the conversion of the office routine into a factory-like process in accordance with the precepts of modern management and available technology. The greatest single obstacle to the proper functioning of such an office is the concentration of information and decision-making capacity in the minds of key clerical employees. Just as Frederick Taylor diagnosed the problem of the management of a machine shop as one of removing craft information from the workers, in the same way the office manager views with horror the possibility of dependence upon the historical knowledge of the office past, or of the rapid flow of information in the present, on the part of some of his or her clerical workers. The recording of everything in mechanical form, and the movement of everything in a mechanical way, is thus the ideal of the office manager. But this conversion of the office flow into a high-speed industrial process requires the conversion of the great mass of office workers into more or less helpless attendants of that process. As an inevitable concomitant of this, the ability of the office worker to cope with deviations from the routine, errors, special cases, etc., all of which require information and training, virtually disappears. The number of people who can operate the system, instead of being operated by it, declines precipitously. In this sense, the modern office becomes a machine which at best functions well only within its routine limits, and functions badly when it is called upon to meet special requirements.*

The Class Position of Clerical Labor

While the working class in production is the result of several centuries of capitalist development, clerical labor is largely the product of the period of monopoly capitalism. Thus the early post-Marx attempts to analyze this phenomenon were severely hampered by the fact that clerical work was as yet little developed as a capitalist labor process. For example, in the discussion of the subject in the German Social-Democracy before the First World War, Emil Lederer (whose *Die Privatangestellten in der Modernen Wirtschaftsentwicklung* was probably the most substantial and important product of the debate) commented on the stagnant technical conditions of the office:

> Indeed, the modern commercial employee resembles the commercial employee of the past more than the labor employed by large-scale industry resembles the journeyman of the Middle Ages. Methods of doing business have hardly changed in the majority of cases. Even large-scale enterprises are only expanded small-scale business. Since no new technique has come to the fore, they exhibit no essentially new methods.[43]

In these discussions, the participants were impressed by the rapid growth of the office; but the changes in office labor, still in their infancy, could not make so great an impression. The general expectation of commentators, as a result, was the rapid increase of office functionaries of the then-dominant varieties. On this basis, the conclusion seemed inescapable: a very large new "middle class" was coming into being.

This conclusion was further guaranteed by the penchant, which continues down to the present day, for defining the class positions of various varieties of office labor on the basis of secondary characteristics. In keeping with this, all the labor of the office is lumped together under such rubrics as "white collar," or "salaried employees." This is nothing but a hangover from the days in which all office labor did share the characteristics of privilege in pay, tenure, authority, etc. In that earlier situation, such designations, when applied to all who worked in offices, served as shorthand expressions for the special position of such employees. It was not the color of the employee's collar, still less the mode of payment on an annual or monthly basis as distinguished from the daily

---

* Managers often wag their heads over the "poor quality of office help" available on the labor market, although it is their own system of office operations which is creating the office population suited to it. This complaint is, unfortunately, too often echoed by unthinking "consumers" when they run into trouble with an office, as they often do. Such difficulties will tend to increase in the same way that the quality of factory production tends to decline and the servicing of consumer appliances tends to worsen even as it becomes more expensive, and for the same reasons.

or hourly wage of the manual worker, that in themselves had a determinate meaning, but rather the whole complex of social position and position in the enterprise and the labor process that these terms symbolized.*

In 1896, Charles Booth was able to write: "The 'average, undifferentiated human labour power' upon which Karl Marx bases his gigantic fallacy does not exist anywhere on this planet, but least of all, I think, is it to be found among clerks."[44] At the time there were few Marxists bold enough to try to counter this thrust. But within less than forty years the development of the capitalist office made it possible for some to comprehend all the essential elements of the process, although it was even then far from being well advanced. Thus Hans Speier, drawing chiefly on German experience, was able to write in 1934:

The social level of the salaried employee sinks with the increasing extent of the group. This qualitative change, which has been termed "the proletarianization of the white collar worker," shows itself in a number of ways. It is most evident, perhaps, in the especially great increase in the women salaried workers, who mostly perform subordinate work. . . . It is the man who typically has the principal authority, the girl who is typically the subordinate. . . . The great increase in salaried employees is especially traceable to a demand for subordinates, not for fully qualified responsible persons. As a result the average chance of advancing has declined. The majority of the subordinate employees in the large offices perform duties which are specialized and schematized down to the minutest detail. They no longer require general training; in part only a very limited and brief training is necessary, in part previous training has become quite unnecessary. The process in the course of which the body of salaried employees become a mass group rests on the successful attempt to replace the personal experience of the individual by a rational scientific

---

* The continued use of this terminology long after the realities behind it have disappeared is one of the greatest sources of confusion in the analysis of this subject. A term which lumps together into a single class grouping the authoritative executive representing capital on the one hand, and the interchangeable parts of the office machine which serves him on the other, can no longer be considered useful. This terminology is, however, considered serviceable by those who are alarmed by the results of a more realistic terminology—those, for instance, whose "sociology" pursues apologetic purposes. For them, such terms as "white-collar employees" conveniently lump into a single category the well-paid, authoritative, and desirable positions at the top of the hierarchy and the mass of proletarianized inferiors in a way that makes possible a rosier picture: higher "average" pay scales, etc. In this use of the term, the "white-collar" category tends to get its occupational flavor from the engineers, managers, and professors at the top of the hierarchy, while its impressive numerical masses are supplied by the millions of clerical workers, in much the same way that the stars of an opera company occupy the front of the stage while the spear-carriers provide the massive chorus.

business administration, so that an increasing proportion of the workers can be changed without danger to the efficiency of the enterprise. One social result of this development is the rise of the unskilled and semi-skilled salaried workers, whose designation already indicates the assimilation of the processes of work in the office to that in the factory. In the case of the salaried workers who serve as subordinates on one of the many modern office machines, or, for example, who sell in a one-price store, the difference in the nature of the duties between such workers and manual workers is completely wiped out . . . especially revealing with regard to the sinking of the social level of the white-collar workers is, finally, the change in the social antecedents. The growing tendency to employ salaried workers of "proletarian origin" indicates that the number of untrained and poorly paid positions is increasing faster than the number of middle and principal positions. In other words, the salaried employees as a whole are being subjected to a process of decreasing social esteem.[45]

This was written before the mechanization of the office. Writing at about the same time, Lewis Corey was anticipating future events when he said: "The mechanization of clerical labor becomes constantly greater; a typical large office is now nothing but a white-collar factory."[46] But by 1951, much of the anticipatory element had disappeared and C. Wright Mills was able to write, upon a solid basis of fact:

The introduction of office machinery and sales devices has been mechanizing the office and the salesroom, the two big locales of white-collar work. Since the 'twenties it has increased the division of white-collar labor, recomposed personnel, and lowered skill levels. Routine operations in minutely subdivided organizations have replaced the bustling interest of work in well-known groups. Even on managerial and professional levels, the growth of rational bureaucracies has made work more like factory production. The managerial demiurge is constantly furthering all these trends, mechanization, more minute division of labor, the use of less skilled and less expensive workers.

In its early stages, a new division of labor may specialize men in such a way as to increase their levels of skill; but later, especially when whole operations are split and mechanized, such division develops certain faculties at the expense of others and narrows all of them. And as it comes more fully under mechanization and centralized management, it levels men off again as automatons. Then there are a few specialists and a mass of automatons; both integrated by the authority which makes them interdependent and keeps each in his own routine. Thus, in the division of labor, the open development and free exercise of skills are managed and closed.

The alienating conditions of modern work now include the salaried employees as well as the wage-workers. There are few, if any, features of wage-work (except heavy toil—which is decreasingly a factor in wage-work) that do not also characterize at least some white-collar work. For here, too, the human traits of the individual, from his physique to his psychic disposition, become units in the functionally rational calculations of managers.

To these pictures of the merging characteristics of clerical and production labor, it is now possible to add a number of important details.

The use of automatic and semi-automatic machine systems in the office has the effect of completely reversing the traditional profile of office costs. A situation in which the cost of operating a large office consisted almost entirely of the salaries paid to clerical employees has changed to one in which a large share of the total is now invested in the purchase (or paid out monthly for the leasing) of expensive equipment. Past or "dead" labor in the form of machinery owned by capital, now employs living labor, in the office just as in the factory. But for the capitalist, the profitability of this employment is very much a function of time, of the rapidity with which dead labor absorbs living. The use of a great deal of expensive equipment thus leads to shift work, which is particularly characteristic of computer operations.

At the same time, the employment of machinery pushes the office installation toward the warehouse and industrial districts of the cities. This is facilitated by the development of remote terminals and other communications devices which annihilate distance and do away with almost all the inconveniences of separate installations, so that executive offices can be maintained in the more expensive and accessible locations while the mass of clerical workers can be moved into lower-rent districts, often together with warehousing or production facilities. Thus the convenience and cachet of working in the central part of town, with its greater shopping interest and more varied lunching facilities, etc., begins for many clerical workers to disappear.

At the same time, the labor market for the two chief varieties of workers, factory and office, begins to lose some of its distinctions of social stratification, education, family, and the like. Not only do clerical workers come increasingly from families of factory background, and vice-versa, but more and more they are merged within the same living family. The chief remaining distinction seems to be a division along the lines of sex. Here the distribution within the clerical and operative groups is strikingly congruent: in 1971, the category of operatives was made up of 9 million men and 4 million women, while that of clerical workers was made up of 10.1 million women and 3.3 million men. The sex barrier that assigns most office jobs to women, and that is enforced both by custom and hiring practice, has made it possible to lower wage rates in the clerical category, as we have seen, below those in any category of manual labor. The growing participation of women in employment has thus far been facilitated by the stronger demand for clerical employees and the relatively stagnating demand for operatives. The existence of two giant categories of labor, operatives and clerical workers, as the two largest major occupational classifications, and the composition by sex of each of these categories, leads to the supposition that one of the most common United States occupational combinations within the family is that in which the husband is an operative and the wife a clerk.

The tendency of modern capitalist employment, in which a vast mass is occupied on a less and less differentiated level of general labor, was recognized early by Theodore Caplow and well portrayed by him in the following passage:

> Near the midpoint of the occupational status scale, where white-collar and manual levels overlap, there are a vast number of employments which are usually called "semiskilled." As a matter of fact, most of them cannot be readily evaluated in terms of skill. Their common characteristic is that no lengthy experience is required to perform the work, and that movement from one occupation to another is easy and frequent. Indeed, the mark of a semiskilled occupation is its vagueness. Unlike the higher and lower portions of the scale, this great central cluster of factory and office jobs is not clearly compartmentalized. Lifetime involvement in a job is rare. Men and women perform comparable work under comparable conditions. Job titles do not correspond to organized social groupings; and each occupation merges into many others. All these factors together contribute to the very high and sustained rate of horizontal mobility which is characteristic of semiskilled workers.[48]

The increasing similarity of the work in factory and office is noted by Caplow, and particularly the similarity of requirements in the form of a high-school diploma to provide the background of general familiarity with the commonplace routines of modern society:

> The characteristic jobs of machine operators in modern factories, of clerical workers in large offices, and of sales clerks, inspectors, and other minor functionaries require a general familiarity with technical and commercial operations, together with a minimum command of the number system, the written language, and the technic of operating such devices as automobiles and cash registers. Although the emphasis upon mechanical insight and manual dexterity is greater in the factory trades than in the office jobs, the two broad branches of semiskilled work tend to become increasingly alike in many ways. Movement from one to the other takes place very readily. Tests carefully devised to measure clerical aptitude sometimes turn out to be better indicators of mechanical aptitude, and vice versa. This is apparently explained by the fact that the tests are patterned after operations actually required in typical jobs, and that operations required in machine production and clerical work are often very similar.
>
> The modern technics of job classification and personnel selection, developed in connection with large-scale production, are designed above all to facilitate the interchangeability of personnel. One method of ensuring interchangeability is to reduce each complex operation to a series of simple operations which

require no extraordinary ability. When this is done, an automatic effect is to standardize output throughout the series of related operations at a point well below the maximum output of which individual workers might be capable. At the same time, the formal qualifications required for employment are standardized by the educational process, so that there are comparatively few differences that matter between one worker and another.[49]

The problem of the so-called employee or white-collar worker which so bothered early generations of Marxists, and which was hailed by anti-Marxists as a proof of the falsity of the "proletarianization" thesis, has thus been unambiguously clarified by the polarization of office employment and the growth at one pole of an immense mass of *wage-workers*. The apparent trend to a large nonproletarian "middle class" has resolved itself into the creation of a large proletariat in a new form. In its conditions of employment, this working population has lost all former superiorities over workers in industry, and in its scales of pay it has sunk almost to the very bottom. But beneath them, in this latter respect at least, are the workers in service occupations and retail trade, whom we must consider next.

Notes

1. David Lockwood, *The Blackcoated Worker: A Study in Class Consciousness* (London, 1958), p. 22.
2. Sidney Pollard, *The Genesis of Modern Management* (Cambridge, Mass., 1965), pp. 137-39, 153-55.
3. F. D. Klingender, *The Condition of Clerical Labour in Britain* (London, 1935), p. 2.
4. Lewis Corey, *The Crisis of the Middle Class* (New York, 1935), pp. 249-50.
5. For the United States: Alba M. Edwards, Sixteenth Census Reports, *Comparative Occupation Statistics in the United States, 1870-1940* (Washington, 1943), p. 112; David M. Kaplan and M. Claire Casey, *Occupational Trends in the United States 1900 to 1950*, Bureau of the Census Working Paper No. 5 (Washington, 1958), Table 1; U.S. Bureau of the Census, *Census of the Population: 1970, Final Report PC (2)-7A, Occupational Characteristics* (Washington, D.C., 1973), Table 1; U.S. Bureau of the Census, *U.S. Census of the Population*: 1960, vol. I (Washington, D.C., 1964), Table 201, p. 523. For Great Britain: Lockwood, *The Blackcoated Worker*, p. 36; George S. Bain, *The Growth of White Collar Unionism* (Oxford, 1970), p. 191.
6. Lockwood, *The Blackcoated Worker*, p. 28.
7. Belton M. Fleisher, *Labor Economics: Theory and Evidence* (Englewood Cliffs, N.J., 1970), p. 219.
8. Stanley Lebergott, *Manpower in Economic Growth: The American Record Since 1800* (New York and London, 1964), p. 500; for production worker pay scales of 1900, see also pp. 525-27.

9. Paul O. Flaim and Nicholas I. Peters, "Usual Weekly Earnings of American Workers," *Monthly Labor Review* (March 1972), pp. 28-38; esp. Table 4, p. 33. This Special Labor Force Report of the Bureau of Labor Statistics covers the 57.6 million workers who worked 35 hours a week or more, excluding the 15 percent of wage and salary workers who worked fewer than 35 hours per week.

10. Lockwood, *The Blackcoated Worker*, p. 49.

11. David M. Gordon, "From Steam Whistles to Coffee Breaks," *Dissent* (Winter 1972), pp. 197-200.

12. Jon M. Shepard, *Automation and Alienation: A Study of Office and Factory Workers* (Cambridge, Mass., 1971), pp. 41-42.

13. Lee Galloway, *Office Management: Its Principles and Practice* (New York, 1918), p. vii.

14. Ibid., pp. 3-4.

15. William Henry Leffingwell, *Scientific Office Management* (New York, Chicago, and London, 1917); see Foreword.

16. Galloway, *Office Management*, pp. 222-26.

17. Leffingwell, *Scientific Office Management*, pp. 27, 32.

18. Galloway, *Office Management*, p. 569.

19. Stanley Vance, *American Industries* (New York, 1955), p. 160.

20. Leffingwell, *Scientific Office Management*, pp. 20-21.

21. Lockwood, *The Blackcoated Worker,* pp. 89-90.

22. Charles Babbage, *On the Economy of Machinery and Manufactures* (London, 1832; reprint ed., New York, 1963), p. 191.

23. Ibid., p. 195.

24. William J. Fuhro, *Work Measurement and Production Control with the F-A-S-T System* (Englewood Cliffs, N.J., 1963), pp. 39-40.

25. Richard J. Morrison, Robert E. Nolan, and James S. Devlin, *Work Measurement in Machine Accounting* (New York, 1963), pp. 69-82.

26. Boris Yavitz and Thomas M. Stanback, Jr., *Electronic Data Processing in New York City* (New York and London, 1967), p. 82.

27. Ibid., p. 83.

28. Ida Russakoff Hoos, *Automation in the Office* (Washington, 1961), p. 53.

29. Ibid., pp. 67-68.

30. Ibid., pp. 78-79.

31. Ibid., pp. 66-68.

32. Yavitz and Stanback, *Electronic Data Processing*, p. 84.

33. Enid Mumford and Olive Banks, *The Computer and the Clerk* (London, 1967), p. 190.

34. Hoos, *Automation in the Office*, p. 57.

35. Joseph P. Newhouse, "Technological Change in Banking," in National Commission on Technology, Automation, and Economic Progress, *The Employment Impact of Technological Change*, Appendix Volume II, *Technology and the American Economy* (Washington, D.C., 1966), p. 167.

36. American Management Association, *Establishing an Integrated Data-Processing System*, Special Report No. 11, 1956, p. 113; cited by Hoos, *Automation in the Office*, p. 85.
37. U.S. Department of Labor, Bureau of Labor Statistics, *Technological Trends in Major American Industries*, Bulletin No. 1474 (Washington, 1966), p. 247.
38. *Business Week*, May 12, 1973, p. 141.
39. "Machines—The New Bank Tellers," *New York Times*, December 2, 1973.
40. *Administrative Management*, May 1972.
41. Ibid., January 1972.
42. Ibid., May 1972.
43. Emil Lederer, *The Problem of the Modern Salaried Employee* (New York, 1937), p. 5. (This is a translation, made by a WPA project, of chapters 2 and 3 of Lederer's book, which was originally published in Tübingen in 1912.)
44. Charles Booth, *Life and Labour of the People in London*, vol. II; quoted in Lockwood, *The Blackcoated Worker*, p. 18.
45. Hans Speier, "The Salaried Employee in Modern Society," *Social Research* (February 1934), pp. 116-118; quoted by Lewis Corey, op. cit., pp. 253-254.
46. Lewis Corey, *The Crisis of the Middle Class*, p. 250.
47. C. Wright Mills, *White Collar* (New York, London, and Oxford, 1951; paperback edition, 1956), pp. 226-27.
48. Theodore Caplow, *The Sociology of Work* (Minneapolis, Minn., 1954), pp. 84-85.
49. Ibid., pp. 85-86.

Chapter 16

Service Occupations and Retail Trade

The giant mass of workers who are relatively homogeneous as to lack of developed skill, low pay, and interchangeability of person and function (although heterogeneous in such particulars as the site and nature of the work they perform) is not limited to offices and factories. Another huge concentration is to be found in the so-called service occupations and in retail trade. We have already discussed, particularly in Chapter 13, "The Universal Market," the reasons for the rapid growth of service occupations in both the corporate and governmental sectors of the economy: the completion by capital of the conquest of goods-producing activities; the displacement of labor from those industries, corresponding to the accumulation of capital in them, and the juncture of these reserves of labor and capital on the ground of new industries; and the inexorable growth of service needs as the new shape of society destroys the older forms of social, community, and family cooperation and self-aid. Now we must examine the labor processes of the service occupations themselves more closely.

"A service," Marx pointed out, "is nothing more than the useful effect of a use-value, be it of a commodity, or be it of labour."[1] The worker who is employed in producing goods renders a service to the capitalist, and it is as a result of this service that a tangible, vendible object takes shape as a commodity. But what if the useful effects of labor are such that they cannot take shape in an object? Such labor must be offered directly to the consumer, since production and consumption are simultaneous. The useful effects of labor, in such cases, do not serve to make up a vendible object which then carries its useful effects with it as part of its existence as a commodity. Instead, the useful effects of labor themselves *become* the commodity. When the worker does not offer this labor directly to the user of its effects, but instead sells it to a capitalist, who re-sells it on the commodity market, then we have the capitalist form of production in the field of services.

Such a strict or scientific definition of services is far more limited than the usual use of the term by statistical agencies, such as the bureaus of the census and of labor statistics in the United States. For example, restaurant labor, which cooks, prepares, assembles, serves, cleans dishes and utensils, etc., carries on tangible production just as much as labor employed in many another manufacturing process; the fact that the consumer is sitting nearby at a counter or table is the chief distinction, in principle, between this industry and those food-processing industries which are classified under "manufacturing." Laundry workers, workers in cleaning and pressing establishments, workers in automobile repair shops and in machine servicing or repair work of other sorts perform the same sort of work as many workers in manufacturing industries, and they are classified, *occupationally*, in the same way, but the Bureau of the Census classifies them in *service industries.** Workers in transportation are often regarded as workers in a "service" industry, but if the location of a commodity is taken as an important *physical* characteristic, transportation is a part of the process of production. And if we do not take this view we fall into insuperable difficulties, because we are forced to extend the distinction between "making" and "moving" back into the factory, where many workers do not play a role in fashioning the object with their own hands but merely *move* it through the plant, or through the process. The distinction so applied becomes meaningless and even ridiculous. Chambermaids are classed as service workers, but their labors are not always different, in principle, from those of many manufacturing workers in that they take shape in a tangible result. When the chambermaids in hotels and motels, or the aides in hospitals and other institutions, make beds they do an assembly operation which is not different from many factory assembly occupations—a fact recognized by management when it conducts motion and time studies of both on the same principles—and the result is a tangible and vendible commodity. Does the fact that porters, charwomen, janitors, or dishwashers perform their cleaning operations not on new goods that are being readied at the factory or construction sites for their first use, but on constantly reused buildings and utensils render their labor different in principle, and any less tangible in form, from that of manufacturing workers who do the factories' final cleaning, polishing, packaging, and so forth?

---

* Stigler has pointed out that in this respect the census practice has changed, and that early in the century all such workers in power laundries, automobile repair shops, and other repair and servicing industries were included in manufacturing, whereas today they are included in service industries. As he notes, this change in statistical practice, when applied to such rapidly growing industries as these, has in itself accounted for a significant part of the shift from "manufacturing" to "services" in the statistics used for long-run comparisons.[2] Today, hand and machine finish pressers, when employed by makers of clothing, are counted as manufacturing workers, but when employed by dry-cleaning plants they are workers in service industries, although the difference in the form of labor is slight; the chief difference is in rates of pay, which is substantially lower in the service industries.[3] The same holds true for a great variety of craftsmen whose work in fabrication is distinguished from repair and servicing; and in fact even when they do the very same work of repair and servicing they are counted as manufacturing workers only when this is done as plant maintenance work.

These are only some of the many difficulties that arise from the attempts to draw strict classifications of the labor in capitalist society on the basis of its determinate form—the particular operations it pursues. They merely illustrate the principle that for capitalism, what is important is not the determinate form of labor but its *social form*, its capacity to produce, as wage labor, a profit for the capitalist. The capitalist is indifferent to the particular form of labor; he does not care, in the last analysis, whether he hires workers to produce automobiles, wash them, repair them, repaint them, fill them with gasoline and oil, rent them by the day, drive them for hire, park them, or convert them into scrap metal. His concern is the difference between the price he pays for an aggregate of labor and other commodities, and the price he receives for the commodities—whether goods or "services"—produced or rendered.

From this point of view, the distinction between commodities in the form of goods and commodities in the form of services is important only to the economist or statistician, not to the capitalist. What counts for him is not the determinate form of the labor, but whether it has been drawn into the network of capitalist social relations, whether the worker who carries it on has been transformed into a wage-worker, and whether the labor of the worker has been transformed into productive labor—that is, labor which produces a profit for capital. Beds were made, floors were scrubbed, food prepared and served, children minded, the sick tended long before people were hired to do any of these things. And even after the hiring of servants to do them had begun, these activities were of no interest to the capitalist except in terms of his comfort and household expenses. They became of interest to him *as a capitalist* when he began to hire people to do services as a profitable activity, a part of his business, a form of the capitalist mode of production. And this began on a large scale only with the era of monopoly capitalism which created the universal market-place and transformed into a commodity every form of the activity of human-kind including what had heretofore been the many things that people did for themselves or for each other. With this began the changed attitude of the capitalist toward service labor, a change which can be seen both in his own massive ventures into the field and, on the ideological side, in the change in the view of service labor taken by economists.

Thus, service occupations have formed a large share in the social division of labor throughout the capitalist era—not to speak of earlier times—but they have not formed a "productive" or *profitable* part until recently. The multitude of personal servants was, in the early period of capitalism, both a heritage of feudal and semi-feudal relations in the form of a vast employment furnished by the landowning aristocracy, and a reflection of the riches created by the Industrial Revolution in the form of similar employment furnished by capital-ists and the upper middle class. In the United States in 1820, according to the first occupational census, employment in domestic and personal services was three-fourths as great as the combined employment of the manufacturing, mining, fishing, and lumbering industries; even in 1870 such employment was not much less than half as great as these nonagricultural employments.[4] (A statistician who calculated the amount of domestic and personal service employment as a percent of the population between 1820 and 1920 found it remarkably stable, in the range between 4.5 and 6 percent.)[5] In England, according to the census of 1861, more than 1.2 million people were employed as servants, and this does not include male or female servants on farms. This, as Marx pointed out, was greater than the total employment in the textile and metal-working industries.*

But from the capitalist point of view, such employment was not an addition to national wealth or income, but a deduction from it. This view, as set forth by classical political economy and especially in Adam Smith, had nothing to do with the nature of the duties performed by these workers (although this point was sometimes confused) but arose rather from the fact that these duties were not performed under the auspices of capital *qua* capital. It was not when he was accumulating capital that the capitalist employed service labor, but when he was spending his profits. "Thus," said Adam Smith, "the labour of a manufacturer adds, generally, to the value of the materials which he works upon, that of his own maintenance and of his master's profit. The labour of a menial servant, on the contrary, adds to the value of nothing. . . . A man grows rich by employing a multitude of manufacturers: he grows poor, by maintaining a multitude of menial servants." And so zealous was Adam Smith in his pursuit of this point that he turned it against all "service" labor in general and found the fault to be not in the fact that the master was so foolish as to employ servants instead of investing in more workers, but rather in the fact that "service" labor did not congeal into a tangible commodity. The clarification of this error on Smith's part occupies many pages of Marx's *Theories of Surplus Value*. Smith's modern editor, Edwin Cannan, more familiar with the profitable uses to which service labor can be put, corrected him by pointing out that "this is only true when the manufacturers are employed to produce commodities for sale and when the menial servants are employed merely for the comfort of the employer. A man may and often does grow poor by employing people to make 'particular

---

* This is cited by Marx, significantly, in the section of *Capital* called "The Theory of Compensation as Regards the Workpeople Displaced by Machinery."[6] In his *Theories of Surplus Value*, this thought is rendered more fully: "According to the latest report (1861 or 1862), on the factories, the total number of persons (managers included) employed in the factories properly so called of the United Kingdom was only 775,534, while the number of female servants in England alone amounted to 1 million. What a convenient arrangement it is that makes a factory girl to sweat twelve hours in a factory, so that the factory proprietor, with a part of her unpaid labour, can take into his personal service her sister as maid, her brother as groom and her cousin as soldier or policeman!"[7]

subjects or vendible commodities' for his own consumption, and an innkeeper may and often does grow rich by employing menial servants."[8]

In modern bourgeois economics, service labor which does not in Adam Smith's words "fix or realize itself in any particular subject or vendible commodity" is no longer held in disfavor, but is rather, since it has been developed as a prime source of profit, celebrated. Colin Clark found "the most important concomitant of economic progress" to be "the movement of the working population from agriculture to manufacture and from manufacture to commerce and services."[9] Few economists would today call service labor "unproductive"—except when performed by the worker on his or her own account, as the housewife does at home. Instead, they tend to extol service as the characteristic form of production of our time, superior to manufacturing and with a greater future before it. In this we see a continuation of the succession of economic theories which assigned the most productive role to the particular form of labor that was most important or growing most rapidly at the time: the mercantilists to labor which brought precious metals into the country; the physiocrats to agricultural labor; the classical economists to manufacturing labor.

In the history of capitalism, while one or another form of productive labor may play a greater role in particular eras, the tendency is toward the eradication of distinctions among its various forms. Particularly in the era of monopoly capitalism, it makes little sense to ground any theory of the economy upon any specially favored variety of labor process. As these varied forms come under the auspices of capital and become part of the domain of profitable investment, they enter for the capitalist into the realm of general or abstract labor, labor which enlarges capital. In the modern corporation, all forms of labor are employed without distinction, and in the modern "conglomerate" corporation some divisions carry on manufacturing, others carry on trade, others banking, others mining, and still others "service" processes. All live peacefully together, and in the final result as recorded in balance sheets the forms of labor disappear entirely in the forms of value.

The service occupations (excluding private household employment, which has not grown in the form of servants directly hired, and is being replaced by commercial companies which contract to perform household cleaning) now include a mass of labor some nine times larger than the million workers they accounted for at the turn of the century. This represents a much more rapid growth than that of employment as a whole, which in the same period (1900-1970), less than tripled.* The nature of these occupations and the labor

---

* Because the term "service labor" is used by statistical agencies of the United States in two different connotations, one *industrial* and the other *occupational*, the

processes which they carry on will be readily understood from the listing as given in the 1970 census.[10]

To this 9 million should be added, as workers of the same general classification and wage level, that portion of sales workers employed in retail trade, or some 3 million out of the total of 5.5 million sales workers of all kinds (the rest being employed in wholesale trade, as manufacturers' representatives, and as salesmen of advertising, insurance, real estate, stocks and bonds, etc., and thus representing a different order of work). These service and retail sales workers, taken together, account for a massive total of more than 12 million workers.

The occupations classified in these two categories require little description and analysis because they are conducted, for the most part, in the public eye, and the labor tasks assigned to most of them are readily visualized. In the case of almost every occupation in the service and retail groups the mass of labor is drawn into these growing fields of employment from a vast pool of common labor which is made available by the relative falling off of employment in other fields. The average pay scales confirm this: the median of the usual weekly earnings of full-time wage and salary workers in the service occupations is lower than that of any occupational group except farmworkers. In May 1971 it was $91 a week (if one includes the half million private household workers; excluding these it was $96), as against $115 for clerical workers, $117 for laborers (nonfarm), and $120 for operatives. In the same month, the median for full-time retail sales workers was $95, which in terms of pay located that grouping closer to the service occupation than to any other major occupational category.[11]

Except for the special cases of police and firemen, the incidence of developed skill, knowledge, and authority in the labor processes of society is naturally very small in these categories, and can be found only in that small layer of housekeepers and stewards who have the function of superintending institutional labor, and among the tiny number of cooks who practice the art

---

following distinction must be kept in mind: The Commerce Department groups enterprises according to a Standard Industrial Classification, and the broad groups within this classification, such as Agriculture, Manufacturing, Mining, Trade, etc. include a group called Service Industries. Occupational figures for this group of industries are available, and employment in the group is sometimes referred to as "service employment." But this employment includes workers in a great many occupations: in 1970 it included more than 3 million clerical workers, over a million craftsmen, another million operatives, and almost 7.5 million professional and technical employees; at the same time, it did *not* include all the service occupations, but only about three-quarters of them, the rest being scattered through all the other industrial classifications. To confuse labor in so-called "service industries" with the service *occupations* would mean, therefore, to duplicate much of the employment that has been and will be herein discussed in other connections. Our present discussion therefore deals only with those workers who are grouped in the *occupational* statistics as service workers, and not those so grouped in the *industrial* statistics.

Service Occupations, 1970

	Both sexes	Male		Female	
	Total	Total	Median earnings (dollars)	Total	Median earnings (dollars)
Service workers, except private household	9 074 154	4 012 814	5 086	5 061 340	2 323
Cleaning service workers	1 939 551	1 310 884	4 636	628 667	2 288
Chambermaids and maids, except private household	217 743	10 515	3 296	207 228	2 048
Cleaners and charwomen	458 290	197 447	4 063	260 843	2 445
Janitors and sextons	1 263 518	1 102 922	4 771	160 596	2 404
Food service workers	2 974 238	932 039	2 899	2 042 199	1 808
Bartenders	197 676	155 307	5 656	42 369	3 008
Busboys	107 124	92 034	943	15 090	925
Cooks, except private household	873 062	327 317	4 076	545 745	2 157
Dishwashers	185 973	115 763	1 238	70 210	1 235
Food counter and fountain workers	156 749	37 547	1 413	119 202	1 382
Waiters	1 110 309	120 050	2 894	990 259	1 662
Food service workers, n.e.c., except private household	343 345	84 021	1 917	259 324	1 839
Health service workers	1 230 454	147 617	4 448	1 082 837	3 247
Dental assistants	93 324	1 996	4 094	91 328	3 405
Health aides, except nursing	124 334	19 897	4 354	104 437	3 460
Health trainees	19 163	1 172	2 413	17 991	871
Lay midwives	963	226		737	2 626
Nursing aides, orderlies, and attendants	751 983	115 357	4 401	636 626	2 969
Practical nurses	240 687	8 969	5 745	231 718	4 205

Personal service workers	1 209 421	406 220	5 072	803 201	2 735
Airline stewardesses	34 794	1 322	8 857	33 472	6 123
Attendants, recreation and amusement	80 564	60 863	1 923	19 701	979
Attendants, personal service, n.e.c.	64 527	24 184	3 983	40 343	2 576
Baggage porters and bellhops	20 277	19 836	3 746	441	...
Barbers	171 004	163 081	5 686	7 923	3 382
Boarding and lodging housekeepers	7 549	1 972	4 256	5 577	2 852
Bootblacks	4 064	3 728	1 176	336	...
Child-care workers, except private household	132 723	9 101	3 936	123 622	1 375
Elevator operators	38 653	28 191	5 329	10 462	3 071
Hairdressers and cosmetologists	492 758	48 907	6 731	443 851	3 041
Personal service apprentices	1 457	604	2 576	853	946
Housekeepers, except private household	105 834	28 955	5 777	76 879	3 142
School monitors	27 045	2 423	1 153	24 622	647
Ushers, recreation and amusement	14 615	10 053	895	4 562	781
Welfare service aides	15 014	3 604	5 487	11 410	3 192
Protective service workers	972 671	911 723	8 009	60 948	2 406
Crossing guards and bridge tenders	43 296	17 626	2 620	25 670	1 494
Firemen, fire protection	180 386	178 115	9 423	2 271	7 809
Guards and watchmen	331 775	315 299	5 891	16 476	3 687
Marshals and constables	5 591	5 363	7 130	228	...
Policemen and detectives	376 618	362 440	8 989	14 178	4 941
Public	358 150	347 121	9 051	11 029	5 582
Private	18 468	15 319	6 989	3 149	3 588
Sheriffs and bailiffs	35 005	32 880	7 346	2 125	5 328
Service workers, except private household—allocated	747 819	304 331	4 633	443 488	2 330

on the chef level. Those who supervise labor in institutions correspond to the foremen who supervise factory labor, or to lower-level managers having the same function in every labor process. Chefs and cooks of superior grades, the highest skill of the service category, offer an instructive instance of the manner in which an ancient and valuable craft is being destroyed even in its last stronghold, luxury and gourmet cooking. The technological means employed in this case is that of food freezing, including its more recent forms, flash freezing and drying at sub-zero temperatures, and cryogenic freezing at temperatures at least 300 degrees below zero. In such processes, cell walls are destroyed and texture and flavor damaged. Moreover, pre-cooked frozen foods tend in the long run to be more expensive than fresh foods because of the expensive equipment required for freezing, transporting these foods in a frozen state, and thawing them in microwave or convection pressure ovens. That moneyed clienteles now pay "luxury prices for slot machine food"—so that a rack of lamb ordered rare in a famous Connecticut inn is brought to the table cold and the client told that rare lamb must be cold[12]—is not what concerns us here. More to the point is the manner in which a precious craft is destroyed and how this destructive tendency feeds on itself. As in so many other fields of work, the simplification and rationalization of skills in the end destroy these skills, and, with the skills becoming ever more scarce, the new processes become ever more inevitable-because of the shortage of skilled labor! The food editor of the *New York Times* wrote, in describing this process:

> Many restaurant owners say the shortage and high price of skilled help are major reasons they turn to frozen foods. But kitchen wages are among the lowest in all industries, and the shortage of help may be a result, rather than a cause, of conditions in the trade.
>
> A reader says his wife applied for a job with the Stouffer's chain and was told that they didn't need any cooks, only "thawer-outers." An executive acknowledged that the chain was "not a chef system but a food management system."[13]

So far as retail trade is concerned, it is worth noting that although the "skills" of store operations have long since been disassembled and in all decisive respects vested in management,* a revolution is now being prepared which will make of retail workers, by and large, something closer to factory operatives than anyone had ever imagined possible. In retail food trading, for example, the demand for the all-around grocery clerk, fruiterer and vegetable dealer, dairyman, butcher, and so forth has long ago been replaced by a labor configuration in the supermarkets which calls for truck unloaders, shelf

---

* In 1892, F. W. Woolworth wrote in a letter to his store managers: "We must have cheap help or we cannot sell cheap goods."[14] Chain stores in the notion and novelty, as well as in the food trades, and nationwide mail order houses, pioneered the fractionalization of retail labor.

stockers, checkout clerks, meat wrappers, and meatcutters; of these, only the last retain any semblance of skill, and none require any general knowledge of retail trade. The use of mechanical equipment for the shelving, display, and sale of commodities has thus far remained in a primitive state, in part because of the ready availability of low-cost labor and in part because of the nature of the process itself. With the perfecting of a number of computerized semi-automatic checkout systems, however, an increasing number of national chains in retail trade—in other fields as well as in food marketing—have committed themselves to replacing their present cash-register systems with new systems that, they estimate, will almost double the number of customers handled by each checkout clerk in a given time. The system will require affixing to each item a tag or label which carries the proper stock number (a universal ten-digit code has been adopted by the food industry) and perhaps a price, printed in characters which may be recognized by an optical scanner. Thus the clerk will simply pass the item over the scanner (or hold a scanner lens to the tag), and the register will transmit the operation to a computer which can either supply the price or check it against the current price list. The effects of this system on inventory control, quick and general price changes, and sales reporting to a central point require no comment. But the checkout counter then adopts as its own the assembly line or factory pace in its most complete form. The "production" of each register can be controlled from a single central station and laggards noted for future action; and, since no knowledge of prices is required, the production speed of a checkout clerk can be pegged at the highest level within a few hours after that clerk has begun the job, instead of the few weeks of learning time that are now allowed. Of course, the slowest operation will then become that of bagging, and various mechanical systems which will eliminate the separate "bagger" and enable the checkout clerk to sweep the item over the optical scanner and into the bag with a single motion are being devised and tested.[15]

The trend to automatic filling stations, where the customer, in return for a small saving, fills his or her own tank while the transaction is monitored on a screen in the station is also worth mentioning, if only for the manner in which it combines a displacement of labor with a shift from male to female labor; the new gasoline station attendants are generally "girls," who, as everyone knows, offer a further saving to the thrifty employer.

As a quick glance at the list of service occupations will make apparent, the bulk of the work is concentrated in two areas: cleaning and building care, and kitchen work and food service. Female workers outnumber male, as in retail sales work. Training prerequisites for most of these occupations are minimal, a job ladder leading upward is virtually nonexistent, and unemployment rates are higher than average. In this occupational category are found the housekeeping jobs of a society of concentrated life and labor that masses workers and residents in multiple-dwelling units, giant office blocks, and immense factory units, and which thus develops extraordinary requirements for cleaning, care-taking, and catering. We see here the obverse face of the heralded "service economy," which is supposed to free workers from the tyranny of industry, call into existence a "higher order" of educated labor, and transform the condition of the average man. When this picture is drawn by enthusiastic publicists and press agents of capitalism (with or without advanced degrees in sociology and econom-ics), it is given a semblance of reality by reference to professional occupations. When numbers are required to lend mass to the conception, the categories of clerical, sales, and service workers are called upon. But these workers are not asked to show their diplomas, their pay stubs, or their labor processes.*

Notes

1. Karl Marx, *Capital*, vol. I (Moscow, n.d.), p. 187.
2. George J. Stigler, *Trends in Output and Employment* (New York, 1947), p. 23.
3. U.S. Bureau of Labor Statistics, *Handbook of Labor Statistics 1969* (Wash-ington, 1969), pp. 242-43, 257.
4. P. K. Whelpton, "Occupational Groups in the United States, 1820-1920," *Journal of the American Statistical Association*, vol. XXI (September 1926), p. 339.
5. Ibid., p. 341.
6. Marx, *Capital*, vol. I, pp. 420-21.
7. Karl Marx, *Theories of Surplus-Value*, Part I (Moscow, 1963), p. 201.
8. Adam Smith, *The Wealth of Nations* (New York, 1937), p. 314.
9. Colin Clark, *The Conditions of Economic Progress* (London, 1940), p. 176.
10. U.S. Bureau of the Census, *Census of Population: 1970, Final Report PC(2)-7A, Occupational Characteristics* (Washington, D.C., 1973), pp. 10-11.
11. Paul O. Flaim and Nicholas I. Peters, "Usual Weekly Earnings of American Workers," *Monthly Labor Review* (March 1972), p. 33.
12. John L. Hess, "Restaurant Food: Frozen, Cooked, Then Refrozen and Re-cooked," *New York Times*, August 16, 1973.
13. Ibid.
14. Edward C. Kirkland, *Industry Comes of Age: Business, Labor, and Public Policy, 1860-1897* (New York, 1962), p. 271.
15. John D. Morris, "Revolution Near at Check-Out Counter," *New York Times*, May 21, 1973; Alan Eck, "The Great American Cornucopia," *Occupational Outlook Quarterly* (Fall 1973).
16. Harold L. Sheppard and Neal Q. Herrick, *Where Have All the Robots Gone?: Worker Dissatisfaction in the '70s* (New York and London, 1972), p. 5; see also Appendix A, p. 193.

---

* We may note here that according to sociological surveys—take them for what they are worth—job dissatisfaction, "negative attitudes toward work and life," while high among workers in manufacturing and in machine trades, are much higher among workers in service, clerical, and sales jobs."[16]

Part V

The Working Class

Chapter 17

The Structure of the Working Class
and its Reserve Armies

Labor and capital are the opposite poles of capitalist society. This polarity begins in each enterprise and is realized on a national and even international scale as a giant duality of classes which dominates the social structure. And yet this polarity is incorporated in a necessary identity between the two. Whatever its form, whether as money or commodities or means of production, *capital is labor:* it is labor that has been performed in the past, the objectified product of preceding phases of the cycle of production which becomes capital only through appropriation by the capitalist and its use in the accumulation of more capital. At the same time, as living labor which is purchased by the capitalist to set the production process into motion, *labor is capital.* That portion of money capital which is set aside for the payment of labor, the portion which in each cycle is converted into living labor power, is the portion of capital which stands for and corresponds to the working population, and upon which the latter subsists.

Before it is anything else, therefore, the working class is the animate part of capital, the part which will set in motion the process that yields to the total capital its increment of surplus value. As such, the working class is first of all raw material for exploitation.

This working class lives a social and political existence of its own, outside the direct grip of capital. It protests and submits, rebels or is integrated into bourgeois society, sees itself as a class or loses sight of its own existence, in accordance with the forces that act upon it and the moods, conjunctures, and conflicts of social and political life. But since, in its permanent existence, it is the living part of capital, its occupational structure, modes of work, and distribution through the industries of society are determined by the ongoing processes of the accumulation of capital. It is seized, released, flung into various parts of the social machinery and expelled by others, not in accord with its own will or self-activity, but in accord with the movement of capital.

From this is derived the formal definition of the working class as that class which, possessing nothing but its power to labor, sells that power to capital in return for its subsistence. As we shall see, this, like all definitions, is limited by its static quality. But in itself it is perfectly correct and forms the only adequate starting point for any attempt to visualize the working class in modern society.

We may gain a rough first approximation of the working class in this century by considering at the outset the mass occupational categories which embrace, with a few anomalies and exceptions, the unmistakably working-class population. These, as classified by the U.S. bureaus of the census and labor statistics, are the craftsmen, clerical workers, operatives, sales workers, service workers, and nonfarm laborers. We exclude from these groups foremen, who are usually classified in the craftsman's category; from among the sales workers, we exclude the salesmen, agents, and brokers of advertising, insurance, real estate, and stocks and bonds, as well as manufacturers' representatives and salesmen in wholesale trade, the latter being generally higher-paid and privileged sales workers, thus leaving in this category chiefly salespersons in retail trade.* In these six categories, so modified, we find the overwhelming bulk of the nonagricultural working class, whose growth and changes of composition can be seen in the following table:[1]

| | *Workers (in millions) 1900-1970* | | | | | | | |
	1900	1910	1920	1930	1940	1950	1960	1970
Operatives and laborers	7.3	9.9	11.5	13.0	14.4	15.5	16.4	18.1
Craftsmen	2.9	4.0	5.0	5.7	5.6	7.3	8.0	9.5
Clerical workers	.9	2.0	3.4	4.3	5.0	7.1	9.6	14.3
Service and sales workers	3.6	4.9	4.9	7.3	8.8	8.7	10.6	13.4
Total workers	14.7	20.8	24.8	30.3	33.8	38.6	44.6	55.3
Total "active" or "experienced labor force"	29.0	37.3	42.2	48.7	51.7	57.9	64.5	80.0
	Workers (as percent of total "labor force")							
Percentage	**50.7**	**55.8**	**58.8**	**62.2**	**65.4**	**66.7**	**69.1**	**69.1**

---

* Since for our tabulation we use the census figures for the "economically active civilian population"—the term used in the early part of this century—or, in later censuses, the "experienced civilian labor force," this tabulation includes all workers whose occupations can be defined, employed or unemployed, but not those who have "dropped out of the labor force."

Using major occupational categories in this way, even if modified as described, leaves much to be desired in statistical precision. For example, it has already been pointed out that even the lowest of the occupational categories included in this table—that of service workers—includes among its hundreds of thousands of cooks some of whom, as chefs, manage the labor processes of large kitchens, are paid on a managerial scale, and are thus strictly speaking far from being "working class" in the same sense as the rest of the category. The same is undoubtedly true of some who are classified as bookkeepers, or even secretaries, within the clerical category. One might also raise objections to the classification of police as workers. The numbers involved, however, are small in relation to the size of the categories as a whole. On the other hand, some parts of other major occupational groups not included in this tabulation are just as much a part of the unmistakable and self-evident working class as those major groups we have included above. In that group called "managers, officials, and proprietors," for instance, there are considerable numbers of railroad conductors, union officials, and especially "managers," so called, of retail stores, eating and drinking places, gasoline service stations, repair and personal services, and the like. In a large number of cases the classification of such workers as managers owes more to convention than to reality. The inclusion of draftsmen, medical, dental, engineering and other such technicians among the professional and technical grouping also, in a large and increasing number of cases, conceals a genuinely working-class situation for those involved.

Moreover, a very rapidly growing category reported in the census is that which falls outside of any occupational group and is given the rubric "occupation not reported." This category of the occupational census included 1,369,621 people in 1950, and 3,453,279 in 1960. Furthermore, the growing number of those who are not counted as part of the "labor force" because they have stopped the active search for employment, as well as the enormous undercounting of the population in the working-class portions of the cities now admitted by census officials, also affect the trends. All in all, we must suppose these forms of undercounting result, particularly in recent censuses, in an underestimate of the size of the working-class population. These considerations, rough though they may be, tend toward the conclusion that the nonagricultural working-class portion of the "experienced civilian labor force" has grown since the start of the century from half to well over two-thirds, perhaps as high as three-quarters, of the total at the present time.

The conversion of an ever larger proportion of the population into labor power on the working-class level devoted to the increase of capital, has taken place primarily at the expense of the farming population, which at the turn of the century embraced nearly 40 percent of the "economically active," while by 1970 it had fallen below 4 percent. The most substantial proportional increases have taken place in three categories: operatives, clerical workers, and the combined service and retail-sales sectors. As the employment effects of the technological revolution began to be felt, however, the steady proportional increase of operatives ceased, and after 1950 this group fell backward as a proportion of the total (although numerically it continued to increase). But the continued, and even accelerated, increase of the other two groups, clerical and sales-service, has taken up the workers released from factory employment (or never hired).

It takes but a moment's reflection to see that the new mass working-class occupations tend to grow, not in contradiction to the speedy mechanization and "automation" of industry, but in harmony with it. As a result of this mechanization, the numbers of workers required by the manufacturing, mining, transportation, communications, public utilities, and even to some extent construction industries are held down and do not increase as rapidly as their material products, so that the labor requirements of these industries, measured as a proportion of the total employed population, are held in check. Thus the scientific-technological revolution possesses, in the long run, this trait: that with its spread, the proportion of the population connected with scientifically and technologically advanced industry, even if only in the form of helots, eventually shrinks. The fastest growing industrial and occupational sectors in the "automated" age tend, therefore, in the long run to be those labor-intensive areas which have not yet been or cannot be subjected to high technology.

The masses of labor sloughed off by the rapid mechanization of industry (and this includes not just those who lose their jobs, but, much more important numerically, those who keep coming into the employment market at a time when traditional opportunities for industrial employment are shrinking) furnish the labor supply for the clerical, service, and sales fields. The mechanization of industry produces a relative surplus of population available for employment at the lower pay rates that characterize these new mass occupations. In other words, as capital moves into new fields in search of profitable investment, the laws of capital accumulation in the older fields operate to bring into existence the "labor force" required by capital in its new incarnations. This process was given its classic formulation by Marx in the chapter of the first volume of *Capital* called "The General Law of Capitalist Accumulation," in the section in which he describes the continuous formation in capitalist production, after it emerges from its "childhood," of a "relative surplus-population." We have already extracted a portion of this passage in Chapter 11, but since Marx's description of the movement of capital and labor in the nineteenth century is extraordinarily helpful for understanding our present theme, and since the matter can hardly be given a more forceful and precise formulation, it bears quotation here at greater length:

But if a surplus labouring population is a necessary product of accumulation or of the development of wealth on a capitalist basis, this surplus-population becomes, conversely, the lever of capitalistic accumulation, nay, a condition of existence of the capitalist mode of production. It forms a disposable industrial reserve army, that belongs to capital quite as absolutely as if the latter had bred it at its own cost. Independently of the limits of the actual increase of population, it creates, for the changing needs of the self-expansion of capital, a mass of human material always ready for exploitation. With accumulation, and the development of the productiveness of labour that accompanies it, the power of sudden expansion of capital grows also; it grows, not merely because the elasticity of the capital already functioning increases, not merely because the absolute wealth of society expands, of which capital only forms an elastic part, not merely because credit, under every special stimulus, at once places an unusual part of this wealth at the disposal of production in the form of additional capital; it grows, also, because the technical conditions of the process of production themselves—machinery, means of transport, &c.—now admit of the rapidest transformation of masses of surplus-product into additional means of production. The mass of social wealth, overflowing with the advance of accumulation, and transformable into additional capital, thrusts itself frantic-ally into old branches of production, whose market suddenly expands, or into newly formed branches, such as railways, &c., the need for which grows out of the development of the old ones. In all such cases, there must be the possibility of throwing great masses of men suddenly on the decisive points without injury to the scale of production in other spheres. Overpopulation supplies these masses. . . . This increase is effected by the simple process that constantly "sets free" a part of the labourers; by methods which lessen the number of labourers employed in proportion to the increased production. The whole form of the movement of modern industry depends, therefore, upon the constant transformation of a part of the labouring population into unemployed or half-employed hands.[2]

Those industries and labor processes subjected to mechanization release masses of labor for exploitation in other, generally less mechanized, areas of capital accumulation. With the repeated manifestations of this cycle, labor tends to pile up in the industries and occupations which are less susceptible to engineered improvements in labor productivity. Wage rates in these "new" industries and occupations are held down by the continuous availability of the relative surplus population created by the steadily increasing productivity of labor in the machine occupations. This in turn encourages the investment of capital in forms of the labor process which require masses of low-wage hand labor. As a result, we see in capitalist industry a secular trend to accumulate labor in those portions of industry and trade which are least affected by the scientific-technical revolution: service work, sales and other forms of marketing, clerical work insofar as it has not yet been mechanized, etc. The paradox that the most rapidly growing mass occupations in an era of scientific-technical revolution are those which have least to do with science and technology need not surprise us. The purpose of machinery is not to increase but to decrease the number of workers attached to it. Thus it is by no means illogical that with the development of science and technology, the numbers of those cheaply available for dancing attendance upon capital in all of its least mechanized functional forms continues to increase at a rapid pace.

In periods of rapid capital accumulation, such as that which has taken place throughout the capitalist world since World War II, the relative surplus population which is the "natural" product of the capital accumulation process is supplemented with other sources of labor. In northern Europe and the United States, the capitalist economies have increasingly made use of the masses of former agricultural labor in the colonies and neocolonies. These masses are thrown off by the process of imperialist penetration itself, which has disrupted the traditional forms of labor and subsistence. They become available to capital as its own agricultural surplus labor (that part of the relative surplus population which Marx called the "latent" portion) is used up. As a result of this, the movement of labor has to some extent become internationalized, although still regulated in each country by government action in an attempt to make it conform to the national needs of capital. Thus Western Europe and the United States now draw upon a labor reservoir which extends in a broad band from India and Pakistan in the east across northern Africa and southernmost Europe all the way to the Caribbean and other portions of Latin America in the west. Indian, Pakistani, Turkish, Greek, Italian, African, Spanish, West Indian, and other workers supplement the indigenous underclass in northern Europe and make up its lowest layers. In the United States, the same role is occupied by Puerto Rican, Mexican, and other Latin American workers, who have been added to the pool of lowest-paid labor which is made up chiefly of black workers.

At the same time, in a process which cuts across racial and national lines, the female portion of the population has become the prime supplementary reservoir of labor. In all the most rapidly growing sectors of the working class, women make up the majority, and in some instances the overwhelming majority, of the workers. Women form the ideal reservoir of labor for the new mass occupations. The barrier which confines women to much lower pay scales is reinforced by the vast numbers in which they are available to capital. These vast numbers are in turn guaranteed, for a considerable period of time, by the lower rate of participation in the working population with which women entered into the era of monopoly capital. While the male population, even in its prime working ages, is suffering a slowly declining labor force participation rate (which is only a concealed form of the rise in unemployment), women have been participating in employment at a very rapidly rising rate throughout this century. For capital, this is an expression of the movement to the poorly paid, menial, and "supplementary" occupations. For the working class, it is in part an expression of the increasing difficulty of keeping up with customary and unavoidable needs of subsistence in the society created by capital, without having two or more family members at work at the same time. In this manner, an ever increasing portion of human work is incorporated into capital.

The Reserve Army of Labor

Thus the mass of employment cannot be separated from its associated mass of unemployment. Under conditions of capitalism, unemployment is not an aberration but a necessary part of the working mechanism of the capitalist mode of production. It is continuously produced and absorbed by the energy of the accumulation process itself. And unemployment is only the officially counted part of the relative surplus of working population which is necessary for the accumulation of capital and which is itself produced by it. This relative surplus population, the industrial reserve army, takes a variety of forms in modern society, including the unemployed; the sporadically employed; the part-time employed; the mass of women who, as houseworkers, form a reserve for the "female occupations"; the armies of migrant labor, both agricultural and industrial; the black population with its extraordinarily high rates of unemployment; and the foreign reserves of labor.

Marx distinguished three forms of the reserve army of labor, or relative surplus population: the floating, the latent, and the stagnant. The *floating* form is found in the centers of industry and employment, in the form of workers who move from job to job, attracted and repelled (that is to say, hired and discarded) by the movements of technology and capital, and suffering a certain amount of unemployment in the course of this motion. With the simplification of job operations and the spread of the number and variety of jobs for which the "qualifications" have become reduced to the minimums of simple labor, this stratum has grown to encompass large parts of the working population. The extraordinary mobility provided by automobile transport in the United States has widened the geographical range of such jobs for each worker, has greatly enlarged the "labor pool" available to each factory, office, warehouse, retail establishment, etc., and has broken down ties to localities and communities. An ordinary working life for many workers now consists of movement among a considerable number of jobs, so that such workers are in turn part of the employed and the reserve labor populations. This has been reflected in the system of unemployment insurance, which provides for periods of unemployment at a reduced wage with monies collected during periods of employment; it is in part a safeguard against the economic, social, and political effects of widespread and prolonged unemployment, and in part a recognition of the roles workers play, now as part of the employed and now as part of the reserve armies of labor.

The *latent* relative surplus population is, in Marx's definition, that which is found in the agricultural areas. In these areas, unlike in the centers of capitalist industry, there exists no counter-movement of attraction to offset the repulsion of those "set free" by the revolution in agricultural technology, and hence the movement of labor is out of the agricultural regions and into the cities or metropolitan areas. In the most developed capitalist countries in northern Europe and North America, this pool of latent relative surplus population has been largely absorbed, although in the United States the black population of the rural areas still remains, in dwindling numbers, as part of this pool. The latent form of surplus population now exists chiefly in the neocolonies, and, as has been noted, the capitalist countries attempt a regulated absorption and repulsion of such labor, in accord with the needs of accumulation. This regulated internationalization of the labor market is supplemented by the export of various industrial processes to cheap labor areas in the countries which are kept in subjugation as "undeveloped regions."

Finally, Marx speaks of the *stagnant* relative surplus population, whose employment is irregular, casual, marginal, and which merges with the "sediment," as Marx called it, of relative surplus population which dwells in the world of pauperism: "Pauperism is the hospital of the active labour-army and the dead weight of the industrial reserve army . . . ; along with the surplus-population, pauperism forms a condition of capitalist production, and of the capitalist development of wealth. It enters into the *faux frais* of capitalist production; but capital knows how to throw these, for the most part, from its own shoulders on to those of the working class and the lower middle class."[3]

The stagnant relative surplus population, irregularly and casually employed, "furnishes to capital," in Marx's words, "an inexhaustible reservoir of disposable labour-power. Its conditions of life sink below the average normal level of the working-class; this makes it at once the broad basis of special branches of capitalist exploitation."[4] The importance of this branch of surplus population for the types of employment that have been increasing rapidly is clear. We will consider it at greater length below.

The activity of capital in breeding masses of labor for its various needs is summarized by Marx in the following familiar paragraph:

> The greater the social wealth, the functioning capital, the extent and energy of its growth, and, therefore, also the absolute mass of the proletariat and the productiveness of its labour, the greater is the industrial reserve army. The same causes which develop the expansive power of capital, develop also the labour-power at its disposal. The relative mass of the industrial reserve army increases therefore with the potential energy of wealth. But the greater this reserve army

in proportion to the active labour-army, the greater is the mass of a consolidated surplus-population, whose misery is in inverse ratio to its torment of labour. The more extensive, finally, the lazarus-layers of the working-class, and the industrial reserve army, the greater is official pauperism. *This is the absolute general law of capitalist accumulation.* Like all other laws it is modified in its working by many circumstances, the analysis of which does not concern us here.[5]

This law, Marx maintained, "always equilibrates the relative surplus-population, or industrial reserve army, to the extent and energy of accumulation. . . . It establishes an accumulation of misery, corresponding with the accumulation of capital."[6] During the 1940s and early 1950s, when the tendencies of the immense upward surge in the accumulation of capital that began (for the United States) in the Second World War were not yet developed or clearly manifest, this "absolute general law of capitalist accumulation" was widely taken to be the weakest aspect of the Marxian analysis. From our present vantage point, when the consequences of this cycle of accumulation have worked themselves out more fully and have been given greater visibility by the unrest of the 1960s, the matter takes on a somewhat different appearance.

The scope and energy of the accumulation process that began at the start of the 1940s has completed the annihilation of the agricultural population in the United States and largely transformed it, black and white alike, into an urban "labor force," and this has been supplemented by the import of workers on a considerable scale from Latin America. This immense increase in "the absolute mass of the proletariat" has been accompanied by an equally immense increase in the industrial reserve army. Statistics show a doubling of the number of officially counted unemployed, so that in the early 1970s this part of the working class had mounted into the 4 to 5 million range, but this is the least significant indicator of the growth of the industrial reserve army. Far more significant is the statistical series known as the "labor force participation rate."

This series attempts to establish, by the technique of household sampling interviews, the proportion of the population which is part of the labor market. It starts from the assumption that some significant part of the population over the age of sixteen cannot be counted as part of the "labor force" because it is made up of people who are in school, running a household full time, sick or disabled, or retired for reasons of age. All these categories of presumed nonseekers after employment are obviously elastic: when one considers that the total embraced in this "not-in-the-labor-force" group exceeded 55 million persons in 1971, there is clearly plenty of room in it for concealed unemployment—all the more so as it also includes those who are not seeking work because they believe they cannot find it. This conclusion is confirmed by the fact that some 4 to 5 million persons in the group, in the last years of the 1960s and the early 1970s, regularly expressed themselves as "wanting a job now," although they are counted as not having been part of the labor force for the preceding period. This alone either doubles or more than doubles the official unemployment rate in most of those years.[7] *

The movement of the labor force participation rate in the years since World War II, *taken as a whole*, is a relatively unenlightening trend. The percent of the noninstitutionalized population found in the total labor force (including the armed forces) has moved since 1947 in a narrow range between 59 and 61 percent. But this static condition conceals changes of a most striking kind, which become visible as soon as one breaks down the overall figures by sex. The nonmovement of the index as a whole is produced by violently contrary movements of the male and female populations.[9]

For the male population during the period 1947 to 1971, a strong and consistent decline since the 1940s and early 1950s has reduced the participation rate from some 87 percent to only 80 percent. This decline is only partly attributable to the increase in school attendance during the student years and to retirement; it is to be found in every age category, and is most particularly marked in male workers between the ages of 55 and 64, for whom the participation rate declined from 89.6 in 1947 to 82.2 in 1971. Unless we are to make untenable assumptions (such as, as Sweezy and Magdoff point out, the assumption of a growing leisure class among workers), this clearly indicates that a portion of the male working population (and the figures point to white workers almost as much as to black) has been and is being moved into the reserve army of labor without this showing up in the unemployment statistics.

For the female population, the trend is precisely the opposite. Here the figures, across the board for all age groups, indicate a very great movement *into* the labor force, from a participation rate of 31.8 percent in 1947 to 43.4 percent in 1971. And just as among males the largest decrease takes place in the 55- to 64-year-old age bracket, so among females the largest *increase* takes place in the age groups from 45 to 54 and from 55 to 64; for the former, from 32.7 percent in 1947 to 54.3 percent in 1971, and for the latter, from 24.3 percent to 42.9 percent.

These two opposing statistical movements of male and female workers are contradictory in form only. In essence, they represent two sides of the same phenomenon, the increase in the relative mass of the industrial reserve army. Among male workers this takes the form of a sloughing off into the ranks of the so-called nonparticipants in the labor force, or in other words an increase of the "stagnant" portion. Among female workers it takes the form of a growing body of female labor which is drawn from the mass of women who previously

---

* This conclusion is also arrived at, by other and much fuller methods of computation, by Paul Sweezy and Harry Magdoff in their analysis of the labor force participation rate in *Monthly Review.*[8]

did not work, and hence represents an enlargement of the "floating" and "stagnant" reserve army of labor by additional hundreds of thousands and even millions each year. As the available pool of unemployed labor is expanded among men by their relative *repulsion* from industry and trade, it is expanded even more among women by their increasing *attraction* into industry and trade. The opposing forms taken by this basically unitary movement simply reflect the different starting points of male and female labor at the beginning of the period we have been considering, as well as the strong demand for female labor in the expanding mass occupations in contrast to the relative stagnation of the male mass occupations.

The logical culmination of these trends is an equalization of the labor force participation rates between men and women, and the stabilization of a uniform rate for the population as a whole—in other words, the transformation of as much as one-third or more of the male population into a reserve army of labor, along with a similar part of the female population. But for purposes of this analysis there is no need to enter into risky extrapolations from existing statistical trends. It is enough to notice *what has in fact been happening*, without trying to assess the extent to which it can proceed, an extent which is limited by future trends in the accumulation process of capital as well as by social trends having to do with the structure of the family, etc. And what has been happening is that, along with an increasing mass of the proletariat, there is also the consolidation of an increasing mass of relative surplus population which takes place by way of a market repulsion of male labor and an attraction of female labor, both on a very great scale.

The well-established fact that women are generally paid on a substantially lower scale than men, either by way of their concentration in lower-paid occupations or within the same occupation, immediately draws our attention to a significant long-term consequence of the statistical movement we have been discussing. The concentration of better-paid employment among crafts-men (as well as professional and managerial males) on the one side, and the further tendency of the mass of working-class jobs to shift in the direction of lower-paid female occupations, clearly brings about a polarization of income among job holders. This is reflected in the fact that the industrial sectors in the United States in which employment is relatively stagnant are the sectors with wage rates above the average, while the sectors in which employment is growing most rapidly are those with lower-than-average wage rates (see table, next page).[10]

An important corroboration of this trend toward a polarization of income among job holders emerges from the work of Victor R. Fuchs for the National Bureau of Economic Research. Fuchs is a celebrant of the growing importance of the service industries, and the information we shall cite here arose as a by-product of his effort to establish the shift to service industries and the consequent characteristics of the emerging economic structure. He divided the

Gross Average Weekly Earnings of Production or Nonsupervisory Workers on Private Nonagricultural Payrolls, 1971

Relatively stagnant industries		*Rapidly growing industries*	
Mining	$171.74	Wholesale	
Contract construction	212.24	and retail trade	$100.74
Manufacturing	142.04	Finance, insurance,	
Transportation		and real estate	121.36
and public utilities	168.84	Service industries	102.94

economy into two sectors, The first, which he called "Industry," included mining, construction, manufacturing, transport, communications and public utilities, and government enterprises. The second, which he called "Service," included wholesale trade, retail trade, finance and insurance, real estate, and household and institutional employment, professional, personal, business, and repair services, and general government including the armed forces.

The rationale of such a separation, and the significance of the results obtained by making these particular groupings, does not here concern us; this I have already discussed in the chapters on the universal market and on the service and retail-trade occupations. What is interesting at this point is that these groupings correspond precisely to the stagnating and the growing portions of the American economy. Each of the industrial classifications listed by Fuchs as belonging to Industry has been either stagnating or declining in terms of the percentage of national employment it represents, and this is true for *every* classification in the group since the 1950s and for *almost every* classification since the 1920s. On the other side, *every* classification (except household employment) included by Fuchs in the Service sector has been a rapidly growing area of employment throughout the last hundred years, again in terms of its percentage of total employment.[11] The Service sector, as defined by Fuchs, grew from approximately 40 percent of total employment in 1929 to over 55 percent in 1967. Between 1947 and 1965 alone, there was an increase of 13 million jobs in this sector, compared with an increase of only 4 million in the Industry sector.*[12]

---

* This increase, we may note in passing, was not, according to Fuchs, accompanied by any increase in the share of output produced in the Service sector. Measured as a share in Gross National Product, the output of the Service sector did not increase at all between 1929 and 1965, despite the great increase in its share of employment.[13] This estimate is interesting, as far as it goes, in highlighting the increasingly wasteful allocation of labor, but since Fuchs is bound by the fictitious concepts of "output" used in calculating the Gross National Product, it does not go nearly as far as it should. The "output" of great portions of the Service sector exists only in the balance sheets of the corporations operating within it, and in the national product accounts of statisticians and economists, while adding little or nothing to the social product calculated in noncapitalist terms.

The most striking finding reported by Fuchs is the growing gap between the pay levels in the Industry sector and those in the Service sector. With remarkable consistency, the average rates of pay in the Service sector each year slipped further behind the average rates of pay in the Industry sector, so that by 1959 Industry rates were on the average 17 percent higher, and thereafter the gap continued to widen.[14] Since the Service sector employs a disproportionately large share of nonwhite, female, and very young workers, Fuchs next investigates whether this widening wage gap is perhaps simply the effect of the contrasting compositions of the two sectors, by color, age, sex, and education—in other words, whether it is not just another way of looking at the well-known fact that blacks, women, young workers, etc., receive less pay. This proves to be only part of the explanation: the differing compositions of the two sectors of employment "explain" only about one-half the great and growing spread in pay. This means that while the Service sector contains a disproportionate share of those who, throughout the whole economy, get lower pay, and this pulls down the average for the sector, at the same time *all* kinds of workers in the Service sector, no matter what their age, color, or sex, receive on the average lower rates of pay.*[15]

The levels of pay in the low-wage industries and occupations are below the subsistence level; that is to say, unlike the scales of the highest paid occupational groups, they do not approach the income required to support a family at the levels of spending necessary in modern society. But, because these industries and occupations are also the most rapidly growing ones, an ever larger mass of workers has become dependent upon them as the sole source of support for their families. It is this continual enlargement of the mass of lower-paid occupations that is at the root of the tendencies, which began to be publicized only during the 1960s but which existed before, toward "poverty in the midst of plenty" in the United States; it is this that accounts for the rapid expansion of the welfare rolls to take in ever larger masses of *employed* workers.

This tendency, which is but one of the factors leading to what Marx called an "accumulation of misery, corresponding to the accumulation of capital," is so marked that even when one abstracts from the effects of the rapid influx of female labor into ill-paid employment and considers only male employment,

---

* Another investigation of the same subject matter, by Barry Bluestone, reaches this conclusion: "In tracing wage histories since the Second World War, one finds that the wage differential between 'high-wage' and 'low-wage' industries has increased secularly. In 1947 the set of industries with lowest wages paid straight-time hourly rates which averaged 75 percent of the average wages prevailing in the highest wage industries in the nation. Apart from slight cyclical variation in wage increases during the ensuing period, the wage ratio between these two sets of industries fell to 60 percent by 1966. The low-wage industries granted smaller wage increases (in percentage as well as absolute terms) in all but four years during the two-decade period."[16]

it is still visible and measurable. A study of the distribution of earned income made by Peter Henle of the U.S. Department of Labor follows the widespread custom of disregarding female employment, which is considered to be somehow temporary, incidental, and fortuitous, when it should actually be placed at the very center of all occupational studies today. Henle considers only the distribution of earned income among males, and his conclusion for the years 1958 to 1970 is as follows: "Over the 12-year span covered by this study, there has been a slow but persistent trend toward inequality in the distribution of earnings and in the distribution of wages and salaries. The trend is evident not only for the work force as a whole, but also for many individual occupational and industrial groups. If the effect of fringe benefits could have been included in the calculations, the trend would undoubtedly have been even more pronounced." "All in all," he notes, "the net effect of the shifting occupational composition of the economy seems clearly in the direction of a more elongated earnings distribution, helping to produce the trend toward inequality."[17] But the "shifting occupational and industrial composition of the economy" is far less significant for the male population alone; it is female employment, as has been noted, that accounts for the bulk of the occupational and industrial shift, and thus it is female employment that constitutes the bulk of the new working-class occupations. We cannot doubt, therefore, that if Henle's analysis were repeated for the total of the wage and salary earning population, it would show a rapid and intense, rather than a slow, trend toward polarization of income.

The problem of immense numbers of jobs which pay less than a "living wage," that is to say, less than the wage necessary to support a working-class family, to provide for the subsistence and reproduction of labor power, is, it is often assumed, resolved by the fact that multiple job holding within the same family is widely practiced. Indeed, in one way this must temper the problem, since the average number of jobs per family is between one-and-a-half and two, and this provides more income to many family units, although it increases the level of spending necessary for subsistence. But when one reflects upon the modes of life brought into being by this rapid change, and the tensions which result from the fact that millions of families are driven to multiple job holding in the absence of suitable conditions for child care, household care, etc., such a conclusion is far from certain. Surveys point out that discontent among workers goes up sharply in families that have more than one wage earner, despite the fact that income also goes up.[18] Further, there is another factor that influences any conclusion here, and that is the existence of a large number of families that have difficulty keeping even one family member occupied full time. An article on the crisis of the underemployed in the *New York Times Magazine* points out:

> It is true that, nationwide, the *average* family has 1.7 full-time equivalent workers. But the majority of *low-income* families in America are unable to *find*

enough work to occupy more than one "full-time-equivalent" member. In 1970, the average number of "full-time-equivalent" workers per low-income family was *less than one!* In other words, one person (usually the male head) worked nearly (but not totally) full time, or several family members worked, but very sporadically. It is therefore useless—and cynical—to tell those for whom jobs do not exist that they could relieve their poverty if only they would be more willing to work.[19]

That portion of the relative surplus population which Marx called "stagnant," irregularly employed and living in conditions of life that have fallen below the average normal level of the working class, and furnishing a "broad basis" for "special branches of capitalist exploitation," has grown to encompass huge proportions of the inner-city populations, considerable numbers in the depressed rural areas, and is on the increase in suburban regions. Its extent, at least in the core areas of the large cities of the United States, was carefully measured during the 1970 census by means of a questionnaire designed to study the relation between poverty and the job market. This Census Employment Survey (C.E.S.) produced some sixty-eight volumes of raw statistics, the analysis of which has been undertaken by the Subcommittee on Employment, Manpower, and Poverty of the United States Senate. The above-quoted article on underemployment, one of whose three authors is a staff member of that subcommittee, offers a summary of some of the findings of the C.E.S., and in particular of the effort to develop what is called a "subemployment index":

> The failure of the social and economic system to provide people with adequate wages is hidden from view under the surface of traditional unemployment statistics. These statistics are excellent for measuring fluctuations in the economy but they do not go far enough as measures of the labor market. To gauge the degree of labor-market failure, it is necessary to know not only the magnitude of overt unemployment, but also the extent of worker discouragement ("discouraged workers" are those who have given up looking for jobs); the number of people who can find only part-time work; and the number who hold jobs but at inadequate pay. The subemployment index attempts to encompass all these factors.
>
> In 1970, nationwide unemployment amounted to 4.9 per cent of the labor force (since then, it has hovered close to the 6 per cent mark month after month). In the C.E.S. central-city survey areas, the unemployment rate in 1970 was 9.6 per cent. This is *very* high. In France, the labor unions took to the streets last February when unemployment reached 2.6 per cent. But as high as it is here, the employment rate alone falls far short of revealing the full extent of urban crisis. When we look at the official definition of unemployment, we note that one cannot be "unemployed" unless one is currently looking for a job. It does not count those people who have given up looking for jobs after failing repeatedly to find work.

How many such discouraged nonseekers are there? The C.E.S. enables us to make a dependable estimate. For example, in New York City, the conventional unemployment rate in 1970 averaged 8.1 per cent in the survey areas (compared with 4.4 per cent for the labor force of the city as a whole), but jumped to 11 per cent when the discouraged workers were added.

This adjustment begins to give us a picture of realities of economic life at the bottom of a city's social structure. But to this we must now add another category—part-time employed workers who would like to work full time but cannot find full-time jobs. The C.E.S. survey carefully separates people who *wanted* to work only part time from those who wanted to work full time, and in this way adds (again, for New York) another 2.3 percentage points to our emerging index of urban poverty. In other words, adding together the officially unemployed, the discouraged jobless and the involuntary part-time workers, we can now account for at least 13.3 per cent of the labor force in the New York City sample areas.

Our adjustments have nearly doubled the official unemployment figures for the sample areas and tripled the national rate of unemployment. But, still, they are far from complete. The last and most important part of the index is the worker who has a full-time job but does not earn enough to make ends meet.[20]

For a definition of the income needed to "make ends meet," the authors go to the Bureau of Labor Statistics' itemized budget of consumption needs for a family of four in New York City. The Bureau compiled three such budgets, for the upper level at about $19,000, for the middle level at about $12,000, and for the lower levels at about $7,000, all before taxes. The nature of the lower-level budget may be judged from the fact that it allows only $100 a month for rent; all the rest of the budgeting is in line with this.

> If we accept the B.L.S. figure of $7,183 as the least a family of four must earn to keep its head above water in New York City in 1970 (the B.L.S.'s national urban average for 1970 was $6,960), what does this require for the family's income earner? If he or she works 50 weeks a year, 40 hours a week (which is itself unlikely in the inner city), the answer is $3.50 an hour. Here is the final link in our chain of employment statistics. For when we add those individuals who earn less than $3.50 an hour to the discouraged nonseekers, the involuntary part-timers and the officially unemployed, the statistics take a horrifying leap. In the seven New York City sample areas, the subemployment rate rises to between 39.9 per cent and 66.6 per cent of the labor force. Indeed, the average for all the sampled areas in the country comes to 61.2 per cent.[21]

What other result could have been expected, when, as we have seen, in May 1971 the median usual weekly earnings of full-time workers in *all occupational categories of the working class with the exception only of craftsmen and foremen were far below this minimal earnings level,* and when the fastest growing occupational categories, those of clerical and service workers, were lowest of all?

Finally, the immense reservoir of subemployed labor holds on its lowest levels the pauperized layers of the population, that bottom sediment which is drawn into employment only infrequently, sporadically, and at peaks of "prosperity." "The more extensive, finally, the lazarus-layers of the working-class," Marx wrote, "and the industrial reserve army, the greater is official pauperism." According to his figures, the official list of paupers in England and Wales in 1865 was 971,433, and since the population count in the 1861 census was just over 20 million, official pauperism then constituted some 4.6 percent of the total population. In the United States, the closest thing we have to an official paupers' list is the roll of those requiring welfare assistance. In 1973, these rolls contained 14.8 million persons out of a total population of 210.4 million or 7 percent of the population (and 1973 was the fourth successive year when 7 percent or more of the population was to be found on the welfare rolls).[22] In this startling proportion one may see the post-World War II "prosperity" cycle in accordance with Marx's absolute general law of capitalist accumulation: the immense mass of social wealth and functioning capital, the extent and energy of capital accumulation, the growth of the absolute mass of the proletariat and the productiveness of its labor, the increasing relative mass of the industrial reserve army, of the mass of consolidated surplus population, and finally, the misery of "official pauperism." That this is a chain in which each link presupposes the rest, and in which "accumulation of wealth at one pole is, therefore, at the same time accumulation of misery" at the other, may no longer be doubted.

Notes

1. Alba Edwards (Sixteenth Census Reports), *Comparative Occupation Statistics for the United States, 1870-1940* (Washington, D.C., 1943), chapter XIII; David L. Kaplan and M. Claire Casey, *Occupational Trends in the United States: 1900 to 1950*, Bureau of the Census Working Paper No. 5 (Washington, 1958); U.S. Bureau of the Census, *U.S. Census of the Population: 1960*, vol. I (Washington, 1964), Part I, Table 201, p. 522; U.S. Bureau of the Census, *U.S. Census of the Population: 1970, Final Report PC(2)-7A, Occupational Characteristics* (Washington, D.C., 1973), Table 1.
2. Karl Marx, *Capital*, vol. I (Moscow, n.d.), pp. 592-93.
3. Ibid., p. 603.
4. Ibid., p. 602.
5. Ibid., p. 603.
6. Ibid., p. 604.
7. *Manpower Report of the President, March 1972*, Table A-8, p. 167.
8. Paul M. Sweezy and Harry Magdoff, "Economic Stagnation and Stagnation of Economics," *Monthly Review* (April 1971), pp. 1-11.

9. *Manpower Report of the President, March 1972*, Table A-1, p.157; Table A-2, pp. 158-59.
10. *Monthly Labor Review* (December 1972), Table 22, p. 96.
11. Victor R. Fuchs, *The Service Economy* (New York and London, 1968), p. 19.
12. Ibid., p. 2.
13. Ibid., pp. 19, 37.
14. Ibid., pp. 61, 129, 156.
15. Ibid., chapter 6.
16. Barry Bluestone, "Capitalism and Poverty in America: A Discussion," *Monthly Review* (June 1972), pp. 66-67.
17. Peter Henle, "Exploring the Distribution of Earned Income," *Monthly Labor Review* (December 1972), pp. 23-25.
18. Harold L. Sheppard and Neal Q. Herrick, *Where Have All the Robots Gone?: Worker Dissatisfaction in the '70s* (New York and London, 1972), pp. 25-27.
19. William Spring, Bennett Harrison, and Thomas Vietorisz, "In Much of the Inner City 60% Don't Earn Enough for a Decent Standard of Living," *New York Times Magazine*, November 5, 1972, p. 48.
20. Ibid., pp. 43-44.
21. Ibid., pp. 46-48.
22. Marx, *Capital*, pp. 611-12; *New York Times*, October 31, 1973.

Chapter 18

The "Middle Layers" of Employment

In the discussion thus far we have restricted ourselves to that portion of the population, embracing as we have seen some two-thirds to three-fourths of the total, which appears readily to conform to the dispossessed condition of a proletariat. But the system of monopoly capitalism has brought into being a further mass of employment, not inconsiderable in size, that does not answer so readily to such a definition. Like the petty bourgeoisie of pre-monopoly capitalism (the petty proprietors in farming, trade, services, the professions, and artisan occupations), it does not fit easily into the polar conception of economy and society. But unlike that earlier middle-class mass, which has so largely evaporated, it corresponds increasingly to the formal definition of a working class. That is, like the working class it possesses no economic or occupational independence, is employed by capital and its offshoots, possesses no access to the labor process or the means of production outside that employment, and must renew its labors for capital incessantly in order to subsist. This portion of employment embraces the engineering, technical, and scientific cadre, the lower ranks of supervision and management, the considerable numbers of specialized and "professional" employees occupied in marketing, financial and organizational administration, and the like, as well as, outside of capitalist industry proper, in hospitals, schools, government administration, and so forth. Relatively, it is nowhere near so large as the old petty bourgeoisie which, on the basis of independent entrepreneurship, occupied as much as half or more of the population in the pre-monopoly stage of capitalism. It embraces in the United States today perhaps over 15 but less than 20 percent of total employment. Its rapid growth as a partial replacement for the old middle class, however, makes its definition a matter of special interest, all the more so since its purely formal character is similar to that of the clearly proletarianized working-class population.

The complexities of the class structure of pre-monopoly capitalism arose from the fact that so large a proportion of the working population, being neither employed by capital nor itself employing labor to any significant extent, fell outside the capital-labor polarity. The complexity of the class structure of modern monopoly capitalism arises from the very opposite consideration: namely, that *almost all of the population has been transformed into employees of capital*. Almost every working association with the modern corporation, or with its imitative offshoots in governmental or so-called nonprofit organizations, is given the form of the purchase and sale of labor power.

The purchase and sale of labor power is the classic form for the creation and continued existence of the working class. Insofar as the working class is concerned, this form embodies social relations of production, the relations of subordination to authority and exploitation. We must now consider the possibility of the same form being made to conceal, embody, and express other relations of production. To take a most extreme example, the fact that the operating executives of a giant corporation are employed by that corporation, and in that capacity do not own its plants and bank accounts, is merely the form given to capitalist rule in modern society. These operating executives, by virtue of their high managerial positions, personal investment portfolios, independent power of decision, place in the hierarchy of the labor process, position in the community of capitalists at large, etc., etc., are the rulers of industry, act "professionally" for capital, and are themselves part of the class that personifies capital and employs labor. Their formal attribute of being part of the same payroll as the production workers, clerks, and porters of the corporation no more robs them of the powers of decision and command over the others in the enterprise than does the fact that the general, like the private, wears the military uniform, or the pope and cardinal pronounce the same liturgy as the parish priest. The form of hired employment gives expression to two totally different realities: in one case, capital hires a "labor force" whose duty it is to work, under external direction, to increase capital; in the other, by a process of selection within the capitalist class and chiefly from its own ranks, capital chooses a management staff to represent it on the spot, and in representing it to supervise and organize the labors of the working population.

Thus far the difference is clear, but between these two extremes there is a range of intermediate categories, sharing the characteristics of worker on the one side and manager on the other in varying degrees. The gradations of position in the line of management may be seen chiefly in terms of authority, while gradations in staff positions are indicated by the levels of technical expertise. Since the authority and expertise of the middle ranks in the capitalist corporation represent an unavoidable delegation of responsibility, the position of such functionaries may best be judged by their relation to the power and wealth that commands them from above, and to the mass of labor beneath them which they in turn help to control, command, and organize. Their pay level is significant because beyond a certain point it, like the pay of the commanders of the corporation, clearly represents not just the exchange of their labor power for money—a commodity exchange—but a *share in the surplus* produced in the corporation, and thus is intended to attach them to the success or failure of the corporation and give them a "management stake," even if a small one. The same is true insofar as they share in a recognized guarantee of employment, in the semi-independence of their mode of labor within the production process, in authority over the labor of others, the right to hire and fire, and the other prerogatives of command.

Judged by these and similar standards, the middle levels of administrative and technical employment clearly encompass a broad range of types. The engineering heads who design the production process merge into management at the top, and the hierarchy that stretches beneath them terminates in large drafting and design rooms which have been organized, in many instances, on the same principles as the factory or office production line, and are staffed by serried ranks of detail workers whose pay scales, if they are better than those of factory operatives or clerical workers, are perhaps not so good as those of craftsmen, and who dispose of little more working independence and authority than the production worker. In between are the subalterns and noncommissioned officers of the industrial army, the foremen, the petty "managers" of all sorts, the technical specialists who retain, if not authority, at least a tenuous working independence. And outside the corporations proper, in governmental, educational, and health establishments, these gradations are reproduced in forms peculiar to the work processes carried on in each of these areas.

Among these intermediate groupings are parceled out the bits of specialized knowledge and delegated authority without which the machinery of production, distribution, and administration would cease to operate. Each of the groupings serves as the recruiting ground for those above, up to and including top management. Their conditions of employment are affected by the need of top management to have within its orbit buffer layers, responsive and "loyal" subordinates, transmission agents for the exercise of control and the collection of information, so that management does not confront unaided a hostile or indifferent mass. These conditions are affected, moreover, by the privileged market position which specialized and technically trained labor possesses in the earlier phase of its development, at a time when the supply of such labor is only in the process of catching up with the needs of capital accumulation. All in all, therefore, those in this area of capitalist employment enjoy, in greater or lesser degree depending upon their specific place in the hierarchy, the privileges of exemption from the worst features of the proletarian situation, including, as a rule, significantly higher scales of pay.

If we are to call this a "new middle class," however, as many have done, we must do so with certain reservations. The old middle class occupied that position by virtue of its place outside the polar class structure; it possessed the attributes of neither capitalist nor worker; it played no direct role in the capital accumulation process, whether on one side or the other. This "new middle class," by contrast, occupies its intermediate position not because it is *outside* the process of increasing capital, but because, as part of this process, it takes its characteristics from *both sides*. Not only does it receive its petty share in the prerogatives and rewards of capital, but it also bears the mark of the proletarian condition. For these employees the social form taken by their work, their true place in the relations of production, their fundamental condition of subordination as so much hired labor, increasingly makes itself felt, especially in the mass occupations that are part of this stratum. We may cite here particularly the mass employments of draftsmen and technicians, engineers and accountants, nurses and teachers, and the multiplying ranks of supervisors, foremen, and petty managers. First, these become part of a mass labor market that assumes the characteristics of all labor markets, including the necessary existence of a reserve army of unemployed exercising a downward pressure on pay levels.* And second, capital, as soon as it disposes of a mass of labor in any specialty—a mass adequate in size to repay the application of its principles of the technical division of labor and hierarchical control over execution by means of a firm grasp on the links of conception—subjects that specialty to some of the forms of "rationalization" characteristic of the capitalist mode of production.

In such occupations, the proletarian form begins to assert itself and to impress itself upon the consciousness of these employees. Feeling the insecurities of their role as sellers of labor power and the frustrations of a controlled and mechanically organized workplace, they begin, despite their remaining privileges, to know those symptoms of dissociation which are popularly called "alienation" and which the working class has lived with for so long that they have become part of its second nature.

In the chapter devoted to clerical labor, we have already described the manner in which an intermediate stratum was enlarged into a mass of working-class employment, and in the process divested of all its privileges and intermediate characteristics. It is not necessary to anticipate here a similar evolution of the specialized and lower-managerial employees in any near-term future. But it should be recognized that the difficulties experienced by those who, in the period before World War I, attempted to arrive at a "definition" of the class position of clerical employees are somewhat the same as the difficulties one must today confront in defining the intermediate strata of modern employment. These difficulties arise, in the last analysis, from the fact that classes, the class structure, the social structure as a whole, are not fixed entities but rather ongoing processes, rich in change, transition, variation, and

---

* The first major instance of this came with the Depression of the 1930s, but in the rapid surge of capital accumulation and the transformation of industry that began with the Second World War this tendency was overcome. By the end of the 1960s, however, rising rates of unemployment among "professionals" of various kinds once more brought home to them that they were not the free agents they thought they were, who deigned to "associate themselves" with one or another corporation, but truly part of a labor market, hired and fired like those beneath them.

incapable of being encapsulated in formulas, no matter how analytically proper such formulas may be.* The analysis of this process requires an understanding of the internal relations and connections which serve as its motive power, so that its direction as a process may be understood. Only secondarily does the problem arise of "defining" the place of particular elements in the process, and this problem cannot always be solved neatly and definitively, nor, it should be added, does science require that it must be so solved.

Notes

1.   E. P. Thompson, *The Making of the English Working Class* (New York, 1964), pp. 10-11.

---

* E. P. Thompson writes: "There is today an ever-present temptation to suppose that class is a thing. This was not Marx's meaning, in his own historical writing, yet the error vitiates much latter-day 'Marxist' writing. 'It,' the working class, is assumed to have a real existence, which can be defined almost mathematically—so many men who stand in a certain relation to the means of production. . . .

"If we remember that class is a relationship, and not a thing, we cannot think in this way."[1]

Chapter 19

Productive and Unproductive Labor

In an earlier chapter devoted to the labor which produces services, we arrived at the conclusion that the existence of a working class as such does not depend upon the various concrete forms of labor which it is called upon to exercise, but rather its social form. Labor which is put to work in the production of goods is not thereby sharply divided from labor applied to the production of services, since both are forms of production of commodities, and of production on a capitalist basis, the object of which is the production not only of value-in-exchange but of surplus value for the capitalist. The variety of determinate forms of labor may affect the consciousness, cohesiveness, or economic and political activity of the working class, but they do not affect its existence as a class. The various forms of labor which produce commodities for the capitalist are all to be counted as productive labor. The worker who builds an office building and the worker who cleans it every night alike produce value and surplus value. Because they are productive for the capitalist, the capitalist allows them to work and produce; insofar as such workers alone are productive, society lives at their expense.

The question then arises: What of those whose labor is unproductive? If, as Marx said, the difference between the Roman proletariat and the modern proletariat is that while the former lived at the expense of society, the latter supports society upon its shoulders, are unproductive workers to be omitted from the modern proletariat? To answer this question we must first gain a clear idea of the various kinds of unproductive labor that exist in capitalist society and their historical development.

The terms "productive" and "unproductive" labor derive from the extensive discussion which took place among the classical economists, and which Marx analyzed so thoroughly in the first part of his *Theories of Surplus-Value*, the uncompleted work that was drafted as a fourth volume of *Capital*. In order to understand the terminology it is necessary to grasp first of all that the discussion of productive and unproductive labor, as it was conducted by Marx, implied no judgment about the nature of the work processes under discussion or their usefulness to humans in particular or society at large, but was concerned specifically and entirely with the role of labor in the *capitalist* mode of production. Thus the discussion is in reality an analysis of the relations of production and, ultimately, of the class structure of society, rather than of the utility of particular varieties of labor.

Essentially, Marx defined productive labor under capitalism as labor which produces commodity value, and hence surplus value, for capital. This excludes all labor which is not *exchanged against capital*. Self-employed proprietors—farmers, artisans, handicraftsman, tradesmen, professionals, all other self-employed—are according to this definition not productive workers because their labor is not exchanged for capital and does not directly contribute to the increase of capital.* Nor is the servant a productive worker, even though employed by the capitalist, because the labor of the servant is exchanged not against capital but against *revenue*. The capitalist who hires servants is not making profits, but spending them. It is clear that this definition has nothing to do with the utility of the labor employed, or even its concrete form. The very same labor may be either productive or unproductive, depending upon its *social* form. To hire the neighbor's boy to cut the lawn is to set in motion unproductive labor; to call a gardening firm which sends out a boy to do the job (perhaps even the same boy) is another thing entirely. Or, to put the matter from the point of view of the capitalist, to hire gardening labor to maintain his family's lawn is unproductive consumption, while to hire the very same gardening labor in order to realize a profit from its work is to set in motion productive labor for the purpose of accumulating capital.

A moment's reflection will show the importance of this distinction for the evolution of capitalist society during the past two hundred years. The change in the social form of labor from that which is, from the capitalist standpoint, unproductive to that which is productive, means the transformation from self-employment to capitalist employment, from simple commodity production to capitalist commodity production, from relations between persons to relations between things, from a society of scattered producers to a society of corporate capitalism. Thus the distinction between productive and unproductive labor, which disregards its concrete form in order to analyze it as a social form, far from being a useless abstraction, represents a decisive point in the analysis of capitalism, and shows us once more how social forms dominate and transform the significance of material things and processes.

The tailor who makes a suit on order for a customer creates a useful object in the form of a commodity; he exchanges it for money and out of this pays his own expenses and means of subsistence; the customer who hires this done purchases a useful object and expects nothing for the money other than the suit. But the capitalist who hires a roomful of tailors to make suits brings into

---

* Even more, they *fall outside* of the distinction between productive and unproductive labor, because they are *outside the capitalist mode of production*. See the clear and comprehensive presentation of Marx's theory of productive and unproductive labor by Ian Gough.[1]

being a social relation. In this relation, the tailors now create far more than suits; they create themselves as productive workers and their employer as capitalist. Capital is thus not just money exchanged for labor; it is money exchanged for labor with the purpose of appropriating that value which it creates over and above what is paid, the *surplus* value. In each case where money is exchanged for labor with this purpose it creates a social relation, and as this relation is generalized throughout the productive processes it creates social classes. Therefore, the transformation of unproductive labor into labor which is, for the capitalist's purpose of extracting surplus value, productive, is the very process of the creation of capitalist society.

Classical political economy, both Ricardian and Marxian, confronted a world in which the largest part of labor could still be reckoned as unproductive (according to the above definitions) because it did not contribute directly to the increase of capital. Much of the history of the capitalist nations during the past two centuries is the account of the destruction of these forms of labor, so that from a dominant share of social labor these forms have been reduced to an insignificant share. This is another way of saying what was pointed out earlier: that the capitalist mode of production has subordinated to itself all forms of work, and all labor processes now pass through the sieve of capital, leaving behind their tribute of surplus.

However, all labor that enters into the capital accumulation process and is necessary for it is not thereby rendered productive. For it is also true that productive labor which serves as the foundation of capitalist society is labor which produces commodity value. just as capitalism, as a system, cannot escape from the productive processes upon which society is based, no matter how remote from production its upper reaches may become, so commodity value is the ultimate foundation upon which all forms of value—money, credit instruments, insurance policies, shares, etc., etc.—depend. For the capitalist who is in the business of producing commodity values, the aim is always to capture as great a margin over his costs as possible. But in order to do this, he must *realize* the commodity values, transforming them into money form. Thus even for the industrial capitalist, who is producing in order to sell, commercial functions arise within the firm. For the commercial capitalist, who, apart from the functions of distribution, storage, packaging, transportation, display, etc., simply buys in order to sell, this realization problem constitutes the essence of his business altogether.

With the routinization of the processes of producing value and surplus value, the attention of the capitalist is increasingly centered upon this realization problem, the solution of which becomes even more important than the creation of value. At the same time, as the surpluses created in production become ever more immense, the use of capital simply for purposes of credit, speculation, etc., increases enormously. In this latter case, what is involved is the appropriation of portions of the surplus commodity value which arises in production. These two functions, the *realization* and the *appropriation* by capital of surplus value, engage, as we have seen, enormous masses of labor, and this labor, while necessary to the capitalist mode of production, is in itself unproductive, since it does not enlarge the value or surplus value available to society or to the capitalist class by one iota.

The receivables clerk who keeps track of outstanding accounts, the insurance clerk who records payments, the bank clerk who receives deposits—all of these forms of commercial and financial labor add nothing to the value of the commodities represented by the figures or papers which they handle. Yet this lack of effect is not due to the determinate form of their labors—the fact that they are clerical in nature. Clerical labor of similar and sometimes identical kinds is used in production, storage, transportation, and other such processes, all of which *do* contribute productively to commodity value, according to the division of productive labor into mental and manual sides. It is due rather to their occupation with tasks which contribute only to the realization of value in the market, or to the struggle of competing capitals over value, and its transfer and redistribution according to individual claims, speculations, and the "services" of capital in the form of credit, etc.

Labor may thus be unproductive simply because it takes place outside the capitalist mode of production, or because, while taking place within it, it is used by the capitalist, in his drive for accumulation, for unproductive rather than productive functions. And it is now clear that *while unproductive labor has declined outside the grasp of capital, it has increased within its ambit.* The great mass of labor which was reckoned as unproductive because it did not work for capital has now been transformed into a mass of labor which is unproductive because it works for capital, and because the needs of capital for unproductive labor have increased so remarkably. The more productive capitalist industry has become—that is to say, the greater the mass of surplus value it extracts from the productive population—the greater has become the mass of capital seeking its shares in this surplus. And the greater the mass of capital, the greater the mass of unproductive activities which serve only the diversion of this surplus and its distribution among various capitals.

Modern bourgeois economics has completely lost the power to treat the question of productive and unproductive labor, in part because of this historical change. Since, in the days of Smith and Ricardo, unproductive labor existed primarily outside the ambit of capital, classical bourgeois economics found it wasteful, and urged its reduction to the minimum. But ever since the mass of unproductive labor has been virtually destroyed *outside* the corporation and recreated on a different foundation *within* it, bourgeois economics, which, as a branch of management science, views all things through the eyes of the bourgeoisie, finds it impossible to retain its old attitude. The modern corporation has developed unproductive labor in this form out of necessity, and out of necessity has given over the narrow and pennypinching ways of its predecessors, whose first rule was to "keep overhead down" and to devote all possible resources to production. "Spend millions to make millions" has become the slogan, and this phrase, in all its variations in modern corporate chatter, is generally understood to indicate the spending of millions in marketing, advertising, promotion, speculation; these are the areas into which disposable corporate income is channeled, while production has become relatively routinized and expenditures in that field flow in measured and predictable amounts.

For economists today, therefore, the question of "productive" or "unproductive" labor has lost the great interest which it had for the early bourgeois economists, just as it has lost interest for capitalist management itself. Instead, the measuring of the *productivity of labor* has come to be applied to labor of all sorts, *even labor which has no productivity*. It refers, in bourgeois parlance, to the economy with which labor can perform any task to which it is set by capital, even those tasks which add nothing whatever to the wealth of the nation. And the very idea of the "wealth of nations" has faded, to be supplanted by the concept of "prosperity," a notion which has nothing to do with the efficacy of labor in producing useful goods and services, but refers rather to the velocity of flow within the circuits of capital and commodities in the marketplace.

The enormous quantities of socially useless labor that enter into this circulation, therefore, are in the minds of the modern ideologists of capital merged into the general processes of labor, just as they are so merged in the minds of the managers. All labor processes are adjudged equally useful—including those which produce, realize, or divert the surplus. The productive and unproductive forms of labor are mingled, in individual firms and in the economy as a whole, on an equal footing. And the organization of labor in the unproductive aspects of corporate activity follows the lines laid down in the productive sector; the labor of both sectors becomes, increasingly, an undifferentiated mass.

In early capitalist enterprises the unproductive labor employed in small quantities was, generally speaking, a favored stratum, closely associated with the employer and the recipient of special privileges. Those who worked with him in fulfilling the sales, accounting, speculative, and manipulative functions represented to him associates in the guarding and expansion of his capital *as capital*, in distinction from those in production who represented his capital only in its temporary form *as labor*. The few who kept his books, sold his products, negotiated on his behalf with the outside world, and in general were privy to his secrets, hopes, and plans, were in fact associates in the exploitation of productive workers, even if they themselves were only employees. The productive worker, on the other hand, represented the social relation between capital and labor, since this worker was the "direct means of creating surplus-value." "To be a productive worker is, therefore," Marx wrote, "not a piece of luck, but a misfortune."[2] Those who aided the capitalist in the circulation of his capital, the realization of his profit, and the management of his labor, gained privileges, security, and status from this function, and thus to be an unproductive worker was in itself a piece of good fortune that contrasted with the misfortune of the worker in production.

Now, however, marked changes have occurred in the relations between productive and unproductive workers within the corporation. On the one hand, the process of productive labor has become, more than ever before, a collective process. It is only the body of productive workers which fashions the ultimate product; each worker can no longer be considered productive in the individual sense, and the definition of productive labor applies only to the body of workers taken as a whole. On the other side, the unproductive labor of the corporation, having been so tremendously expanded, has been given the same twofold structure as productive work by the capitalist division of labor. The individual functionary, closely associated with the capitalist, has, as we have described, given way to the department or division of the corporation, in which only the heads remain associated with capitalist management while the rest occupy positions akin to those of workers in production. Thus while, on the side of productive labor, the individual worker loses those characteristics as producer of a finished commodity which made him or her a productive worker, and retains those characteristics only in the mass, on the side of unproductive labor a mass has been created which shares in the subjugation and oppression that characterizes the lives of the productive workers.

The unproductive functions, having evolved from special and privileged occupations closely associated with capital into divisions of corporate activity or even into capitalist "industries" separate and complete in themselves, have now produced their armies of wage-workers whose conditions are generally like those of the armies of labor organized in production. And just as, for corporate management, the problems of the organization of the labor process in production and outside production become increasingly similar, just so for workers the distinction between the various determinate forms of labor—punch press or typewriter, key punch or assembly line, stockroom or filing room, machine tool or bookkeeping machine—become less and less significant. In the modern office and factory the gap between the forms and conditions of labor that loomed so large in the early counting house and shop now dwindles. Although they were at one time a means of escaping the "misfortune" of being a productive worker, the unproductive occupations have, in the armies of labor employed at their bases, for the most part lost their attractiveness and become merely another form of exploitation. From being privileged positions in which one could to a small extent share in the benefits derived by capital from productive labor, they have become mere cogs in the total machinery designed to multiply capital. And this remains true despite the fact that, technically speaking, all those who do not themselves produce commodity values must perforce consume a portion of the commodity values produced by others. In the modern corporation, and for the mass of labor which it employs, this distinction has lost its social force as a line of division between proletarians and middle class: that line can no longer be drawn as roughly corresponding to the division between productive and unproductive workers, but must be inscribed elsewhere in the social structure. Thus Marx's aphorism must be modified, and it must now be said that *to be a wage-worker is a misfortune.*

It must be pointed out, finally, that Marx himself never drew a sharp distinction, in terms of the class structure of society, between productive and unproductive workers in the employ of the capitalist functioning as capitalist. He called production workers and commercial employees alike *wage-workers.** "In one respect," he said, "such a commercial employee is a wage-worker like any other. In the first place, his labour-power is bought with the variable capital of the merchant, not with money expended as revenue, and consequently it is not bought for private service, but for the purpose of expanding the value of the capital advanced for it. In the second place, the value of his labour-power, and thus his wages, are determined as those of other wage-workers, i.e., by the cost of production and reproduction of his specific labour-power, not by the product of his labour." And to this he adds: "Just as the labourer's unpaid labour directly creates surplus-value for productive capital, so the unpaid labour of the commercial wage-worker secures a share of this surplus-value for merchant's capital."[5]

Marx was not, however, completely convinced by his own argumentation, since he went on to point out that this "seems to conflict with the nature of merchant's capital, since this kind of capital does not act as capital by setting in motion the labour of others, as industrial capital does, but rather by doing its own work, i.e., performing the functions of buying and selling, this being precisely the means and the reason why it receives a portion of the surplus-value produced by the industrial capital."[6] Here his question is essentially: If commercial capital receives its return out of the surplus created by industrial capital, for the function purely of buying and selling, what happens when commercial capital grows so large, as it necessarily must, that it has to employ its own wage-workers, and thus convert a portion of its own capital into

---

* He did not, however, call them the "commercial proletariat"; Gough is mistaken in this, since the term occurs in a footnote added and signed by Engels.[3] The fact that Marx did not use this term, but that Engels found it possible to use it some two decades later, is itself significant, and the significance is made partly clear by Engels himself in the same footnote, in which he points out that clerks trained in commercial operations and acquainted with three or four languages "offer their services in vain in London City at 25 shillings per week, which is far below the wages of a good machinist."[4]

variable capital? Since such variable capital, as Marx points out, creates no value, it can grow only as a *result* of the growth of surplus value, never as a *cause*. But if that is the case, the portion of commercial capital converted into variable capital (i.e., into wage labor) is different from all other variable capital that creates value and surplus value. This difference between the capital laid out as wages for production workers and for commercial workers, Marx refers to as a "difficulty." He does not completely provide a solution, as is indicated by the facts that, first, he reminds himself parenthetically in the text to deal with the analysis of various points, including merchant's variable capital, "the law of necessary labour in the sphere of circulation," and other points including "money-dealing" capital; and second, his discussion of commercial wage labor breaks off and is followed by two blank pages, indicating, as Engels points out, that this matter was to have been treated at greater length. But in terms of what interests us here, Marx's discussion is substantially complete, and contains the following conclusions dealing with commercial labor:[7]

1. Mercantile capital must be analyzed first as a branch of industrial capital, and therefore within the office of the industrial capitalist rather than as a separate capital.

2. Such an office is "from the outset infinitesimally small compared to the industrial workshop." But as the scale of production grows, the commercial office grows too, which "necessitates the employment of commercial wage-workers who make up the actual office staff."

3. This is true also for separate merchant capital (and by inference for financial capital in banking, insurance, etc.), since "if every merchant had only as much capital as he himself were able to turn over by his own labour, there would be an infinite fragmentation of merchant's capital," which is not to be expected for reasons he explains. Thus in the commercial offices of merchant as well as banking capital the employment of commercial wage-workers may be expected to grow.

4. The commercial worker is like the production worker in basic respects, that is, in the worker's sale and the capitalist's purchase of labor power. Yet commercial workers are unlike wage-workers in two special respects. First, since their employment is not a cause of the increase of surplus value, but a result, profit is a precondition of outlays on their wages rather than a conse- quence of outlays to hire them. (As an expression of this, Marx points out, a part of commercial salaries was "frequently paid by a share in the profit.") And second, since the concrete form of their labors is generally different from that of production workers, commercial workers "belong to the better-paid class of wage-workers—to those whose labour is classed as skilled and stands above average labour."

5. But, since Marx would have been the last to regard the determinate forms of labor of any sort as fixed and final under capitalism, he immediately

adds to this that commercial wages "tend to fall," partly because of the "division of labour in the office," and partly because the "universality of public education" devalues the labor power of commercial workers with the progress of capitalist production.

Having marked out these various characteristics of commercial labor, Marx has, it is clear, outlined the problem as it exists in all its modern dimensions. The unproductive labor hired by the capitalist to help in the realization or appropriation of surplus value is in Marx's mind like productive labor in all respects save one: it does not produce value and surplus value, and hence grows not as a cause but rather as a result of the expansion of surplus value.

What is also clear, however, is that Marx neither anticipated nor attempted to anticipate the extent of the growth of a commercial wage-working stratum and its transformation into a commercial proletariat. In this, as everywhere else in Marx, the limits of speculation are clear and definite: analysis is used to lay down the principles and never to speculate on the eventual result should those principles continue to operate indefinitely or over a prolonged period of time.* It is also clear that Marx grasped the principles with his customary profundity and comprehensiveness, in a manner which neglected no part of the architecture of the capitalist system and its dynamics of self-reproduction.

That which in Marx was a subordinate and inconsequential part of the analysis has thus for us become a major consequence of the capitalist mode of production. The few commercial wage-workers who puzzled Marx as a conscientious scientist have become the vast and complicated structure of occupations characteristic of unproductive labor in modern capitalism. But in so becoming they have lost many of the last characteristics which separated them from production workers. When they were few they were unlike productive labor, and having become many they are like productive labor. Although productive and unproductive labor are technically distinct, although productive labor has tended to decrease in proportion as its productivity has grown, while nonproductive labor has increased *only as a result of the increase in surpluses thrown off by productive labor*—despite these distinctions, the two masses of labor are not otherwise in striking contrast and need not be counterposed to each other. They form a continuous mass of employment which, at present and unlike the situation in Marx's day, has everything in common.

---

* To understand this, it is necessary to keep in mind that Marx was not only a scientist but also a revolutionary; that so far as he was concerned the capitalist mode of production had already operated for a sufficiently long period of time; and that he anticipated not its prolonged continuation but its imminent destruction, a conviction which is part of the armament of all working revolutionaries.

Notes

1. Ian Gough, "Marx's Theory of Productive and Unproductive Labor," *New Left Review*, no. 76 (November-December 1972), pp. 47-72.
2. Karl Marx, *Capital*, vol. I (Moscow, n.d.), p. 477.
3. Gough, "Marx's Theory of Productive and Unproductive Labor," p. 70.
4. Karl Marx, *Capital*, vol. III (Moscow, 1966), p. 301.
5. Ibid., pp. 292, 294.
6. Ibid., p. 294.
7. Ibid., pp. 292-301.

Chapter 20

A Final Note on Skill

In a study of the mechanization of industry conducted for the National Bureau of Economic Research in the 1930s, Harry Jerome concluded: "As to the effect on skill of further mechanization in the future . . . there is considerable reason to believe that the effect of further changes will be to raise the average skill required."[1] Forty years later there are few who would disagree with this judgment. The idea that the changing conditions of industrial and office work require an increasingly "better-trained," "better-educated," and thus "up-graded" working population is an almost universally accepted proposition in popular and academic discourse. Since the argument that has been thus far made in this work appears to clash directly with this popular idea, it is now necessary to confront the conventional view. The concepts of "skill," "train-ing," and "education" are themselves sufficiently vague, and a precise inves-tigation of the arguments which are used to support the thesis of "upgrading" is further hampered by the fact that they have never been made the subject of a coherent and systematic presentation. We can grapple with the issue only by attempting to give coherence to what is essentially an impressionistic theory, one which is obviously considered so self-evident as to stand above the need for demonstration.

In the form given to it by Jerome in the sentence cited above, the phrase upon which the issue turns is "average skill." Since, with the development of technology and the application to it of the fundamental sciences, the labor processes of society have come to embody a greater amount of scientific knowledge, clearly the "average" scientific, technical, and in that sense "skill" content of these labor processes is much greater now than in the past. But this is nothing but a tautology. The question is precisely whether the scientific and "educated" content of labor tends toward *averaging*, or, on the contrary, toward *polarization*. If the latter is the case, to then say that the "average" skill has been raised is to adopt the logic of the statistician who, with one foot in the fire and the other in ice water, will tell you that "on the average," he is perfectly comfortable. The mass of workers gain nothing from the fact that the decline in their command over the labor process is more than compensated for by the increasing command on the part of managers and engineers. On the contrary, not only does their skill fall in an absolute sense (in that they lose craft and traditional abilities without gaining new abilities adequate to compensate the loss), but it falls even more in a *relative* sense. The more science is incorporated into the labor process, the less the worker understands of the process; the more sophisticated an intellectual product the machine becomes, the less control and comprehension of the machine the worker has. In other words, the more the worker needs to know in order to remain a human being at work, the less does he or she know. This is the chasm which the notion of "average skill" conceals.

The same ambiguity is to be seen in another common formulation of the "upgrading" thesis, one which points to the proliferation of trained and educated specialties. Omar Pancoast, for instance, says: "It is an historical fact that an increasing number of positions require special skills. The evidence for this is well summarized by J. K. Norton with the comment: 'No extensive study of occupational trends arrives at an opposite conclusion.' "[2] In this form the claim is probably unexceptionable, but it may not be taken, as it often is, to mean that an *increasing portion of the working population* occupies positions that require special skills, if the word "skill" is given an interpretation of substance. This approach tends to rest exclusively upon the increase in the number of specialized technical occupations, without recognizing that the multiplication of technical specialties is the condition for dispossessing the mass of workers from the realms of science, knowledge, and skill.

For most of those who hold it, the "upgrading" thesis seems to rest upon two marked trends. The first is the shift of workers from some major occupational groups into others; the second is the prolongation of the average period of education. It will repay our efforts to consider both of these matters in some detail, not only because such a consideration is necessary to establish a realistic picture of the historical trends of skill, but also because in this consideration we shall see a splendid example of the manner in which conventional social science accepts carefully tailored appearances as a substitute for reality.

Let us begin first with the shifts that have taken place within the occupational categories used by statisticians to identify the various portions of the "manual" working class. At the turn of the century the three classifications of workers today known as *craftsmen, foremen, and kindred, operatives and kindred, and nonfarm laborers* together made up slightly less than 36 percent of employed persons. Seventy years later these three categories made up just over 36 percent (although in the intervening decades their total had risen to around 40 percent—in the 1920 to 1950 censuses—and then fallen back again). But during these seventy years the distribution of this group among its three statistical components had changed sharply. In terms of percentages of the entire employed population, the changes were as follows:[3]

	1900	1970
Craftsmen, foremen, and kindred	10.5	13.9
Operatives and kindred	12.8	17.9
Nonfarm laborers	12.5	4.7
Total	35.8	36.5

The most marked feature of this tabulation is the decline in laborers. A large part of this classification had become operatives (we are still speaking in terms of percentages, since in terms of absolute numbers the total of the three groups was about $22\frac{2}{3}$ times larger in 1970 than at the turn of the century, and each percentage point now represents about $22\frac{2}{3}$ times as many people) and the rest had become craftsmen and foremen. This shift is taken, on its face, to represent a massive "upgrading" of workers to higher categories of skill.*

Classifications of workers, however, are neither "natural" nor self-evident, nor is the degree of skill a self-evident quality which can simply be read from the labels given to various such classifications. The first socioeconomic occupational classifications used in the United States were those of William C. Hunt, an employee of the Bureau of the Census who, in 1897, grouped all gainful workers into four categories: proprietors, clerical employees, skilled workers, and laborers. The group we now call "operatives" did not exist in this classification, and the division of manual workers into two classes was a clear and unambiguous one: There were the craftsmen—the mechanics in various trades, whose admission into this category of skilled workers was thus dependent upon satisfying the traditional requirements of craft mastery. Laborers were all others; they were thus a residual category.

---

* It would be wrong to try to derive any comforting conclusions from the rise in the category of craftsmen and foremen between 1900 and 1970. We have already discussed the dispersal and deterioration of craft skills in the machine shop, for example, and many of the possessors of partial skills continue to carry the label of craftsmanship. In a discussion of traditional apprenticeships in British industry, for example, one British authority points out that "although apprentices theoretically emerge as skilled craftsmen much of the work they are put to would be regarded as semi-skilled, because of the fragmentation of many industrial processes." Because, this writer says, the need is for "semi-skilled" workers, "the apprenticeship system encourages unrealistic and rigid job definitions."[4] In the United States such attacks against the apprenticeship system are no longer necessary, since there is little left of it. And it should also be noted that much of the growth of the craftsmen classification is due to the rapid increase of the "mechanics and repairmen" category (the largest grouping of which is that of automobile mechanics) which does not conform to traditional standards of craftsmanship and represents an ever slighter level of technical capacity and training.

In the 1930s a revision of these classifications was carried out by Dr. Alba Edwards, for many years an official of the Bureau of the Census, who reconstructed the conceptual basis of occupational statistics in a fundamental fashion. The change which he made that is of concern to this discussion is his division of the former group of laborers into two parts. Those who tended or operated machines, or attended mechanized processes, he called operatives. Laborers, still a residual category, now consisted of those nonfarm workers who were neither craftsmen nor machine operatives. These classifications were first applied in the census of 1930. Edwards, however, did the massive work of reconstructing the census data back to the turn of the century, and even earlier, in accord with his new classification scheme. The class of workers known as "operatives," therefore, insofar as we find it in the census statistics earlier than those of 1930, is a backward projection of a category that did not exist in these earlier censuses. Edwards' work has been the chief basis for all similar reconstructions since done by others.[5]

The three Edwards classifications were taken to correspond, both in official terminology and in common parlance, to levels of skill. Craftsmen continued to be called skilled workers and laborers "unskilled"; operatives were now called "semiskilled." But it must be noted that the distinction between the skills of the two latter categories was based not upon a study of the occupational tasks involved, as is generally assumed by the users of the categories, but upon a simple *mechanical* criterion, in the fullest sense of the word. The creation of "semi-skill" by Edwards thus brought into existence, retroactively to the turn of the century and with a mere stroke of the pen, a massive "upgrading" of the skills of the working population. By making a connection with machinery—such as machine tending or watching, machine feeding, machine operating—a criterion of skill, it guaranteed that with the increasing mechanization of industry the category of the "unskilled" would register a precipitous decline, while that of the "semiskilled" would show an equally striking rise. This statistical process has been automatic ever since, without reference to the actual exercise or distribution of "skills."

Let us take as an example the categories of teamster on the one side, and the operators of motor vehicles (such as truckdrivers, chauffeurs and taxi drivers, routemen and deliverymen, etc.) on the other. These categories are important because that of teamster was, before World War I, one of the largest of occupational groups, while the drivers of various sorts are, taken together, one of the largest today. The former are classified, retroactively, among the "unskilled" laborers, while the latter, because of their connection with machinery, are classed as operatives and hence "semi-skilled." When the Edwards scale is applied in this fashion, a skill upgrading takes place as a consequence of the displacement of horse-drawn transport by motorized. Yet it is impossible to see this as a true comparison of human work skills. In the circumstances of an earlier day, when a largely rural population learned the arts of managing horses as part of the process of growing up, while few as yet knew how to operate motorized vehicles, it might have made sense to characterize the former as part of the common heritage and thus no skill at all, while driving, as a learned ability, would have been thought of as a "skill." Today, it would be more proper to regard those who are able to drive vehicles as unskilled in that respect at least, while those who can care for, harness, and manage a team of horses are certainly the possessors of a marked and uncommon ability. In reality, this way of comparing occupational skill leaves much to be desired, depending as it does on relativistic or contemporary notions. But there is certainly little reason to suppose that the ability to drive a motor vehicle is more demanding, requires longer training or habituation time, and thus represents a higher or intrinsically more rewarding skill than the ability to manage a team of horses.

It is only in the world of census statistics, and not in terms of direct assessment, that an assembly line worker is presumed to have greater skill than a fisherman or oysterman, the forklift operator greater skill than the gardener or groundskeeper, the machine feeder greater skill than the longshoreman, the parking lot attendant greater skill than the lumberman or raftsman. And with the routinization of machine operation, there is less and less reason to rate the operative above many other classifications of laborers, such as craftsmen's helpers. The entire concept of "semi-skill," as applied to operatives, is an increasingly delusory one. The prefix *semi* means "half" or "partly." When this prefix is attached to the noun *skill*, the resulting compound word leaves the impression of a level of training and ability that lies somewhere—perhaps about halfway—between skill and the total lack of it. But for the category of operatives, training requirements and the demands of the job upon the abilities of the worker are now so low that one can hardly imagine jobs that lie significantly below them on any scale of skill. If we turn, for example, to the United States Department of Labor's *Occupational Outlook Handbook*, which is virtually the only systematic and official attempt to describe occupational skills and training, we find the category of operatives described as follows:

> Semiskilled workers ordinarily receive only brief on-the-job training. Usually they are told exactly what to do and how to do it, and their work is supervised closely. They often repeat the same motions or the same jobs throughout the working day.
>
> Semiskilled workers do not need to invest many years in learning their jobs. The simplest repetitive and routine semiskilled jobs can be learned in a day and mastered in a few weeks. Even those jobs that require a higher degree of skill, such as truckdriver, can be learned in a few months. At the same time, adaptability—the ability to learn new jobs quickly, including the operation of new machines—is an important qualification for semiskilled workers.

New employees starting out in semiskilled jobs are not expected to be highly proficient. After a short training period, however, they must work at a standard, fast, and steady pace. Frequently, good eyesight and good coordination are required.[6]

Jobs which require merely the ordinary physical characteristics of human beings in a fair state of health; where duties are learned in periods ranging from as little as a day to, at a maximum, a few months; in which the worker is "told exactly what to do and how to do it"; which are "supervised closely," repeat the "same motions or the same jobs throughout the working day," and of which the Department of Labor analysts can find nothing more favorable to say than that they demand "adaptability"—is this not a definition of unskilled labor? Here is another description, by a British authority:

> The oldest and most traditional differentiation between hourly-paid workers in British industry is based upon skill; skilled, semi-skilled, and unskilled categories being recognized in the wage structure of most industries, and in the class structure of society. Although it is impossible to define these categories with any degree of precision, the terms are commonly used and understood throughout industry. It is generally accepted that a skilled worker is a craftsman whose training has been spread over several years and is formally recognized outside an individual firm; a semi-skilled worker is one who, during a limited period of training, usually between two and twelve weeks, has acquired the manual dexterity or mechanical knowledge needed for his immediate job, and an unskilled worker is one whose job requires no formal training of any kind.[7]

If we take Joan Woodward at her word, the gap between the skilled and the semi-skilled worker is a matter of "years" of training, while the creation of "semi-skill" as against "no skill" is accomplished in "two to twelve weeks." Clearly, what we have here is not a realistic distinction but an artifact of the classifiers (which, at least in United States industry, is not reflected in wage structure or class structure). There are few if any jobs, including all those classified as "unskilled," in which the training period is actually zero. The carpenter's helper (or other craft helpers classified as "unskilled labor" because they fall neither into the craft nor into the machine-operative categories) is of little use to the carpenter until he learns a great variety of tools and materials in their various sizes and dimensions, and until he gains a familiarity with the craftsman's operations; it is unquestionable that this large section of the "laborers" grouping requires a longer training period than most operatives. Even pick and shovel work takes more learning before it can be done to required standards than many assembly or machine-feeding jobs. "Studies of final assembly line work in a major automobile company by the Technology Project of Yale University found the average time cycle for jobs to be 3 minutes. As to learning time, a few hours to a week sufficed. Learning time for 65 percent of the work force was less than a month."[8] And yet assembly jobs are the most representative type of operative jobs into which there has been so great an influx in the past three-quarters of a century, and which, by a marvel of definition, have produced a striking upgrading of the skills of the working population.*

The imaginary creation of higher categories of skill by nomenclatural exercises does not end with the transformation of most urban labor into "semi-skilled" work. We have yet to consider the phenomenon of the decline of farm laborers. Here the statistical category involved was especially large and the transformation especially illusory. At the turn of the century, 17.7 percent of the working population was classified as "farm laborers and foremen" (almost all of them "laborers," few of them foremen). But here there is not even a hint in the census classification of an attempt to sort workers by skill. For the population employed on farms, the census has no differentiated categories at all, no class of "skilled farmers," or "farming craftsmen." *All* farm labor employed by farm owners is classified in the "farm laborers and foremen" category. The only distinction drawn by the census is a purely proprietary one, between owners on the one side (with a very small group of managers included with owners), and "laborers and foremen" on the other. Among the 17.7 percent of the working population of the United States which, at the time of the 1900 census, was employed by farm proprietors, a great many—perhaps most— were fully qualified farmers who had themselves owned and operated farms and lost them, or who had grown up in farm families and learned the entire broad craft. The farm hired hand was able to be of assistance to the farmer because he was the product of years of farm life and had a mastery of a great many skills involving a knowledge of land, fertilizer, animals, tools, farm machinery, construction skills, etc., and the traditional abilities and dexterities in the handling of farm tasks. Only in this way could he be set to work by the farmer in plowing, milking, caring for animals, mending fence, harvesting, etc. To be sure, there was unquestionably a distribution of skills, and many farmworkers, such as those employed in cotton or fruit picking and other such "plantation" tasks, did not possess the all-around skills of the working farmer. But to disregard, as is now customary, the broad range of abilities required of so many farmworkers and to be deceived by the use of the catch-all designation

---

* It must not be imagined that these training times—so short as to mock the very term "training"—are characteristic only of assembly line and other factory work. Charles Silberman, a *Fortune* editor, reports: "A detailed manpower survey by the New York State Department of Labor, for example, revealed that approximately two-thirds of all the jobs in existence in that state involve such simple skills that they can be—and are—learned in a few days, weeks, or at most months of on-the-job training."[9] "Two-thirds of all the jobs in existence" would have to include all operatives, clerical workers, service workers, sales workers on the retail level, laborers—and some portions of other occupational categories as well.

of "laborer" is to deal not in social science but in promotional labeling. Of all categories of labor, this one has suffered the most complete decimation, having plunged to 1.7 percent by 1970. In the world of the sociologists, this represents a triumphant ascent of an enormous mass of workers to higher levels, since *every* classification of labor is rated by them above farm labor in "skill."

On the other side, the labor classifications whose names conceal a woeful lack of skill or training have, like the "semi-skilled," grown rapidly. For example, beginning with the 1950 census another change was introduced into the classification schema. The Alba Edwards system was modified, for that and subsequent censuses, by the introduction of the new category of nonhousehold "service" workers, and again this classification was used to reinterpret the figures of earlier censuses. At one stroke this reclassification significantly reduced the major occupational groups usually included in the so-called blue-collar categories. The new service category was composed of approximately one-fourth of workers who had previously been classified as "semi-skilled," and three-fourths of workers previously classed as "unskilled." Since, by the common consent of social scientists, "service workers" are at least several cuts above "laborers," and since some even think that because they produce "services" instead of working in factories and wearing "blue collars" while producing goods, they should be rated above operatives, another substantial "upgrading" was brought about. There is no need to add here to what is known about the jobs of the mass of service workers as shown in the listing of the occupations in this category (see pp. 274-75 above), or the relative pay of these workers compared not only to operatives but even to laborers (see p. 226 above).

We must finally mention the strength drawn by the illusory upgrading of skills from the statistics which show the very rapid growth of clerical and sales occupations. The reflex response which causes governmental and academic social scientists automatically to accord a higher grade of skill, training, prestige, and class position to any form of office work as against any and all forms of manual work is a tradition of long standing in American sociology which few have ventured to challenge. Caplow has pointed out that the "superiority of white-collar work" is "undoubtedly the most important" of the assumptions underlying not only the census scale but a number of other socioeconomic occupational scales used by American sociology.[10] (Those scales which break with this tradition go no further than to put skilled craftsmen on approximately the same level as clerical workers!) The weight of the prejudice which rates all "white-collar" above all "blue-collar" work is such that the growth of the former at the expense of the latter is again taken as evidence of an increase in skill and training for which no real factual backing is required, so self-evident is this conclusion for the conventional wisdom.*

The lengthening of the average period spent in school before entry into the "labor force," which is the other common ground for assuming that a better-educated working population is needed by modern industry and trade, must also be analyzed and separated into its component parts. Time spent in school has been increasing: the median years of school completed by the employed civilian working population rose from 10.6 in 1948 to 12.4 by the end of the 1960s;[12] and this was merely the culmination of a secular trend which had been going on for a century. In this we see first of all the fact that the requirements of literacy and familiarity with the numbers system have become generalized throughout the society. The ability to read, write, and perform simple arithmetical operations is demanded by the urban environment, not just in jobs but also for consumption, for conformity to the rules of society and obedience to the law. Reading and figuring are, apart from all their other meanings, the elementary attributes of a manageable population, which could no more be sold, cajoled, and controlled without them than can symbols be handled by a computer if they lack the elementary characteristics of identity and position. Beyond this need for basic literacy there is also the function of the schools in providing an attempted socialization to city life, which now replaces the socialization through farm, family, community, and church which once took place in a predominantly rural setting. Thus the average length of schooling is generally higher for urban populations, and the shift of a population from farm to city brings with it, almost as an automatic function, an increase in the term of education.

During the past century, moreover, the vastly increased practice of the scientific and technical specialties in production, research, management, administration, medicine, and in education itself have called into being a greatly expanded apparatus of higher education for the provision of professional specialists in all these areas. This, of course, has also had a marked effect upon the average length of school attendance.

These two factors, which tend to define educational requirements from an occupational standpoint, obviously explain some of the increase in mass schooling, but just as clearly they do not explain all of it. A complete picture of the functions and functioning of education in the United States and other capitalist countries would require a thorough historical study of the manner in

---

* That self-evident, conventional wisdom can vary with time, place, and social circumstances was strikingly displayed by Jerome Davis in a study he made of the social attitudes of Soviet schoolchildren in the mid-twenties. In rating a list of occupations adapted from one of the common U.S. "prestige" scales, these children reversed the order of rank found in the use of the scale in the United States, putting farmers first and bankers last.[11]

which the present standards came into being, and how they were related, at each step of their formation, to the social forces of the society at large. But even a sketch of the recent period suffices to show that many causes, most of them bearing no direct relationship to the educational requirements of the job structure, have been at work.

The Depression was responsible for the enactment, late in the 1930s, of legislation restricting the labor-force participation of youths, the object of which was to reduce unemployment by eliminating a segment of the population from the job market. The anticipated consequence of this was the postponement of the school-leaving age. World War II temporarily solved this problem with its immense mobilization of the population for production and service in the armed forces, but as the war drew to an end fears revived that the return of the demobilized soldiers and sailors, together with the cutback of war orders, would renew the Great Depression. Among the measures enacted to ward this off was the veterans' educational subsidy, which, after both World War II and the Korean War, swelled school enrollment, subsidized educational institutions, and contributed further to the prolongation of the average schooling period. Throughout the postwar period the rapid pace of capital accumulation stimulated demand for specialized managerial and semi-managerial employees and other professionals, and this demand, in the situation of governmental subsidy to education, brought forth, not unexpectedly, so great a supply of college-trained people that by the end of the 1960s it began to manifest itself as an oversupply. The encouragement to an entire generation to train itself for "careers," when all that would be available for at least three-quarters of that generation were working-class jobs requiring minimal education and offering working-class pay, began to backfire.

In the meanwhile, as a result of the generalization of secondary education, employers tended to raise their screening requirements for job applicants, not because of educational needs but simply because of the mass availability of high school graduates. Herbert Bienstock, New York regional director of the Bureau of Labor Statistics, described this trend in these words: "The completion of a high school education has become an important requirement for entry into the labor market of today. Employers, finding persons with high school diplomas becoming more available in a period of rising educational attainment, have come to use the diploma as a screening device, often seeking people with higher levels of education even when job content is not necessarily becoming more complex or requiring higher levels of skill. This has been true in many of the rapidly growing job categories in the clerical, sales, and service fields."[13] This spreading policy reinforced the other pressures tending to postpone the school-leaving age by making the "diploma" a ticket of admission to almost any kind of job. It was used in factory as well as office: "Most factory type jobs require only *6th grade competency* in arithmetic, spelling, reading, and writing, and speaking," we are told by the personnel director of the Inorganic Chemicals Division of the Monsanto Chemical Company. "Too often," he continues, "business has used the requirement of a high school diploma or certificate as an easy means of screening out job applicants."[14]

Thus the continuing extension of mass education for the nonprofessional categories of labor increasingly lost its connection with occupational requirements. At the same time, its place in the social and economic structure became ever more firmly guaranteed by functions which have little or nothing to do with either job training or any other strictly educational needs. The postponement of school leaving to an average age of eighteen has become indispensable for keeping unemployment within reasonable bounds. In the interest of working parents (the two-parent-job-holding family having become ever more common during this period), and in the interest of social stability and the orderly management of an increasingly rootless urban population, the schools have developed into immense teen-sitting organizations, their functions having less and less to do with imparting to the young those things that society thinks they must learn. In this situation the content of education deteriorated as its duration lengthened. The knowledge imparted in the course of an elementary education was more or less expanded to fill the prevalent twelve-year educational sojourn, and in a great many cases school systems have difficulty in instilling in twelve years the basic skills of literacy and numbers that, several generations ago, occupied eight. This in turn gave a greater impetus to employers to demand of job applicants a high school diploma, as a guarantee—not always valid—of getting workers who can read.

We cannot neglect the direct economic impact of the enlarged school system. Not only does the postponement of the school-leaving age limit the growth of recognized unemployment, but it also furnishes employment for a considerable mass of teachers, administrators, construction and service workers, etc. Moreover, education has become an immensely profitable area of capital accumulation for the construction industry, for suppliers of all sorts, and for a host of subsidiary enterprises. For all these reasons—which have nothing to do with either education or occupational training—it is difficult to imagine United States society without its immense "educational" structure, and in fact, as has been seen in recent years, the closing of even a single segment of the schools for a period of weeks is enough to create a social crisis in the city in which this happens. The schools, as caretakers of children and young people, are indispensable for family functioning, community stability, and social order in general (although they fulfill even these functions badly). In a word, there is no longer any place for the young in this society other than school. Serving to fill a vacuum, schools have themselves become that vacuum, increasingly emptied of content and reduced to little more than their own form. Just as in the labor process, where the more there is to know the less the worker need know, in the schools the mass of future workers attend the more there is to learn, the less reason there is for teachers to teach and students to learn. In this more than in any other single factor—the purposelessness, futility, and empty forms of the educational system—we have the source of the growing antagonism between the young and their schools which threatens to tear the schools apart.

It follows that the growing recognition among corporate managers and educational researchers that the commonly made connection between education and job content is, for the mass of jobs, a false one, will not necessarily result in a reversal of the educational trend and bring about an earlier school-leaving age. Capitalist society in the United States has little choice but to maintain this educational establishment as a social institution with transcendent functions. Yet the recognition of how little is accomplished in the years of elementary and high school attendance in the way of job preparation, and how little in the way of educational preparation these jobs require, is spreading.

Ivar Berg, for example, in one of the more detailed examinations of this subject carried out in recent years, arrives at the conclusion that educational "achievements" have already "exceeded requirements in most job categories," and that the demand for "better-educated" labor cannot therefore be explained by "technological and related changes attending most jobs."[15] His most startling finding is that investigations show that education may in fact be a *liability* for the employer. His study of productivity, turnover, and absenteeism in a group of textile workers found that "educational achievement was *inversely* related to performance thus conceived."[16] A sample study in the clerical field yielded the same conclusion: "Performance in 125 branch offices of a major New York bank, measured by turnover data and by the number of lost accounts per teller, was inversely associated with the educational achievements of these 500 workers. The branches with the worst performance records were those in which a disproportionately (and significantly) high number of employees were attending educational programs after working hours! There was also evidence that performance was worst in precisely those branches in which, besides the educational achievements being higher, the managers stressed education in consultation with tellers concerning their futures with the bank."[17] Berg was able to report instances in which managers automatically assumed that their most competent workers had more education, when the opposite was true, "as in one company in which managers reported that the better-educated technicians in their employ were the 'best' technicians." The data from this company showed that "the less-educated technicians received higher evaluations from supervisors and had longer service than technicians with higher educational achievements in comparable jobs; the managers, however, assumed that these 'better' employees had completed more years of schooling!"[18] In part, the explanation for this may lie in the finding, also reported by Berg, that "education is more often than not an important factor accounting for dissatis-faction among workers in many occupational categories. . . ."[19]

As one consequence of the recognition by managers of these facts, the emphasis on more years of education has begun to disappear from the hiring policies of many firms. During the period when high school education had not yet become so general as it is now, unemployment tended to settle more heavily among those with less formal schooling. This was of course given enormous publicity during the 1950s and early 1960s, both as evidence for the educational requirements of modern scientific industry and also in the simpleminded hope that giving everyone a high school education would eliminate unemployment. The latter conclusion, of course, rested upon the assumption that unemployment was a consequence of the functional inadequacy of the unemployed in an economy that demanded higher educational attainments. This notion, as Stanley Lebergott pointed out, "misapprehends at least one fundamental characteristic of the unemployed," which is that they "are marginal in the existing state of offer and demand in the labor market. If all workers in the labor force had their education improved, some would still be marginal," but "their marginality would then appear to be associated with some other simple single characteristic."[20]

This is in fact what has happened, although the change has not received the same publicity as the earlier disparity between educational levels of employed and unemployed. A study by the Bureau of Labor Statistics in 1971 reaches this unequivocal conclusion: "In the past, jobholders had more educa-tion than did jobseekers—in 1959, for example, the median education of the employed was 12.0 years, while that of the unemployed was only 9.9 years. Since then, the average education of unemployed workers has risen so that by 1971 the difference between the median education of employed and unem-ployed workers, 12.4 and 12.2 years respectively, is no longer statistically significant."[21] This convergence between the schooling of employed and unemployed has been more rapid for women than for men, so that by the mid-1960s there was no longer any significant difference between the median educational attainments of employed and unemployed women. In the case of men, the difference in the late 1950s was much greater than it was for women, but by the start of the 1970s that gap had also been closed. Thus a chart of educational attainments by sex and employment status begins as a broad fan in 1957, with unemployed men averaging below 9 years of school, unemployed women 10½ years, employed men above 11 years, and employed women just above 12 years. By the date of the above-cited study, March 1971, this fan had closed completely and all were bunched together in the same narrow range between 12 and 12½ years: men and women, employed and unemployed.

For the worker, the concept of skill is traditionally bound up with craft mastery—that is to say, the combination of knowledge of materials and processes with the practiced manual dexterities required to carry on a specific branch of production. The breakup of craft skills and the reconstruction of production as a collective or social process have destroyed the traditional concept of skill and opened up only one way for mastery over labor processes to develop: in and through scientific, technical, and engineering knowledge. But the extreme concentration of this knowledge in the hands of management and its closely associated staff organizations have closed this avenue to the working population. What is left to workers is a reinterpreted and woefully inadequate concept of skill: a specific dexterity, a limited and repetitious operation, "speed as skill," etc.* With the development of the capitalist mode of production, the very concept of skill becomes degraded along with the degradation of labor and the yardstick by which it is measured shrinks to such a point that today the worker is considered to possess a "skill" if his or her job requires a few days' or weeks' training, several months of training is regarded as unusually demanding, and the job that calls for a learning period of six months or a year—such as computer programming—inspires a paroxysm of awe. (We may compare this with the traditional craft apprenticeship, which rarely lasted less than four years and which was not uncommonly seven years long.)

In the early 1920s, Georges Sorel wrote that "the modern factory is a field of experiment constantly enlisting the worker in scientific research," and Albert Thierry said in the same vein: "Our entire civilization is a system of physics, the simplest worker is a physicist."[23] Georges Friedmann quotes these two remarks with his customary ambiguity, not knowing whether to applaud them for their optimism or deprecate them as pious but unfounded hopes. The past half-century has removed all doubt, if there ever was any, about the falsity of these views.

The worker can regain mastery over collective and socialized production only by assuming the scientific, design, and operational prerogatives of modern engineering; short of this, there is no mastery over the labor process. The extension of the time of education which modern capitalism has brought about for its own reasons provides the framework; the number of years spent in school has become

---

* "With reference to Marshall and Smith on the subject of 'dexterity,' " says M. C. Kennedy in his unpublished Ph.D. dissertation on the division of labor, "one thing should be made clear. Both men confuse increased dexterity with skill or talent. When a cabinet maker is skilled in his craft, skill covers his ability to imagine how things would appear in final form if such and such tools and materials were used. When he can estimate accurately both aesthetic appeal and functional utility, organize his tools, his power and his materials in a way which accomplishes his task and gives him livelihood and recognition—then, we are speaking of his skill. But if the man should be able rapidly and with facility to do nothing but snap his fingers over and over again for livelihood, then we would be speaking of dexterity. It is the latter that Marshall calls skill. Yet, in large industry today, increased dexterity means decreased skill."[22]

generally adequate for the provision of a comprehensive polytechnical education for the workers of most industries. But such an education can take effect only if it is combined with the practice of labor during the school years, and only if education continues throughout the life of the worker after the end of formal schooling. Such education can engage the interest and attention of workers only when they become masters of industry in the true sense, which is to say when the antagonisms in the labor process between controllers and workers, conception and execution, mental and manual labor are overthrown, and when the labor process is united in the collective body which conducts it.*

---

* The demands for "workers' participation" and "workers' control," from this point of view, fall far short of the Marxist vision. The conception of a democracy in the workplace based simply upon the imposition of a formal structure of parliamentarism—election of directors, the making of production and other decisions by ballot, etc.—upon the existing organization of production is delusory. Without the return of requisite technical knowledge to the mass of workers and the reshaping of the organization of labor—without, in a word, a new and truly collective mode of production—balloting within factories and offices does not alter the fact that the workers remain as dependent as before upon "experts," and can only choose among them, or vote for alternatives presented by them. Thus genuine workers' control has as its prerequisite the demystifying of technology and the reorganization of the mode of production. This does not mean, of course, that the seizure of power within industry through demands for workers' control is not a revolutionary act. It means rather that a true workers' democracy cannot subsist on a purely formal parliamentary scheme.

It is a mistake to think, therefore, as some apparently do, that the raising of the idea of workers' control in industry—in the sense of an electoral structure within each workplace—is a demand that goes *beyond* Marxism. Those who incline to this belief should note how Marx's entire discussion of the capitalist mode of production in the first volume of *Capital* is permeated by a much more revolutionary conception, which is the return of the process of production itself to the control of the workers in the fullest and most direct way. Marx would have viewed a philosophy of "workers' control" which made no mention of this kind of a revolution in the mode of production to be a feeble and illusory remedy, just as he would have considered a revolution, such as that in the Soviet Union, which altered property relations but left the mode of production untouched, as a hybrid form which, so long as it went no further, remained only the abortive *first stage* of revolution.

In this connection, see Paul Blumberg's book on workers' control. Blumberg, although he provides one of the best surveys available on the subject, fails, like so many others, to grasp the Marxist view when he complains of the "silence" of Marx and Engels on workers' control; he attributes this chiefly to "their reluctance to spell out the nature of the coming Communist social order," and goes on to say: "Nevertheless, taking their work as a whole, it is clear that, had they been more articulate about the nature of Socialism, they might have expressed sympathy for the idea of workers' control. Such sympathy is often implied in their works."[24] There is no question that Marx and Engels *took for granted* the democratic control of workers over their own workplace and their own society as a whole. But they were concerned with a far more revolutionary concept, and one without which the idea of "industrial democracy" becomes an illusion.

In the capitalist mode of production, the prolongation of an ever emptier "education" combined with the reduction of labor to simple and ignorant tasks represent a waste of the educational years and a wasting of humanity in the years thereafter. This system is understood by its apologists to exemplify efficiency raised to its highest point; where one engineer can direct fifty workers, they argue, there is no need for "wasting" the resources of society in educating all to the engineering standard. So goes the logic of the capitalist mode of production, which, rather than threaten the hierarchical social relations by which it accumulates wealth in the hands of the owners of society, prefers to leave the worker ignorant despite years of schooling, and to rob humanity of its birthright of conscious and masterful labor.

The perfect expression of the concept of skill in capitalist society is to be found in the bald and forthright dictums of the early Taylorians, who had discovered the great truth of capitalism that the worker must become the instrument of labor in the hands of the capitalist, but had not yet learned the wisdom of adorning, obfuscating, and confusing this straightforward necessity in the manner of modern management and sociology. "What happens to unskilled labor under Scientific Management?" ask the Gilbreths in their *Primer* on this subject. "Under Scientific Management there is no unskilled labor; or, at least, labor does not remain unskilled. Unskilled labor is taught the best method obtainable. . . . No labor is unskilled after it is taught."[25] The instruction of the worker in the simple requirements of capital: here, in the minds of managers, is the secret of the upgrading of skills so celebrated in the annals of modern industrial sociology. The worker may remain a creature without knowledge or capacity, a mere "hand" by which capital does its work, but so long as he or she is *adequate to the needs of capital* the worker is no longer to be considered or called unskilled. It is this conception that lies behind the shabby nominal sociology in which the sociologists find "upgrading" in the new names given to classifications by the statisticians. "Training a worker," wrote Frank Gilbreth, "means merely enabling him to carry out the directions of his work schedule. Once he can do this, his training is over, whatever his age." Is this not a perfect description of the mass of jobs in modern industry, trade, and offices?

Notes

1. Harry Jerome, *Mechanization in Industry* (New York, 1934), p. 402.
2. Omar Pancoast, Jr., *Occupational Mobility* (New York, 1941), p. 14.
3. For 1900, see David L. Kaplan and M. Claire Casey, *Occupational Trends in the United States: 1900 to 1950*, Bureau of the Census Working Paper No. 5 (Washington, 1958), Table 2. For 1970, see U.S. Bureau of the Census, *Census of Population: 1970, Final Report PC(2)-7A* (Washington, D.C., 1973), Table 1.
4. S. R. Parker, "Industry and Education," in S. R. Parker, R. K. Brown, J. Child, and M. A. Smith, *The Sociology of Industry* (rev. ed.; London, 1972), p. 36.

5. Theodore Caplow, *The Sociology of Work* (Minneapolis, 1954), Chapter 2, esp. pp. 31-36; Joseph A. Kahl, *The American Class Structure* (New York, 1957), pp. 64-65; J. E. Morton, *On the Evolution of Manpower Statistics* (Kalamazoo, Mich., 1969), p. 46.
6. U.S. Department of Labor, Bureau of Labor Statistics, *Occupational Outlook Handbook*, Bulletin No. 1550, 1968-1969 edition (Washington, n.d.), p. 316.
7. Joan Woodward, *Industrial Organization: Theory and Practice* (London, 1965), pp. 28-29.
8. Charles R. Walker, "Changing Character of Human Work Under the Impact of Technological Change," in National Commission on Technology, Automation, and Economic Progress, *The Employment Impact of Technological Change*, Appendix Volume II, *Technology and the American Economy* (Washington, D.C., 1966), p. 299.
9. Charles Silberman, *The Myths of Automation* (New York, 1966), p. 52.
10. Caplow, *The Sociology of Work*, pp. 42-43.
11. Jerome Davis, "Testing the Social Attitudes of Children in the Government Schools in Russia," *American Journal of Sociology* (May 1927); cited in ibid., p. 40.
12. *Manpower Report of the President* (Washington, 1972), p. 207.
13. *Collective Bargaining Today*, Proceedings of the Collective Bargaining Forum (1969), p. 334.
14. K. B. Bernhardt, speaking to the Community Relations Division (Justice Department) Conference on Job Opportunities for Minorities, Chicago, June 1967; quoted in R. A. Nixon, *The Labor Market Framework of Job Development: Some Problems and Prospects* (New York, 1967), p. 41.
15. Ivar Berg, *Education and Jobs: The Great Training Robbery* (Boston, 1971), pp. 14-15.
16. Ibid., p. 87.
17. Ibid., pp. 93-94.
18. Ibid., pp. 16-17.
19. Ibid., p. 17.
20. Stanley Lebergott, *Men Without Work: The Economics of Unemployment* (Englewood Cliffs, N.J., 1964), p. 11.
21. William V. Deutermann, "Educational Attainment of Workers, March 1971," *Monthly Labor Review* (November 1971), p. 31.
22. M. C. Kennedy, *The Division of Labor and the Culture of Capitalism: A Critique* (Ann Arbor, Mich., 1968), p. 172n.
23. Georges Sorel, *Les illusions du progrès* (Paris, 1921), p. 282; Albert Thierry, *Réflexions sur l'education* (Paris, 1923), pp. 99-100; quoted by Friedmann in *Industrial Society* (Glencoe, Ill., 1955), p. 240.
24. Paul Blumberg, *Industrial Democracy: The Sociology of Participation* (New York, 1969), p. 190.
25. William R. Spriegel and Clark E. Myers, eds., *The Writings of the Gilbreths* (Homewood, Ill., 1953), p. 110.

Appendix 1

Two Comments

In the following notes, Harry Braverman responded to a number of contributors to a special issue of Monthly Review *(Vol. 28, no. 3, July-August, 1976) entitled "Technology, the Labor Process, and the Working Class."*

I would like to take this opportunity to comment on two of the many issues that have been raised in the accompanying articles. The same issues have been raised in a number of other reviews and communications on *Labor and Monopoly Capital.* The first has to do with the connections between the subject matter of the book and the women's movement. The second has to do with the consciousness of the working class as a class *for itself,* struggling in its own behalf, apart from its objective existence *in itself.*

I

The authors of "The Working Class Has Two Sexes" (Rosalyn Baxandall, Elizabeth Ewen, and Linda Gordon) generously conclude that *"Labor and Monopoly Capital . . .* makes a major contribution, perhaps unbeknownst to its author, to feminist analysis." Be that as it may, the connection did not come as a post-publication surprise to me. During the earliest period of my research, I became convinced of the importance of recent trends in the working population for the feminist movement. I have been gratified to see that many of the conclusions I had drawn in my own mind have now been drawn by readers, and particularly by women readers.

In comments both public and private, many of these readers have expressed some disappointment that I omitted from my discussion any direct comments on matters of special concern to the women's movement, and particularly household, or non-wage family, labor. Since these readers have all been most understanding of the self-imposed limits of my study, and (as in the two articles contained in this collection which address themselves directly to the subject) have adapted their critiques to these limits, I do not raise this here in order to make an unnecessary explanation. But I would like to add one thing to what has been said on this particular point. Beyond the fact that a consideration of household work would have fallen far outside the bounds of my subject (not to mention my competence), there is also this to consider; that household work, although it has been the special domain of women, is not thereby necessarily so central to the issues of women's liberation as might appear from this fact. On the contrary, it is the breakdown of the traditional household economy which has produced the present-day feminist movement. This movement in its modern form is almost entirely a product of women who have been summoned from the household by the requirements of the capital accumulation process, and subjected to experiences and stresses unknown in the previous thousands of years of household labor under a variety of social arrangements. Thus it is the analysis of this new situation that in my opinion occupies the place of first importance in the theory of modern feminism.

Let me add at once that none of this is said in order to disparage the need for an understanding of the specific forms and issues of household labor, of the working-class family, and of sexual divisions and tensions both within and outside the family. But the unraveling of every complex of social reality requires a starting point, and it is my strong conviction that the best starting point in every case is the analysis of the dynamic elements rather than the traditional and static aspects of a given problem. Thus I have a feeling that the most light will be shed on the totality of problems and issues embraced in the feminist movement, including those of household work, by an analysis that begins not with the forms of household work that have been practiced for thousands of years, but by their weakening and by the dissociation of an increasing number of women from them in the last few decades.

To move to a different, although related, point, which has figured in a number of reviews as well as private comments that have reached me: Baxandall, Ewen, and Gordon raise in this connection my use of the distinction between the *social* and the *technical* or *detailed* division of labor. In common with some other reviewers, they treat this as my own invention, calling it "Braverman's distinction." Actually, as my references to this chapter and my use of quoted materials from Marx should make clear, the entire treatment comes from Chapter 14, especially Section 4 of the first volume of *Capital,* called by Marx "Division of Labor in Manufacture, and Division of Labor in Society." In connection with this topic, there is nothing more important to be studied by any modern reader. On the one hand, it is a brilliant example of Marx's historical method. On the other, it contains in fully developed form Marx's most mature conclusions on the subject of the division of labor, and it becomes ever more mystifying with every passing day how so many can discuss Marx's opinions on this subject as though all he ever wrote on it is contained in the few scrappy paragraphs of *The German Ideology* or other early manuscripts unpublished by him, which represent his first reactions to the problem.

Baxandall, Ewen, and Gordon comment that "Braverman's distinction between the social division of labor and the detail division of labor in capitalist industry is not adequate" for an understanding of the whole of the damage wrought by the divisions of labor in society, and they cite specifically the sexual division of labor. They could not be more right. The distinction in question is adequate only to the purposes for which it was fashioned.

Readers who study Marx's chapter carefully will see how he uses one of his most characteristic tools of analysis: He dissociates the elements of the problem historically specific to capitalism from those generally characteristic of human societies, and treats these not just as continuities, one of the other, but in their polar opposition. From this opposition between abstract social categories and specific social forms in which they are cast in a given epoch of history, Marx works up an analysis of extraordinary penetration.

This does not, however, mean that the analysis is directed toward the clarification of the sexual division of labor which originates in the long hunting period of human pre-history, and which requires considerably different tools of analysis. On the other hand, an approach so broadened as to include this problem would require a level of abstraction and generality—in relation to the division of labor in the factory and similar institutions—so extreme as to make it relatively useless for the latter. It is this, I believe, which dictated the approach taken by Marx and followed by me. What I am trying to emphasize here is that an attempt to combine these two analyses—of the division of labor in modern society and of the most general forms of the sexual division of labor—into a single step would only defeat the object of both analyses and create a muddle all around.

II

Labor and Monopoly Capital has been criticized also for its omission of any discussion of the future of working-class consciousness, although in this case too the critics have, like John and Barbara Ehrenreich in their article in this collection ("Work and Consciousness"), understood and explained the self-imposed limits of my analysis and thus relieved me of the need to repeat any explanations. Nevertheless, a few further words may be usefully said.

Marxism is not merely an exercise in satisfying intellectual curiosity, nor an academic pursuit, but a theory of revolution and thus a tool of combat. From that point of view the value of any analysis of the composition and social trends within the working population can only lie in precisely how well it helps us to answer questions about class consciousness. Thus I do not quarrel with critics who are anxious to see further progress made in that most important side of the analysis. It was my interest in that very question of class consciousness, in fact, which led to my taking up the entire study in the first place.

When I did so, however, I already had the firm conviction that little purpose would be served by a direct attack on the subject, since it did not appear to me to be in any condition to yield to such an attack. Two major preconditions seemed to me to be lacking. The first has to do with the lack of a concrete picture of the working class, what it is made up of, the trends of income, skill, exploitation, "alienation," and so forth among workers, the place of the working population as a segment of the entire population, etc. I thought that my efforts would best be directed toward helping to fill this gap. I might add that since this is still far from accomplished, I believe that many more essays (along the lines of some of those in this collection) will be appearing in the near future.

The second precondition is considerably more difficult to satisfy. It may be described simply by saying that while social conditions have been changing rapidly over the past half century, and the working class along with them, the class struggle has been in a state of relative quiescence in the United States, Western Europe, and Japan—the countries of developed capitalism for which the analysis must be made. We are therefore lacking in concrete experience, for the most part, of the sort which will indicate the forms and laws of struggle which will predominate in the new social conditions which characterize the epoch of monopoly capital—although we do have some interesting indications from the sixties, of which the French events of 1968 are perhaps the most suggestive. Those who have been wrestling with this problem since the thirties best realize how, in the absence of further concrete experience, discussion tends to degenerate into cliche, apologia, and the repetition of old formulas, and how difficult it has become to say anything new or fresh about it.

It seems to me that a fruitful discussion of the working class as a class conscious of and struggling in behalf of its own interests will begin to revive as two conditions begin to be satisfied: first, as a clear picture of the class in its present conditions of existence is formed by patient and realistic investigation; and second, as experience begins to accumulate of the sort which will teach us to better understand the state of mind and modes of struggle of this class.

I would like to make one further comment, having to do with my own attitude on this subject, since there seem to be some questions as well as some misconceptions on this score. Some readers have concluded, chiefly on the evidence of my description of a process of "degradation of labor," that I myself am "pessimistic" about the future of working-class consciousness. But if readers will take the trouble to compare, they will find that the wording which I have used to describe the effects of the capitalist mode of production on the physical, moral, and mental constitution of the working population differs from Marx's only in being milder. A new study by Steven Marcus of Engels's classic first work, which in many ways set the tone for Marx, notes that "The descriptive or characterizing term used with the greatest frequency throughout *The Condition of the Working Class* consists of variations of the word 'demoralize'—demoralized, demoralizing, demoralization and so on."*

---

* Steven Marcus, *Engels, Manchester, and the Working Class* (New York: Random House, 1976), 133.

But neither Marx nor Engels considered themselves "pessimists" on that account; on the contrary, they found in this unremitting assault of capital upon the humanity of labor the precondition for revolt.

This therefore I regard as a specious clue to my own state of mind; there is, moreover, no need for mind reading, since I have a clear conviction and no hesitancy in stating it. I have every confidence in the revolutionary potential of the working classes of the so-called developed capitalist countries. Capitalism will not, over the long run, leave any choice to these classes, but will force upon them the fulfillment of the task which they alone can perform. This presupposes an enormous intensification of the pressures which have only just begun to bear upon the working class, but I think there is no question that it will happen. I have long tended to agree with those who think it will still be a long time in coming. But time is a social and historical concept, not a purely chronological one. When I look at the great changes that have occurred during the past ten or fifteen years, I believe I see this time passing rather more quickly than I used to think would be the case. In any event, historical time is difficult to forecast, and may be measured out in generations; it sets its own pace and not a pace to satisfy our wishes. But pass it will, whether rapidly or slowly, and bring in its train those explosive developments which for the past few decades have appeared limited to "other" parts of the world.

Appendix 2

The Degradation of Work
in the Twentieth Century

The following talk, given by Harry Braverman in the spring of 1975 at the West Virginia Institute of Technology, is his last known recorded presentation before his death on August 2, 1976. It was slightly edited for posthumous publication by Monthly Review *in 1982 (vol. 34., no. 1).*

My topic this evening is the "degradation of work in the twentieth century," and there is one firm generalization with which we may begin—that is, that humanity is a working species. Our relationship with nature is not merely one of food-gathering or seeking shelter in the crevices provided ready-made by nature. Rather humanity takes the materials provided by nature and alters them into objects more useful to itself. Humanity works in order to live, to provide itself with the means and provisions of life. Thus even though men and women often have occasion to complain of work as a constraint laid upon the species, there is never any doubt that work as a species characteristic is as natural to human life as grazing or hunting are to other species. But it would be the greatest of all possible mistakes to take any simple truisms of this sort, whether in the form of Biblical laments or biological and evolutionary constraints, as the direct basis for an analysis of work in modern society. Between biology and sociology, civilization—with all of its social relations and institutions—intervenes. In capitalist society, which is the society in which we live, work is organized in institutions that have long since separated us from simple production for our own use and indeed have as a basis for their activity something very different from any kind of production for use.

The purpose of a capitalist enterprise, as we know it, is to use the surplus that may be extracted from the process of production. Thus while humans work to provide for their needs, in capitalist society nobody works who does not at the same time provide for the needs of capital. It is only by creating a surplus for the corporations that we obtain permission to create necessities for ourselves. In capitalist society this is rule number one, or if you like you might call it Catch-22. Whatever you call it, it is the underlying law of the system.

Now it's true that there have been other forms in which ruling groups extracted a surplus for themselves from the working population. In slave societies the masters directly appropriated the labor of others. In feudal societies the rulers took from the produce of others what they themselves required under rules that obligated the peasantry to surrender to the manorial lord a portion of their product or of their labor. Thus it has been said of feudalism that the nobility defended all, the clergy prayed for all, and the commoners fed all. But in capitalist society the manner in which a surplus is extracted is very special and has had during the past two hundred years the most extraordinary consequences. The foremost of these is that the capitalists have taken into their own hands the direct control over all processes of labor and production; and this in itself constitutes an enormous change from anything that has existed in previous societies. In previous societies the work of artisans or of that immense mass of the population then engaged in crop or animal husbandry as farmers, peasants, and serfs was as a rule conducted autonomously. So far as the direct processes of labor are concerned, the artisans or peasants worked according to traditional methods generally under their own control. It is only under capitalist conditions that the masters take over the entire process, repeatedly reshape and reorganize it to suit their own needs, and parcel it out as tasks to workers for whom the process as a whole is now lost.

Labor that has been subjected to these conditions is sometimes referred to as *alienated labor.* Now this is a vague phrase, and its vagueness has increased with its popularity. Indeed, we may suspect that its present popularity in official sociology and popular journalism is dependent upon its vagueness. In their usage its connection with the specific conditions of capitalist social relations and capitalist production has all but disappeared, and alienated labor is understood to mean merely the worker who suffers from a feeling of distress, a malaise, a bellyache about his or her work. But the term may still be useful if its significant content is restored and clearly understood.

It must be understood first of all in accordance with the prime definition of the verb *to alienate,* that is, to transfer ownership to another. The ownership of the tools and instruments of production is in capitalist society alienated, that is, transferred to others. The ownership of the product is alienated in the same sense. The same applies to the ownership of the proceeds from the sale of the product, and finally the process of production too is alienated. It too is transferred to alien control and becomes the property of others. In the end, everything about the productive process becomes alien to the worker in the sense that everything is outside his or her interests, claim, and control—the wage becomes the sole equity of the worker in the job.

Thus in capitalist society production is carried on in an atmosphere of hostility or indifference by a mass of workers who have lost all stake in or concern for the process, and this in turn makes necessary certain extraordinary means of control and management. It is thus that management for the first time comes into existence and is brought into the world by capitalist society. This necessitates ever more extraordinary means of control and management as well as an ever more alienating reorganization of the work of production, so that we have here an alienation which feeds on itself and becomes ever deeper until it emerges as a profound antagonism between those who work and those who manage them. In this situation it is not at all surprising that work is seen as a curse—what is surprising is only that it is tolerated at all. The manner in which this step-by-step alienation of the process of production from the worker has developed historically is too large a subject to be dealt with in any short presentation. Suffice it to say that it existed only in exceptional instances in ancient and medieval societies; that it grew rapidly in the workshops of the sixteenth, seventeenth, and eighteenth centuries during the rise of early capitalism, that it became generalized in the workshops and factories of the nineteenth century, and that it has become virtually universal in the factories, mills, warehouses, offices, farms, wholesale and retail establishments, hospitals, offices of public administration, and even to some extent in the schools of the twentieth century in the countries of fully developed capitalism.

Now once capitalists take control of the process of production, they seek out every means whereby the output of the worker will be increased so that an ever larger surplus may remain with them. At first this was accomplished by prolonging the working day, but in more recent times intensive methods have replaced extensive ones. This means the reduction of the labor time required in the production process, and it means also the cheapening of labor power. How is labor power cheapened? There are a variety of ways. By far the most important in modern production is the breakdown of complex processes into simple tasks that are performed by workers whose knowledge is virtually nil, whose so-called training is brief, and who may thereby be treated as interchangeable parts. In this way the requirements of production are satisfied not through small pools of highly skilled labor in each craft but by labor of the simplest sort. The consequence is that for most jobs the whole of society becomes a labor pool upon which to draw, and this helps to keep the value of labor power at the level of subsistence for the individual or below the level of subsistence for the family.

In speaking in this way about the capitalists or the corporate organization of capitalism it is not my intention to assault them personally as conscienceless or to malign them. Taken as a class they are no doubt, like all of us, only what society makes of them. But this is precisely the point—we must deal not with the capitalist as a person but with the way the capitalist mode of production operates and the conduct it enforces upon the capitalists themselves. After Henry Ford introduced the moving conveyor (between 1912 and 1914) as the means of sub-assembly and final assembly of automobiles, none of the hundreds of automobile firms then in existence could hope to continue long in business without adopting this process. From the moment the first food-retailing organization adopted self-service methods of shelving and checking out commodities in its stores, no food-retailing organization could hope to prosper or perhaps even to survive without these methods. Or, to take as an instance a process that is just now getting underway, every office manager now understands that since the means have become available to segregate secretarial work in specialized production units connected to executive offices by modern telephonic and recording equipment, no office employing a large number of scattered secretaries can long afford to neglect this innovation; and many are beginning to reorganize secretarial work as the office equivalent of factory production work.

Thus the tendency of the capitalist mode of production from its earliest days some 200 or 250 years ago to the present, when this tendency has become a headlong rush, is the incessant breakdown of labor processes into simplified operations taught to workers as tasks. This leads to the conversion of the greatest possible mass of labor into work of the most elementary form, labor from which all conceptual elements have been removed and along with them most of the skill, knowledge, and understanding of production processes. Thus the more complex the process becomes, the less the worker understands. The more science is incorporated into technology, the less science the worker possesses; and the more machinery that has been developed as an aid to labor, the more labor becomes a servant of machinery.

Although there is a general impression, which is fostered by official academic and journalistic opinion, that all of this is happening because of the rise of scientific technology and the development of machinery, this process of degradation of work is not really dependent upon technology at all. It will be remembered that this mode of the organization of labor arose in the workshops of early capitalism at a time when modern technology did not exist. One need only read Adam Smith's description of the division of labor in pin manufacture to see that the key to the matter is the organization of labor. In modern industry the worst examples of the division of labor are still found chiefly in those processes which exist in the gap left open by technology, those things which cannot be mechanized or cannot be economically mechanized by the capitalists at the prevailing rates of pay. Let us just remind ourselves that one of the most abominable forms of labor, the one in fact that is often mistakenly taken as an instance of the horrors of modern machinery, the assembly line, is just such a case—it has little or nothing to do with machinery since it is a hand process of the crudest sort, its technological feature being merely a primitive device for hauling the work past the worker. Even this device is dispensable, and dispensed with, in the case of smaller and lighter units of production which can be pushed along the work tables to the next station. As a rule, however, the powered endless belt or chain conveyor is favored by management not just as an aid to labor, but chiefly because it enables management to control the pace of production.

Modern technology in fact has a powerful tendency to break down ancient divisions of labor by re-unifying production processes. Adam Smith's pins, for example, are no longer made by a worker who straightens the wire, another who cuts the length, a third who fashions the heads, a fourth who affixes them to the pins, a fifth who points the pins, a sixth who tins or whitens, another who inserts them into the paper, and so on. The entire process is re-unified in a single machine which transforms great coils of wire into millions of pins each day already papered and ready for sale. Now go back and read Adam Smith's arguments for the division of labor, arguments having to do with the dexterity gained in the constant application to one operation of a hand process over and over again and so on. You will notice that this modern technology has made a complete hash of these arguments. Not one remains with any force today. The re-unified process in which the execution of all the steps is built into the working mechanism of a single machine would seem now to render it suitable for a collective of associated producers, none of whom need spend all of their lives at any single function and all of whom can participate in the engineering, design, improvement, repair, and operation of these ever more productive machines. Such a system would entail no loss of production, and it would represent the re-unification of the craft in a body of workers far superior to the old craftsworkers. Workers can now become masters of the technology of their process on an engineering level and can apportion among themselves in an equitable way the various tasks connected with this form of production that has become so effortless and automatic.

The division of labor in a capitalist society, however, has to do with many other things besides the pace of production, which in most cases would not be injured if it were wiped out. It has to do, as Charles Babbage pointed out in the early nineteenth century, with differential pay rates, which dictate that the ignorance of the great masses of the workers and the concentration of all engineering knowledge in a few specialists are desirable and, in fact, essential conditions rather than, as it would seem from a human point of view, an abomination. Thus the capitalist mode of production enforces upon new processes devised by technology an ever deeper division of labor no matter how many possibilities for the opposite are opened by machinery. In this way two worlds of work are created: the world in which a very few managers and engineers grasp the process as a whole as their special monopoly, and the world of scheduling clerks, inventory clerks, timekeepers, machine tenders, machine repairers, stock chasers, forklift operators, warehouse attendants, and so on, each of whom performs simple labor in service to a complex machine and each of whom is expected to make a working life of from forty to fifty years out of these scraps of duties, none of which can engage the interests or capacities of a mature human or even of a child for more than a few weeks or a few months, after which they become sheer and mindless drudgery. Thus we may say that while production has become collective and the individual worker has been incorporated into the collective body of workers, this is a body the brain of which has been lobotomized, or worse, removed entirely. Its very brain has been separated from its body, having been appropriated by modern management as a means of controlling and cheapening labor power and labor processes.

We have briefly considered the production process. Let us turn now to its outcome. Let me say at once what cannot be denied and what is in fact capitalism's chief historic role. This unremitting drive on the part of the capitalists to extract an ever greater surplus from the working population, a drive in which the immense powers of science and technology have been enlisted in the service of the accumulation of capital, this drive has brought about an extraordinary development of the human powers of production. The productivity of labor and hence the surplus which it makes available for further expansion have risen most remarkably in the developed capitalist countries. The owners of the corporations never tire of reminding us that they require great surpluses if they are to constantly enlarge the scale of production, and this is quite true. No change of social system can do away with it as a technical fact. If production is to grow, a portion of the product must be reinvested in the process of production rather than be consumed at once. This we may treat as a natural law, but it is no natural law that this surplus must become and remain the property of a tiny ruling class. This is rather a law of capitalism, and as a result of its workings there has been an immense accumulation of property at one pole of society, greater than at any time in human history.

How about the working population, by which I mean that portion of the population excluding the managers and the proprietors of industry and even excluding those somewhat privileged intermediate strata in professional occupations and in middle management who today make up what might be called a new middle class? The remaining mass, which I have called the working population but which one might call labor or the working class, this remaining mass which constitutes perhaps three quarters of all employment in the United States, is described in the census and in Labor Department statistics under six headings: craftsworkers, operative and kindred workers, laborers, clerical workers, service workers, and sales workers. Here we find close to 60 million out of the approximately 80 million persons, including owners, counted by the census of 1970 as among the working population, and here too we find those jobs characteristically of the sort which I have been describing. Now earlier in this talk I noted that the reduction of the typical job to the level of a few simplified tasks is one of the chief means of cheapening labor power, and I added that this helps to keep the value of labor power at the level of subsistence for the individual or below the level of subsistence for the family.

Lest this be thought an exaggeration, let me now substantiate it with estimates based upon the pay scales for workers in all of these six classifications in 1971, and official estimates of the cost of maintaining a family of four above the poverty line in that same year—and it's worth noting that the situation since then can only have gotten worse, not only because of the economic crisis, but also because during these four years inflation has outstripped wages, thus lowering real wages. Some 80 percent of service workers and workers in retail trades did not receive enough pay to support a family of four above the poverty level. The same is true of at least 75 percent of all clerical workers and laborers, both of whom are paid on about the same level, the laborers maybe a little higher than clerical workers. It is also true of close to 70 percent of all operatives and kindred workers. Only craftsworkers earn in their majority enough to lift a family of four out of the officially defined poverty category, and even in this grouping the wages of 40 percent, if used to support a family of four, were below the poverty level.

Now, one result of these earnings levels is that very large numbers of families do live below the poverty level; that a big majority of families is not put in that position is due only to multiple job-holding within the same family. This we know. But what I am trying to highlight is the startling fact that a pretty large majority of the jobs in the economy have now been transformed by the workings of the capitalist division of labor into the kinds of work one usually thinks of as second jobs, the mythical pin-money jobs which women and teenagers are supposed to be the only ones to take to supplement the major family income. The result is that most of the people, whether they are supplementary earners or heads of households, now occupy such so-called second jobs with their pitiful and demeaning duties and meager pay. That this is so is due not only to the kind of division of labor we have been discussing, but also to the occupational and industrial shifts which have resulted from the accumulation of capital in the United States.

Let me try to make this clear. In striving to economize on labor time, the corporation is also striving to reduce the number of workers required for a given quantity or output, or—and this comes to much the same thing—to produce a rapidly growing output without a proportional growth in the number of workers. To use Marx's memorable way of putting it, unlike the generals who win their wars by recruiting armies, the captains of industry win their wars by discharging armies. The practical consequences of this can be seen in any analysis of United States employment in the manufacturing industries over any reasonable period of time. Thus in the United States between 1947 and 1964, a seventeen-year period, the output of the textile industries grew by more than 40 percent but employment was cut by one third. Other industries, such as iron and steel foundries, lumber and wood products, malt liquors, and footwear, showed production increases of from 15 percent to 40 percent in the same period, accompanied by employment drops of 10 percent to 25 percent. The petroleum industry poured out five-sixths more product at the end of the period than at the beginning, but its employment was one-fourth lower. Even the construction industry, which by the nature of its production processes is notably resistant to technological change, doubled its output while adding only 50 percent to its labor force. Only the most rapidly growing industries showed substantial increases in employment. Thus electrical machinery and motor freights added respectively 50 percent and 70 percent to their employment, but in the process they roughly tripled their output. The aluminum industry more than doubled its employment, but this was the result of a quadrupled output. An extreme case is that of air transport, which enlarged its output some eight times while increasing employment by only one and one-third times.

Now, the figures that I have been giving you deal only with a seventeen-year period; but, taking a much longer-term view, you can very clearly see the trend by focusing on the changes in manufacturing and related industries like construction. For at least a century these industries occupied close to half of all non-farm employment, usually between 45 percent and 50 percent. But after the 1920 census, about fifty years ago, this began to change; and by the time we come to the most recent census, that of 1970, these industries occupy only one-third of non-farm employment. There has therefore been an immense shift of labor out of the traditional manufacturing, mining and construction, and transportation industries into the very rapidly growing areas of real estate, insurance, finance, services, and wholesale and retail trade. But these rapidly growing fields of industry are precisely the low-wage portions of the economy; while the higher-wage sector is the stagnant or declining portion. None of this is accidental; there are profound structural reasons why the most rapid growth of capital has taken place in the low-wage areas and also in the enlargement of nonproductive as against productive work. In any case, this trend is not a matter for doubt, and it is this trend, along with the rapid growth of the lowest-wage occupations, such as clerical, service, and retail trade, that in good measure accounts for the fact that we live increasingly in an economy of so-called second jobs and that true first jobs in the traditional sense—jobs that are rewarding in themselves and pay enough to support a family—are fewer than ever.

If the captains of industry win their war, as Marx put it, by discharging armies, how do we know that the rapidity of the accumulation of capital will keep up with it and that new products, services, or unproductive industries will develop rapidly enough to absorb all of the labor freed by the capitalist drive for higher productivity? Well, we do not know, and in fact in capitalist society there is always a pool of unused labor power, an industrial reserve army. It has almost always been a very sizable mass in United States industrial history, at least during this century. And it shrinks to a small size only on those rare occasions when the upswings in the business cycle are unusually strong and correspond as well to longer-term upswings in the process of capitalist accumulation, especially during wars.

Apart from the natural growth of the population, the freeing of workers from their jobs by the continuous revolution in production creates, again to use Marx's words, a disposable industrial reserve army that belongs to capital quite as absolutely as if the latter had bred it at its own cost. If we try to verify this from the United States statistics we run up against the difficulty that unemployment figures are kept on very different principles from those embraced by the concept of the industrial reserve army, but these statistics nevertheless have the value attaching to any set of figures that is kept on more or less constant principles over a long period of time. The most striking thing to emerge from an examination of the unemployment statistics from the Second World War to the present is the long-run trend of gradual but persistent enlargement of the pool of officially counted unemployed. There has been throughout this whole period a business cycle, so that the line is a jagged one, but even so it is a line which constantly trends upward. The levels of unemployment, which at the start of the period meant recession, are now regarded as perfectly acceptable prosperity rates. I clipped from yesterday's *New York Times* an article with the headline "High Joblessness Expected to Persist as a Condition of United States Throughout the Decade." This article points out that although we began immediately after the Second World War aiming for an unemployment rate of 2 percent or 3 percent, we soon gave this up, that the 4 percent unemployment target embraced by President Kennedy in 1962 has been abandoned, and the 5 percent goal of the Nixon administration economists has also lost support. Most economists today, regardless of their political affiliation, believe that 5.5 percent to 6 percent of unemployment is probably the lowest the government can achieve without stirring up virulent inflation again, and even that modest target is a long way from attainment—1979 at the earliest. In other words, the target for unemployment and prosperity nowadays is higher than what was regarded as a recession rate of unemployment only twenty-five years ago.

Now I said a moment ago that these unemployment rates are not the same as the concept of an industrial reserve army, the latter being much larger. This is because the measuring of unemployment is a relatively restrictive count. Let me give you a very graphic instance of this: when the unemployment figures for February of this year were released a month or two ago, they proved to be about 8.3 million, only slightly changed from the 8.2 million counted as unemployed in the previous month of January—but we were told at the same time that employment had fallen by a full half-million persons. How do we explain this paradox? Well, the answer that they give is that in official parlance almost 600,000 persons had dropped out of the labor force between one month and the next. What does that remarkable statistic mean? It simply means the following: since capitalism does not recognize that every able-bodied adult has either the responsibility or the opportunity to work and contribute to society, the theory is that one cannot distinguish the unemployed from the leisure class except by asking the individual whether he or she had been actively seeking employment during the previous four weeks. Those who cannot show that they have been doing so—and in the largest majority of cases this would mean those who have given up hope of getting a job—are no longer counted as part of the labor force and hence cannot be counted as unemployed. Nothing in official statistics distinguishes them from the housewife who has never worked or from the millionaire in Palm Springs. Thus there is clearly a large mass of non-working people who constitute a reserve army of labor, only a portion of which is counted. Those who rise to the surface in active search of jobs are counted as unemployed; those who sink to the bottom and are forced onto the welfare roll are counted as paupers. The size of this pauperized mass is now between 14 and 15 million persons, and this enormous size was attained back in 1970 and bids fair to go much higher. From all of this we can see that the accumulation of wealth which takes place at one pole of society in the capitalist system is matched at the other pole by an accumulation of misery.

Index

Abstract labor, 220
  Marx's theory of, 125
Administrative Management (magazine), 237, 238
Administrators. *See* Managers
Ætna Life Insurance Co., 223–24
Agricultural workers, 268
  1880-1970, 177
Agriculture, U.S. Department of, 113
Air Force, U.S., 136
Alienation, 39
  Schmidt on Marx's theory of, 19, 19*n*
American Chemical Society, 111n
American Management Association, 230, 233
American Society of Mechanical Engineers, 137*n*
American Tobacco Company, 99
Animals, 37–38, 50
  human labor and, 31–34
Apprenticeship, 92
  craftsmanship and, 76
  German technical education and, 110–11
Aptitude tests, 99–100
Argyle, Michael, 34*n*
Aristotle, 31*n*, 36*n*
Arkwright, Sir Richard, 181
Assembly line, 134, 135–36, 298,299–300
  at Ford, 101–3
  modern technology and, 223
Automation, 231–32
  Bright's study of management and, 146–53
  Friedmann on progressive aspect of, 159*n*
Automobile industry, 141–42, 168
  at Ford, 101–3
  job dissatisfaction and, 22–23

Babbage, Charles, 52n, 59, 138, 235
  on disciplinary function of machinery, 134*n*
  on division of labor, 55–57, 218–19
  Taylor and, 61–62, 81
Baker, Newton, 111*n*
Banking, 305
  clerical work within, 26, 208, 233–35
Baran, Paul A., 37*n*, 175, 177, 200
  on monopoly capitalism, 176
Barber, Bernard, 109, 160
Belidor (French engineer), 61
Bell, Daniel, 73*n*
Bell Telephone Laboratories, 113
Bentham, Jeremy, 110
Berg, Ivar, 305
Bernal, J. D., 91
Bernhardt, K. B., 303–4
Bethlehem Steel Company, Taylor at, 70–73
Bienstock, Herbert, 303
Bierce, Ambrose, 134
Blank, David M., 167–68
Blauner, Robert, 20, 129, 155
Blue-collar workers. *See also* Manual laborers
  job dissatisfaction among, 21–22, 23–24
  white-collar workers and, 205–6, 225, 301–2
Bluestone, Barry, 273*n*
Blumberg, Paul, 308*n*
Boiler shop, 140
Bookkeeping, 53, 170
  merchant capitalism and, 45, 207
  by modern corporation, 209–10
Booth, Charles, 241

338   *Labor and Monopoly Capital*

class consciousness of, 20
defining, 17–18
integration of unionized, 8
job dissatisfaction among, 21–25
machine and creation of, 133–34
"middle layers" of employment and, 279–83
"new working class" and, 17–18, 19n
occupational shifts and, 262–64
proportion of population in, 269–71, 274
regaining control over production process, 307–9
reserve army of labor and, 266–67

scientific-technological revolution and, 264–66
simplified tasks and, 88, 89–90
social form of labor and, 284
World of the Office Worker, The (Crozier), 90
Wundt, Wilhelm, 97

Yale University Technology Project, 299
Yavitz, Boris, 229, 232
Young workers, job dissatisfaction among, 24

Zwerman, William J., 14n